Latinos and
the 2016 Election

LATINOS IN THE UNITED STATES SERIES

SERIES EDITOR
Rubén O. Martinez, *Michigan State University*

EDITORIAL BOARD
Adalberto Aguirre Jr., *University of California–Riverside*
Robert Aponte, *Indiana University–Purdue University Indianapolis*
Teresa Cordova, *University of Illinois at Chicago*
Julie Leininger Pycior, *Manhattan College*
Rogelio Saenz, *University of Texas San Antonio*

Latinos and the 2016 Election

LATINO RESISTANCE AND THE ELECTION OF DONALD TRUMP

Edited by
Gabriel R. Sanchez, Luis Ricardo Fraga,
and Ricardo Ramírez

Michigan State University Press • *East Lansing*

⊛ The paper used in this publication meets the minimum requirements
of ANSI/NISO Z39.48–1992 (R 1997) (Permanence of Paper).

Michigan State University Press
East Lansing, Michigan 48823-5245

LIBRARY OF CONGRESS CATALOGING-IN-PUBLICATION DATA
Names: Sanchez, Gabriel R., 1979– editor. | Fraga, Luis Ricardo, editor.
| Ramírez, Ricardo, 1973– editor.
Title: Latinos and the 2016 election : Latino resistance and the election of Donald Trump
/ edited by Gabriel R. Sanchez, Luis Ricardo Fraga, and Ricardo Ramírez.
Description: East Lansing : Michigan State University Press, 2020.
| Series: Latinos in the United States series | Includes bibliographical references.
Identifiers: LCCN 2019028394 | ISBN 9781611863611 (paperback)
| ISBN 9781609176365 (PDF) | ISBN 9781628953985 (EPUB) | ISBN 9781628963991 (Kindle)
Subjects: LCSH: Hispanic Americans—Politics and government. | Presidents—United States—
Election—2016. | United States. Congress—Elections, 2016. | Voting research—United States.
| Political participation—United States. | Trump, Donald, 1946–
Classification: LCC JK1968 2016 .L37 2020 | DDC 324.973/093208968—dc23
LC record available at https://lccn.loc.gov/2019028394

Book and cover design by Charlie Sharp, Sharp Des!gns, East Lansing, MI

Michigan State University Press is a member of the Green Press Initiative and is
committed to developing and encouraging ecologically responsible publishing
practices. For more information about the Green Press Initiative and the use of
recycled paper in book publishing, please visit *www.greenpressinitiative.org*.

Visit Michigan State University Press at *www.msupress.org*

Contents

Foreword

Rubén O. Martinez

THE ELECTION OF DONALD TRUMP AS PRESIDENT OF THE UNITED STATES on November 8, 2016, shocked the nation and traumatized millions of Americans. This was especially the case given that Hillary Clinton was expected to win the election. How did this happen? How could a man with a history of shady business deals, of endlessly hurling insults at opponents, and of directly and indirectly promoting racism and violence win the presidency? What role did Latino voters have in the outcome? Did they support Trump? Six of the ten states with the largest number of Latinos voted for Clinton. Trump lost the popular vote by 2.8 million votes, but won the Electoral College votes. The outcome reflected representational unreliability; that is, the electoral votes contradicted the popular vote. Only five candidates have ever won the presidency despite losing the popular vote. Trump is the most recent and he lost by the widest margin of all of them. Interestingly, in 2012, when Trump mistakenly thought that President Barack Obama would be re-elected despite losing the popular vote, he called the Electoral College "a disaster for democracy." But in 2016, when the Electoral College handed him the presidency, he referred to it as an "instrument of genius."

Perhaps it is this factless feature of his public comments and his continual shift in positions that best define his presidency. He asserted that his loss of the popular vote was due to votes cast against him by more than a million undocumented immigrants, thereby continuing to promote his anti-immigrant agenda.

The campaign and the results of the 2016 General Election took American politics to a new low. Candidate Trump, if he was not gloating about his wealth and supposed intelligence, spent most of his time ridiculing and taunting his competitors without engaging in serious discussions about the issues. And there were many issues to discuss, including access to health care, immigration, national debt, and national security. He promised health care for all, a wall at the southern border paid for by Mexico to stop immigration, elimination of the national debt in eight years, and meaningful engagement with allies. Since his election, he has sought to reduce, if not eliminate, health coverage for millions of Americans, passed the costs of building a border wall onto American taxpayers, increased the national debt by reducing taxes for the wealthy, and isolated the country from its historical allies. His populist rhetoric "won" him the election, but he has since turned his back on ordinary Americans and promoted the neoliberal agenda of reducing government, deregulating the economy, and disempowering organized labor. He has also demonstrated tyrannical tendencies by chumming up to right-wing dictators, attacking the free press, judges, and intelligence agencies, attempting to use political appointees as his protectors, and undermining the balance of power between the branches of government.

The recently released "Mueller Report" provides ample evidence of Trump's corrupt tendencies and his lack of fitness to be president, yet he is in the White House. Consequently, the United States is at a point in its history that threatens the very foundations of democracy—a threat perhaps worse than that posed by the secessionist efforts of the Southern Confederacy. He has promoted dysfunctions in government, undermined the nation's moral order, and deeply divided American citizens. The demise of democracy could usher in a period of violence against Americans by their own government at a scale never before seen in this country. Dictators tend to promote simple solutions to complex problems and they use punitive measures to maintain themselves and their regimes in power. Trump has repeatedly expressed intentions to use government to go after persons and organizations he defines as his enemies. How could a man with such corruptive tendencies get elected president of the United States?

Today's American social order is characterized by the economic features of neoliberalism, the political values and practices of conservatism, and the right-wing populist movement that has risen in the form of Trumpism. Neoliberal ideology has been institutionalized in the form of free-market fundamentalism, which is grounded in extreme individualism, antigovernment sentiments, manipulation of the masses through propaganda, privatization of government functions, deregulation of the economy, economic freedom in the form of unleashed greed, and anti-labor and anti-job-tenure views. The institutionalization of this ideology is marked by increased income and wealth inequalities, economic instability, social atomization, and the penetration of the private sphere by market logic and relations. At the same time, conservatism has politically divided Americans along several dimensions and given rise to the intensification of xenophobia, homophobia, nativism, misogyny, and White nationalism, among other forms of factionalism. The downward socioeconomic mobility experienced by many Americans generated intense frustration. When coupled with social atomization, produced by both extreme individualism and communications technology, and the relative lack of sociality they engender, that frustration produced conditions rife with the potential for the emergence of a mass movement—one in which the direction could be determined by charismatic leadership, which we saw with both the Sanders and Trump campaigns.

The 2016 General Election saw the rise of Bernie Sanders and Donald Trump, diametrically opposed populist leaders, the former a progressive who envisioned a better society and the other a regressive leader who sought absolute power at the expense of the social order and vulnerable groups. These diametrically opposed leaders reflect the intensification of political and material divisions brought about by neoliberalism and conservatism. Latino voters were about equally split between Sanders and Clinton, but they opposed Trump by a wide margin. Clinton beat Sanders by taking the largest states: California, Texas, Florida, and New York, which have the largest Latino populations, and together have about 56% of the entire Latino population.

The authors of this volume edited by Gabriel R. Sanchez, Luis Ricardo Fraga, and Ricardo Ramírez address key questions about the role Latino voters played in the 2016 General Election. The volume consists of fourteen substantive chapters, an introduction, a concluding chapter, and an appendix describing the data and methodology used by the authors. The major finding is that Latino voters supported Hillary Clinton and opposed Donald Trump. While there are variations by gender, generations, subethnic populations, and states, the majority of Latino voters rejected Trump. It is not surprising that Latinos opposed Trump as his campaign rhetoric was overtly hostile to both immigrants and Latinos. His endless assertions that he would build a huge border wall and make Mexico pay for it gained support among his loyal supporters, but it mobilized Latino voters against him. Trump even managed to lose by a slight margin among Cuban Americans, a Latino population segment that traditionally has supported Republican candidates.

This volume provides the most comprehensive analysis to date of Latino voting patterns at the national level, and reflects the achievements made in the collection of data on Latino voters. Long neglected by mainstream pollsters and analysts, the study of Latino voting has matured among Latino scholars as the demographic shift has unfolded and Latinos have become the largest ethnoracial minority group in the nation at the turn of the century. The full influence of Latino voters has not yet been felt given their relatively low voter registration and low voter turnout levels. However, as demonstrated by the studies in this volume, this is changing. The technical and analytical achievements in the examination of Latino voting patterns have been long in coming, and as this phase in the study of Latino voters develops it sets the platform for the next stage, and that is contextual analyses of the patterns identified and described. The next stage involves interpreting the patterns within the context of the neoliberal social order in which we currently live. This will not only link Latino voting patterns to their subjective and objective interests, it will link their voting patterns to the trajectory of the social order. Moving forward, this volume sets a new standard for the study of Latino voters and provides the basis upon which we can interpret Latino voting patterns within the context of today's political economic order.

Preface

Gabriel R. Sanchez

THE 2016 ELECTION PROVIDES AN IMPORTANT OPPORTUNITY TO REFLECT on the state of Latino politics years removed from a 2012 election season that was in many ways a watershed moment for the Latino electorate. The study of Latino voters in the 2012 election published in this book series opened by stating that this was the first election in which the Latino electorate was consequential to a presidential election outcome and that the strong performance of the Latino electorate had finally put to bed the stereotype of Latino voters as a "sleeping giant." In contrast, Trump's victory in 2016 despite a campaign that by all accounts attacked Latino and immigrant communities leaves many wondering whether this outcome is an indicator of the lack of power Latino voters in the United States, or worse, whether Latino voters helped propel Trump to victory. In many ways this volume intends to address the central question many pundits, scholars, and journalists have been asking themselves since the final votes were tallied late into the evening on Election Day: How did this happen? Our authors tackle this important question from a Latino lens, addressing the role

Latinos played in an election that will be remembered as one of the biggest surprises in a presidential election history.

The book is organized around a few major themes that advance our collective understanding of Latino voting behavior in 2016. The first and arguably the most important finding from the book is that Latino voters emphatically rejected Trump's racialized campaign. In fact, the data reported from Latino Decisions' Election Eve Poll across this volume found that 79% of Latino voters polled in that massive sample reported that they voted for Hillary Clinton in 2016, an improvement on Obama's performance with Latino voters in both 2008 and 2012. In contrast, only 18% of Latino voters supported Trump, the lowest number for a candidate among Latino voters on record. This trend held across all of the states included in the Election Eve Poll. In fact, even in Florida, a state where Cuban American and other Latino voters have provided relatively high support for Republican candidates, 67% of Latino voters supported Clinton, including a majority (52%) of Cuban American voters. The "Latino Rejection of Trump" chapter in the volume draws from several data sets to make clear that the campaign rhetoric that attacked immigrants and Latinos more broadly and policy issues important to the Latino community, including killing the Affordable Care Act (ACA) and building a massive wall along the United States-Mexico border, did not gain traction with Latino voters. This overall finding was reinforced by authors across several chapters, noting that Latino voter registration and turnout were higher in 2016 than in 2012, with the Trump campaign leading to mobilization of the Latino electorate.

The book uses the extensive data provided to our author team by Latino Decisions to evaluate the feasibility of Trump outperforming Romney with Latino voters, as was suggested by the National Exit Poll. This was addressed most directly by the Texas-specific chapter that uses ecological inference to conclude that the National Exit Poll numbers for Latino voters should not be referenced in discussions of the 2016 election, or any election for that matter. When taken collectively, the book makes clear that Latino voters should not be blamed for the inability of Hillary Clinton to defeat candidate Trump. In fact, as our opening substantive chapter concludes, when one moves away from an "all-or-nothing" approach to evaluate group influence,

Latinos were in fact a highly influential voting bloc that made the 2016 election much tighter than it would have been otherwise.

Another major theme of the volume is that despite strong cohesion in vote choice, the Latino electorate is not a monolithic community. Our authors investigate potential variation across some of the most important demographic and political factors within the Latino electorate through the large and rich data sets made available to them for their analyses. This is most clear in the inclusion of several state-specific chapters that allow for deep dives into how Latinos behaved politically within states that varied in competitiveness, Latino demographic prowess, and overall ideology. By including four battleground states (Florida, Colorado, Arizona, and Nevada) where Latinos were a key constituent group targeted extensively by the campaigns and independent mobilization, along with some high-population states that were not competitive (California and Texas), we are able to speak to the important role Latinos played across each state, noting differences in contact rates in these states relative to the national markers, as well as to each other. The book also includes key battleground states where Latinos are emerging as politically influential, including Virginia and North Carolina. This depth in regional coverage is key and will provide the opportunity to use this book in courses focused on state and local politics, as well as on Latino and racial and ethnic politics.

In addition to state-level variation, our authors also emphasize important differences across other important factors identified in the Latino politics literature to be meaningful. For example, several authors note differences in vote choice, most important policy issues that drove vote choice, and other political attitudes by national origin, age/generation, and gender. The book has chapters focused specifically on Latina, Puerto Rican, and millennial voters, three subgroups of the larger Latino electorate that received a lot of attention during the 2016 election season. In the case of gender, the Election Eve Poll found identified a meaningful gap in vote choice based on gender, with Latinas supporting Clinton at a rate of 87%, but Latino men supporting her at 76%. Jessica Lavariega Monforti, national expert in Latina politics, dives deep into this apparent gender gap in her chapter, looking for factors that help explain why there was an important difference based on gender and what this suggests for the future of Latino politics. Given that millennial Latinos comprise essentially half of all eligible Latino voters, we include a specific chapter dedicated to this critically important subgroup. The authors of this chapter pull from several data sets collected by Latino Decisions during the election season that were focused specifically on understanding the views of millennials with a goal of mobilizing them to vote. Aileen Cardona-Arroyo's chapter focuses on the Puerto Rican electorate, a Latino subgroup with an immigration experience unique among other Latinos. This chapter describes the major migration patterns of Puerto Ricans historically and explores whether this context influences the voting behavior of Latinos from this national-origin group.

Although the book does a great job of exploring meaningful points of variation across the Latino community, one of the big-picture findings across the full volume is that we collectively found greater similarity across region/state, national origin, gender, age, and other factors than there were differences. In short, Latinos spoke loudly in one voice, supporting Hillary Clinton at an overwhelmingly high rate and continuing to indicate that immigration and a general concern for representing the Latino community were driving factors influencing how they approached the decision of how to vote in 2016.

The power of this book remains the combination of the expertise of the set of scholars recruited to participate in this project, along with the rich data they were provided by Latino Decisions to complete their individual chapters. In partnership with America's Voice, UnidosUS (formally National Council of La Raza), Latino Victory Project, Service Employees International Union, and Mi Familia Vota, among other leading national civic engagement organizations, Latino Decisions conducted a series of surveys of Latino likely voters in battleground states during the 2016 election season, culminating in the widely cited Latino Decisions 2016 Latino Election Eve Poll, which provided the definitive data on the Latino electorate. One of the goals of the overall book project is to introduce a wider audience to the rich data available to conduct research on Latino politics. We therefore include a specific chapter that provides a detailed description of the methodology for the surveys, along with leads to additional content and analytical tools available through Latino Decisions. Therefore, while each substantive chapter may provide some discussion of the specific measures the authors used in their analyses, this chapter presents essentially the data and methods for the entire volume. This approach not only saves valuable page space for state-specific content in each chapter, but it also provides readers with the opportunity to learn more about data they can use for their research interests.

The volume closes with a projection into the future of Latino electoral politics from one of the premier authorities on Latino politics, Dr. Luis Fraga from Notre Dame, who is also one of the editors of the volume. In addition to summarizing some of the overall findings across the chapters in the book, Dr. Fraga makes some projections regarding the future of Latino politics based on what we observed in 2016. Among other important considerations, Dr. Fraga tackles whether the greater cohesion in voting patterns among Latino voters over the past few presidential election cycles has some unintended consequences. Most importantly, does a perception that Latinos are solidly Democratic voters lead to less outreach among both parties, a similar concern to what scholars of African American politics have suggested to be the case for the African American electorate?

Our team of authors convened just after the 2016 presidential election at Notre Dame University for a conference hosted by the Institute for Latino Studies, where most of the authors in the volume presented their outline for the chapter they were going to write for the book project. Our team collectively set a goal of completing a book that would provide a comprehensive overview of the 2016 election as it pertained to the Latino electorate so that the book is the definitive place to turn to for answers to all questions related to how Latinos voted and why in 2016. After two years of hard work, we are confident that we have met this goal and have produced a book that is a must read for anyone interested in learning more about how Latino voters contributed to the 2016 election and what this monumental election season has taught us about Latino politics that we can utilize as we look toward 2020 and beyond.

Although the timing of the release of this book did not allow for a deep analysis of how Latinos contributed to the 2018 election outcomes across every chapter of the volume, we wanted to pull some data points from the 2018 Latino Decisions Election Eve Survey in this introduction to add to the overall power of this book. In 2018 Latino Decisions collaborated with Asian American Decisions and the African American Research Collaborative on large-scale election polls of Latino, Asian American, and African American voters in key states and congressional districts, as well as Native American voters nationwide. Overall, the election eve poll interviewed 9,400 (2,600 Latino) voters in final days before the election, offering exclusive information about the electorate, including congressional, Senate, and gubernatorial vote choices, issue priorities, and evaluations of both major parties. Results are broken out across battleground congressional districts, as well as critical states in 2018, including Arizona, California, Florida, Georgia, Nevada, and Texas.

The Election Eve Survey identified that 74% of Latino voters in 2018 voted for a Democratic candidate for Congress, compared to 24% who voted for a Republican candidate, with the remaining 2% indicating that they support someone from a third party. This is down slightly from the 79% of Latinos we discuss in this book supporting Hillary Clinton in 2016. When we look at variation across the states included in the survey, we see a range from 59% Democratic vote in Florida to a high of 86% Democratic vote in California. Texas (70%), Nevada (72%), and Arizona (76%) were all more than 70% Democratic support. One of the more surprising findings from the 2018 election data is regarding the "most important issue" Latino voters identified, as immigration reform, although among the top three issues, trailed health care and the economy/jobs in issue salience among Latino voters. The strategy of the Democratic party to focus messaging to voters on health care and Obamacare proved successful, as 31% identified this policy area as the most important to them, and those who identified this issue area as important were more supportive of Democratic candidates.

Consistent with the overall finding across the chapters of this book, President Trump appeared to mobilize Latinos in 2018. The president's approval rating was only 30% among Latinos, compared to 54% among Whites, and a robust 74% of Latino voters in 2018 indicated that something the president had said or done made them angry. Finally, nearly half of Latino voters (48%) indicated in the Election Eve Survey that they felt President Trump is a "racist whose policies are intended to hurt my community," compared to only 18% who believe that the president "has a positive impact on my community." Interestingly, the 18% who perceive that the president is having a positive impact on their community is identical to the percentage of Latinos in the 2016 survey who reported that they voted for President Trump. We encourage readers of this book to take a look at the rest of the findings from the 2018 survey to see whether there are any interesting differences in the midterm from what we discuss here for the 2016 presidential election (http://www.latinodecisions.com/2018-election-eve-poll). For instructors, we have also assembled a test bank available on the book's webpage to assist you with utilizing the book in your courses.

Latino Influence in the 2016 Presidential Election

Beyond All or Nothing

Justin H. Gross and Ivelisse Cuevas-Molina

EVERY FOUR YEARS, THE SPECULATION GAME BEGINS ANEW: WILL THIS BE the election in which Latinos finally become the electoral juggernaut that forever changes the political calculus of presidential campaigns? When it comes to Latino influence on presidential elections, journalists and academics alike are prone to all-or-nothing thinking. Depending on who you ask, either they will be the decisive factor or they are completely "irrelevant," a "myth" even (Yanez 2008; Zoellner 2012). The 2016 presidential contest was supposed to be a tipping-point election: the Republicans could no longer win the presidency while alienating the vast majority of Latino voters. Scant months after Romney's loss in 2012, the GOP released its so-called autopsy, calling for, among other things, a more inclusive approach that would avoid alienating Latino, Black, Asian American, and other groups of voters who felt unwelcome in the party. At the very least, the reasoning went, they would need to avoid explicit or even implicit appeals to nativism and racism if they wished to have any chance of winning; with the White, non-Latino proportion of the electorate continuing to shrink, they could no longer afford to settle for less than one-third of the Latino vote.[1] Yet Mitt Romney's talk of "self-deportation" (Madison 2012) and his praise for Arizona's SB1070 in 2012 seem almost mild in comparison to what we witnessed in the run up to the 2016 presidential election. Donald Trump—who launched his candidacy with a speech that included the claim that Mexican immigrants were "bringing drugs, they're bringing crime, they're rapists"[2]—appeared at times to revel in antagonizing Latinos. For instance, he made the call-and-response of "We're going to build a wall! And who's gonna pay for the wall? Mexico!"[3] a favorite routine at his rallies. He repeatedly insisted that U.S. District Judge Gonzalo P. Curiel, a federal judge, could not rule impartially on a civil case against Trump due to the judge's Mexican heritage[4]: "I've been treated very unfairly by this judge. Now, this judge is of Mexican heritage. I'm building a wall, OK?" (Kertscher 2016). And past slurs—such as his repeated references to Miss Universe Alicia Machado as "Miss Housekeeping" (Ross 2016)—attracted increased scrutiny over the course of the campaign. If anyone could mobilize Latino voters via antipathy, this was surely the candidate.

Indeed, it is clear from the Latino Decisions 2016 Election Eve Poll that "Latino consciousness" surged during the most recent election cycle, with a large number of Latino voters citing support for the Latino community as the reason why they went out to vote in 2016. No doubt, the Trump factor was a major reason why; a full 55% identified Trump as "hostile" toward Latinos (Sanchez and Barreto 2016), compared to just 18% who said the same about Romney on the eve of the 2012 election. And yet it wasn't enough. The conventional wisdom that Latinos could no longer be safely ignored and certainly not openly antagonized by a candidate who had any chance of winning seems to have been incorrect. After all, if the candidate overwhelmingly preferred by a group of voters loses the election, then this group must not have been all that influential, right? Yet, as a number of authors (e.g., Fraga and Ramirez 2004; Barreto et al. 2010; Ramírez 2013; Gross and Barreto 2015) have convincingly argued, such all-or-nothing notions of group influence offer only limited insight, leading analysts to mistake random fluctuations for meaningful trends. As an antidote to such simplistic assessments, we offer an analysis of the 2016 presidential election that considers multiple aspects of influence while recognizing the inherent randomness that leads to any observed outcome in a single election. The complex dynamics of group influence are especially apparent in U.S. presidential elections, due to the role of the Electoral College and the uneven distribution of eligible voters by race and ethnicity throughout the nation. Overall, it is important to remember that every electoral outcome is the result of myriad systematic and random forces. It is tempting, especially in close elections, to fixate on some unforeseeable minor phenomenon as "decisive." Our goal is to measure systematic influence without being led astray by random fluctuation.

Consider, by way of analogy, a fanciful scenario in which an election result is to be determined by a single draw from a deck of playing cards. In the first "election," imagine that I, the candidate, will win if any card showing the suit of clubs is drawn. I have a 25% chance of winning. Suppose I draw an eight of clubs—I win the election. In the next election, imagine a slightly different scenario: I will win if a card of either black suit (clubs or spades) is drawn. This time, I have a 50% chance of winning. Now suppose I draw the jack of hearts, losing the election. Were I to fixate on the particular results, I would claim incorrectly that the former game was more advantageous to my candidacy. It would be similarly naive for us to jump to the conclusion that Latinos were less influential in the 2016 presidential election than in 2012 simply because the candidate preferred by a majority of Latinos won in 2012 and lost in 2016. Our goal is to measure Latinos' role in affecting the odds of a given outcome, as well as in the public perception of their power to change these odds. With this in mind, we shall employ computer simulations using information from the Latino Decisions 2016 Election Eve Poll, Census data, and state-by-state election results in order to ascertain Latino electoral power as a probability of being relevant to the outcome. First, however, we turn our attention to a few other indicators of Latino electoral influence: media attention, outreach efforts by campaigns, and demographic trends.

Power through Attention I: Media Coverage

The 2016 presidential race began in earnest with Cuban American Senator Ted Cruz of Texas announcing his bid for the Republican nomination on March 23, 2015, making him the first major candidate of either party to formally announce. Another Cuban American, Senator Marco Rubio of Florida, announced his own run for the GOP nomination less than a month later. Their two candidacies sparked early media speculation regarding the potential for Republican candidates to peel away some of the strong Latino support typically enjoyed by Democrats. Candidates Cruz and Rubio thus found themselves compared on their "Latino-ness" and on their ability to garner support from Latino voters across the United States (Attanasio 2016). Lost in much of this speculation was the fact that neither had attracted overwhelming Latino support in their previous elections. Cruz earned just 35% of the Latino vote in Texas while winning his Senate seat in 2012.[5] Rubio, on the other hand, did manage to garner 62% of Latino votes when he first ran for the Senate in 2010, but this was in Florida, which traditionally housed the most Republican-friendly Latino voters, many themselves of Cuban heritage.[6] Nationwide, Latinos' mixed feelings about these two Republicans made their candidacies a less obvious opportunity to attract new voters to their party. Their prominence did, however, ensure that media-led conversations about Latino voters—and their ethnic and regional diversity—started early.

During the primary election season, journalists regularly noted the growth in the population of eligible Latino voters since 2012, but were divided on whether their participation at the polls would follow suit. As it became evident that Donald Trump would secure the Republican nomination, articles discussing the Latino electorate increasingly turned to the theme of their overwhelming antipathy for Trump, frequently providing anecdotes of Latinos registering to vote for the first time specifically to cast their votes against Trump. Such reports characterized him—correctly, for the most part—as a mobilizing figure, primarily due to his anti-immigrant and specifically anti-Mexican rhetoric. Taking advantage of the apparent opportunity, Univision, the most-watched Spanish language network, created programming to promote voter registration among Spanish-speaking Latinos. Such participation by a Spanish-language media organization was hardly unprecedented. Univision itself had previously partnered with political advocacy organizations such as NCLR and NALEO, as in its "Ya Es

Hora" mobilization effort of 2012 and an election-oriented naturalization campaign in 2008, while competitor Telemundo even planted election and Census-related plotlines in its soap operas during its 2012 "Vota por Tu Futuro" campaign (Ali 2012). Even more than in previous years, though, the personal stakes were clear and attempts at journalistic impartiality had become strained. Dramatic footage of Univision's longtime Spanish-language news anchor Jorge Ramos being physically removed by security from a Trump press conference in Iowa in August 2015 (Gabriel 2015) drew early attention to growing tensions between the Trump campaign and Latinos. A number of high-profile Spanish-speaking supporters of previous Republican presidential candidates, such as Representative Ileana Ros-Lehtinen (R-FL) and Republican political consultant Ana Navarro, refused to endorse candidate Trump. The few prominent Latinos to back him tended to be reserved in their support; Representative Mario Diaz-Balart (R-FL), for example, avoided referring to Trump by name while acknowledging that he would vote for "the Republican nominee" (Mazzei 2016). Univision's Ramos and his evening news co-host Maria Elena Salinas frequently reminded viewers of their unsuccessful attempts to get anyone from the Trump campaign to agree to an interview with the network during the course of the long campaign, a snub Ramos claimed would not likely be repeated, regardless of the election results (Stelter 2016).

In the final stretch leading up to the general election, the press emphasized the importance of Latino voters to Clinton's potential victory, including reports of increased registration of Latino voters and a surge in early voting by Latinos (Levitz 2016). The press reported on Latinos' extremely high rates of support for Clinton's candidacy, further feeding into the "Latino influence" narrative. Largely missed was the possibility that an increase in White, non-Latino voters and a decrease in African American turnout might change the group influence calculus enough to make a difference in the outcome.

The media seem to have paid at least as much attention to Latino voters in 2016 as they had in 2012 and likely slightly more. We selected eleven high-circulation newspapers and compared their election coverage during five comparable periods in each election (August, September, October, the week before Election Day, and the week after Election Day).[7] Although this was a purposive sample, chosen to reflect prominence and regional diversity, the choices were made independently of any obvious factors that might lead results to be systematically different from a randomly selected set of prominent newspapers. Within the selected set of newspapers, we searched for all stories designated by LexisNexis as pertaining to the subject "elections" and counted the proportion of these that additionally contained either the word "Latino" or "Hispanic" within the article text. In four of the five comparison periods—all but the week following Election Day—most of these newspapers increased their proportional coverage of Latinos in election stories from 2012 to 2016, including ten of eleven in October. In these same four periods, the average difference represented an increase in 2016.

Overall, we observe a small but statistically detectable increase in media coverage of Latinos in election coverage from 2012 to 2016. In table 1, there are eleven rows (one per newspaper) and five pairs of columns, with each pair indicating the percentage of election articles mentioning Latinos in corresponding time periods during 2012 versus 2016—fifty-five pairwise comparisons in all (or fifty-four if we disregard the August *Minneapolis Star-Tribune*, which had no discernible Latino election coverage in August of either election year). All but one of eleven newspapers showed an average increase in Latino-related election coverage over the three months leading up to Election Day in 2016 compared to 2012. On average, we observe a small increase in proportional Latino election coverage over corresponding periods within a newspaper (+1.19% across all eleven newspapers and +2.35% over just the three full months measured, August through October). If we restrict our attention to the comparison periods prior to Election Day, before the election outcome is known, we note a statistically distinguishable but modest increase in attention to Latinos in election coverage. Thirty-one of forty-three valid newspaper-period pairs registered an increase (table 1, first eight columns—the unshaded cells represent an increase in coverage of Latinos in electoral stories). Were there in fact no change in any of the underlying rates of mention within any newspaper at corresponding periods in 2012 versus 2016, the probability of observing at least this many increases in the data by chance alone would be less than one in a thousand.[8]

Table 1. Media Attention on Latino Voters: Proportion of Stories in Each Newspaper Period Mentioning Elections That Also Mention the Term "Latino" or "Hispanic" (LexisNexis)

	3 months before election		2 months before election		1 month before election		1 week before election		1 week after election	
	Aug. 2012	Aug. 2016	Sept. 2012	Sept. 2016	Oct. 2012	Oct. 2016	Oct. 30–Nov. 5, 2012	Nov. 1–7, 2016	Nov. 7–13, 2012	Nov. 9–15, 2016
USA Today (US)	8.59%	6.33%	5.06%	6.92%	5.41%	8.85%	7.25%	8.96%	12.61%	14.53%
New York Times (NY)	6.61%	11.55%	7.64%	7.31%	6.00%	9.73%	6.56%	12.25%	15.28%	11.67%
Tampa Bay Times (FL)	5.64%	7.38%	8.24%	9.84%	6.72%	10.70%	5.10%	14.12%	11.51%	10.20%
Philadelphia Inquirer (PA)	2.82%	6.25%	4.24%	3.92%	4.71%	4.17%	11.76%	4.60%	17.50%	23.40%
Washington Post (DC)	3.59%	11.35%	3.67%	7.45%	3.46%	7.71%	4.93%	11.83%	11.40%	9.86%
Las Cruces Sun-News (NM)	8.93%	8.33%	9.33%	3.33%	4.46%	6.98%	9.09%	5.88%	25.00%	18.18%
Minneapolis Star-Tribune (MN)	0.00%	0.00%	2.25%	1.67%	2.88%	4.24%	2.50%	2.38%	0.00%	4.00%
Christian Science Monitor (US)	11.59%	9.38%	4.80%	14.09%	5.96%	8.60%	15.91%	7.55%	18.64%	14.29%
Wisconsin State Journal (WI)	0.75%	2.78%	1.22%	3.85%	0.00%	3.52%	0.00%	2.33%	0.00%	6.52%
Durham Herald-Sun (NC)	6.61%	9.09%	2.13%	13.73%	2.44%	4.35%	5.88%	0.00%	7.69%	0.00%
Denver Post (CO)	7.80%	10.94%	7.28%	10.37%	2.72%	6.42%	8.82%	11.36%	21.25%	11.71%

Note: For each newspaper, the proportion of election coverage mentioning the term "Hispanic" or "Latino" in a particular month or week in 2012 (measured relative to Election Day) is compared to the corresponding month or week in 2016. Paired observations in which this estimated coverage dropped in 2016 appear in gray.

Treating the newspapers as distinct, seven out of ten papers registering a change in August saw an increase in proportional coverage of Latinos, as well as seven out of eleven in September, ten out of eleven in October, and seven of eleven in the final week before Election Day. If there were no change in underlying reporting rates at each newspaper, the probability of observing at least this much of a shift by chance would be just 0.0066.[9] During the week immediately after the election, however, the upward trend is absent from the data. Six of eleven newspapers had fewer mentions of Latinos in election coverage in the immediate aftermath of the 2016 election than in 2012, with an average drop of 1.5% in our sample—statistically indistinguishable from no change. Were Hillary Clinton the victor, one anticipates a narrative emphasizing realized Latino influence. Instead, the coverage in the immediate aftermath focused on the shock of the outcome, the possible problems with polling, campaign missteps, and possible reasons behind the shifts in Pennsylvania, Michigan, and Wisconsin.

Power through Attention II: The Presidential Campaigns

When it comes to campaign indicators of group influence, perception is reality. That is, if a candidate and his or her team pay particular attention to a specific subset of voters, using scarce resources to win their support and/or mobilize them to show up to vote, it is because they believe the group is an important component of a winning strategy. They recognize the group's potentially pivotal role in a number of plausible paths to 270 Electoral College votes and acknowledge the importance of motivating these voters. Moreover, this means that the candidate will be loath to take any policy positions or public stances that would likely alienate such voters. Thus, for example, we witnessed a number of uncomfortable moments for both Bernie Sanders and Hillary Clinton during the primaries, as African American activists affiliated with Black Lives Matter heckled them at campaign rallies, pushing the candidates to more vocally support their cause. Despite long-standing concerns among Black voters that Democrats take their support for granted, surely the recognition that strong Black turnout would be essential to a

Democratic victory helped push candidates to increasingly embrace these activists and become more outspoken on their behalf. The fact that they did so—rather than, say, dismissing them as too radical—was a clear indication of latent African American voting power. What then of campaign overtures to Latino voting power?

The Democratic and Republican presidential campaigns diverged in their approach to mobilizing Latino voters in 2016. Hillary Rodham Clinton's presidential campaign made Latino outreach an important feature of her run for the White House. This was demonstrated in many dimensions of the campaign, including hiring of key staff, selection of the vice presidential candidate, its online platforms, and ad campaigns (Beckel 2016). For starters, Amanda Rentería, the daughter of a former farm worker, became the national political director of the Hillary for America campaign in March 2015; moreover, she became the first Latina to take on such a role for a major party candidate. A few months later a DREAMer,[10] Lorella Praeli, was hired to head Latino outreach for the campaign. Having secured the nomination in June 2016, Clinton selected Senator Tim Kaine of Virginia, a person who has spent significant time in Latin America and speaks fluent Spanish, as her running mate. During the campaign, Senator Kaine made several appearances in which he was interviewed in Spanish or made full speeches in Spanish. Latino supporters could access a Spanish-language version of the campaign's official website, which also included a link to "Latinos for Hillary."[11] Furthermore, the campaign itself and the political action committees (PACs) supporting the Clinton-Kaine ticket ran many advertisements in both Spanish and English, referencing Trump's remarks about Mexican immigrants. This is not to say the Clinton campaign avoided all missteps with the Latino community. Most notable was the backlash to a blog post written during the primary campaign by a Latina staffer comparing Hillary Clinton to "your abuela," Spanish for grandmother (Luisi 2015), sparking widespread use of the hashtag #NotMyAbuela (Easley 2015).

The Trump presidential campaign relied almost completely on the Republican National Committee (RNC) for Latino outreach. No official efforts were made by the Trump campaign to reach Latino voters other than convening with the RNC and a National Latino Advisory Committee formed of "business, civic, and faith-based Latino leaders" in August 2016 (Collins 2016). The committee had the purpose of serving as an intermediary between the Trump campaign and the Latino community. A week or so after the Trump campaign met with this committee, several of its members either resigned or considered resigning from their posts because of disagreements with Trump's proposed immigration policies. Though an organization named "Latinos for Trump" was active during the election, it was an independently organized group, not sponsored by the Trump campaign. Additionally, the press characterized the campaign as an English-only campaign, in that the campaign was run entirely in the English language (Goldmacher 2016).

The only Spanish-language ads aired in late October 2016, and even these were created and funded by a PAC supporting Trump's candidacy rather than by the campaign itself. Such weak efforts to reach Latinos and Spanish-speaking voters were typified by the ubiquitous signs at rallies reading "Latinos para Trump," a grammatically incorrect translation of "Latinos for Trump" (Rupert 2016; Saxena 2016). By way of contrast, the 2012 Romney campaign actively engaged Latino voters, creating a Latino outreach team named "Juntos with Romney" (Together with Romney); membership in this team was almost entirely made of current or former Latino Republican politicians from state governments and Congress. The Romney campaign had a Spanish-language website and ran ad campaigns and Web videos targeting Latinos voters, while having full-time Latino outreach staffers in Florida, Nevada, North Carolina, Colorado, and New Mexico.

A number of high-profile Latino Republicans either declined to endorse Trump or publicly opposed him. Prominent Republican strategist Ana Navarro, despite a long history of supporting Republican candidates—including stints as National Latino Co-Chair for the John McCain and John Huntsman presidential campaigns—quickly became a passionate critic of candidate Trump. The Republican nominee's offensive characterization of Mexican immigrants in the announcement of his presidential bid may have been the initial catalyst for her staunch opposition to his run, but the reasons she provides for her grudging decision to actually vote for Hillary Clinton include concern for the members of the intersecting communities of which she is a part—immigrants, Latinos, women, and Republicans—as well as those that count her friends and family among its members—for example, Jews, veterans, African Americans, and disabled people (Navarro 2016). Navarro's account highlights the opportunities for members of different aggrieved groups to leverage their joint voting power.

The Changing Electorate: Demographics and Ethnic Diversity

According to Barreto et al. (2010), "A prerequisite for group influence is a minimum group size, and preferably one that is cohesive or mobilized" (913). Demographic trends can contribute to changes in cohesion and thus to variation in group voting influence, not only through relative population growth, but also via ethnic and ideological diversity. For instance, the distinctiveness of Florida subsides as Cuban American voters become less dominant in the state (Cordeiro 2016) and overall Latino voting patterns there begin to more closely mirror that in the rest of the country. Additionally, the shared perception of animosity directed at all Latino communities, without ethnic or regional distinction, provides an incentive for development of a shared pan-ethnic Latino identity. Indeed, the continuing rise in the number of Latinos naming "immigration reform" as the most important issue facing the Latino community—a plurality of 39% in the LD 2016 Election Eve poll—is a sign that candidate Trump's rhetoric—his promises of mass deportations, of building a border wall while demanding that Mexico foot the bill, and derogatory statements about Mexican American Judge Gonzalo Curiel and Venezuelan American former Miss Universe Alicia Machado—may have had the unintended consequence of bringing together Latinos of different ethnicities. Indeed, in 2016, immigration reform became the most important issue for Latinos in all twelve states included in Latino Decisions' 2016 Election Eve Poll. This is quite a change from 2012, when Arizona was the only state out of the eleven polled demonstrating a similar pattern.

While Florida continues to stand out as having the lowest rate of Latino support for Democratic presidential candidates, it looks more like other states with each election. Just 67% of Florida's Latinos voted for Clinton in 2016 (compared to around 79% nationwide), but this gap is narrower than

58% (Florida) versus 73% (nationally) for Obama in 2012 or just 44% (Florida) versus 58% (nationally) for Kerry in 2004, according to the Pew Research Center (Suro et al. 2005). Demographic changes in Florida's Latino community over the past twenty years—particularly the influx of Puerto Ricans to Central Florida—appear to have produced an increase in support of Democratic candidates.

One additional sign that pan-Latino identity was on the rise during the 2016 election season was the increase in reports of voting specifically with the "Latino community" in mind. Latino Decisions asked Latino respondents a similar question in 2012 and 2016 on the reason for their decision to vote, allowing them to choose among three alternatives, (1) to support Democratic candidates, (2) to support Republican candidates, and (3) to support (and represent) the Latino community.[12] Forty-two percent of Latinos reported they were voting "to support and represent the Latino community" in 2016, while just 36% said there were voting "to support the Latino community" in 2012, an estimated six-point increase. Thus, Latino identity seems to have been at least as salient during this election cycle than the last, with feelings of Latino-linked fate likely a key attitude mobilizing Latinos to vote.

Influence at the Electoral College: Measuring the Probability of Group Relevance

Journalists and bloggers understandably use dramatic language when assessing Latino voting influence. Breathless headlines, such as "Trump Awakens a Sleeping Giant" (Scotti 2016) or "This year, Latino voters . . . really might decide this election" (Cohn 2016), stir excitement and draw attention. Readers would be less likely to click on a headline that reads "Latino Voters Likely to Be Somewhat More Influential This Year." Even ignoring the multifaceted nature of group voting influence discussed earlier, the popular notion of some group or groups having a "decisive" role in an election's outcome is hardly well defined. Counterfactual reasoning makes intuitive sense and we thus often treat electoral voting patterns like physical causal scenarios: Striking the match was decisive in starting the fire because were it not for this act, the flame would not have erupted; likewise, we may say that college-educated women were decisive in an election because if they hadn't voted, the other candidate would have won. Indeed, it can be interesting to consider such extreme counterfactuals—see, for instance, the various electoral maps showing women-only, men-only, and so on (Gilson 2017).

The problem is that, while they may be of some descriptive value, such scenarios are too implausible to be meaningful in a conversation about electoral influence. It makes more sense to consider counterfactuals that are within the realm of possibility; fanciful scenarios such as an electorate consisting of all Latinos or non-Latinos are irrelevant to decision makers such as eligible voters, actual voters, and campaigns. We take up the modeling and simulation strategy introduced in Gross and Barreto (2015)—which in turn is based on insights by Andrew Gelman and coauthors (2002, 2004)—using data from Latino Decisions' 2016 Election Eve poll and Census voting and registration data to assess the probability of group voting influence.[13] The basic idea is to answer the following question, given our best current information: What was the probability that the election would be decided by a set of states whose electoral votes in turn hinged on the turnout and vote choice of Latinos? That is, we define Latino voting power as the estimated probability of obtaining Electoral College results in which both (1) the winning candidate could be switched by a set of states casting their electoral votes differently and (2) the margins of victory in those pivotal states are close enough that Latinos could have flipped the state victor by a plausibly different turnout and/or vote share per candidate. Our claim is that voting influence is intimately tied to uncertainty; if a group's behavior is too predictable, in terms of either turnout or preference, or lacks the cohesion that allows its members to be reached through a coherent and efficient strategy, the group can exert little influence either on the outcome or on subsequent policy positions by the candidate. In terms of the preceding analogy, we tend to think of striking the match as more influential than the presence of oxygen, although the fire would not have been initiated in the absence of either. Similarly, although it is the case that Obama wouldn't have won the 2012 election if people in cities hadn't voted, we would not typically think of "urban voters" as an influential bloc. There was no plausible threat that urban voters would abstain en masse (or vote heavily Republican). If urban voters (or women, middle class, etc.) are the oxygen, the question for us is whether Latino voters may serve as the matchstick.

We do not treat Latino votes for each candidate probabilistically—instead, we identify a range of plausible outcomes using Latino Decisions' polling in current and previous elections, together with Census and Exit Poll data, and then treat the non-Latino White vote probabilistically. Although these plausible ranges are somewhat arbitrary, they are far more realistic than considering outcomes with and without the entire Latino electorate, as is commonplace. We presume that Latinos as a percentage of a state's voters will remain close to recent precedent, corrected for known demographic shifts, and that the percentage of Latinos voting for the Republican or Democrat will also not stray beyond a few points below or above polling by state over the past three elections. Where no state information is available (e.g., Michigan, Minnesota, Maine's Second District), we use national figures or neighboring states as a proxy).

Key to our assessment is the understanding that even after an election has occurred, we must resist the temptation to treat the outcome as predetermined; the inherent randomness of what has transpired must be addressed in the measurement itself. We thus use data on actual voting together with historical information on variability on the national and state level in order to estimate how likely, in retrospect, various electoral college outcomes were and in what proportion of such hypothetical outcomes a plausible change in Latino turnout and/or vote choice would have resulted in a different winner. We use a common statistical approach called random effects modeling. To understand this intuitively, imagine that Hillary Clinton and Donald Trump are playing tug-of-war, with states (and their respective electoral votes) dangling from the rope so that the states most supportive of each are closest to them on the rope, from Washington, DC, (on Clinton's end) to West Virginia (on Trump's end), in this past election. The object for each candidate is to pull the rope far enough that states worth more than 270 electoral votes cross the threshold marker placed on the ground between them. Neither campaign knows the exact ordering of states along the rope, but many arrangements are virtually impossible (for example, Massachusetts closer to Trump than

Alabama). We assume there is a nationwide component to the electoral dynamics (the rope, with all states, moving back and forth)—this is called the *national effect* and it varies from election to election or even across polls in the same election. We may assume that certain shocks (e.g., renewed investigations into Clinton's e-mails or a big endorsement) may nudge national support in one direction or the other. However, many dynamics are state specific—represented by *state effects*, akin to individual states leapfrogging one another along the rope. We restrict ourselves to consideration of those states with a nonnegligible chance of voting for either candidate: Arizona, Colorado, Florida, Georgia, Iowa, Michigan, Minnesota, North Carolina, New Hampshire, New Mexico, Nevada, Ohio, Pennsylvania, Virginia, Wisconsin, Maine's statewide vote, and Nebraska's Second District.[14]

The simulation begins with the actual outcome and then uses estimated probability distributions for the nationwide and state-specific random effects to generate different plausible outcomes in proportion to their likelihood. Thus, the overall national voting may move in either direction from the actual outcome, as may the individual state votes per candidate. For ease of comparison, we employ the same normal distributions of random effects used in Gross and Barreto (2015), estimated from hierarchical linear models fit to polling variation in 2012, actual historical electoral outcomes, and variants on these for the purpose of sensitivity analysis. One possible limitation is the lack of regional random effects in the model. In general, this is hard to do well, since regional cohesion ebbs and flows over time, making historical data unreliable for the task. While the lack of independence within particular groups of states is not typically a major concern, the fact that we cannot effectively model regional dynamics means that our assessment will necessarily fail to take account of the rust-belt bump enjoyed by Trump in 2016 (in particular, in Wisconsin, Michigan, Ohio, and Pennsylvania).

In each of 100,000 simulation runs, Clinton starts with 184 safe electoral votes and Trump with 164 safe electoral votes. The remaining 190 electoral votes from sixteen states in closest contention—and one district, Nebraska's Second District—are awarded according the outcomes of each simulation in the following manner. We begin by fixing Latino turnout based on Census estimates and Latino vote choice (proportion voting for Trump and

Clinton, respectively) according to Latino Decisions Election Eve polling where available (and a combination of past polling, national average, and imputation by substituting figures from similar states where it is not). Using this information and the final vote tallies, we algebraically obtain our starting estimate for non-Latino turnout and vote choice. A nationwide random effect is drawn from a normal distribution with mean zero and standard deviation from each model's parameter estimates, and state-specific random effects are drawn in a similar fashion for each state/district.[15] The common nationwide effect and individual state effect are added to each state's estimate of actual non-Latino vote proportion, resulting in the simulated non-Latino popular vote within each state in contention. Finally, we calculate the Latino vote in each of the states under two scenarios—one most beneficial to Trump and the other most beneficial to Clinton.[16] In each run of this simulation, we record whether each state's electoral votes would change according to scenario—if so, we say that the outcome falls within the range of plausible Latino variation, making this group relevant to the outcome. Most importantly, we calculate the total electoral votes under the Trump-optimal and Clinton-optimal Latino vote and note whether the change results in a different candidate moving past the 270-vote threshold to win the election.

We operationalize Latino voting influence here as the estimated probability that a set of states could together determine the outcome of the election. This probability depends on the Latino turnout and vote choice within plausible limits in each of these states. In table 2, we provide this probability of Latino voting influence (PLVI) under each of four simulations and compare it to the counterpart estimate from 2012 (Gross and Barreto 2015). The featured simulation (column 1), in which the national random effect has standard deviation 0.02 and state random effects have standard deviation 0.01, assumes the same polling variability as existed in the months leading up to the 2012 general election, allowing simulated elections to bounce around in a fashion similar to what we witnessed in those national and state polls. In the simulation that assumes the widest distribution of national and state random effects, based on the Gelman HLM estimates from long-term differences over multiple elections, the PLVI drops to 22%, not too far from the estimate of 19% from 2012. That set of simulations presumes that we had

Table 2. Probability of Group Relevance in the Electoral College 2016

| | $\sigma_{nation} = 0.02$ $\sigma_{state} = 0.01$ | $\sigma_{nation} = 0.030$ $\sigma_{state} = 0.015$ | $\sigma_{nation} = 0.06$ $\sigma_{state} = 0.04$ | $\sigma_{nation} = 0.01$ $\sigma_{state} = 0.03$ |
	Short-term estimates, based on polls	Greater uncertainty	Gelman estimates over a few decades	High uncertainty for states, not overall
Latinos (2016)	0.364	0.368	0.217	0.317
Latinos (2012)	0.167	0.232	0.189	0.138

Note: Proportion of simulations in which Latino voters would have been relevant, in the sense that there was some set of states together determining the outcome of the simulated election, each of which individually had results that could have plausibly been different given realistic variation in Latino turnout and vote choice. The first column estimates uncertainty at the national and state level, where uncertainty over national and state-specific effects is estimated from movement in average polls provided by Real Clear Politics over the three months prior to the 2012 general election. This most naturally captures the short-term variability and a sense of what might have been possible, given the actual final votes within the states. The second column assumes an additional 50% standard deviation in both sets of random effects; this may be considered an allowance for additional uncertainty beyond variation in recent polls. Simulation results in the third column were generated using long-term estimates of variance in state and nation effects, and the final column is based on a hypothetical situation in which the overall nationwide figures are precisely measured, but we are less sure how individual states will vary (100,000 elections simulated).

Table 3. Probability of Group Influence by State

| | Short-term variability (polling) | | Long-term variability (Gelman estimates) | |
	P(Latino state influence)	P(state is member of Latino-influence states pivotal in election)	P(Latino state influence)	P(state is member of Latino-influence states pivotal in election)
Arizona	0.960	0.364	0.522	0.174
Florida	0.850	0.364	0.433	0.183
Nevada	0.413	0.304	0.339	0.131
New Mexico	0.288	0.244	0.434	0.139
Pennsylvania	0.201	0.191	0.083	0.042
Wisconsin	0.141	0.135	0.094	0.043
Michigan	0.081	0.080	0.047	0.024
North Carolina	0.278	0.077	0.088	0.033
Nebraska second district	0.071	0.040	0.024	0.008
Virginia	0.022	0.019	0.078	0.037
Georgia	0.236	0.017	0.089	0.027
New Hampshire	0.017	0.017	0.014	0.006
Minnesota	0.011	0.010	0.044	0.020
Iowa	0.111	0.009	0.039	0.011
Colorado	0.012	0.008	0.127	0.048
Maine (at large)	0.006	0.003	0.134	0.044
Ohio	0.083	0.003	0.036	0.010

Note: In 100,000 simulations, centered on actual outcome of 2016 election, assuming nation- and state-level variability normally distributed with given standard deviations, P(Latino state influence) gives the proportion of simulations in which a given state's candidate preference could be flipped based only on realistic variation in Latino turnout and vote choice (i.e., simulated voting puts the state in the interval of Latino voting power). P(state is member of Latino-influence states pivotal in election) gives the proportion of simulations in which Latino voters would have been relevant to the overall national outcome (in the sense of table 2) and in which the given state is in the pivotal set of states.

very little knowledge specific to the 2016 election and that the national vote and state-specific votes might vary as widely as they have over the course of the past several elections.

Concentrating on simulations that best reflect our uncertainty just before the election (i.e., that based on polling variability alone), the PLVI is 36% in 2016, compared to 17% in 2012. A PLVI of 36% means that there was an estimated 36% chance that Latinos would be a relevant voting bloc (compared to 17% in 2012). From the perspective of a campaign, one would be less inclined to take a group for granted if there was a 36% (around 1 in 3) chance that their voting behavior would prove pivotal than if there was only a 17% (or around 1 in 6 chance), though a cautious campaign with sufficient resources would hardly wish to ignore such a group in either scenario. Among the comparisons corresponding to each of four sets of random effect distributions, only those stemming from the third set are somewhat close across the two elections (0.217 in 2016 vs. 0.189 in 2012). Loosely, this reflects the narrow victory by Trump, bringing Latinos and many other groups into positions of influence; various slight differences in voting dynamics would have reversed his victory. A wider distribution on national and state-level random effects is equivalent to allowing greater overall swing of Democratic versus Republican support, as well as greater sorting of individual states relative to one another. The bottom line is that, despite Donald Trump's victory, Latino group relevance to the Electoral College vote was no less—and likely a bit greater—than in the previous presidential election.

Conclusion: Targeted Voter Suppression as an Indicator of Latino Influence

While we tend to focus on voter mobilization as a component of group electoral influence, attempts at demobilization may also be viewed as indicators of voting power. After all, targeting specific classes of voters and making it more difficult for them to vote is tricky business; not only may it run the risk of a legal response (as when courts have turned back attempts at redistricting and voter ID laws that would have the effect of disenfranchising black voters), but it may also lead to voter backlash and have the opposite of its intended effect.

Influence of Latinos on the 2016 election is dependent on the existing institutional limitations on their ability to participate in elections. In recent years state governments across the United States have passed legislation that has it made more difficult for Latinos, and people of color in general, to both get registered and vote in elections. Furthermore, the 2013 Supreme Court decision in *Shelby County v. Holder* has resulted in a severe wound to the Voting Rights Act (VRA) that may have hampered the electoral power of Latinos in the 2016 election.

A study commissioned by the Leadership Conference Education Fund (2016) found that in the wake of the 2013 Supreme Court decision that eliminated VRA Section 5 coverage of nine full states and some jurisdictions within six other states, in total 868 polling places have been closed in Alabama, Arizona, Louisiana, Mississippi, North Carolina, South Carolina, and Texas. The state of Texas closed the largest number polling places, with 403 closures, 46% of all closures, followed by Arizona with 212 poll closures, 24% of all closures (Thompson 2016). This means that two of the top ten Latino population states have seen greatest number of poll closures since Shelby County; Texas is the state with the second highest population of Latinos in the United States and Arizona is sixth. More than 10 million Texas residents are Latinos, 39% of the state population (López and Stepler 2016b), and Arizona has a population of little more than 2 million Latinos, who make up 31% of the total state population (López and Stepler 2016a). Overall, the total poll closures represent a 16% reduction in polling places among counties in the study that were once covered by Section 5 of the VRA, and 46% of the 381 counties in the study have fewer voting locations.

In addition to the hundreds of polling place closures, many other voting restrictions were in place at the time of the 2016 General Election. Fourteen states had new voting restrictions active for the first time in this election, ranging from registration restrictions to limits on early voting; these include Alabama, Arizona, Indiana, Kansas, Mississippi, Nebraska, New Hampshire, Ohio, Rhode Island, South Carolina, Tennessee, Texas, Virginia, and Wisconsin. Eleven of these states have new photo ID or proof of citizenship requirements for voting, with Texas being one of them. Another six states now have greater registration restrictions, including Illinois, Florida, and Texas, with Illinois being the state with the fifth highest Latino population in the United States and Florida the third highest. Eight states reduced the time period for early voting, with Florida among them (The Brennan Center for Justice 2016).

Looking ahead, the clearest sign of Latino electoral influence may be, oddly enough, the extent to which it attracts attempts to suppress Latino voters. That newly elected President Trump clings to baseless claims that millions of noncitizen ineligible voters unlawfully voted against him simply as an explanation for his popular vote loss may be a signal that he and his supporters will continue to push aggressively for policies that make voting more difficult, particularly for Latinos and other communities of color. A broad view of group voting influence will allow us to approach externally enforced demobilization as the counterpart to voter mobilization, a sign that minority populations' growing influence is great enough to invite risky countermeasures.

Notes

1. Mitt Romney's presidential campaign declared 38% as the "magic number" of Latino voters needed in order to win the 2012 election (Joseph 2012). In the end, he only managed to get 27%.

2. Washington Post Staff (June 15, 2015). Full text: "Donald Trump Announces Presidential Bid." *The Washington Post.* https://www.washingtonpost.com/news/post-politics/wp/2015/06/16/full-text-donald-trump-announces-a-presidential-bid.

3. See, for example, footage here: https://www.youtube.com/watch?v=z5YCExZE0rw

4. Totenberg, Nina. "Who Is Judge Gonzalo Curiel, The Man Trump Attacked for His Mexican Heritage?" *NPR: Politics,* June 7.

5. Texas results from the ImpreMedia-Latino Decisions Election Eve Poll at http://www.latinovote2012.com/app/#all-tx-all.

6. He would only earn 40% of the Latino vote when—after losing the presidential nomination to Trump—he won re-election to his Senate seat.

7. We began by identifying top circulation newspapers available through

LexisNexis without including more than one from a single state (http://www.cision.com/us/2014/06/top-10-us-daily-newspapers and https://www.agilitypr.com/resources/top-media-outlets/top-15-daily-american-newspapers). This resulted in the following: *USA Today, New York Times, Los Angeles Times, Washington Post, Denver Post,* and *Tampa Bay Times,* the final two of which are from swing states Colorado and Florida. (*Los Angeles Times* had to be dropped, as 2012 was not available in the database. We replaced it with the highest circulation California newspaper available: *San Jose Mercury News.*) We then chose the highest circulation newspapers in the database for each of several states, chosen to emphasize potential swing states in different regions, giving us the *Philadelphia Inquirer* (Pennsylvania) (a top-twenty national paper), the *Minneapolis Star-Tribune* (Minnesota), the *Wisconsin State Journal* (Wisconsin), the *Durham Sun-Herald* (North Carolina), and the *Las Cruces Sun-News* (New Mexico). Finally, we added another national newspaper, the Christian Science Monitor, a highly regarded paper that was one of the first to abandon print completely in favor of online journalism, bringing the total to eleven.

8. Formally, a one-tailed hypothesis test assuming a binomial distribution with probability of increase and probability of decrease both equal to 0.5 yields a *p* value of 0.00096 (the probability of 31 or more increases in 43 chances), meaning we can reject the null of no difference at all conventional significance levels. This is a simple nonparametric test that considers only direction of observed change, not magnitude.

9. The probability of at least 7 of 10 in one month, 7 of 11 in two months, and 10 of 11 in one month is 0.00055 times 12 ways that these outcomes can be arranged. (The multinomial coefficient corresponding to the number of arrangements is 4!/2!1!1! = 12)

10. Noncitizens born outside the United States but living here since childhood would be eligible under the DREAM Act (Development, Relief, and Education for Alien Minors)—first introduced in the U.S. Senate in 2001—to apply for legal residency. Individuals covered by the bill have come to refer to themselves as DREAMers.

11. https://www.hillaryclinton.com/es

12. The wording in parentheses was added in 2016.

13. https://www.census.gov/data/tables/time-series/demo/voting-and-registration/p20-580.html.

14. Maine and Nebraska are the only states that currently may split their electoral votes. The only ones in contention were the two electoral votes that Maine

allots by popular vote winner and the one Nebraska vote based on the popular vote in their Second Congressional District.

15. We use the term "state" here to indicate each of the fifteen states with all electoral votes at stake, as well as for Maine's two at-large electoral votes awarded to the winner of the statewide vote and the single electoral vote awarded to the winner of Nebraska's Second District.

16. We define the boundaries of plausible Latino turnout as ranging from 35% to 65% of eligible Latino voters within a state, centered on the actual national average of around 50% and encompassing actual state estimates ranging from 36% (Michigan and Minnesota) to 64% (Virginia). We define limits of plausible vote choice based on recent elections, specific to state but generally ranging from around 10% to 34% of Latinos supporting the Republican among those voting for one of the two major-party candidates. (The exception is Florida, with low and high limits assumed to be 17% and 45%, respectively.)

References

Ali, Ambreen. 2012. "GOTV: A Mission of Hispanic Media." *Roll Call*, March 3.

Attanasio, Cedar. 2016. "Are Ted Cruz and Marco Rubio 'Latino' Presidential Candidates? 4 Factors to Consider Ahead of Nevada." *Latin Times*, February 19.

Beckel, Michael. 2016. "Hillary Clinton Campaign, Super PACs Targeting Latino Voters." *Time Magazine*, September 28.

Barreto, Matt A., Loren Collingwood, and Sylvia Manzano. 2010. "A New Measure of Group Influence in Presidential Elections: Assessing Latino Influence in 2008." *Political Research Quarterly* 63 (4): 908–21.

The Brennan Center for Justice. 2016. "Voting Restrictions in Place for 2016 Presidential Election." August 2. http://www.brennancenter.org.

Collins, Eliza. 2016. "Trump Relying on RNC for Latino Outreach." *USA Today*, August 30.

Cohn, Nate. 2016. "This Time, There Really is a Hispanic Voter Surge." *New York Times*, November 7. https://www.nytimes.com/2016/11/08/upshot/this-time-there-really-is-a-hispanic-voter-surge.html.

Cordeiro, Monivette. 2016. "Puerto Ricans Will Surpass Cubans in Florida by 2020, New Report Says." *Orlando Weekly*, September 12.

Easley, Jonathan. 2015. "Clinton's Latino Outreach Sparks Online Backlash." *The Hill*, December 22. http://www.thehill.com.

Fraga, Luis Ricardo, and Ricardo Ramírez. 2004. "Demography and Political

Influence: Disentangling the Latino Vote." *Harvard Journal of Latino Policy* 16: 69–96.

Gabriel, Trip. 2015. "At Donald Trump Event, Jorge Ramos of Univision Is Snubbed, Ejected and Debated." *New York Times*, August 25.

Gelman, Andrew, Jonathan N. Katz, and Francis Tuerlinckx. 2002. "The Mathematics and Statistics of Voting Power." *Statistical Science* 17 (4): 420–35.

Gelman, Andrew, Jonathan N. Katz, and Joseph Bafumi. 2004. "Standard Voting Power Indexes Do Not Work: An Empirical Analysis." *British Journal of Political Science* 34 (4): 657–74.

Gilson, Dave. 2016. "How the Candidates' Demographic Base Stacks Up, State by State." *Mother Jones*, November 1.

Goldmacher, Shane. 2016. "Trump's English-Only Campaign." *Politico*, September 23.

Gross, Justin H., and Matt A. Barreto. 2015. "Latino Influence and the Electoral College: Assessing the Probability of Group Relevance." In *Latinos and the 2012 Election: The New Face of the American Voter*, edited by Gabriel R. Sanchez, 1–18. East Lansing: Michigan State University Press.

Joseph, Cameron. 2012. "Mitt's Target Number to Take Hispanic Vote from Obama: 38 Percent." *The Hill*, August 22. http://thehill.com.

Kertscher, Tom. 2016. "Donald Trump's Racial Comments about Latino Judge in Trump University Case." *Politifact Wisconsin*, June 8. http://www.politifact.com.

Levitz, Eric. 2016. "Latino Turnout Surges in Early Voting." *New York Magazine: Intelligencer*, November 4.

López, Gustavo, and Renee Stepler. 2016a. "Latinos in the 2016 Election: Arizona." *Pew Research Center: Latino Trends*, January 19. http://www.pewLatino.org.

———. 2016b. "Latinos in the 2016 Election: Texas." *Pew Research Center: Latino Trends*, January 19. http://www.pewLatino.org.

Luisi, Paola. 2015. "7 Things Hillary Clinton Has in Common with Your Abuela." *HillaryClinton.com*, December 22.

Madison, Lucy. 2012. "Romney on Immigration: I'm for 'Self-Deportation.'" *CBS News*, January 24.

Mazzei, Patricia. 2016. "Diaz-Balart's Awkward Position When It Comes to Trump." *Miami Herald*, August 17.

Navarro, Ana. 2016. "I'm Voting for Hillary Clinton—and Against Donald Trump." *CNN*, November 8.

Ramírez, Ricardo. 2013. *Mobilizing Opportunities: The Evolving Latino Electorate and the*

Future of American Politics. Charlottesville: University of Virginia Press.

Ross, Janell. 2016. "Alicia Machado, the Woman Trump Called Miss Housekeeping, Is Ready to Vote Against Donald Trump." *The Washington Post: The Fix,* September 27.

Rupert, Evelyn. 2016. "Convention Bungles 'Latinos for Trump' Sign." *The Hill,* July 21.

Sanchez, Gabriel, and Matt A. Barreto. 2016. "In Record Numbers, Latinos Voted Overwhelmingly Against Trump. We Did the Research." *Monkey Cage* (blog), *Washington Post,* November 11.

Saxena, Jaya. 2016. "This 'Latinos Para Trump' Doesn't Seem Right." *Daily Dot,* July 22.

Scotti, Ciro. 2016. "Trump Awakens a Sleeping Giant: Record Turnout for Latinos." *Fiscal Times,* November 7.

Stelter, Brian. 2016. "Univision's Jorge Ramos Says Trump's Snub of Latino Media Will Cost Him." *CNN,* November 8.

Suro, Roberto, Richard Fry, and Jeffrey Passel. 2005. "Hispanics and the 2004 Election: Population, Electorate, and Voters." June 27. https://pewhispanic.org.

Thompson, Scott. 2016. "The Great Poll Closure." The Leadership Conference Education Fund, November. http://civilrightsdocs.

Yanez, Alonso. 2008. "Myth of the Latino Vote." *Latino Link News,* October 29. http://news.newamericamedia.org.

Zoellner, Tom. 2012. "The Myth of the Latino Vote." *Atlantic,* September.

The Latino Rejection of the Trump Campaign

The Biggest Voter Gap on Record

Barbara Gomez-Aguinaga and Gabriel R. Sanchez

ONE OF THE MOST DISCUSSED QUESTIONS IN THE RUN UP TO THE AN-nouncement that Donald Trump had won the presidency was how the Latino population would react to the Trump campaign, which included rhetoric regarding immigrants, Mexico, and Latinos and led many people to state that the presidential campaign of Donald Trump was unprecedented in modern American elections (Damore 2016; Elmer and Todd 2016; Pantoja 2016; Slaughter 2016; VanSickle-Ward and Pantoja 2016). The Trump campaign's hostility toward Latinos has been well documented. We do not elaborate extensively on the specifics of the campaign in this regard.

Donald Trump set the tone for his campaign when he announced his candidacy for the nomination of the Republican Party with the following statement: "When Mexico sends its people, they're not sending their best . . . They're bringing drugs. They're bringing crime. They're rapists . . . It's coming from all over South and Latin America." The Trump campaign extended the racialization of Latinos for political gain when he openly criticized other GOP candidates based on their direct and indirect con-nections to Latinos and particularly Latino immigrants. This included personalized jabs at Jeb Bush, whose wife is a Mexican immigrant who has since become a naturalized citizen, and Ted Cruz, for having a Cuban-born father (Schleifer 2015; Smith 2015). Although some might contend that Trump's tactics were not distinct from those of other candidates looking to win their party's nomination, his decision to heighten race by connecting his opposition to Latino immigrants disparaged not only these candidates, but the Latino population as a whole.

As the Trump campaign picked up steam and saw the electoral benefits associated with racializing Latinos, the campaign continued this general approach by utilizing Latino elites as a mechanism to alienate the Latino community more broadly. This included being openly critical of New Mexico governor and fellow Republican Susana Martinez during a campaign visit to the state of New Mexico in May. In his speech, Donald Trump had the following quote that was reported widely by national media outlets: "Hey! Maybe I'll run for governor of New Mexico. I'll get this place going. She's not doing the job. We've got to get her moving. Come on: Let's go, governor" (Sullivan 2016).

Consistent with this more general approach, but more widely discussed in the national media, was Trump's statements regarding federal judge Gonzalo Curiel, a U.S.-born son of Mexican immigrants who oversaw the lawsuit against Trump University, a case that became a major national discussion, given the unfortunate timing of the case from Trump's perspective (Kendall 2016; Parker and Martin 2016). In short, Trump suggested that Judge Curiel could not be unbiased in his decision regarding Trump University due to his "Mexican heritage," given Trump's policy views regarding immigration. These actions generated concern among GOP leadership, who recognized the implications for engaging the Latino electorate with the party beyond the 2016 election. Speaker of the House Paul Ryan distanced himself from Trump's comments against Judge Curiel, stating that they were "the textbook definition of a racist comment" (Steinhauer, Martin, and Herszenhorn 2016).

Against this backdrop of hostile rhetoric directed at Latino elites, Latino immigrants, and Latinos more broadly, we examine how Donald Trump's campaign resonated with Latino voters. We utilize the Latino

Decisions 2016 Election Eve Poll, as well as other Latino Decisions polls conducted during the 2016, 2012, and 2008 presidential campaigns, to compare the Latino vote and attitudes toward Trump and former Republican presidential candidates. We ground our analysis within the wider academic literature that discusses how campaigns influence the voting behavior of the electorate. This approach allows us to situate the reaction of Latino voters to the Trump campaign within the broader context of how Latinos have been increasingly racialized over the past several election cycles, as well as whether the Trump victory will lead to continued alienation of the Latino population for electoral gain.

Candidate Effects on Latino Presidential Voting Behavior

Throughout U.S. history, some presidential and gubernatorial candidates have proposed racialized policies or have included negative discourses against racial and ethnic groups during their campaigns for different purposes. In the presidential election of 1964, for example, Barry Goldwater aimed to appeal to conservative voters and members of far-right interest groups through racialized speeches and policy proposals (Hammerback 1999). One of Goldwater's policy positions openly rejected the principles of the Civil Rights Act (CRA) of 1964, which was supported by 54% of the American public and opposed by only 28% (UConn Communications 2014). Similarly to opponents of the CRA, Goldwater framed this act as a trade that would grant rights and opportunities for minorities, but would lead to a loss in rights and opportunities for White Americans. "I reject . . . executive actions which seek to provide opportunities for some by restricting or limiting opportunities for others," Goldwater said (Krock 1964). In this way, Goldwater became the unofficial spokesman for the emerging conservative movement that opposed the CRA (Hammerback 1999; Taylor 2016).

Besides being a critical event for the emerging conservative movement in the United States, Goldwater's presidential campaign marked a historical turning point for African American voters. In 1964, Goldwater obtained 6% of the African American vote, compared to 32% and 39% from fellow

Republican presidential candidates in 1960 and 1956, respectively. Additionally, this presidential campaign marked a historical trend that currently exists, given that Republican presidential candidates have not been able to win more than 15% of the African American vote in presidential elections since 1964 (Bositis 2012). Experts claim that Goldwater's presidential campaign has been one of the most consequential in U.S. history in terms of voting blocks and the emergence of the conservative movement (Middendorf 2008; Perlstein 2009; Rincón 2010; Yosso and Garcia 2007).

In addition to political discourse and policy preferences involving issues affecting African Americans, Latinos have also been the target of racialized policies. For example, in 1994, Republican lawmakers from California introduced Proposition 187, also known as the "Save Our State" (SOS) initiative, which, in addition to depriving unauthorized immigrants of welfare benefits, education, and medical care, aimed to facilitate the deportation of noncitizens by forcing state employees to report unauthorized immigrants to the Immigration and Naturalization Service for removal (Alvarez and Butterfield 2000; Lee and Ottati 2000; Lee, Ottati, and Hussain 2001; Michelson 2007). Although 59% of California voters supported this initiative, Proposition 187 "resulted in significant backlash and political mobilization among California Latino voters," many of whom participated in rallies and challenged the constitutionality of the bill (Barreto 2013). Experts have argued that the perceived anti-immigrant sentiment in California in the 1990s motivated immigrants to naturalize to not only protect their rights but also participate in future elections (Barreto et al. 2009; Nowrasteh 2016; Pantoja, Ramirez, and Segura 2001; Varsanyi 2008). Overall, Proposition 187 has been considered "the progenitor of all contemporary grassroots local and state anti-immigration legislation" (Varsanyi 2008).

Although Proposition 187 increased the levels of political participation of Latinos in California and pushed the politics of the state to the left, these types of racialized policies have unfortunately spread across the country, especially after the Great Recession of 2007–2009 (Ybarra, Sanchez, and Sanchez 2016), and have continued to target immigrants and racial minorities (Gómez-Aguiñaga 2016; O'Leary and Romero 2011; Ybarra, Sanchez, and Sanchez 2016). We believe that it is critical that we do not overlook this larger anti-Latino political climate, which provided the context for the Trump campaign to take the extreme approach of racializing the Latino community.

The Latino Vote in Presidential Elections

In the past five presidential elections, the Latino vote for Republican candidates has varied, peaking in 2004 with 40% to George W. Bush (Lopez and Taylor 2012) and decreasing to 23% for Mitt Romney in 2012 (ImpreMedia/ Latino Decisions 2012 Election Eve Poll). Immigration has been a major factor driving the Latino vote, particularly in the last few election cycles. In 2000, for example, George W. Bush obtained 30% of the Latino vote with a campaign that promised to reform the U.S. immigration system by improving the processing time of immigration applications, encouraging family reunification of legal permanent residents, and increasing border enforcement (Schmitt 2001). Although George W. Bush failed to enact immigration reform in his first term, he obtained 40% of the Latino vote in his 2004 reelection (Suro, Fry, and Passel 2005). Similarly, President Barack Obama won 72% of the Latino vote in 2008, promising to enact immigration reform with a path to citizenship for unauthorized immigrants (Barreto 2008). Although he was unable to achieve his goal, in 2012, President Obama introduced the Deferred Action for Childhood Arrivals (DACA), an executive order that provided work authorization and a two-year reprieve from deportation to young, unauthorized immigrants (U.S. Citizenship and Immigration Services2016). Experts claim that regardless of the unprecedented number of deportations under the Obama Administration in his first term, DACA helped President Obama retain and increase the Latino vote in 2012. In that election, 75% of Latino voters cast ballots for President Obama, and 58% of them said that DACA "made them more enthusiastic about voting for Obama," particularly in swing states such as Colorado and Nevada (Barreto, Schaller, and Segura 2016).

In the presidential election of 2012, Republican presidential candidate Mitt Romney gained one of the lowest shares of the Latino vote in the past thirty years. During the Republican primaries, Romney brought up the philosophy of "self-deportation," in which the lives of unauthorized immigrants would be so unbearable that they would voluntarily decide to go back to their home countries (Charen 2012; Thrush 2012). While Romney did not openly support state-level restrictive immigration policies, such as Arizona SB1070 and Alabama HB56, he had referred to Arizona as "a 'model' for the nation" regarding immigration policies (*Washington Post* 2012). Some experts have claimed that Romney's tough stances on immigration represented a problem to Latino voters, who, according to GOP fundraiser Ana Navarro, "were disillusioned with Barack Obama, but ... are absolutely terrified by the idea of Mitt Romney" (Charen 2012; Hamby 2012). Clearly, immigration policies have deployed race-based appeals, particularly in favor of and against Latinos. This history of racialization toward both Latinos and immigrants allowed Trump to take this rhetoric to a new level.

Results and Analysis

The presidential campaign of Donald J. Trump was constantly fueled with hostile rhetoric against the Latino electorate, immigrants from Latin America, and even Latino elites. To examine this assumption, we draw heavily from the Latino Decisions 2016 Election Eve Poll, which, simply stated, is the best data set available for analysis of Latino voting behavior in the 2016 election, as well as the 2016 Latino Victory Project-Republican National Convention (RNC) Reaction Poll, to examine Latinos' responses to the RNC and Donald Trump's campaign over the course of the election. The Latino Decisions 2016 Election Eve Poll is a national survey of 5,600 Latino voters, with state-specific results in twelve states in addition to a fifty-state weighted national result. Interviews were conducted in English or Spanish from a random sample of Latino voters in the final days before the election, offering exclusive information about the Latino electorate including presidential and senate vote choices, issue priorities, and evaluations of both major parties. The national sample carries an overall margin of error of ±1.8 percentage points. Florida has 800 completed interviews and carries a margin of error of ±3.5 percentage points. The remaining individual states sampled—Arizona, California, Colorado, Illinois, New York, Nevada, North Carolina Ohio, Texas, Wisconsin, and Virginia—have 400 complete interviews each and carry a margin of error of ±4.9 percentage points. The Latino Victory Project—RNC Reaction Poll is an online national survey of 1,200 registered Latino voters conducted between July 18 and July 21, 2016, in either English or Spanish, depending on the respondent's preference; this survey carries a margin of error of ±2.8 percentage points.

In addition to surveys conducted during the 2016 presidential election, we also make use of the ImpreMedia/Latino Decisions 2012 Election Eve Poll and the Latino Decisions/NALEO/ImpreMedia National Post-Election Survey 2008 to compare the turnout rates and vote choice of Latino voters in the 2008, 2012 and 2016 presidential elections. The extensive data collection effort from Latino Decisions throughout the past presidential elections allows us to determine whether Latino views toward the president-elect have varied at several major points during the 2016, 2012, and 2008 campaign seasons, culminating in the identification of factors that explain Latino vote support for Donald Trump and previous Republican presidential candidates.

The 2016 Republican National Convention and Latino Attitudes

Similar to the racialized and divisive campaign of the Republican Presidential Candidate Donald Trump, the Latino electorate perceived the 2016 Republican National Convention as an offensive event that targeted the immigrant and Latino communities in the United States. The results of the Latino Victory Project—RNC Reaction Poll revealed that 72% of the respondents said they watched or followed the 2016 Republican National Convention; however, the vast majority of them had negative reactions of the Republican nominee, Donald Trump, and the Republican Party.

Contrary to his bigoted rhetoric against Latinos and immigrants from Latin America throughout his presidential campaign, Trump constantly stated that he loved Hispanics and that Hispanics loved him back (Guadalupe 2016; Parker 2016). However, the results of the Latino Victory Project show that the latter claim was false, with 88% of respondents stating that they did not love the Republican presidential nominee. Additionally, 80% of Latinos said that they had unfavorable views of Donald Trump, and when asked about what words described the Republican presidential nominee, more than 80% of respondents said that Trump was "racist," "unstable," "foolish," "dangerous," and a bully who made America more divided. Clearly, negative views of Donald Trump were evident among Latino voters.

During the 2016 presidential campaign, registered Latino voters' negative feelings about Trump's rhetoric translated to negative views of the Republican Party. For example, 75% of respondents agreed that Donald Trump made the Republican Party more hostile to Latino voters; additionally, 85% of respondents said that both Donald Trump and Republicans had worsened their image with Latino voters. Additionally, 59% of respondents said that the 2016 RNC showed that the Republican Party was more hostile to Latino voters than before. When asked about words to describe the GOP, more than 70% of respondents said that the Republican Party was "anti-immigrant," "angry," "dangerous," "old," and "had a negative attitude."

The results of the Latino Victory Project—RNC Reaction Poll not only show that Latinos rejected the negative rhetoric of Donald Trump against Hispanics, but also convey that there is a growing negative perception of the Republican Party, which did little to stop the bigoted attacks against Latinos, immigrants, and other minority groups of the country. The next section explores how and to what extent Latino voters transferred these feelings to the ballots, given that Donald Trump received the lowest support among Latino voters that has been recorded in presidential elections.

The Trump Effect and Latino Voter Turnout

In 2016, the Latino turnout was substantially different and Latinos had distinct motivations to vote, compared to the 2012 presidential election. In 2016, Latinos turned out in high numbers, and they turned out early, outpacing early voting numbers from 2012 in essentially all key battleground states, including Florida, where Latinos improved their early vote numbers

Table 1. Latino Vote Share, Selected Precincts/Counties, 2012 and 2016

Precinct	Share of Latinos	2012 turnout	2016 turnout	Turnout change
Florida				
MD309	97%	60%	66%	6
MD342	96%	60%	69%	9
MD410	97%	59%	65%	6
MD322	95%	64%	70%	6
MD416	95%	64%	71%	7
MD388	95%	55%	74%	16
KISS210	78%	64%	70%	6
KISS200	69%	62%	68%	6
KISS314	69%	56%	64%	8
KISS 411	71%	60%	68%	8
New Mexico				
D.A. 93	86%	49%	59%	10
D.A. 97	96%	42%	50%	8
D.A. 13	99%	40%	49%	9
Dal. 24	94%	40%	47%	7
S.F. 79	87%	56%	63%	7
S.M. 17	91%	38%	42%	4
Texas (counties)				
Starr	96%	45%	47%	2
Jim Hogg	94%	44%	54%	10
Maverick	94%	38%	44%	6
Hidalgo	86%	46%	49%	3
Cameron	89%	48%	53%	5
Brooks	92%	46%	46%	6

Sources: Latino Decisions 2016 Election Eve Poll, and ImpreMedia/Latino Decisions 2012 Election Eve Poll.

from 2012 by nearly 90% (Cohen 2016; Diaz 2016; Fraga and Schaffner 2016; Latino Decisions 2016b). Additionally, more Latinos in Texas, Nevada, and New Mexico cast votes for the 2016 presidential election when compared to 2012, and, in specific counties, the Latino vote went through the roof (Ralston 2016; Schwartz and Hill 2016; Texas Secretary of State n.d.). Evidence of this growth was everywhere. In the Rio Grande Valley of Texas, for example, heavily Latino counties saw turnout increases of 4% to 10% over 2012. Likewise, heavily Latino precincts across Miami and Osceola Counties in Florida showed larger increases in voter participation of 6 to 16 percentage points. Similarly in New Mexico, majority-Latino precincts in Las Cruces showed consistent increases in voter turnout in 2016 over 2012. Table 1 shows the Latino share of electorate and turnout of 2012 and 2016 in selected precincts or counties.

The polling of Latino Decisions throughout the election season indicated that the high levels of enthusiasm among Latino voters were driven largely by a goal to keep Donald Trump from winning the election; scholars have referred to this cycle as the "Trump Bump" (Latino Decisions 2016b; Mascaro 2016; Sanchez 2016). For example, in the America's Voice/Latino Decisions National and Battleground State Poll conducted in August 2016, respondents who voted in 2012 were asked whether they were more enthusiastic about voting in 2016 and whether they felt it was more important to vote in 2016 compared to 2012. A robust 76% of respondents said it was "more important" to vote in 2016, and 51% said they were "more enthusiastic about voting" in 2016. When those respondents were asked the follow-up question of why they were more enthusiastic or felt it was more important to vote in 2016, the modal category in both cases was to block/stop Trump from becoming president: 51% for the importance to vote question and 47% for enthusiasm (Latino Decisions 2016a).

This "Trump Bump" that occurred during the 2016 campaign translated into to an outstanding 53% of Latino respondents to the Latino Decisions Election Eve Poll saying they voted early either by mail/absentee ballot or through an early voting location (24% by mail/absentee and 29% at voting location), concurring with the early vote numbers reported before Election Day (Latino Decisions 2016a; Martin 2016; Sanchez and Barreto 2016). This was a significant increase of early voting when compared to the 2012 and 2008 presidential elections. While there was a 3-percentage-point increase in voting early from 2008 to 2012, there was a 10-percentage-point increase from 2012 to 2016, as shown in table 2. Furthermore, for the first time in the past three presidential elections, the share of the Latino early vote in 2016 (53%) was greater than the percentage of those who voted on Election Day in 2012 (43%) and 2008 (40%). The data clearly shows that the early vote numbers among Latinos in the 2016 elections were noteworthy, particularly when compared to previous presidential elections.

Table 2. Latino Early Vote in the 2016, 2012, and 2008 Presidential Elections

	2016	2012	2008
Voted early/absentee ballot	53%	43%	40%
Polls on election day	47%	57%	59%
Difference with respect to early voting	+6%	−14%	−19%

Sources: Latino Decisions 2016 Election Eve Poll, ImpreMedia/Latino Decisions 2012 Election Eve Poll, and Latino Decisions/NALEO/ImpreMedia National Post-Election Survey–November 2008.

Figure 1. Perceptions of 2012 and 2016 Republican Candidates' Degree of Caring for the Latino Community

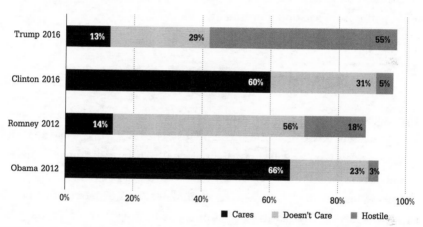

Sources: Latino Decisions 2016 Election Eve Poll, ImpreMedia/Latino Decisions 2012 Election Eve Poll, and Latino Decisions/NALEO/ImpreMedia National Post-Election Survey–November 2008.

The volatile comments made by the GOP nominee throughout the entire campaign season appeared to energize the Latino electorate, and the Latino Decisions 2016 Election Eve poll confirms these trends. While 55% of Latino voters stated that Donald Trump was "hostile" toward Latinos or Hispanics and another 29% expressed that he "did not care too much" about Latinos, Democratic Presidential Nominee Hillary R. Clinton was perceived significantly more positively, with 60% of respondents stating that Clinton cared about the Latino community and only 5% stating that she was "hostile" toward Latinos or Hispanics, as shown in figure 1. For comparison, Trump was viewed more negatively on this question than the Republican

Party overall, as 30% of Latinos in the poll believed that the Republican Party was hostile toward Latinos during the 2016 campaign.

Additionally, Latinos' perceptions of Donald Trump were much worse than those of 2012 Republican Presidential Nominee Mitt Romney, as figure 1 shows. While the majority of respondents (56%) in 2012 stated that Romney did not care about the Latino community, only 18% stated that Romney was hostile towards Latinos or Hispanics. The 37-percentage-point increase in the perceived hostility against Hispanics that occurred from Romney in 2012 to Trump in 2016 shows that Donald Trump was viewed very negatively by Latino voters and that this led to high enthusiasm and a collective goal to keep him from becoming president.

Latino Voters Give Trump Lowest Level of Support on Record

The huge turnout of Latinos coincided with the most lopsided vote choice for Latinos ever recorded in American history. The results of the Latino Decisions 2016 Election Eve Poll show that nationally Hillary Clinton dominated Donald Trump with an astonishing 79% to 18% advantage, with another 3% voting for one of the third-party candidates. This 61-percentage-point gap is the largest that Latino Decisions polls have ever recorded, outpacing Obama's 2012 advantage over Romney (52-percentage-point gap) and Obama's 2008 advantage over John McCain (47-percentage-point gap), as shown in figure 2. Clinton's 79% is the highest level of Latino support that has ever been recorded in Latino Decisions polls, and 18% for Trump is the low for any candidate.

When we look at variation across states, we see that Latino support was as high as 88% in New York, and well above 80% across every state except for Florida. Even in Florida, where the Latino vote split is the closest, there was a 36-percentage-point gap, with Clinton at 67% and Trump at 31%.

In table 3 we see that there were only a few bright spots for Donald Trump among Latino voters, when compared to the 2012 and 2008 presidential elections. As expected, partisanship is the factor with the greatest impact on presidential vote choice for Latinos during the 2016 election.

Figure 2. Latino Turnout and Vote Gap in the 2016, 2012, and 2008 Presidential Elections

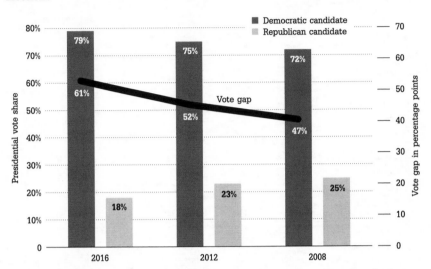

Sources: Latino Decisions 2016 Election Eve Poll, ImpreMedia/Latino Decisions 2012 Election Eve Poll, and Latino Decisions/NALEO/ImpreMedia National Post-Election Survey–November 2008.

There was essentially no Latino crossover voting, as only 2% of self-identified Democrats reported that they voted or intended to vote for Donald Trump. Conversely, 22% of self-identified Latino Republicans crossed over and supported Democratic nominee Hillary Clinton. Clinton also won the lion's share of Latino independent and "other" party respondents, with 65% compared to 26% for Trump.

There was a small but meaningful gender gap in the vote choice of Latinos in the 2016 presidential election: Only 12% of Latinas voted for Trump, compared to 24% of Latino males. In the 2012 and 2008 presidential elections, 21% of Hispanic women reported voting for Republican presidential candidates, compared to 25% and 28% of Hispanic males in the 2012 and 2008 presidential elections, respectively.

Nativity and dominant language also had a pronounced effect on support for Trump in the 2016 presidential election. While only 13% of naturalized Latinos reported voting for Trump, 19% of U.S.-born Latinos cast votes for the Republican presidential candidate. Romney in 2012 and McCain in

Table 3. Latino Vote Choice in the 2016, 2012 and 2008 Presidential Elections by Party ID, Gender, Nativity, and Dominant Language

	2016		2012		2008	
	Hillary Clinton	Donald Trump	Barack Obama	Mitt Romney	Barack Obama	John McCain
All respondents	79%	18%	75%	23%	72%	25%
Party ID						
Democrat	97%	2%	97%	2%	88%	10%
Republican	22%	75%	9%	90%	28%	66%
Other	65%	26%	60%	34%	73%	23%
Gender						
Female	86%	12%	77%	21%	77%	21%
Male	71%	24%	73%	25%	68%	28%
Nativity						
Naturalized immigrant	84%	13%	80%	18%	76%	22%
U.S. born	72%	19%	71%	27%	71%	26%
Language of interview						
English	75%	21%	67%	25%	69%	27%
Spanish	89%	9%	69%	19%	78%	18%

Sources: Latino Decisions 2016 Election Eve Poll, ImpreMedia/Latino Decisions 2012 Election Eve Poll, and Latino Decisions/ NALEO/ImpreMedia National Post-Election Survey–November 2008.

2008 obtained a higher vote share from naturalized Latinos with 18% and 22% respectively, as well as from U.S.-born Latinos with 27% for Romney and 26% for John McCain. Although Trump's harsh campaign and policy proposals against immigrants helped him win the Republican presidential nomination, it also mobilized naturalized Latinos to vote against Trump.

The nativity findings were reinforced by language, suggesting strongly that Trump's divisive comments about Mexican and Latin American immigrants, along with his immigration policy views, impacted support among Latinos closer to the immigrant experience themselves. As table 3 shows, while 21% of English-dominant Latinos voted for Trump, only 9% of Latinos who completed the survey interview in Spanish cast their ballots for the Republican nominee. Compared to the 2012 and 2008 Republican presidential candidates, Trump obtained less than half of the vote share of Spanish-speaking Latinos, as table 3 shows.

There were some notable differences in voting behavior by national origin, as shown in table 4. In the 2016 presidential election, we see that Latinos who trace their origin to the Dominican Republic were at the low end of the distribution with only 8% supporting Trump and Cuban Americans being the most supportive with 48% for Trump. Additionally, 19% of Puerto Ricans, 15% of Mexican Americans and Central Americans, and 16% of South Americans reported voting for Trump in 2016. When compared to the Latino support for the Republican presidential nominee in 2012, Trump lost Latino supporters who trace their origin to Cuba and Central America (-7 percentage points each), Mexico (-5 percentage points), and South America (-3 percentage points); however, Trump performed better than Romney among Latinos who trace their origin to Dominican Republic (+4 percentage points) and Puerto Rico (+5 percentage points). Perhaps this divide can be explained by the anti-immigrant rhetoric that Trump used against Mexican and Central Americans, along with those who came to the United States as refugees.

Education was one of the most discussed demographic factors in post-election analysis, with most of the discussion focused on Trump's support among low-educated Whites. Although Latino support for Trump is low regardless of educational attainment, there is a 10-percentage-point gap in Trump support based on college education: 24% of college-educated Latinos voted for Trump, compared to 14% among Latinos without a college education, as table 4 shows. Furthermore, we see that only 11% of first-time voters cast their ballots for Donald Trump, compared to 16% of Latinos who cast a vote for the first time in the 2012 presidential election. This is consistent with our suggestion that Trump's campaign mobilized lower propensity voters.

The high level of consistency found in Latino vote choice over the full course of the 2016 election season is largely explained by how early in the campaign many Latino voters made up their minds. When asked when they decided which presidential candidate they would vote for in the 2016 presidential election, 21% of respondents noted that this important decision was made over the summer, and 57% made their choice more than six months before Election Day. This reminds us that the clear distinction in immigration policy between Clinton and Trump very early in the campaign, along

Table 4. Latino Vote Choice in the 2016 and 2012 by Level of Education and Country of Origin

	2016		2012	
	Hillary Clinton	Donald Trump	Barack Obama	Mitt Romney
All respondents	79%	18%	75%	23%
First-time voters	83%	11%	81%	16%
Education level				
College +	73%	24%	71%	26%
Less than college	82%	14%	81%	18%
Nativity				
Mexico	81%	15%	78%	20%
Puerto Rico	79%	19%	83%	14%
Cuba	50%	48%	44%	55%
Dominican Republic	89%	8%	96%	4%
Central America	82%	15%	76%	22%
South America	81%	16%	79%	19%

Sources: Latino Decisions 2016 Election Eve Poll, ImpreMedia/Latino Decisions 2012 Election Eve Poll, and Latino Decisions/NALEO/ImpreMedia National Post-Election Survey—November 2008.

with Trump's harsh campaign against Latinos, was critical to establishing a clear vote choice for many Latinos early.

Most Important Issues Facing the Latino Community

The Latino Decisions 2016 Election Eve Poll also asked respondents directly in an open-ended question what are "the most important issues facing the [Latino/Hispanic] community that our politicians should address," allowing respondents to provide up to two policy issues in both 2016 and 2012. The results reveal that immigration was the dominant issue on the minds of Latino voters as they cast ballots in 2016. More specifically, 39% of Latinos identified "Immigration Reform/Deportations" as the top one or two policy issues, compared to 33% for "Fix Economy/Jobs/Unemployment." As shown in figure 3, other top issues in the 2016 presidential election include education reform (15%), health care (13%), anti-immigrant or Latino discrimination (10%), and stopping Donald Trump from becoming president (8%).

In contrast to 2016, the most important policy issues for Latino voters

Figure 3. Perceived Most Important Issues Facing the Latino Community by Presidential Election

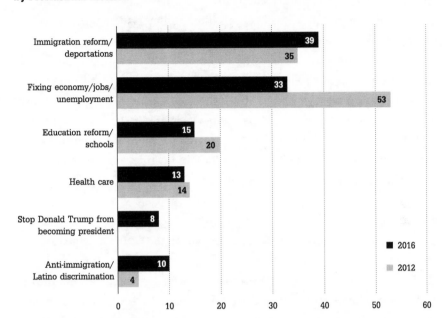

Sources: Latino Decisions 2016 Election Eve Poll, ImpreMedia/Latino Decisions 2012 Election Eve Poll.

Notes: The results were obtained from the following open-ended question: "Thinking about the 2016/2012 election, what are the most important issues facing the [Hispanic/Latino] community that our politicians should address?" Each bar reports the percentage of respondents indicating the category as one of the top policy issues for the corresponding year.

in the 2012 presidential election was fixing the economy and/or addressing unemployment (53%), followed by immigration reform (35%), as figure 3 shows. Other important policy issues in the 2012 election include education reform (20%), health care (14%), and anti-immigrant/Latino discrimination (4%). The fact that immigration reform and anti-immigrant/Latino discrimination played a much more significant role among the most important policy issues in 2016 when compared to 2012 suggests that the anti-immigrant/Latino rhetoric used by Trump also impacted the policy perceptions of Latino voters.

We have stressed that the prominent role of immigration in the minds of Latino voters has been driven by a personal connection to the issue among Latinos, and this poll confirms this trend, as 60% of Latinos who voted in 2016 indicate that they have an undocumented immigrant in their personal network (Latino Decisions 2016).

Immigration policy has been a salient policy issue for Latino voters over the last two election cycles, and the build-the-wall policy approach for Trump, not to mention the negative comments regarding Mexican immigrants and threats to terminate DACA, helped ensure that immigration became a prominent issue for Latinos in 2016 (Hipsman, Gomez-Aguinaga, and Capps 2016; Jaffe 2015; Kopan 2016; Ross 2016). The high turnout of Latinos, coupled with the prominent role that immigration policy played in both turnout and vote choice, makes clear that Latino voters are not happy with the outcome of the 2016 election.

Conclusion: Trump's Long-Term Impact on the Latino Electorate

It is clear from our data that Latinos outperformed expectations in 2016 when compared to the 2012 and 2008 presidential elections. Nevertheless, it simply did not matter enough to swing the 2016 election in the direction that Latinos and Clinton's supporters desired. Our discussion of the extant literature on the racialization of the Latino population through hostile campaign rhetoric and punitive immigration policy platforms suggests that Trump should not have done well among this electorate. The Latino Decisions 2016 Election Eve Poll data support this presumption, as the GOP nominee had the lowest level of support ever recorded for the Latino electorate, and Latinos turned out with high enthusiasm driven by a desire to keep him from winning. This analysis concludes with the finding that Latinos thoroughly rejected the Trump campaign's hostile and divisive comments, as well as Trump's harsh policy proposals directed toward Latinos, immigrants, and other marginalized communities.

Whether 2016 represents a high point for Latino voter engagement or a continuation of increased turnout in presidential races will hinge largely on whether President Trump attempts to repair a clearly damaged relationship with the Latino electorate during his first term in office. In his appointing no Latinos to his cabinet as of the time of this book's submission, we do not see any reason to expect that the president will help rekindle a relationship between the GOP and the most prominent subgroup for that party's long-term success.

References

Alvarez, R. Michael, and Tara L. Butterfield. 2000. "The Resurgence of Nativism in California? The Case of Proposition 187 and Illegal Immigration." *Social Science Quarterly* 81 (1): 167-79.

America's Voice/Latino Decisions National and Battleground State Poll. 2016. http://www.latinodecisions.com.

Barreto, Matt. 2008. "Record Latino Voter Turnout in 2008 Helps Obama Win Key Battleground States." *Latino Decisions*, November 19.

———. 2013. "The Prop 187 Effect: How the California GOP Lost Their Way and Implications for 2014 and Beyond." *Latino Decisions*, October 17.

Barreto, Matt A., Sylvia Manzano, Ricardo Ramirez, and Kathy Rim. 2009. "Mobilization, Participation, and Solidaridad Latino Participation in the 2006 Immigration Protest Rallies." *Urban Affairs Review* 44 (5): 736-64.

Barreto, Matt A., and Gabriel R. Sanchez. 2014. "Accepted Photo Identification and Different Subgroups in the Eligible Voter Population, State of Texas, 2014." http://www.latinodecisions.com.

Barreto, Matt A., Thomas F. Schaller, and Gary Segura. 2016. "DACA's Three-Year Anniversary." *Huffington Post*, June 15.

Bositis, David A. 2012. "Blacks and the 2012 Democratic National Convention." *Joint Center for Political and Economic Studies.* http://jointcenter.org.

Charen, Mona. 2012. "Why Romney Lost the Hispanic Vote." *National Review*, November 9.

Cohen, Marshall. 2016. "Democrats Take the Lead in Florida Early Voting." *CNN Politics,* November 5. http://catalist.us.

Damore, David. 2016. "Translating Trump: When He Talks Immigration, What Latino Voters Hear." *Latino Decisions,* September 8.

Davidson, Chandler. 2009. "The Historical Context of Voter Photo-ID Laws." *PS: Political Science and Politics* 42 (1): 93-96.

Diamond, Jeremy. 2016. "Donald Trump Outlines Plan to Get Mexico to Pay for Border Wall." *CNN,* April 5.

Diaz, Daniella. 2016. "Early Voting Data in 3 Key States Show Spike in Latino

Turnout." *CNN Politics,* November 7. http://catalist.us.

Elmer, Greg, and Paula Todd. 2016. "Don't Be a Loser: Or How Trump Turned the Republican Primaries into an Episode of *The Apprentice.*" *Television & New Media* 17 (7): 660-62.

Fox News. 2016. "Donald Trump: Miss Universe Alicia Machado Was 'The Absolute Worst.'" September 27.

Fraga, Bernard L., and Brian Schaffner. 2016. "Who's Voting Early? Latino Turnout Is Surging, but White Turnout Is, Too." *Washington Post,* November 4.

Gómez-Aguiñaga, Bárbara. 2016. "Stepping into the Vacuum: State and Cities Act on Immigration, But Do Restrictions Work?" *Migration Information Source,* November 3. http://www.migrationpolicy.org.

Guadalupe, Patricia. 2016. "Trump Says He Loves Latinos. Do They Love Him Back?" *The Hill,* February 29.

Hamby, Peter. 2012. "Analysis: Why Romney lost." *CNN,* November 7.

Hammerback, John C. 1999. "Barry Goldwater's Rhetorical Legacy." *Southern Communication Journal* 64: 323-32.

Hershey, Marjorie R. 2009. "What We Know about Voter-ID Laws, Registration, and Turnout," *PS: Political Science and Politics* 42 (1): 87-91.

Hipsman, Faye, Barbara Gomez-Aguinaga, and Randy Capps. 2016. "DACA at Four: Participation in the Deferred Action Program and Impacts on Recipients." *Migration Policy Institute,* August. http://www.migrationpolicy.org.

Holpuch, Amanda. 2016. "Trump Re-ups Controversial Muslim Ban and Mexico Wall in First Campaign Ad." *The Guardian,* January 4.

ImpreMedia/Latino Decisions. 2012. "2012 Latino Election Eve Poll." http://www.latinovote2012.com.

Jaffe, Alexandra. 2015. "Donald Trump: Undocumented Immigrants 'Have to Go.'" *NBC News,* August 16.

Kendall, Brent. 2016. "Trump Says Judge's Mexican Heritage Presents 'Absolute Conflict.'" *Wall Street Journal,* June 3.

Kopan, Tal. 2016. "What Donald Trump Has Said About Mexico and Vice Versa." *CNN,* August 31.

Krock, Arthur. 1964. "A Clear Line of Republican Cleavage." *New York Times,* May 28.

Latino Decisions. 2016a. "2016 Election Eve Poll." http://www.latinodecisions.com.

———. 2016b. "NALEO Educational Fund/Noticias Telemundo/Latino Decisions Weekly Tracking Poll—September–November 2016." http://www.

latinodecisions.com.

Lee, Yueh-Ting, and Victor Ottati. 2002. "Attitudes toward US Immigration Policy: The Roles of In-Group-Out-Group Bias, Economic Concern, and Obedience to Law." *Journal of Social Psychology* 142 (5): 617–34.

Lee, Yueh-Ting, Victor Ottati, and Imtiaz Hussain. 2001. "Attitudes Toward 'Illegal' Immigration into the United States: California Proposition 187." *Hispanic Journal of Behavioral Sciences* 23 (4): 430–43.

Lopez, Mark H., and Paul Taylor. 2012. "Latino Voters in the 2012 Election." Pew Research Center. http://www.pewhispanic.org.

Martin, Jonathan. 2016. "Hillary Clinton Appears to Gain Late Momentum on Surge of Latino Voters." *New York Times*, November 5.

Mascaro, Lisa. 2016. "Latinos Could Set a Record by Casting Almost 15 Million Ballots for President. Activists Call It the Trump Bump." *Los Angeles Times*, November 3.

McIlwain, Charlton, and Stephen M. Caliendo. 2011. *Race Appeal: How Candidates Invoke Race in US Political Campaigns*. Philadelphia: Temple University Press.

Michelson, Melissa. 2007. "All Roads Lead to Rust: How Acculturation Erodes Latino Immigrant Trust in Government." *Aztlán: A Journal of Chicano Studies* 32 (2): 21–46.

Middendorf, John William. 2006. *A Glorious Disaster: Barry Goldwater's Presidential Campaign and the Origins of the Conservative Movement*. New York: Basic Books.

Nowrasteh, Alex. 2016. "Proposition 187 Turned California Blue." *The Cato Institute*, July 20. https://www.cato.org.

O'Leary, Anna, and Andrea Romero. 2011. "Chicana/o Students Respond to Arizona's Anti-Ethnic Studies Bill, SB 1108: Civic Engagement, Ethnic Identity, and Well-Being." *Aztlán: A Journal of Chicano Studies* 36 (1): 9–36.

Pantoja, Adrian. 2016. "The Trump Effect and the Latino Vote." *Latino Decisions*, November 1. http://www.latinodecisions.com.

Pantoja, Adrian D., Ricardo Ramirez, and Gary M. Segura. 2001. "Citizens by Choice, Voters by Necessity: Patterns in Political Mobilization by Naturalized Latinos." *Political Research Quarterly* 54 (4): 729–50.

Parker, Ashley. 2016. "Donald Trump's 'Taco Bowl' Message: 'I Love Hispanics.'" *New York Times*, May 5.

Parker, Ashley, and Jonathan Martin. 2016. "Donald Trump Gives Gov. Susana Martinez a Poor Performance Review." *New York Times*, May 25.

Perlstein, Rick. 2009. *Before the Storm: Barry Goldwater and the Unmaking of the American Consensus.* New York: Nation Books.

Ralston, Jon. 2016. "Ralston: How Deep Does the Blue Wave Go?" *Reno Gazette-Journal,* November 5.

Rincón, Alejandra. 2010. "Undocumented Immigrants and Higher Education: Sí Se Puede!" *Aztlán: A Journal of Chicano Studies* 36 (2): 233-36.

Ross, Janell. 2016. "From Mexican Rapists to Bad Hombres, the Trump Campaign in Two Moments." *Washington Post,* October 20.

Sanchez, Gabriel R. 2016. "Don't Believe Those Exit Polls Saying 25 Percent of Latinos Voted for Trump." *Vox,* November 10.

Sanchez, Gabriel, and Matt Barreto. 2016. "In Record Numbers, Latinos Voted Overwhelmingly against Trump. We Did the Research." *Washington Post,* November 11.

Schleifer, Theodore. 2015. "Donald Trump Launches First Attacks Against Ted Cruz." *CNN,* December 12.

———. 2016. "McConnell Worries Trump Could Have Goldwater Effect on Latino Voters." *CNN,* June 13.

Schmitt, Eric. 2001. "Bush Aides Weigh Legalizing Status of Mexicans in U.S." *New York Times,* July 15.

Schwartz, Jeremy, and Dan Hill. 2017. "Number of Texas Latino Voters Climbed 29 Percent in 2016, Records Show." *My Statesman,* February 10.

Segura, Garry. 2013. "Democrats Crush Republicans Among Latino and Asian American Voters in Virginia." *Latino Decisions,* November 5. http://www.latinodecisions.com.

Slaughter, Stephany. 2016. "#TrumpEffects: Creating Rhetorical Spaces for Latinx Political Engagement." *Latin Americanist* 60 (4): 541-76.

Smith, Candice. 2015. "Donald Trump Deletes Tweet About Jeb Bush's Wife." *ABC News,* July 6.

Sobel, Richard, and Robert Ellis Smith. 2009. "Voter-ID Laws Discourage Participation, Particularly Among Minorities, and Trigger a Constitutional Remedy in Lost Representation," *PS: Political Science and Politics* 42 (1): 107-10.

Steinhauer, Jennifer, Jonathan Martin, and David M. Herszenhorn. 2016. "Paul Ryan Calls Donald Trump's Attack on Judge 'Racist,' but Still Backs Him." *New York Times,* June 7.

Sullivan, Sean. 2016. "After Criticizing New Mexico's Gov. Martinez, Trump Now

Says He Wants Her Endorsement." *Washington Post*, June 3.

Suro, Roberto, Richard Fry, and Jeffrey S. Passel. 2006. "How Latinos Voted in 2004." *Pew Research Center*, June 27. http://www.pewhispanic.org.

Taylor, Andrew. 2016. "Barry Goldwater: Insurgent Conservatism as Constitutive Rhetoric." *Journal of Political Ideologies* 21 (3): 242-60.

Texas Secretary of State. n.d. "Election Results." https://www.sos.state.tx.us.

Thrush, Glenn. 2012. "How Romney Lost Latinos." *Politico*, March 14.

UConn Communications. 2014. "The Civil Rights Act of 1964 Revisited." *UConn Today*, July 2. http://today.uconn.edu.

U.S. Citizenship and Immigration Services. 2016. "Consideration of Deferred Action for Childhood Arrivals (DACA)." https://www.uscis.gov.

VanSickle-Ward, Rachel, and Adrian D. Pantoja. 2016. "Latina Voters Say Adiós to Trump." *Latino Decisions*, October 15. http://www.latinodecisions.com.

Varsanyi, Monica W. 2008. "Rescaling the 'Alien,' Rescaling Personhood: Neoliberalism, Immigration and the State." *Annals of the Association of American Geographers* 98 (4): 877-96.

Washington Post. 2012. "Obama and Romney on the Issues: Immigration." October 5.

Wright, David, Dan Merica, and Jim Acosta. 2016. "Ryan, Clinton Slam Trump over Racial Criticism of Judge." *CNN*, June 4.

Ybarra, Vickie D., Lisa M. Sanchez, and Gabriel R. Sanchez. 2016. "Anti-Immigrant Anxieties in State Policy: The Great Recession and Punitive Immigration Policy in the American States, 2005-2012." *State Politics & Policy Quarterly* 16 (3): 313-39.

Yosso, Tara, and David García. 2007. "'This Is No Slum!': A Critical Race Theory Analysis of Community Cultural Wealth in Culture Clash's Chavez Ravine." *Aztlán: A Journal of Chicano Studies* 32 (1): 145-79.

The Latinx Gender Gap in the 2016 Election

Jessica Lavariega Monforti

AS THE LARGEST MINORITY GROUP IN THE UNITED STATES, HISPANICS ARE playing an increasingly impactful role in national politics (Barreto and Segura 2014). The population is only expected to grow, and much of that growth will be U.S.-born. By 2060, the U.S. Census Bureau projects Hispanics will make up 29% of the population in what by then will be a majority-minority nation. At the same time, Hispanics' demographic power has been offset by their historically low turnout on Election Day. For example, in presidential years since 2000, Hispanics have barely edged out Asian American turnout, and that population comprises just 5% of the U.S. population whereas Hispanics comprise about 17%. For example, 48% of eligible Latinx voters showed up at the polls on Election Day in 2012.[1] Meanwhile, 67% of Blacks and 64% of Whites came out to cast a vote. There was a slight uptick in Latina/o voter turnout for the 2016 presidential election.

In the 2016 presidential election there has been much talk about the role of identity—specifically, ethnicity, immigration, and gender. On the right, Donald Trump kicked off his campaign by squarely targeting Mexicans and undocumented immigrants, promulgating the idea of building a border wall and having Mexico pay for it, and massive deportations. Targeting immigrants as problematic and a national security threat became a centerpiece of his campaign. Overall, his primary and general election campaigns were hypermasculine in tone, and there were several major issues around gender, from his treatment of female journalists and candidates to accusations of sexual assault. On the left, the historic nature of Hillary Clinton's campaign for the Democratic nominee for president and her eventual general election campaign placed her identity as a woman front and center. Her role as a mother and grandmother and her many years of working on behalf of women and children were put alongside her years of elective and diplomatic experience. She also campaigned on the importance of immigration reform and providing a pathway to citizenship for undocumented workers.

As a result of these election season trends, much was made of the anticipated reaction of Latino and female voters on Election Day. For example Charlie Cook said, "The 2016 election is going to be a test of the character of the Latino community," referring particularly to negative comments about immigrants from Republican presidential candidate Donald Trump. He continued, "When someone engages in demagoguery at your expense, do you pull back or do you double your efforts?"[2] Record Latino voter registration and mobilization efforts took place, and a tsunami of Latino turnout was expected. Further, the media focused extensively on the power of the female vote in 2016. For instance, Leah Askarinam (2016) wrote the following in an *Atlantic* article:

> Hillary Clinton became the first truly viable woman presidential nominee the nation had ever seen—and used Trump's alleged behavior toward women as a weapon against him . . . thanks to a collision of cultural and demographic change that's occurred this election cycle, this voting bloc, representing half the country, could be more influential over an election's outcome than ever before.[3]

Despite the attention paid to Latino and women voters, little was said or written about the population that stands at the interaction of these ethnic and gender identities: Latinas. Nevertheless, over the last century, Hispanic women[4] have been agents of change in their communities, in elective office and as campaign staff, and as voters. In this work, we examine the intersection of gender and ethnicity in the 2016 presidential election. Specifically, we investigate whether there exists a gender gap among Hispanic voters in this election. Using theories of intersectionality and the concept of the Latinx gender gap, this chapter focuses on the importance of gender and country of origin as contextualizing variables that help us better understand Latinx public opinion and political behavior.

Importance of the Latina Voter Turnout

Studies have shown that Latinas' levels of participation, political preferences, and motivations for engaging in the political arena are unique from those of both their ethnic and gendered counterparts (Montoya 1996; García Bedolla et al. 2007). Fraga et al. (2008) and Jaramillo (2010) posit that elected Latinas have a distinctive approach to politics as a result of their intersectional identities as women and Hispanics. That is to say, their intersecting identities of ethnorace and gender, along with other sociopolitical identities such as language, immigration status, and history, shape their political worldviews and behavior. As a result of their intersectional identity, Latinas may prefer and/or hold salient policies and ideas that others do not. When a Latino gender gap in public opinion is evident, the size of the gaps has also varied by national origin group (Montoya 1996; García Bedolla et al. 2007).

Let's begin with an examination of political engagement, specifically voter turnout in 2016. One interesting fact to note is that the 2016 election marked the most diverse electorate in U.S. history. Approximately one-third of eligible voters (U.S. citizens ages eighteen and older) were from racial and ethnic minorities; this represents a net increase of 7.5 million eligible voters.[5] In particular, Latinos increased their number of eligible voters by another 4 million to reach a record-setting 27.3 million eligible voters, which is the largest increase of any racial/ethnic group.[6]

Further, voter turnout, the proportion of eligible voters who cast a ballot in an election, regardless of ethnicity, in 2016 was approximately 58%—setting a new record high.[7] In recent elections, voter turnout rates for women have equaled or exceeded voter turnout rates for men—regardless of ethnicity. Women, who constitute more than half the population, have cast between 4 and 7 million more votes than men in prior elections.[8] According to the Edison National Exit Poll, more women (52%) turned out to vote than their male (48%) counterparts by a margin of 4%.

Moreover, when we examine ethnorace using the Latino Decisions 2016 Election Eve Poll (Latino Decisions 2016), Latinx voter turnout was up significantly compared with 2012. Specifically, Sanchez and Barreto estimate that 13.1 million to 14.7 million Latinos cast ballots in the 2016 election—a significant increase from the 11.2 million Latinx votes cast in 2012.[9] An all-time high of Latinx voters nationwide voted; 20% of 2016's Latinx voters were exercising their franchise for the first time.[10] When we examine the intersection of gender and ethnorace, historically, young Hispanic male citizens have turned out to vote at lower rates than their female counterparts.[11] Ethnorace is a hybridized identity category that bridges racial and ethnic categories and enhances our ability to conceptualize the treatment of most if not all Latinos in the United States. And as in previous elections, Latinas turned out to vote at a higher rate than their male co-ethnics, and therefore played a critical role in this historic 2016 election.[12]

Policy, Policy, and More Policy

In the United States since the 1980s, women generally have held more liberal policy positions than men. In terms of specific policy views, women are often more supportive of a more activist role for government, more supportive of affirmative action and efforts to achieve racial equality, and more supportive of programs to guarantee quality health care and meet basic human needs (Center for American Women and Politics [CAWP] 2012).

Latinx generally support more liberal policy views than their non-Latinx counterparts, with Latinas generally more liberal than Latino men. The policy areas include gender-related issues, reach of government policies (government income support, support the Affordable Care Act continuing as law), and immigration-related policies (such as disapproval of workplace raids). A key set of government policies relates to the debate over immigration reform (Bejarano 2013). To illustrate, more Latinas (70%) than Latino males (62%) agree the government should ensure access to health insurance.[13] The majority of Latinxs, 78%, favor raising the federal minimum wage from $7.25 to $10.10 per hour. In terms of the environment, 84% of Latinxs also believe it is important that the federal government take measures to reduce carbon pollution that is causing global warming or climate change. In both cases, Latinas report higher levels of support than do their male co-ethics. Additional support is provided by Manzano (2012), who found a significant gender gap in support of more liberal public policies among Latinxs during the 2012 and 2014 elections. For example, when respondents were asked about how much trust they have for political parties on "women's issues," Manzano found that Latinas had overwhelming support for the Democrats over the Republicans in 2012: 78% compared to 13% (Manzano 2012). Based on these ethnoracial and gender trends, we would expect Latinas to also demonstrate a modern gender gap, with more liberal political views than their male counterparts.

The Latino Decisions 2016 Election Eve Poll also provides us with information about policy preferences among Latinx voters in 2016. The poll asked, "Thinking about the 2016 election, what are the most important issues facing the (Hispanic/Latino) community that our politicians should address?" Respondents were able to answer by naming two issues. The top response, with 39.4%, was immigration reform/deportations, followed by fixing the economy/jobs and unemployment with 32.7%, and education reform and schools with 28.6%. We want to examine whether adding gender, and interacting gender with country of origin, change our results. The general order of the importance of these three policy issues remains unchanged when examining Latinas and Latinos. However, fewer Latinas indicated that fixing the economy/job/unemployment is a top issue than their male co-ethnic counterparts by almost 9 percentage points.[14] Also more Latinas indicated that education reforms and schools is a top issue in comparison.[15] While there is a gap of 5.9 percentage points between

Latinos and Latinas on immigration reform/deportations, the difference is not significant.

The picture becomes more nuanced when country of origin is added to the puzzle. The top three issues vary across country-of-origin populations. The top three policy concerns for Mexican origin as well as Dominican origin respondents are (1) immigration reform/deportation, (2) fix the economy/jobs/unemployment, and (3) education reform/schools. For Puerto Rican respondents, we find that the economy is at the top of the list, followed by immigration reform/deportations, and stop Trump from being President. Finally, Cuban origin respondents reported their top issues to be (1) fix the economy/jobs/unemployment, (2) immigration reform/deportation, and (3) terrorism/ISIS/homeland security. Again, let's add gender to our calculations across country of origin information.

Examining the intersection of gender and country-of-origin identities may provide us with a clearer picture of opinion preferences across Latinx subgroups. All of the variables in table 1 are dichotomous, coded 0 for no, and 1 for yes. We use a difference of proportions test to determine whether the differences between Latinas and Latinos within each group are statistically significant. The bold numbers highlight statistically significant differences within each respective country-of-origin group. We do not find a consistent gender gap among Latino subgroups across their choices for most important issues facing their communities. Rather, we find a gender gap among Mexican origin respondents such that a significantly higher percentage of women said that immigration reform/deportations is a top issue in comparison to their male co-ethnics by more than 9 percentage points. This result is consistent with previous research that finds that Latinas tend to be more ideologically liberal in terms of their policy preferences than their males counterparts across country-of-origin subgroups (García Bedolla et al. 2007).

We also find that Puerto Ricans are more divided by gender than Cuban, Dominican, and Mexican origin respondents in terms of their top policy concerns. For example, by a margin of almost 16 percentage points, Puerto Rican men support the economy as a top issue in comparison to their female co-ethnics. They also stated that stopping Donald Trump from being president

Table 1. Public Opinion by Issue, Country of Origin, and Gender

	All Latinos		Mexican origin		Puerto Rican origin		Dominican origin		Cuban origin	
	Female	Male	Female	Male	Female	Male	Female	Male	Female	Male
Fix economy/jobs/ unemployment	**28.5%** (734)	**37.4%** (845)	26.5% (84)	30.2% (78)	**26.2%** (72)	**42%** (92)	43.9% (43)	43% (44)	42.4% (42)	41.4% (48)
Immigration reform/ deportations	40.3 (1038)	34.4 (863)	**34.6** (89)	**25.5** (80)	26.9 (74)	24.2 (53)	31.8 (34)	40.6 (41)	34.3 (34)	35.9 (42)
Education reform/ schools	**30.3** (779)	**26.7** (603)	22.4 (71)	23.7 (61)	**25.8** (71)	**18.2** (40)	27.1 (29)	23.5 (24)	20.2 (20)	25 (29)
Stop Trump					11.6 (32)	18.6 (41)				
Terrorism/ISIS/ national security									18 (18)	17.2 (20)

Note: Bolded font indicates 0.05 significance level or greater.

Source: Latino Decisions 2016 Election Eve Poll (Latino Decisions 2016).

was a top priority by a 7-percentage-point margin. Puerto Rican women showed more support for education reform/schools as a top issue by a margin of almost 8 percentage points. For Dominican and Cuban origin populations, no statistically significant gender gap exists across the top three issues for Latino respondents. Nor does a statistically significant gap exist for those top three issues within their country-of-origin group, respectively.

Given the consistency of immigration reform as a top concern across Hispanic subgroups, it is worth taking a deeper look into this issue. The survey provides us with three additional questions on immigration to investigate. The survey asks respondents: (1) "Do you support or oppose President Obama's 2012 executive action on immigration, sometimes called DACA, that currently provides undocumented youth, called DREAMERS, with legal work permits and temporary relief from deportation? And is that strongly or just somewhat?"; (2) "President Obama announced executive actions on immigration in 2012 and 2014 (DACA/DAPA) that would allow a small proportion of the undocumented immigrant population to obtain legal work permits and temporary relief from deportation. Republican governors and attorney generals from twenty-six states, with the support of Republicans in Congress, sued the Obama administration to stop some of these policies from taking effect. Do you support or oppose the Republican effort

Figure 1. Immigration Support by Country of Origin

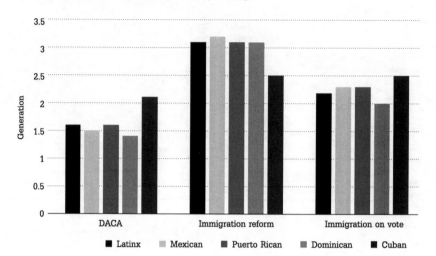

that has, for now, stopped some of President Obamas executive actions on immigration?"; and (3) "How important is the issue of immigration in your decision to vote, and who to vote for in this election? Is it the top, most important issue, one of the important issues, somewhat important, or not really important to your voting decision?" All three are ordinal variables. For the first two questions, the responses are coded 1 for strongly support and 4 for strongly oppose. The mean for the question about DACA is 1.6, and the mean for the question about immigration reforms of 2012 and 2014 is 3.1. The latter is coded 1 for top issue and 4 for not really important. The mean for this last question is 2.2.

First, let's examine country of origin differences in means across these three questions. In figure 1 we observe that Dominican-origin respondents most strongly support DACA, followed by Mexican- and then Puerto Rican-origin populations. Cuban-origin respondents, while still supportive, voiced their support least intensely. On the question of immigration reform efforts of 2012 and 2014, the data in figure 1 demonstrate that Mexican-origin respondents have the strongest preference for opposing restrictions, followed by a tie between Puerto Ricans and Dominican respondents. Again,

Table 2. Mean Score of Immigration Policy Preferences, Country of Origin, and Gender

	All Latinos		Mexican origin		Puerto Rican origin		Dominican origin		Cuban origin	
	Female	Male	Female	Male	Female	Male	Female	Male	Female	Male
DACA	**1.42** (SD = 0.76)	**1.77** (SD = 1.09)	**1.48** (SD = .97)	**1.88** (SD = 1.1)	**1.46** (SD = 0.87)	**1.74** (SD = 1.10)	1.3 (SD = 0.50)	1.5 (SD = 0.76)	2.1 (SD = 1.16)	2.1 (SD = 1.17)
Immigration reform	**3.15** (1.14)	**3.03** (1.22)	**3.16** (1.16)	**2.59** (1.33)	3.12 (1.15)	3.03 (1.26)	3.1 (1)	3.2 (1.16)	2.5 (1.3)	2.5) (1.2)
Immigration and vote choice	2.15 (0.86)	2.28 (0.88)	2.17 (0.85)	2.37 (0.97)	2.43 (0.80)	2.23 (8)	1.8 (0.84)	**2.16** **(0.92)**	2.3 (0.9)	2.5 (0.92)

Note: Bolded font = 0.05 significance level or greater. Source: Latino Decisions 2016 Election Eve Poll.

Cuban-origin respondents oppose restrictions but less strongly than other groups. Finally, on the question of how important immigration was in respondents' voting decisions, the data in figure 1 show that the issue was most important in the voting decisions of Dominicans, and then Puerto Ricans and Mexicans are tied, followed by Cuban-origin respondents.

The data demonstrate that when we add gender to the analysis we find a gender gap across all three questions on immigration. We utilized a difference of means test to investigate the relationship in table 2. Latinas more strongly support DACA and the immigration reform efforts of 2012 and 2014 than do their male counterparts to a statistically significant degree, yet immigration was slightly less important to their vote decision this election. Based on the country-of-origin and gender differences we found, we expect to find differences across and between subgroups when we examine the intersection of gender and country of origin (see table 2).

The results for Mexican-origin respondents by gender mirror those of the entire sample, and the gender differences are statistically significant. For Puerto Rican respondents there is a significant gender gap only on the questions about DACA and the importance of immigration on vote decision. Puerto Rican women more strongly support DACA than do male co-ethnics; however, they also stated that immigration entered into their voting calculus more heavily than did Puerto Rican men. For Dominican-origin respondents, a gender gap was statistically significant such that women in this country-of-origin group said immigration entered into their voting calculus more heavily than did Dominican men. There is no statistically significant gender gap for Cuban-origin respondents across any of the questions.

Clearly, the results in tables 1 and 2 reveal important differences in Latino men and women's opinions across a variety of issues as well as important national-origin differences, lending support for previous work (Montoya 1996; García Bedolla et al. 2007; Bejarano 2013; Manzano 2012). The national origin and gendered differences suggest that even though some of the differences we found seem to follow along the lines of those found among Hispanics generally, we cannot assume that this automatically means there will be one among one or all Latinx groups. As García Bedolla et al. (2007) note, this finding also suggests that national origin, perhaps operating as a proxy for ideology, geography, socialization, and racialization, interacts with gender in important ways, affecting its impact across different policy issue areas. Furthermore, these findings demonstrate that, using contemporary data, we still cannot have a discussion about a U.S. Latinx community that is united based on the issues; we cannot gloss over the existence of significant national-origin group differences, even in the wake of a unique election year that put Latinx communities and immigration front and center. However, we also need to ask, how do these differences affect vote choice?

Vote Choice and Gender Among Latinos

As a result of Latinas' increased support of more liberal policies, historically and as demonstrated here for the 2016 presidential election, they may also be more likely than Latino males to support the Democratic Party and their candidates. It is imperative that the political parties devise new strategies to appeal to the very diverse Latinx electorate. They should also be determined to focus on Latinas as a key group of Latinx voters (Bejarano 2014). Latinas, particularly those who are mothers, are a key political organizational force within their households and communities; they are more liberal than their male counterparts (Gamboa 2015).

Previous work has shown that Latinas were more inclined towards supporting the Democratic Party because of the party's supportive views of "government involvement in terms of 'compassion issues' and promoting social welfare policies" (García Bedolla, Lavariega Monforti, and Pantoja 2006, 149). The data in table 3 provide a historical review of Latinx voting patterns and the long-standing gender gap among Latinx voters since 1980. In every presidential election we reviewed, the majority of Latinx voters supported the Democratic nominee for president. The margin of support ranges from a low of 18-percentage point gap in favor of Kerry in 2004 to a high of a 62-percentage point gap in favor of H. Clinton in 2016. The second column in table 3 presents the gender gap in Latinx voting in presidential elections—a clear pattern emerges that Latinas have shown more support for Democratic candidates for president in comparison to their male co-ethnics.

So, what causes Latinas to vote differently than Latinos? García Bedolla et al. (2006) discovered that among Latinos, issued-focused studies have found that women and men have distinct positions on 'use of force issues' such as capital punishment, military spending, and gun control. Additionally, they also have different attitudes "on 'compassion issues' such as increases in social welfare spending and other programs designed to help the elderly, children, and the poor" (149). Further, "it appears that there is something about the gendered experiences of women that impacts these views" (154). Women more than men participate in their children's education, having to deal with issues that impact their families, and dedicating themselves to solving the problems of their communities. Therefore, they, more than the men in Hispanic communities, are likely to have different reasons for becoming informed citizens, participating in politics, and encouraging the community to become involved. This is supported by our analysis on policy preferences and priorities.

For a bit more context, let's review the most recent presidential elections. A gender gap in terms of vote choice was found in the 2008 and 2012 elections. For example, there was a noticeable gender gap in 2008 between the women and men who supported Obama (7-point difference) and McCain (5-point difference) (CNN National Exit Poll 2008). Incorporating ethnicity

Table 3. The Hispanic Vote in Presidential Elections, 1980–2016

		Latinx vote margin*	Latinx gender gap[†]				Latinx vote margin*	Latinx gender gap[†]
1980	Reagan Carter	21	5		2000	Bush Gore	27	4[§]
1984	Reagan Mondale	24	9–16		2004	Bush Kerry	18	7[§]
1988	Bush Dukakis	39	2–8		2008	McCain Obama	36	4
1992	Bush Clinton	36	N/A		2012	Romney Obama	44	11[‖]
1996	Dole Clinton	51	13[‡]		2016	Trump Clinton	62	13

Note: The numbers in the table represent percentage points. Positive numbers in the Latinx vote margin column indicate more Latinx voters supported the Democratic nominee. Positive numbers in the gap column indicate that women more strongly supported the Democratic nominee.

* http://www.pewhispanic.org/files/2012/11/2012_Latino_vote_exit_poll_analysis_final_11-07-12.pdf.

† See https://www.jstor.org/stable/pdf/448770.pdf, p. 188, for details.

‡ "See Beyond the Gender Gap: Women of Color in the 1996 Election" by Hardy-Fanta and Cardozo (1997), a paper from the APSA.

§ http://www.pewhispanic.org/2005/06/27/iv-how-latinos-voted-in-2004.

‖ http://www.pewhispanic.org/files/2012/11/2012_Latino_vote_exit_poll_analysis_final_11-07-12.pdf.

into the picture, there is still a noticeable gender gap, as 68% of Latinas supported Obama while 30% supported McCain, and for the Latinos 64% supported Obama while 33% supported McCain. These figures demonstrate, in fact, that women do differ from men, and that this trend holds for Latinx voters. While some may question whether this gender gap is significant substantively, the relatively close outcome of the 2016 election in key states has once again made clear that even small differences in important electorates like Latinos can have meaningful substantive effects on the outcomes.

In 2008 Barack Obama's grassroots, community-level campaign, motivated communities to support him. In a time of dissatisfaction with the Republican Party, Obama focused on the issues that motivated Latinas to participate in the 2008 election and they did. A report by the University of Massachusetts Center for Women in Politics and Public Policy said, "Latinas have become increasingly engaged in politics, making up 5% of total voter turnout" while Latinos make up 4% (Gonzalez-Rojas 2008).

In 2012, Latino Decisions tracking polls included questions asking Hispanic respondents which party was better equipped to address issues

Table 4. Public Opinion by Issue, Country of Origin, and Gender

	All Latinos		Mexican origin		Puerto Rican origin		Dominican origin		Cuban origin	
	Female	Male	Female	Male	Female	Male	Female	Male	Female	Male
Clinton	87.9% (2026)	74.6% (1508)	83.7% (237)	61.3% (136)	83.7% (207)	72.2% (143)	97.8% (87)	85% (68)	50% (47)	52.9% (54)
Trump	12.1 (279)	25.4 (313)	16.3 (46)	38.7 (86)	12.7 (30)	27.8 (55)	2.2 (2)	15 **(12)**	50 (47)	47.1 (48)

Note: Bolded font indicates 0.05 significance level or greater. Fewer than 100 gender-identified respondents said they voted for a third-party candidate. Given this small sample size, these respondents were excluded from the analysis. Source: Latino Decisions 2016 Election Eve Poll.

important to women. Latinx voters agreed that Democrats were better equipped; however, as previous research would signal, a 65-point advantage for the Democrats on women's issues was found among Latinas compared to Latinos. This again highlights the importance of the gender gap within Hispanic communities in terms of both public policy preferences and vote choice. In the 2012 election, we see a similar trend in terms of vote choice as in previous elections—support for President Obama among Latinas was 77%, compared to 21% for Romney; this represents a 56-point gap (Bejarano 2014). Latino male voters planned to vote 61% for Obama and 32% for Romney just before the 2012 election (Manzano 2012). In the end, this leads to an 11-percentage-point gender gap in vote choice that favored Obama.

According to the Latino Decisions 2016 Election Eve poll, 81% of Latinx voters supported Hillary Clinton.[16] Nearly 88% of Latinas reported supporting Clinton (19 points higher than the national exit poll). In the same poll in 2012, 77% of Latinas expressed support for President Obama, so the 2016 results represent an 11-percentage-point gain for the Democratic presidential nominee. Thus, Latinas are a core constituency for the Democratic Party, and as voters they have been key to Democratic candidates' success on the national stage in previous election cycles.[17] We know they also represent a growing electorate that will continue to have a more dramatic impact on U.S. politics. Thus, when we talk about the modern gender gap in support of the Democratic candidates, we need to focus on the growing role of Latinas, along with all women of color.

Multivariate Analyses

Our next step was to test these relationships using multivariate analyses. Multivariate estimations allow us to determine whether the gender gaps in public opinion among various Latino groups are the result of gender differences per se, or rather of differences in socioeconomic status, age, ideology, or other factors between men and women. In short, through multivariate analysis we can assess the extent to which gender is a significant factor that structures Latinx vote choice. The vote choice of Latinx voters in 2016 is the dependent variable and includes eight control variables commonly found in gender gap studies: gender, religion (being "born again"), partisanship, marital status, age, education, income, and nativity.

The primary exogenous variable is *gender,* coded 1 for female and 0 for male. The models include the variable *born-again Christian,* a dichotomous measure, for respondents who consider themselves as born-again or evangelical Christians. Born-again and evangelical Christians are noted for their theological, social, and political conservatism (Jelen, Smidt, and Wilcox 1993), and we anticipate that the variable will play an important role in structuring Latinx attitudes, particularly attitudes related to traditional women's roles. Further, gender roles in the United States have been altered as a result of women entering the workforce (McDonagh 1982; Andersen and Cook 1985; Segura 1989).

Marital status is also anticipated to have an effect on political attitudes, as the traditional partisan gap is strongly shaped by women's marital status, with married women being less likely to identify as Democrats (Plutzer and McBurnett 1991). The variable *married* is dichotomous, with 1 for married and 0 for nonmarried. Finally, the models include the demographic controls, *age, education, income,* political *ideology,* and *U.S.-born. Age* is a categorical variable ranging from eighteen years to over sixty-five years across 6 categories. *Education* is a categorical variable with 1 for "Grade 1-8" and 6 for "postgraduate/professional degree." *Income* is a dichotomous variable, with 1 for persons whose annual household incomes are below $60,000, and 2 for incomes above $60,000. *Ideology* is a categorical variable of quartiles. Finally, because there is a high percentage of foreign-born Latinxs, we include

Table 5. Multivariate Logit Analysis of Latinx Vote Choice in 2016

	Mexican origin	Puerto Rican origin	Dominican origin	Cuban origin
U.S.-born	0.737* (0.227)		−3.248‡ (1.598)	
Gender	−13.87† (0.210)		−4.018‡ (1.819)	
Born again	1.036* (0.240)	0.931‡ (0.463)		2.040+ (1.209)
Married	−0.469‡ (0.207)			1.304‡ (0.610)
Income	0.746* (0.210)			
Age	−0.163† (0.57)			
Ideology	−1.307* (0.1266)	−19.89* (0.370)	−3.067† (1.311)	−2.719* (0.591)
Constant	1.822† (0.696)			
n	505	435	169	196

*$p \leq 0.000$, †$p \leq 0.001$, ‡$p \leq 0.05$, §$p \leq 0.10$. Source: Latino Decisions 2016 Election Eve Poll.

the variable *U.S.-born,* a dichotomous variable with 1 for persons born in the United States and 0 for persons born outside the United States. In the case of Puerto Ricans, *U.S.-born* captures Puerto Ricans born in the continental United States. The multivariate estimations are presented in table 5.

There are four multivariate models in table 4. Logistic regressions are used when the dependent variable is dichotomous like vote choice for Hillary Clinton or Donald Trump. Although some of the control variables play an important role in our models, we do not discuss them at length, given that our primary interest is in gender differences. After the introduction of the selected control variables, gender differences among Mexican- and Dominican-origin respondents remain significant. Dominican-, Puerto Rican-, and Mexican-origin women were more likely to vote for the Democratic nominee, Hillary Clinton, than were their male co-ethnics. While Cuban-origin women were more likely than their male counterparts to support Clinton, the gender gap in vote choice was not statistically significant in a multivariate model.

We also find that vote choice for Mexican-origin respondents is also shaped by nativity, political ideology, age, income, marital status, and being a born-again Christian. For Puerto Ricans, ideology is an additional significant predictor, while ideology and nativity shape Dominican-origin vote choice. For Cuban-origin respondents, we find that marital status, political ideology, and religion shape vote choice but gender does not.

Taken together, the multivariate models show evidence of a significant gap in attitudes between Latino men and Latinas in vote choice for two out of the four largest Latinx country-of-origin communities. These results suggest that the Latinx gender gap with regard to this question has persisted since Montoya (1996) conducted her landmark study. Our results may be driven by differences in the survey instrument, by the sampling design, or by changes in the sociodemographic and attitudinal characteristics of respondents. We suspect the latter. Regardless of the reasons, our results clearly demonstrate important attitudinal differences between Latino men and Latinas across different national origin groups. However, the size and significance of the gender gap clearly vary by national origin group, suggesting that attitude differences among Latinxs are the result not solely of gender, but also of the unique way in which gender and national origin intersect among these respondents. National origin, the preferred ethnoracial identity of most Latina/os, continues to influence the political attitudes and behaviors of Latinx respondents. The history of when and how certain subgroups immigrated to the United States impacts political socialization in these communities—and ultimately affects opinion formation and political action.

Conclusion and Discussion

This analysis brings us back to our original set of questions. The gap in opinion between Latinas and Latinos was statistically significant across all of the questions we examined, but that was not the case among the four national origin populations we analyzed. Therefore, we do find some support for the idea of a Latinx gender gap, but we also find important national origin differences. So, how can these findings inform our understanding of the intersection of national origin, class, and gender in U.S. politics? In this work, we have employed what McCall (2005, 1785) describes as an "intercategorical approach," an analysis that treats national origin and gender categories as "anchor points." The understanding is that they are not static, and the primary "concern is with the nature of the relationships among social groups and, importantly, how they are changing, rather than with the definition or representation of such groups per se." We understand that there are problems inherent in the representation of "gender," a social construct, with a dichotomous variable. Our intention is not to minimize the complexity of these categories, but rather to use this analysis to highlight the variation and similarities that exist within Latinx national origin groups. For example, there are significant gender gaps for Mexican-, Dominican-, and Puerto Rican-origin group in terms of opinions on immigration, and gender gaps for Mexican- and Dominican-origin respondents in terms of vote choice. Future research is needed to better understand why those differences exist. The ultimate goal is to suggest ways in which gendered marginalization and privilege are operating within U.S. society, and, within the context of this analysis, helping to shape Latinx public opinion.

Our findings contribute to political theory by encouraging scholars to think more deeply about how experiences of ethnicity and gender interact within the United States context. In general, much scholarly work still derives from the proposition that "all the women are White and all the Blacks are men" (Hull, Bell, and Smith 1982; Hancock 2007). Such a simplistic understanding of marginalization and privilege in the U.S. context bears little resemblance to empirical reality, and does little to move forward our theoretical understanding of how systems of racial/ethnic discrimination and patriarchy reinforce and maintain themselves (Gilmore 2019; Browne and Misra 2003). If we believe Omni and Winant's (1994) proposition that race is a socially constructed phenomenon that exists for the sake of particular political projects, only understanding how national origin *and* gender are constructed in concert can we truly understand the nature of these projects and their potential political effects.

This study constitutes an attempt to move the scholarly debate one step toward that deeper understanding. From an empirical standpoint, on the most basic level, these findings support what intersection theorists have long argued–that experiences of marginalization intersect within individuals and can have important political consequences (Crenshaw 1991; Cohen 1999; hooks 2000; McCall 2005). Of interest here are not only the areas of disagreement between Latino men and Latina women, to which we dedicated the bulk of our analysis, but also the areas of agreement. To put this another way, why is gender less salient in this instance? It is possible, as García Bedolla (2005) finds, that the gender differences across Latinx communities are the result of experiences of marginalization. At the very least, the lack of gender difference among Latinxs with regard to certain policy questions suggests that for those issues national origin, perhaps operating as a proxy for marginalization in general, is driving attitudes more than gender.

This is an important point for scholars when considering the concrete political effects of race, national origin, class, and gender. From a policy standpoint, these Latina women, because of their experiences of marginalization across multiple dimensions, potentially could have different policy priorities and a policy focus that is different from that of Latino men. Or those policy positions, with regard to some issues, could be quite similar. From a political mobilization standpoint, this suggests that particular policy issues or ballot propositions may mobilize Latinas to engage in politics more than Latino men, or vice versa. It is because Latinas are out-voting Latinos that they become significantly important. If this trend continues, more attention may be placed on the issues that motivated Latinas. If Latinas, through their participation in politics, manage to seize the interest of political contenders, might these contenders in return begin paying attention to the issues that drive Latinas to become politically active? If they do, it might be the case that Latinas will have had a tremendous impact in politics in the United States and for the foreseeable future.

Note
I thank Ryan O'Neill for his assistance on this research project.

1. http://www.pewresearch.org/fact-tank/2014/04/02/
   hispanics-punch-below-their-weight-in-midterm-elections.

2. http://www.usnews.com/news/blogs/data-mine/2015/10/06/
   hispanics-could-play-huge-role-in-the-2016-elections.

3. https://www.theatlantic.com/politics/archive/2016/11/
   women-election-clinton-trump/506981.

4. *Hispanic women* and *Latinas* are used interchangeably throughout this work.

5. http://www.pewresearch.org/
   fact-tank/2016/02/03/2016-electorate-will-be-the-most-diverse-in-u-s-history.

6. http://www.pewhispanic.org/2016/01/19/
   millennials-make-up-almost-half-of-latino-eligible-voters-in-2016.

7. http://www.electproject.org/2016g.

8. http://presidentialgenderwatch.org/polls/womens-vote-watch/turnout.

9. https://www.washingtonpost.com/news/monkey-cage/wp/2016/11/11/in-
   record-numbers-latinos-voted-overwhelmingly-against-trump-we-did-the-
   research.

10. http://presidentialgenderwatch.org/polls/womens-vote-watch/turnout.

11. http://civicyouth.org/PopUps/turnoutbygender.pdf.

12. http://www.cnn.com/election/results/exit-polls.

13. While more Latino males than Latinas support the Affordable Care Act
    continuing as law and expanding the Medicaid program.

14. The phi score is -0.094 with a significance is 0.000.

15. The phi score is 0.020 and the significance is 0.006.

16. Note that there is disagreement among the national polls over the true level
    of Latinx support for Clinton; I choose to utilize the Latino Decisions polling
    numbers as the most accurate representation of Latino support.

17. http://presidentialgenderwatch.org/
    no-women-didnt-abandon-clinton-fail-win-support/#more-11172.

References

Andersen, Kristi, and Elizabeth A. Cook. 1985. "Women, Work, and Political
    Attitudes." *American Journal of Political Science* 29: 606–25.

Askarinam, Leah. 2016. "Women May Decide the Election." *Atlantic*, November 8.

Barreto, Matt, and Gary Segura. 2014. *Latino America: How America's Most Dynamic
    Population Is Poised to Transform the Politics of the Nation.* New York: Public
    Affairs.

Bejarano, Christina E. 2013. *The Latina Advantage: Gender, Race, and Political Success.* Austin: University of Texas Press.

———. 2014. "The Latino Gender Gap in U.S. Politics." *Latino Decisions,* February 19. http://www.latinodecisions.com.

Browne, Irene, and Joya Misra. 2003. "The Intersection of Gender and Race in the Labor Market." *Annual Review of Sociology* 29 (1): 487–513.

Center for American Women and Politics (CAWP). 2012. "The Gender Gap: Attitudes on Public Policy Issues." http://www.cawp.rutgers.edu.

CNN. 2008. "CNN National Exit Poll. Exit Polls." http://www.cnn.com.

Cohen, Cathy J. 1999. *The Boundaries of Blackness: AIDS and the Breakdown of Black Politics.* Chicago: University of Chicago Press.

Crenshaw, Kimberlé. 1991. "Mapping the Margins: Intersectionality, Identity Politics, and Violence against Women of Color." *Stanford Law Review* 43 (6): 1241–99.

Fraga, Luis Ricardo, Valerie Martinez-Ebers, Linda Lopez, and Ricardo Ramírez. 2008. "Representing Gender *and* Ethnicity: Strategic Intersectionality." In *Legislative Women: Getting Elected, Getting Ahead,* edited by Beth Reingold, 157–74. Boulder, CO: Lynne Reiner Publishers.

Gamboa, Suzanne. 2015. "Opinion: GOP Losing the Latina Mom Vote and Much More." NBCLatino.com. http://nbclatino.tumblr.com.

García Bedolla, Lisa. 2005. *Fluid Borders: Latino Power, Identity, and Politics in Los Angeles.* Oakland: University of California Press.

García Bedolla, Lisa, Jessica Lavariega Monforti, and Adrian Pantoja. 2006. "A Second Look: The Latina/o Gap." *Journal of Women, Politics, & Policy* 28 (3/4): 147–71.

Gilmore, Glenda. 2019. *Gender and Jim Crow: Women and the Politics of White Supremacy in North Carolina, 1896–1920.* Chapel Hill: University of North Carolina Press.

Gonzalez-Rojas, Jessica. 2008. "The Power of the Latina Vote." *HispanicTrending.* http://www.mediaforum.org.

Hancock, Ange-Marie. 2007. "When Multiplication Doesn't Equal Quick Addition: Examining Intersectionality as a Research Paradigm." *Perspectives on Politics* 5 (1): 63–79.

Hardy-Fanta, Carol and Carol Cardozo. 1997. "Beyond the Gender Gap: Women of Color in the 1996 Election." Paper delivered at the Annual Meeting of the American Political Science Association, Washington, DC, August 28–31.

hooks, bell. 2000. *Feminist Theory: From Margin to Center.* Pluto Press.

Hull, Gloria, Patricia Bell, and Barbara Smith. 1982. *All the Women Are White and All the Blacks Are Men, But Some of Us Are Brave.* New York: Feminist.

Jaramillo, Patricia A. 2010. "Building a Theory, Measuring a Concept: Exploring Intersectionality and Latina Activism at the Individual Level." *Journal of Women, Politics and Policy* 31 (3): 193-216.

Jelen, Ted G., Corwin E. Smidt, and Clyde Wilcox. 1993. "The Political Effects of the Born Again Phenomenon." In *Rediscovering the Religious Factor in American Politics,* edited by David C. Leege and Lyman A. Kellstedt, 199-215. New York: M. E. Sharpe.

Latino Decisions. 2016. "2016 Election Eve Poll." http://www.latinodecisions.com.

Manzano, Sylvia. 2012. "The Latino Gender Gap: Latina Voters Prefer Obama by 53 Point Margin." *Latino Decisions,* September 17.

McCall, Leslie. 2005. "The Complexity of Intersectionality." *Signs: Journal of Women in Culture and Society* 30 (3): 1771-800.

McDonagh, E. L. 1982. "To Work or Not to Work: The Differential Impact of Achieved and Derived Status Upon the Political Participation of Women, 1956-1976." *American Journal of Political Science* 26 (2): 280-97.

Montoya, Lisa J. 1996. "Latino Gender Differences in Public Opinion: Results from the Latino National Political Survey." *Hispanic Journal of Behavioral Sciences* 18 (2): 255-76.

Omni, M., and H. Winant. 1994. *Racial Formation in the United States.* New York: Routledge.

Plutzer, E., and M. McBurnett. 1991. "Family Life and American Politics: The 'Marriage Gap' Reconsidered." *Public Opinion Quarterly* 55 (1): 113-27.

Segura, Denise. 1989. "Chicana and Mexican Immigrant Women at Work: The Impact of Class, Race, and Gender on Occupational Mobility." *Gender & Society* 2 (1): 37-52.

Did Latino Millennial Voters Turn Out in 2016?

Maria Livaudais, Edward D. Vargas, and Gabriel R. Sanchez

"MILLENNIAL VOTERS" GARNERED A LOT OF ATTENTION DURING THE 2016 elections as they now represent a larger portion of eligible voters than the baby boomers and are nearly half of the overall eligible voting population among Blacks and Latinos (PEW 2016).[1] In fact, millennials are the most racially/ethnically diverse age cohort (U.S. Census 2015). Despite the potential of this electorate to influence elections and, ultimately, policy, only 50% of millennials, or 24 million, turned out to vote during the 2016 presidential election, compared to 60% of the overall population (Pillsbury and Johannesen 2016).

Of the young adults who voted, Hillary Clinton won 55% of the youth vote, compared to Donald Trump, who won 37% of the youth vote (U.S. Census 2016; CIRCLE 2016). With a lackluster turnout and higher than anticipated support for the GOP nominee, millennial voters were among the subgroups that pundits suggested helped Trump win the election due to underperformance. Despite this suggestion among pundits and the national media, there is surprisingly little work among political scientists specifically focused on the millennial population. Our chapter addresses

Figure 1. Eligible Voters by Race/Ethnicity and Age in 2016

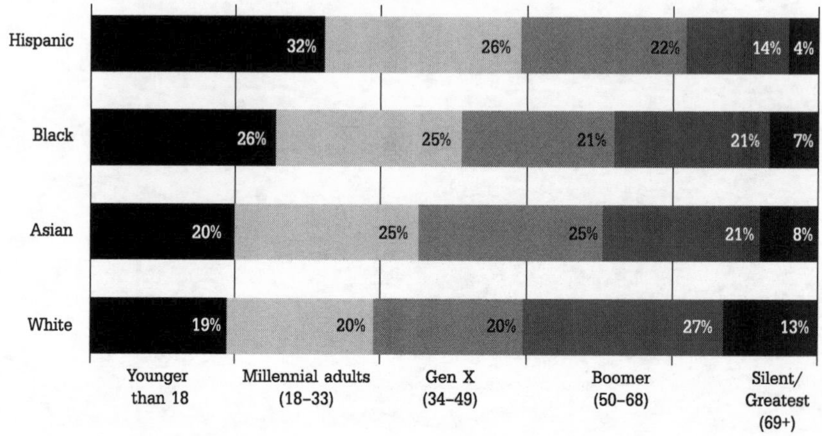

	Younger than 18	Millennial adults (18–33)	Gen X (34–49)	Boomer (50–68)	Silent/ Greatest (69+)
Hispanic	32%	26%	22%	14%	4%
Black	26%	25%	21%	21%	7%
Asian	20%	25%	25%	21%	8%
White	19%	20%	20%	27%	13%

Source: Krogstad et al. (2016).

this limitation with an examination of how Latino millennials engaged in 2016 with an eye toward any lessons learned that could improve turnout among this key electorate moving forward.

Latino millennials are clearly a key subgroup of the Latino electorate that not only played a prominent role in the 2016 election but will continue to be important to Latino politics as they age as a cohort. Within the larger Latino population, Latino millennials represent almost half of eligible Latino voters, as seen in figure 1 (Krogstad et al. 2016). The prominence of Latino millennials shows in key battleground states such as Colorado,[2] North Carolina, and Ohio (America's Voice/Latino Decisions 2016). The high ratio of millennials among the voting eligible Latino population means Latinos will have long-term electoral power as this population ages. However, in the short term, turnout among millennial Latinos is likely to be low, resulting from their lack of experience navigating the political system. We intend to focus our chapter on this critically important yet understudied subgroup with a specific eye toward how, if anything, to better mobilize this specific subgroup of the Latino electorate.

Our chapter focuses specifically on Latino millennials (individuals between eighteen and thirty-three years old) and addresses the following questions: Did Latino millennials support Trump at similar rates as millennials overall? Did a racialized campaign directed at the Latino community mobilize Latino millennials to vote, and what challenges exist for organizations and candidates interested in engaging Latino young adults in electoral politics? In this chapter, we address these central questions by pulling from multiple Latino Decisions data sets to provide a comprehensive analysis specific to the Latino millennial population. There was an increase in millennial Latino voters during the 2016 presidential election, 40.3% who said they voted, relative to 2012, 37.8% who said they voted (Krogstad and Lopez 2017). We find these voters were highly motivated to turn out as a means to support the Latino community and were primarily concerned with immigration policy. Surprisingly, we also found that millennials do not see voting as the best mechanism to bring forth social change in society relative to engaging in protest activities or social media. This along with their more pessimistic views regarding the role of government will make mobilization challenging down the line, and helps explain low turnout in the 2016 campaign. This new reality is important as it impacts get out the vote (GOTV) efforts and will force campaigns to think critically about how they can engage this cohort in traditional politics.

Literature Review: The Powerful Role of Age in Political Behavior

Despite the large numbers of eligible millennial voters, they are characterized as the least involved and least politically active among all age cohorts, which raises concerns for mobilization, turnout, and future political engagement (Kaid, McKinney, and Tedesco 2007). Compared to older generations, millennials are less politically active and civically engaged from the view of traditional political science theory and practice. Voter turnout among adults eighteen to twenty-five years old has steadily declined since 1972 (Levine and Hugo Lopez 2002). Until the 2000 election, youth voter turnout decreased at a faster rate than the rest of American voter turnout (Dalton 2008; Putnam 2000; Wattenberg 2008). However, in 2008, youth voting rates (adults under twenty-nine) increased three times faster than the turnout for Americans older than thirty, for which we must acknowledge President Obama's use of social media during his campaigns (PEW 2008). Immediately after President Obama took office, the momentum of political participation extended to forms other than voting, such as campaign volunteerism (Dalton 2008; Fisher 2012; Sander and Putnam 2010). Since the 2008 presidential election, the millennial voter turnout has returned to its more typical numbers below those of older segments of the electorate (CIRCLE 2016; PEW 2016). A part of this explanation is that young voters are a moving target. In other words, many of those who were mobilized by the 2008 Obama candidacy are no longer "young voters" but may continue to be engaged and mobilized. Demographically speaking, a large share of millennials who were not eligible to vote in 2008 are now part of eligible and registered voters.

The socioeconomic model of participation often explains differences in political participation across generations and race/ethnicity groups, suggesting individuals who are older and have higher socioeconomic (SES) status are more likely to have high levels of political participation and higher levels of voter turnout (Andolina et al. 2003; Beck and Jennings 1982; Blais 2000; Plutzer 2002; Strate et al. 1989; Verba and Nie 1972; Verba et al. 1995; Wolfinger and Rosenstone 1980).

The previously cited scholars argue that the older an individual is, the more time they have to increase their income and educational attainment, which reduces their costs of voting and political participation. Age, income, and education together become characteristics of individuals who are equipped to navigate the political system and bureaucratic barriers to participate. In addition, young adults who come from households with higher SES levels are more likely to talk about politics, vote, and be more engaged in politics. Conversely, young adults with less resources and lower levels of education are less likely to be informed about politics and less likely to participate (PEW 2013; Jennings and Niemi 2014; Sandell and Plutzer 2005; Wolfinger and Rosenstone 1980).

This chapter employs SES theory to explain the low turnout among young Latinos (Garcia-Rios and Barreto 2016; Ramírez 2013; Terriquez 2014, 2017; Zepeda-Millan 2017). For young voters who are often voting for the first time, they uniquely face the highest number of barriers, navigating registration, finding polling locations, and other aspects of the voting process. Furthermore, millennials' high residential mobility may amplify these barriers to voting by undercutting the GOTV efforts employed during the election (Myers 2015). Young Latinos may also face additional language barriers and difficulties understanding party differences and key issues. Despite the fact that millennial Latinos represent such a large portion of the eligible voting bloc, they may not be contacted because of their lack of disposable income to contribute to campaigns. Therefore, they are even further disenfranchised. Like all Latinos, millennial voters may be clustered in non-battleground states like Texas and California that are not receiving substantial GOTV resources (Ramírez, Solano, and Wilcox-Archuleta 2018).

The Latino population is significantly younger than the overall population, which leads to the high concentration of millennials among the Latino electorate. In addition, younger Latinos are more likely to have an even more acute socioeconomic disparity than older Latinos and other groups because they do not have the same amount of time and resources to accumulate wealth and formal education (DeSipio 1996; Highton and Burris 2002; Wolfinger and Rosenstone 1980). Younger Latinos who have gone through the naturalization process are even further disadvantaged because they have not had the time nor experience with the political system (Grenier 1984; Highton and Burris 2002). Ultimately, political science theory would predict that younger Latinos are less likely to participate in politics because they face many challenges navigating the political system and understanding political norms with fewer resources available to them to overcome these challenges.

Not surprisingly, in 2012, millennial Latinos turned out in lower numbers—38% of millennial Latinos—than older Latinos—55% of Gen X, Boomer, and Silent/Greatest Latinos (Krogstad et al. 2016). Latino Millennials' turnout (38%) also fell behind White (47.5%) and Black Millennials (55%) (Krogstad et al. 2016). In the 2016 election, the turnout gap between Latino millennials and White, Black, and Asian millennials increased (Krogstad and Lopez 2017).

This underperformance disproportionately harms Democratic candidates. Registered Latino millennial voters identified as 37% liberal, 38% moderate, and 21% conservative as of 2012 (Lopez et al. 2016). In 2014, half of Millennials identified as Independent, 27% identified as Democrat, and 17% identified as Republican (Taylor et al. 2014). In the 2012 election, Latinas between eighteen and twenty-nine years old were the most liberal compared to other race/gender groups. When compared to older Latino voters, Latina voters were more liberal and less religious (CIRCLE 2012). This backdrop helps inform our specific research questions and hypothesis specific to the 2016 election.

We anticipate that millennial Latinos are more likely to vote in the interest of supporting the Latino community than in support of either the Democratic or Republican Party because of their high independent party identification and strong bonds to immigration, an issue identified as the most salient to Latino voters. Furthermore, we hypothesize that because millennial Latinos represent such a large portion of the Latino electorate, they will have had higher rates of contact by political parties than other age cohorts within the Latino electorate. Fortunately, Latino Decisions conducted several surveys over the course of this election that provide an opportunity to analyze the rates of enthusiasm, policy preferences, and voting behavior among this specific population throughout the election season.

Data and Methods

We draw from the Latino Decisions 2016 Election Eve Survey. Latino Decisions completed 5,600 interviews with high propensity Latino voters who had either voted or reported being certain to vote on Election Day, November 8, 2016, for the presidential election. Because of our focus on millennials, it is important to note that we had 1,172 completed interviews from Latinos aged eighteen to thirty-three years. This provided a large sample for millennial specific analysis, as well as the ability to compare millennials to the wider Latino electorate.

We also draw from two surveys in Colorado conducted in collaboration with the Latino Data Project that were utilized by organizations on the ground in Colorado to engage and mobilize Latino millennials specifically in that state. The power of this data set lies in its ability to look at internal variation within this subgroup, given the large sample size of a statewide poll conducted in May 2016 and a sampling strategy specific to capturing likely millennial voters online in a millennial-focused poll conducted in June 2016. The poll included live interviews of 400 registered Latino voters in Colorado between the ages of eighteen and thirty-three years by telephone through both landlines and cell phones.[3] The Colorado Statewide Issues poll included live interviews with 500 registered Latino voters in Colorado conducted by telephone via both landlines and cell phones.[4]

Results

We utilize descriptive statistics to discuss how Latino millennials reacted to the Clinton and Trump campaign throughout the election, as well as to analyze their voting behavior. One of the core goals of this study is to address the broader question of how to engage Latino millennials in the electoral process, given the challenge we know exists based on the impact of age on voting identified in the literature.

The Colorado data set provides insights on the challenges we will face to mobilize young adult Latinos moving forward. In line with the general finding that age correlates negatively with civic engagement, the pre-election polling in Colorado found a sizable enthusiasm gap between Latino millennials and older Latinos. More specifically, we found that among Latinos in Colorado, only 57% of millennials were certain that they would vote at this stage in the campaign, compared to well over 80% of the other age cohorts in the sample. This trend was consistent with other indicators of enthusiasm from pre-election surveys that consistently revealed a strong enthusiasm gap between Latino millennials and older Latinos.

In an effort to help address this enthusiasm gap we tested several engagement-messaging themes in an online poll specific to millennials in Colorado. While many of the messaging themes underperformed relative to older cohorts, Latino millennials viewed Trump's inflammatory language regarding Mexicans/immigrants as the most persuasive in Colorado. Teachers, community organizations, and family members are much stronger messengers for Latino millennials than either local elected officials or a wide list of celebrities we tested. These celebrities included singer Shakira, America Ferrera, Diane Guerrero, Jennifer Lopez, and Selena Gomez, as well as sports figure Mark Sanchez, and Spanish TV celebrities like Jorge Ramos and Armida y La Flaka.

Finally, and most importantly, we found that some of the core values across this age cohort will require mobilization efforts to focus on the underlying value of voting in their efforts to engage millennials. As reflected in the following, while a robust 86% of Latino millennials want to see major change in the United States, and 82% feel negative about what is happening in politics, many do not view voting as the mechanism to create change in our country (see figure 2). More specifically, there are large percentages of Latino millennials who believe that utilizing social media to influence political outcomes is more effective than voting, and 51% would rather attend a protest or demonstration than vote in an election (see figure 3).

These numbers remind us that millennials have been socialized to politics in a highly polarized era of American politics, since the *Citizens United v. Federal Election Commission* case further enabled the powerful role of money in our political system. Therefore, efforts will need to aim directly at the value of voting for millennials if we are to see their turnout rates improve in 2018 and beyond.

When we look at the numbers from our Election Eve Poll, a sample of 5,500 Latino voters conducted in the final days of the campaign, November 2-7, we see that many of the findings from the pre-election polls continued through Election Day. For example, the enthusiasm gap for millennials translated into a disparity in early voting according to our Election Eve Poll. Here we found that 53% of Latinos nationwide voted early either by mail or absentee (24% by mail or absentee and 28% at voting location), but only 42% among Latinos aged eighteen to thirty-three years.

There was a lot of national discussion about the importance of first-time voters in 2016 among Latinos, fueled by the large number of millennial

Figure 2. How Latino Millennials Describe Their Generation

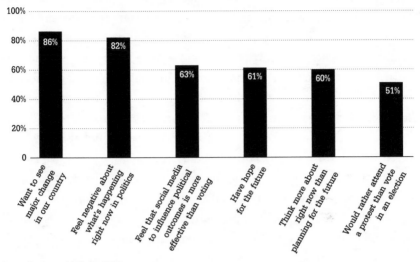

Source: Sanchez and Archuleta (2016).

Figure 3. Latino First-Time Voters in 2016 Presidential Election by Age Cohort

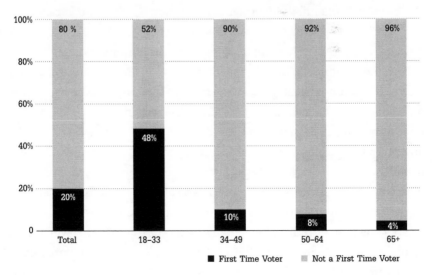

Source: Latino Decisions 2016 Election Eve Poll.

voters who were not old enough to vote in 2012 and the prospect of Trump's rhetoric bringing out Latinos who do not typically vote. According to the Election Eve data, we found that 20% of Latino voters in 2016 were "first-time voters," and not surprisingly, a much higher percentage (48%) of Latinos aged eighteen to thirty-three years reported that they voted for the first time (see figure 3). In addition, campaigns, political parties, and community organizations contacted Latino millennials at a higher rate (44%) than other Latino age cohorts (31%) to encourage them to register and vote.

As discussed throughout the book, Latino voters overwhelmingly supported Hillary Clinton (79%) over Donald Trump (18%). When we isolate the millennial population, we find that 80% of Latino millennials voted for Hillary Clinton, 14% voted for Donald Trump, and the rest for a third party. Given that the National Exit Poll reported only 55% of millennials overall supported Clinton, it is therefore clear that Latino millennials were much stronger supporters of the Clinton campaign than millennials overall.[5]

We asked respondents directly what the most important issues facing the [Latino/Hispanic] community are that our politicians should address and found that immigration was the dominant issue on the minds of Latino voters as they cast ballots (see figure 4). More specifically, we found that 48% of Latino millennials identified immigration reform or deportations as the top issue, compared to 25% for the economy, jobs, and unemployment. This demonstrates an increase in attentiveness to immigration reform and deportations compared to 2012, when millennials identified the economy (42%) and then immigration (40%) as the two most important issues (ImpreMedia/Latino Decisions 2012). We also asked respondents to identify how important immigration was in their decision to vote and who to vote for directly in this election. When asked directly, 22% of Latino millennials said it was the "most important" issue, and another 43% said it was "one of the most important" issues. Furthermore, nearly all (89%) of Latino millennials support President Obama's 2012 executive action, referred to as DACA.

Moving forward, it may be challenging for the GOP to gain favor among young Latinos. When asked whether they were voting to support Democratic candidates, Republican candidates, or the Latino community, young Latinos (ages eighteen to thirty-three years) overwhelmingly (51%) said

Figure 4. Most Important Issues Identified by Latinos across Age Cohorts

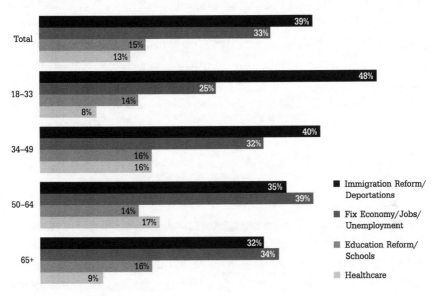

Source: Latino Decisions 2016 Election Eve Poll.

Figure 5. Latino Millennial's Perception of How GOP Cares for Latino Community in 2016 Election

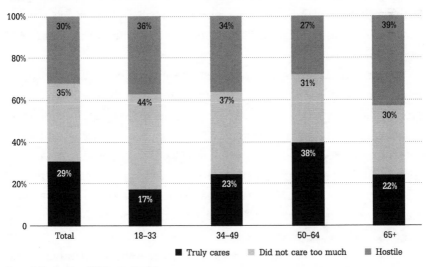

Source: Latino Decisions 2016 Election Eve Poll.

it was to support the Latino community. We found that 21% of younger Latinos voted to support the Democratic candidates and only 8% voted to support Republican candidates. Furthermore, when asked whether the Republican Party truly cares about Latino voters or is hostile toward Latinos, 36% of young Latinos felt the GOP is hostile and 44% felt Republicans do not care too much for Latinos (see figure 5). Of all the age cohorts, younger Latinos perceived the GOP to be the most hostile or indifferent toward the Latino community.

Conclusion

The data presented in this chapter show that blame for the Trump victory should not lie with Latino millennials, as they overwhelmingly supported Hillary Clinton in the 2016 presidential election. Latino millennials' ties to their community and immigration policies were very strong. We also found that Latino millennials were more likely to be mobilized by candidates, parties, and interest groups than older Latinos. However, the story of Latino millennials in 2016 is not all positive. Despite strong mobilization turnout, both the perception that voting is not the most effective means of bringing forth social change and a greater propensity to believe that protest politics and engagement in social media are more effective than voting hampered Latino millennials.

Our chapter suggests that the strong sense of attachment to the Latino community among millennials can be utilized to mobilize them to a greater extent than party-focused messages. Furthermore, given the high numbers of Latino millennials who view the GOP as being hostile and/or indifferent to Latinos, the Republican Party will have a lot of work ahead to repair this relationship and build stronger ones with this large and critical subgroup of the Latino electorate. Our analysis reveals that focusing on comprehensive immigration reform that includes a path to citizenship is the best road to this outcome, assuming, of course, that the GOP is interested in improving their brand among a community for which the members will only become more consequential to electoral politics as they age.

Notes

1. We acknowledge that there is a debate on the age cutoffs for millennials; for this study we define millennials as individuals between eighteen and thirty-three years old.

2. Latino millennials make up one of Colorado's most rapidly growing voting blocs (Sanchez and Archuleta 2016).

3. Respondents answered in English or Spanish at their discretion. We weighted results to known population characteristics using the Current Population Survey. The nominal margin of error for the poll is 4.86%.

4. Respondents answered in English or Spanish at their discretion. We weighted results to known population characteristics using the Current Population Survey. The nominal margin of error for the poll is 4.4%.

5. The National Exit Poll suggested that 70% of Latino millennials voted for Hillary Clinton and 24% voted for Donald Trump. Given our overall strong concerns with the exit poll, we do not recommend referencing the millennial numbers.

References

America's Voice/Latino Decisions. 2016. "America's Voice/LD 2016 Latino Vote State Polls." *America's Voice/Latino Decisions.* http://www.latinodecisions.com.

Andolina, Molly W., Krista Jenkins, Cliff Zukin, and Scott Keeter. 2003. "Habits from Home, Lessons from School: Influences on Youth Civic Engagement." *Political Science and Politics* 36 (2): 275–80.

Beck, Paul Allen, and M. Kent Jennings. 1982. "Pathways to Participation." *American Political Science Review* 76 (1): 94–108.

Blais, André. 2000. *To Vote or Not to Vote? The Merits and Limits of Rational Choice Theory.* Pittsburgh: University of Pittsburgh Press.

CIRCLE. 2012. "Diverse Electorate: A Deeper Look into the Millennial Vote." Center for Information & Research on Civic Engagement. http://civicyouth.org.

———. 2016. "Young Voters in the 2016 General Election." Center for Information & Research on Civic Engagement. http://civicyouth.org.

Dalton, Russell J. 2008. *The Good Citizen: How a Younger Generation Is Reshaping American Politics.* Washington, DC: CQ Press.

DeSipio, Louis. 1996. *Counting on the Latino Vote: Latinos as a New Electorate.* Charlottesville: University of Virginia Press.

Fisher, Dana R. 2012. "Youth Political Participation: Bridging Activism and Electoral Politics." *Annual Review of Sociology* 38: 119-37.

Garcia-Rios, Sergio I., and Matt A. Barreto. 2016. "Politicized Immigrant Identity, Spanish-Language Media, and Political Mobilization in 2012." *RSF* 2 (3): 78-96.

Grenier, Gilles. 1984. "Shifts to English as Usual Language by Americans of Spanish Mother Tongue." *Social Science Quarterly* 65 (2): 537-50.

Highton, Benjamin, and Arthur L. Burris. 2002. "New Perspectives on Latino Voter Turnout in the United States." *American Politics Research* 30 (3): 285-306.

ImpreMedia/Latino Decisions. 2012. "ImpreMedia/Latino Decisions 2012 Latino Election Eve Poll." *Latino Decisions.* http://www.latinovote2012.com.

Jennings, M. Kent, and Richard G. Niemi. 2014. *Generations and Politics: A Panel Study of Young Adults and Their Parents.* Princeton, NJ: Princeton University Press.

Kaid, Lynda Lee, Mitchell S. McKinney, and John C. Tedesco. 2007. "Introduction: Political Information Efficacy and Young Voters." *American Behavioral Scientist* 50 (9): 1093-111.

Krogstad, Jens Manuel, and Mark Hugo Lopez. 2017. "Black Voter Turnout Fell in 2016, Even as a Record Number of Americans Cast Ballots." Pew Research Center. http://www.pewresearch.org.

Krogstad, Jens Manuel, Mark Hugo Lopez, Gustavo Lopez, Jeffery S. Passel, and Eileen Patten. 2016. "Millennials Make Up Almost Half of Latino Eligible Voters in 2016." Pew Research Center. http://www.pewhispanic.org.

Levine, Peter, and Mark Hugo Lopez. 2002. "Youth Voter Turnout Has Declined, by Any Measure." Report from The Center for Information & Research on Civic Learning & Engagement (CIRCLE), College Park, MD.

Lopez, Mark Hugo, Ana Gonzalez-Barrera, Jen Manuel Krogstad, and Gustavo Lopez. 2016. "Democrats Maintain Edge as Party 'More Concerned' for Latinos, but Views Similar to 2012". Pew Research Center. http://www.pewhispanic.org.

Myers, Dowell. 2015. "Peak Millennials: Three Reinforcing Cycles That Amplify the Rise and Fall of Urban Concentration by Millennials." *Housing Policy Debate* 6: 928-47.

Pew Research Center 2008. "Young Voters in 2008 Election." Pew Research Centers Social Demographic Trends Project RSS. https://www.pewresearch.org/2008/11/13/young-voters-in-the-2008-election/

———. 2013. "A Rising Share of Young Adults Live in Their Parents' Home." Pew Research Centers Social Demographic Trends Project RSS. https://www.pewsocialtrends.

org/2013/08/01/a-rising-share-of-young-adults-live-in-their-parents-home/.

———. 2016. "Millennials Approach Baby Boomers as America's Largest Generation in the Electorate" Pew Research Centers Social Demographic Trends Project RSS. https://www.pewresearch.org/fact-tank/2018/04/03/millennials-approach-baby-boomers-as-largest-generation-in-u-s-electorate/.

Pillsbury, George, and Julian Johannesen. 2016. "America Goes to the Polls 2016." Nonprofit Vote and US Election Project, March 16. http://www.nonprofitvote. org.

Plutzer, Eric. 2002. "Becoming a Habitual Voter: Inertia, Resources, and Growth in Young Adulthood." *American Political Science Review* 96 (1): 41-56.

Putnam, Robert D. 2000. *Bowling Alone: America's Declining Social Capital.* New York: Simon & Schuster.

Ramírez, Ricardo. 2013. *Mobilizing Opportunities: The Evolving Latino Electorate and the Future of American Politics.* Charlottesville: University of Virginia Press.

Ramírez, Ricardo, Romelia Solano, and Bryan Wilcox-Archuleta. 2018. "Selective Recruitment or Voter Neglect? Race, Place, and Voter Mobilization in 2016" *Journal of Race, Ethnicity, and Policies* 3(1): 156-184.

Sanchez, Gabriel, and Katherine Archuleta. 2016. "Expanding the Latino Vote in Colorado in 2016 and Beyond." Latino Decisions/Latino Data Project. https://www.scribd.com.

Sandell, Julianna, and Eric Plutzer. 2005. "Families, Divorce and Voter Turnout in the US." *Political Behavior* 27 (2): 133-62.

Sander, Thomas H., and Robert D. Putnam. 2010. "Still Bowling Alone? The Post-9/11 Split." *Journal of Democracy* 21(1): 9-16.

Strate, John M., Charles J. Parrish, Charles D. Elder, and Coit Ford. 1989. "Life Span Civic Development and Voting Participation." *American Political Science Review* 83(2): 443-64.

Taylor, Paul, Carroll Doherty, Kim Parker, and Vidya Krishnamurthy. 2014." Millennials in Adulthood: Detached from Institutions, Networked with Friends." Pew Research Center.

Terriquez, Veronica. 2014. "Trapped in the Working Class? Prospects for the Intergenerational (Im)Mobility of Latino Youth." *Sociological Inquiry* 84 (3): 382-411.

———. 2017. "Legal Status, Civic Organizations, and Political Participation Among Latino Young Adults." *Sociological Quarterly* 58 (2): 315-36.

U.S. Census. 2015. "Millennials Outnumber Baby Boomers and Are Far More

Diverse." Census Bureau Reports. June 25.

U.S. Census. 2016. "Electorate Profiles: Selected Characteristics of the Citizen, 18 and Older Population." Census Bureau Reports. October 28. http://www. census.gov.

Verba, Sidney, Nancy Burns, and Kay Lehman Schlozman. 1997. "Knowing and Caring About Politics: Gender and Political Engagement." *Journal of Politics* 59 (4): 1051–72.

Verba, Sidney, and Norman H. Nie. 1987. *Participation in America: Political Democracy and Social Equality.* Chicago: University of Chicago Press.

Wattenberg, Martin P. 2008. *Is Voting for Young People? With a Postscript on Citizen Engagement.* New York: Pearson Longman.

Wolfinger, Raymond E., and Steven J. Rosenstone. 1980. *Who Votes?* New Haven, CT: Yale University Press.

Zepeda-Millan, Chris. 2017. *Latino Mass Mobilization: Immigration, Racialization, and Activism.* Cambridge: Cambridge University Press.

Colorado

Latinos and the 2016 Election

Robert R. Preuhs

DESPITE THE EXTRAORDINARY 2016 CAMPAIGN SEASON AND ITS WIDELY unexpected national presidential outcome, Colorado's 2016 general election closely followed the trajectory of its recent presidential elections. Democratic Nominee Hillary Clinton's 48.15% of Colorado's popular vote won the state, besting Republican nominee and winner of the Electoral College Donald Trump's 43.27% (Colorado Secretary of State 2016). The 4.88% margin differed only nominally from Barack Obama's 5% margin of victory in 2012 (Colorado Secretary of State 2012). Down the ballot, the status quo reigned. The preferences and participation of Latinos provide an important explanation for Colorado's consistent election results in the midst of surprises at the national level, or, at least, in several states. From candidate and party preferences, policy concerns, enthusiasm, and impact, Latinos in Colorado continued to play a significant role in the state's election outcomes and political climate.

Demographics and Political Preferences

The size of Colorado's Latino population and its political preferences combined to exert a substantial impact on the 2016 election. Latinos accounted for 21.3% of Colorado's population in 2015, up slightly from 20.7% in 2010 (U.S. Census 2016). As in most states, Colorado's Latino population is younger than the non-Latino White population; experiences higher poverty rates and lower homeownership rates; and includes a substantial portion of noncitizen residents and undocumented immigrants (about 18% of Latinos were noncitizens in 2014) (U.S. Census 2016; Passel and Cohn 2014; Pew Center 2014). Combined, these factors, whether due to general correlates of lower voter turnout and registration rates (Rosenstone and Hanson 1993) or obvious legal constraints, result in the estimated Latino share of registered voters at 10% in 2015 (NALEO 2016). Accounting for 1 in 10 of Colorado's voters and potentially more, depending on the level of turnout among other groups, Latinos were situated to play a major role in the 2016 election outcome.

The impact of Latino voters depends on their relative preference for the candidates combined with turnout. For instance, a 50/50 split across parties or candidates among Latino voters results in virtually no impact on the election outcome, as Latino voters supporting opposing candidates equally cancel each other out. Like all other states in this volume, however, such a split fell far from reality, with Latinos in Colorado strongly favoring Democratic candidates in their vote choices up and down the ballot. Figure 1 presents data on national presidential and senatorial candidate preferences from two America's Voice/Latino Decisions polls taken in April 2016 and August 2016, and the Latino Decisions 2016 Election Eve Poll taken November 4–7, 2016. The April and August numbers combine leaners with likely voters, while the Election Eve Poll reports the response to the simple question: "Did or will you vote for one of the candidates (or someone else)?"

As figure 1 demonstrates, Colorado's Latino community strongly supported both Democratic presidential nominee Hillary Clinton and the incumbent Democratic U.S. senatorial candidate Michael Bennet throughout the election. From April through August, Clinton's support among Latinos never fell below 72%, which occurred at mid election season as she secured

Figure 1. Colorado Latinos' Presidential and Senate Preferences, 2016 General Election

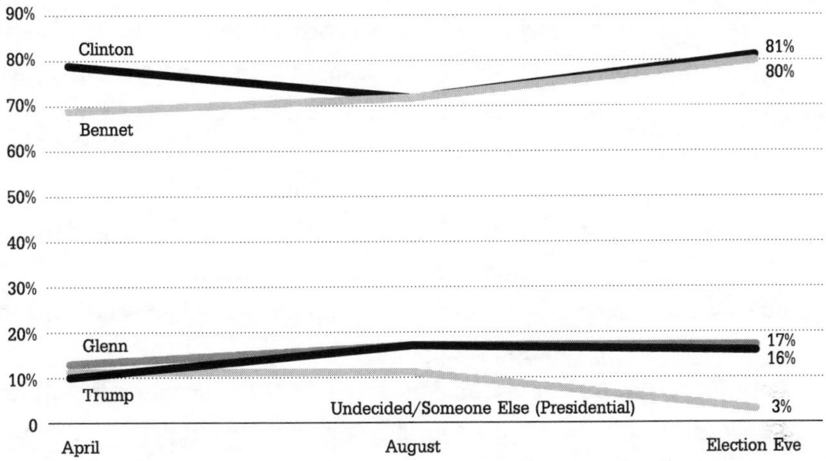

Source: America's Voice/Latino Decisions 2016, 3-State Battleground (April) and National Battleground State Polls (August); Latino Decisions 2016 Election Eve Poll.

the nomination. In the days leading up to the election, her support gained strength and resulted in a high point at 81%. Donald Trump's trajectory of support peaked in the August poll, at 17% leaners or likely supporters, and held steady up until Election Day at 16%. While the margins tightened in August to a 55% lead for Clinton, the polling most proximate to the election revealed a strong preference for Clinton and a margin of 65% (or more than 5 to 1) over Trump. Undecided voters seemed to move toward Clinton, with only 3% ultimately voting for a third- or minor-party candidate (down from 11% undecided in August). There is simply nothing to suggest that Latinos in Colorado did not strongly favor Democrat Hillary Clinton over Republican Donald Trump in 2016.

Democratic preferences among Latinos were not constrained to the top of the ballot's presidential selection. In fact, preferences in the Senate and a generic Congressional candidate match-up by party paralleled those for president so closely that it was almost impossible to graphically distinguish the three. Figure 1's depiction of the senatorial race highlights this point, with support for Democrat Michael Bennet at 80% at the time of the election (which rose throughout the year), compared to support for his

Republican opponent, Darryl Glenn, at 17%. The margin of 63% is statistically indistinguishable from Clinton's 65% margin.

Moreover, margins on the eve of the election for the U.S. House of Representatives fell in line with both the presidential and senatorial margins. Eighty-four percent of Latinos in Colorado indicated that they did or will vote for the Democratic candidate in the election for the U.S. House of Representatives, compared to 14% for the Republican candidate. The 70% margin was the largest of all three, but likely reflected the large populations of Latinos living in Denver and Jefferson County whose incumbent House members were Democrats and benefited from an incumbency advantage and relatively low information campaigns.

Contrary to prominent national narratives, neither down-ballot fallout from opposition to Trump nor a significant decline in support for Clinton seemed at play in the candidate preferences of Latinos in Colorado. While overall support for Clinton was lower than for Obama in 2012 (an issue discussed later in this chapter), she bested Obama's 2008 margin of 50% (70% for Obama vs. 20% for McCain), while Bennet's support remained stable relative to Latinos' 80-20 split in his favor over GOP challenger Ken Buck in 2010 (Latino Decisions 2010; Latino Decisions 2012). Bennet also improved on the 48-point margin favoring incumbent Democratic U.S. Senator Mark Udall (71% of Latinos) in his loss to current Republican Senator Cory Gardner (23%) (Latino Decisions 2014). Democratic support in U.S. House races actually increased from 2014, when 72% of Latinos in Colorado reported voting for the Democrat while 24% supported the Republican candidate (Latino Decisions 2014). In short, while Democratic Presidential support experienced some drop-off relative to four years earlier, Latino preferences and subsequent margins for Democrats remained stable, or even increased, over the three general elections and two mid-term elections since 2008. The lack of significant changes in support up and down the ballot and a consistent orientation toward the Democratic Party's candidates suggest that while nationally this election witnessed a substantive shift in party allegiances among some demographic groups, Colorado's Latinos remained soundly in favor of Democratic candidates, and in some ways even more so than in previous elections.

The degree to which Latinos' clear preferences for Democratic candidates translates into election impacts depends entirely on Latino voter turnout, and, in turn, the overall Latino portion of the electorate. Colorado does not collect registration, and subsequently voter participation, data by race or ethnic background. However, various sources provide a set of estimates for Latino voter impact on the electorate. Depending on the construct, estimates range from around 10% of registered voters in 2015 (NALEO 2016) to about 14.5% of the eligible voters in the state (Pew Center 2016). Taking this range as a reflection of the actual proportion of the state's electorate on Election Day and the Latino margin of support for Clinton reported in the Election Eve Poll, Latinos provided a statewide margin for Clinton of between 6.5% and 9.4%, well in line with the margin provided to Obama in 2012 (Preuhs 2015) and, even at the low end, enough to account for Clinton's popular vote win of 4.9%. The impact of the Senate race was essentially the same, with estimates ranging from a 6.3% to a 9.1% advantage for Bennet, and again, enough to account for Bennet's 5.7% margin of victory. In other words, Latino voters in Colorado accounted for both Clinton's and Bennet's statewide winning margins and thus played a pivotal role in Colorado's electoral outcomes in 2016.

Immigration Policy, General Policy Alignment, and the Latino Vote in Colorado

Why did Latinos prefer Democratic candidates at such high margins and so consistently throughout the campaign season? The answer lies in Latinos' intense concern regarding immigration policy and the candidates' positions on those issues. Coupled with a general orientation toward Democratic policy positions, the issue of immigration solidified Democratic support among Colorado's Latinos in 2016. However, it played a role in pushing Latinos away from the GOP as much as, if not more than, pulling Latinos into the Democratic fold.

Immigration, of course, arose as a key element of Donald Trump's national campaign early in the season. Discarding the advice of downplaying

Table 1. Top Five Most Important Issues Facing the Latino Community

	Polling period		
	April	August	Election eve
Immigration reform/deportations	37%	35%	35%
Jobs/economy	21%	31%	28%
Education reform/schools	17%	11%	13%
Health care	15%	16%	17%
Anti-immigrant/Latino discrimination/race relations	10%	12%	11%

Note: Cells report percentage of respondents indicating the category as one of the top issues. Top five responses reported.

Source: America's Voice/Latino Decisions 2016 3-State Battleground (April) and National Battleground State Polls (August); Latino Decisions 2016 Election Eve Poll.

restrictive immigration policies from the GOP's "autopsy" of the 2012 election, Trump and his campaign heartily embraced an anti-immigrant policy position (Republican National Committee 2013). From the statements calling many immigrants rapists and terrorists to promising to build a border wall, immediate deportation of criminal undocumented immigrants, and eventual removal of all undocumented immigrants, the hard-line stance of the Trump campaign further pushed Colorado's Latinos away from the GOP. President Trump's early executive orders signed in January 2017 that reflect this position on immigration likely cemented Latinos' partisan orientations for the foreseeable future.

At the foundation of this dynamic was the emphasis Colorado Latinos placed on immigration throughout the campaign. Table 1 presents the results of a question asking about the most important issues facing the Latino or Hispanic community that politicians should address. The results are striking in that from the April through Election Eve polls, immigration reform and deportations garnered the most responses. While the economy, education, and health care landed in the top five responses—issues shared with many non-Latinos in the state—none reached the level of importance placed on immigration. Moreover, 10% of Latinos in Colorado cited anti-immigrant/Latino discrimination and race relations as a top concern.

These issues rose to the top due to a combination of Trump's candidacy and positions, as well as an underlying preference for Democrats among Latinos. Trump and other actions associated with the GOP clearly pushed Latino voters away, following a trend established in 2012 by Mitt Romney's call for self-deportations and President Obama's executive order establishing Deferred Action for Childhood Arrivals (DACA). Over 60% of Latinos in Colorado opposed Republican efforts to stop the implementation of President Obama's executive orders on Deferred Action for Parents of Americans (DAPA) and DACA. Trump's views on immigration, per the August poll results, led 61% to be much less likely to vote for Republican candidates and another 10% to be somewhat less likely to do so (similar results emerged when applied to voting for the GOP's Senate candidate, specifically). Seventy-six percent of Latino respondents in that August poll indicated that Donald Trump has made the Republican Party more hostile to Latinos (only 7% indicated he made the party more welcoming). In all, there was a clear push away from the GOP and its presidential nominee.

Did a Democratic pull play a role? To an extent—Hillary Clinton's and, more generally, the Democratic Party's policies aligned with Latino preferences. With 59% of Latinos in Colorado knowing somebody who is an undocumented immigrant, it is not surprising that this was a top issue, and preferences for reform aligned with the Democrat's policies. In August, 64% of Latinos indicated that Clinton's views on immigration made them more likely to vote for Democratic candidates, and 55% said Clinton made the Democratic Party more welcoming to Latinos (only 11% indicated she made the party more hostile). In terms of policy congruence, more than 80% of respondents agreed with DAPA in the August poll, and another 75% indicated that Clinton's support for DACA would make them more likely to vote for Democratic candidates. In short, while Trump pushed voters away, there remained a significant pull from the Democratic Party on the key issue facing the Latino community in Colorado.

But Latinos in Colorado are also generally oriented toward the Democratic Party, and thus, a foundation of party affiliation and more general policy preferences underlie the specific dynamics of immigration policy. For instance, only 16% of Latino respondents in the Election Eve poll indicated that they generally agree with the Republican Party and are likely to vote for them in the future (the number drops to 9% if the statement only asks about agreement and not voting). Only one-third said they would consider supporting the GOP in the future if the party and its candidates changed their position on immigration. Moreover, 60% of respondents cannot recall ever voting for a Republican candidate. This orientation is well established and matches closely with results over the last several election cycles (Preuhs 2015). One item from the 2016 election in Colorado highlights the generally liberal preferences of Latino voters. Amendment 70, a ballot issue to raise the minimum wage, passed statewide by a margin of 55% to 45%. That margin was eclipsed by the 78% to 18% margin of support among Latino voters in the Election Eve poll. As in previous elections and across a variety of topics, Latinos in Colorado maintain a more liberal orientation than the overall electorate, and, coupled with concurrent immigration policies, reasonably voted for Democrats up and down the ballot.

Outreach and Enthusiasm

Colorado's election season was marked by early calls to action by the Latino community. On the day of the Republican presidential debate in October 2015, the "My Country, My Vote" campaign kicked off with a rally in Boulder on the University of Colorado campus. The rally led by high-profile Latino community members, including former Denver mayor and U.S. Secretary of Transportation Federico Peña and Lt. Governor Joe García, kicked off what would be a year-long effort among numerous groups to both solidify support for Democratic candidates as well as register and mobilize Latino voters (Stein 2015). Various groups in Colorado also received support to engage in registration and get out the vote (GOTV) efforts from the Immigrant Voters Win political action committee (PAC), an organization backed by George Soros favoring progressive immigration reform (Gamboa 2016). By October, the group Colorado Latinos Rise reported almost 200,000 attempts to reach out to Latinos via door-knocking strategies (Gamboa 2016). Another Latino group, Mi Familia Vota, reportedly registered more than 10,000 Latino voters in 2016 (Englebart 2016). That figure, if accurate, accounts for just under 10% of the increase in registered voters from 2012 (Colorado Secretary of State 2012, 2016).

On top of the registration and mobilization efforts by independent groups, the Clinton campaign made several stops to Colorado, presumably to shore up support in what was projected to be a close win. Stops in counties with large Latino populations, such as Pueblo, highlighted efforts to garner enthusiasm after she failed to win Colorado's Democratic caucus in March. The ground game was apparent, and Emmy Ruiz, Clinton's Colorado state director, highlighted efforts to garner support across the state, including areas with traditionally low but rapidly growing Latino populations (Gamboa 2016).

Among Colorado Latinos, the Trump campaign remained hampered by a general disaffection for his candidacy and immigration policies. In efforts to bolster support, prominent Latino members of the state's GOP attempted to redirect the message to other conservative issues in more conservative parts of the state. The goal, according to George Rivera, Republican Party chairman in Pueblo County, was to "continue the effort among Hispanics so we didn't lose any ground." In an October 2016 rally in Colorado Springs, Donald Trump proclaimed that "nobody will do more for the Latino Community than Donald Trump" (Englebart 2016).

While both parties claimed to pay attention and devote resources to Latino outreach, the survey evidence clearly indicates a Democratic advantage in both outreach and influence, tempered by the reality of a strong push away from the Trump camp and a weaker pull by Clinton. By Election Day, 52% of Latinos surveyed reported being contacted by a campaign, political party, or community organization asking them to vote or register to vote (Election Eve Poll). That tied Colorado with Nevada and Ohio at the top of the twelve states in the Election Eve Poll in terms of generic Latino outreach. However, among those contacted, 69% were contacted by organizations representing the Democratic Party or its candidates, while only 29% were contacted by the Republican Party or its candidates. Clearly, despite the rhetoric of the GOP and its candidates, the voter registration and outreach efforts aimed at the Latino community were dominated by Democratic-oriented organizations.

Latino voter outreach from the Democrats and their surrogates paid off, at least in terms of generating enthusiasm and delineating the candidates'

Figure 2. Comparison of Perceptions of the 2012 and 2016 Candidates' Degrees of Caring for the Latino Community in Colorado

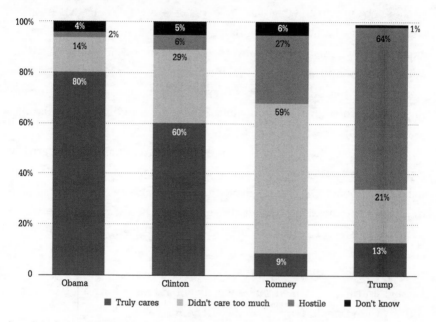

Source: Latino Decisions 2016 Election Eve Poll; ImpreMedia/Latino Decisions 2012 Election Eve Poll.

levels of empathy for the Latino community. The push away from the GOP, however, dominated the pull toward the Democrats. Figure 2 presents responses to questions asking respondents whether the 2016 Donald Trump or Hillary Clinton campaigns showed that the candidates truly care about Latino voters, do not care too much about Latinos, or are hostile to Latinos. The figure also provides the numbers for similar questions about Republican Mitt Romney and Democrat Barack Obama's effects in 2012. Latinos viewed Clinton as much more caring towards the Latino community, with 60% of respondents indicating that she truly cares, compared to just 13% responding that Trump truly cares about the Latino community. Moreover, 64% of respondents reported that Trump was hostile toward the community, compared to just 6% indicating the same about Clinton. In terms of the degree of both perceived empathy and hostility, Clinton bested Trump among Latinos in Colorado. Comparisons between 2016 and 2012 highlight

Figure 3. Enthusiasm Relative to 2012 and Reasons for Enthusiasm

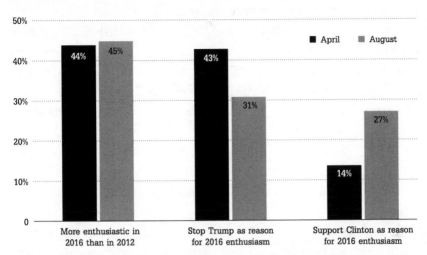

Source: America's Voice/Latino Decisions 2016, 3-State Battleground (April) and National Battleground State Polls (August).

the push/pull dynamic and how it shifted after the earlier presidential election. The percentage of Latinos stating that the candidate truly cares dropped by 20% between Obama in 2012 and Clinton in 2016, indicating a diminished pull toward the Democrats. However, the push away from Trump far outpaced its 2012 strength with Romney. In 2012, only 27% said Romney was hostile to the Latino community (still a high number), compared to 64% saying the same about Trump. The more than twofold increase in perceptions of hostility underscores the strong push away from Trump, which played well for Democratic outreach and left GOP efforts anemic at best.

The extensive push away from Trump and GOP candidates, as well as the pull by the Democrats and Clinton, is reflected in levels of enthusiasm for this election and the reason for that enthusiasm as presented in figure 3. In the April and August 2016 polls, respondents were asked to indicate how important they thought the election was and how enthusiastic they were relative to the 2012 contest. The results indicate a fairly high and consistent level of enthusiasm, with about 45% responding that they were more enthusiastic this year. Moreover, in August, 75% stated that this election was more important than that in 2012. Preventing a Trump presidency, rather than

electing Clinton, formed the basis for this enthusiasm. Early on, 43% of Latinos in Colorado cited stopping Trump as the reason for enthusiasm, while
that number dropped to 31% by August. The drop coincided with an increase
in support for Clinton as a reason for their enthusiasm, up to 27% in August
from 14% in the preconvention April poll. Thus, while the popular narrative
and the data already presented suggest strong opposition to Trump and
tepid support for Clinton, the latter garnered as much positive enthusiasm
as the former did negative.

The Latina/Latino Gender Gap Persists

The candidacy of Hillary Clinton, the first female major party nominee,
juxtaposed with the accusations of past sexual assaults and demeaning
behavior toward women by the Republican nominee, Donald Trump, led to
the potential of a much wider "gender gap" in partisan vote choice. While
the gender gap persisted in Colorado in 2016, the magnitude of the gap
remained similar to that found in 2012 (Preuhs 2012). The stability of the
size of Latina and Latino differences reflected heightened support among
Latinas for Democratic candidates, but also no clear indication of diminishing Latino support.

As in 2012, Latinas generally supported the Democratic candidate at
higher levels than Latinos, with 85% indicating they would vote for Clinton
in the Election Eve Poll, compared to 76% of Latinos. Generic congressional
vote preferences and the U.S. Senate race revealed a similar gender gap,
ranging from 8% to 11% more support from Latinas for Democrats. The
gender gap in voter preferences is reflected in the reasons for those choices
as well. For instance, while 44% of males surveyed indicated that supporting
the Democratic candidate was their reason for voting, only 29% of females
were motivated primarily to support the party. Instead, 52% of females cited
support and representation of the Latino Community as their rationale for
voting (compared to just 35% of males). Immigration was cited at the same
rates by both groups as an important issue for politicians to address as well
as a reason for their vote, but Latinas tended to support DACA at higher

rates (85%) than Latinos (76%). Latinas also tended to support the statewide issue of increasing the minimum wage to a higher degree (84% supporting the initiative) than Latinos (76% supporting the initiative). This more liberal orientation is reflected by females' slightly lower levels of concern about the economy as a whole, and less willingness to vote for Republicans, even if the immigration positions of the party changed to allow for a path to citizenship. Overall, Latinas in Colorado tended to be more liberal and supportive of Democratic candidates than Latinos, a phenomenon that parallels national trends (VanSickle-Ward and Pantoja 2016), but displayed similar levels of concern for immigration as both an issue and rationale for vote choice. Democrats certainly benefited from greater Latina support in Colorado, yet Latinos did not peel off and vote for the Republican in any meaningful way relative to the 2012 election. The underlying unifying element may have been the push away from Donald Trump, as both Latinas (at 65%) and Latinos (at 63%) reported that he was hostile to toward Latino/as.

Continuity and Change in Colorado's Latino Electorate

The evidence thus far reveals a straightforward interpretation of Latinos' (both genders) impact on the 2016 election in Colorado. Latinos strongly favored Democratic candidates up and down the ballot. Democratic and aligned Latino advocacy organizations dominated mobilization efforts. Donald Trump's immigration positions, along with Clinton's promise to continue (and perhaps expand) the Obama administration's favorable immigration policies, resulted in both a strong push away from Trump and a pull toward Clinton. And while the gender gap persisted, both Latinas and Latinos placed immigration as a major consideration and viewed Donald Trump as hostile. Moreover, even at the low end of Latino voter participation in the electorate, Latino voters likely flipped both the presidential and U.S. Senate races in Colorado. This last narrative is a departure from that presented in postelection analyses, suggesting a decline in enthusiasm, turnout, and even vote choice among the Obama coalition, particularly among Black and Latino voters.

Does the popular alternative have merit? Have Colorado's Latino vot-ers experienced some seismic shift from 2012 that is hidden in the overall election results and aggregate 2016 polling data? And, if so, what are the implications for the future role of Latinos as a pivotal block of the electorate and cornerstone of support for the Democratic Party?

The first question can be addressed in two ways. The first, and most straightforward, is to note once again that overall partisan support did shift, at least in terms of the Election Eve Poll results. In 2012, Latinos favored Democrat Barack Obama with 87% to 10% for Republican Mitt Romney. Similar numbers held for generic Congressional candidate preferences. Don-ald Trump, with about 16% support compared to Hillary Clinton's 81%, and his Republican co-partisan Congressional candidates (in both Senate and generic House races) narrowed relative to the 2012 margins. Yet using 2008 as a baseline, Latino support for the Democratic presidential candidate actually rose from the 50% margin benefiting Obama. It may be that 2016 witnessed a decline in support from 2012, but longer term trends suggest 2016 remained one of the most supportive of Democratic candidates among Latinos.

The popular narrative loses more validity in Colorado once we look at the second key element to that argument, suggesting enthusiasm declined among Latino voters. In both 2012 and 2016, about 45% of Colorado Latino likely voters reported being more enthusiastic about the current year's election relative to the previous presidential election in August polling. Comparable data on enthusiasm are not available for Election Eve Polls, but a spike did occur in 2012 that may not have materialized in 2016. Yet in both years, Democratic support jumped in the period between August/Septem-ber and the last few days leading up to the election. In short, very similar patterns of support and enthusiasm emerged. The general narrowing of the partisan gap, while one that should be noted, may have been part of a more national trend attributable to cyclical preferences and the uniqueness of this particular election.

Another general explanation for the rise of Republican support rests in the defection of working-class voters (among Whites in particular). Those without college educations were more supportive of Donald Trump and Republicans candidates than past GOP candidates as a stronger populist message permeated GOP rhetoric. Does this logic hold for Colorado's Latino voters? Quite simply, no. Unlike White voters nationally who gave Trump a strong lead, but one that was particularly strong among those without a college education (67% for non-college-educated Whites, 49% for college-educated Whites; *New York Times* 2016), the relationship reverses among Latinos in Colorado. College-educated voters provided some of the strongest levels of support for Trump among the usual set of demographic groups within the Latino sample. At 23%, the level of support for Trump among college-educated Latinos almost doubled the 12% support for Trump by voters without a college education. Clinton gained 75% of college-educated versus 85% of non-college-educated Latino voters. Similar patterns hold for down-ballot vote choices for Congress. Colorado's non-college-educated voters, counter to the pattern of White voters nationally, were a key source of support for Clinton and at levels greater than college-educated Latinos. While Trump's populist anti-immigrant sentiment likely bolstered some of the Democrat's advantage, it is important to note that other elements of the message simply did not have the same impact on working-class Latino voters in Colorado as they did for Whites across the nation.

In short, the decline in Democratic support and concurrent rise in Republican support is not really a matter of shifting coalitions within Colorado. While overall support declined relative to 2012, it remained in line with 2008 levels of support. Moreover, this does not seem attributable to high levels of support among the working class, or even a lack of enthusiasm. Lowered levels of support, especially compared to 2012 with its remarkably high 87% for Obama and coupled with an expected decline of support for the incumbent party after a two-term presidency, seem well in line with a static interpretation of Latino coalition membership within the Democratic Party in Colorado.

The Future

The 2012 general election left some analysts predicting a continued shift toward Democratic strength in Colorado and, of interest here, a continued role for Latinos as a foundation for that trajectory (Preuhs 2015). As a result of the 2012 election, Democrats took over the legislature, re-elected a Democratic governor, passed legislation providing driver's licenses for undocumented residents, created a new tuition scale for undocumented students at state institutions of higher education, and altered the safe communities program. And in many ways, the outcomes of 2016 maintain that status quo. While the legislature was split after the election (the GOP holds a one-seat majority in the state senate, while the Democrats bolstered their majority by three seats in the House), there is still a Democratic governor, which will remove any possibility of drastic changes in policies of specific interest to Latino voters. County-level support for Clinton and Trump almost perfectly correlated with 2012 levels of support for Obama and Romney, respectively ($r > 0.96$ for both pairings). All seven of the U.S. House seats and the U.S. Senate seat were won by the incumbent (including the contested Sixth Congressional District, where the margin was exactly the same as in 2014). Coloradoans passed an initiative to increase the minimum wage, yet overwhelmingly opposed universal single-payer health care, and thus cemented the moderate-to-blue bent of the electorate. The 2016 election outcome thus presents more like a case of status quo politics in a bluish state than the extraordinary event witnessed at the national level.

This chapter has argued, in many ways, that the heart of this consistency lies in the substantial influence of Latino voters in Colorado politics and policy. But will this influence continue as a source of a directional shift in Colorado's partisan fortunes? Or, in other words, will Latino voters keep Colorado leaning blue?

Forecasting future Latino political influence in Colorado requires both projections of Latino's proportions of the electorate and indicators of future political preferences. Neither are certain, but reasonable ranges can be estimated. The proportion of the electorate provides the potential for influence. Colorado's Latino population in 2015 stood at 21.3% of the total population. Estimates, as reported in the preceding, of its share of the electorate range from about 10% to 14%, depending on turnout. Given Colorado's growth, both in Latino and non-Latino populations, it seems reasonable to assume that Latinos' proportion of the population would remain the same at the low end of the set of potential estimates. At the high end, given marginally diminishing birth rates and a presidential administration promising to reduce immigration (and primarily through Mexico, which is the national origin of most of Colorado's foreign-born Latinos), a 5% increase in the Latino share of the population—to 26% of Colorado's population—over the next decade is a reasonable high-end estimate (and reflects the same rate of growth witnessed from 2000 to 2010) (CensusViewer 2012). Assuming voter participation remains static among Latinos (and other racial/ethnic groups), reflecting the 2016 estimated turnout, between 50% and 65%, the proportion of the electorate that is Latino may be between 10% (the current low estimate) and 16.9% (based on the high estimate of its relative population). That is an admittedly large range, but one that is useful nonetheless as a starting point for projecting future electoral influence.

But does this equate to a marginal advantage for either party? The answer depends on the partisan orientation of Latino vote choice over the next ten years. Predicting group vote choice is a precarious endeavor. However, fairly static orientations are not unheard of, with African Americans being a clear example of consistent support for the Democratic Party over the last several decades. Given Colorado's Latino voter preference for Democratic Presidential candidates over the last twelve years where data are available, as well as a much longer Democratic orientation in state politics generally, the Democratic Party likely holds an advantage over the next decade.

More specific evidence from the Election Eve poll supports this general assertion. Given that voters tend to solidify partisan affiliation in young adulthood and that political context experienced in those years of early political engagement further shapes political outlooks and preferences, one indicator of the future of Latino political preferences lies in the preferences of younger and first-time voters (Jacobson 2016). As younger voters replace older voters, and first-time voters enter the electorate, these two groups should form the foundation of the Latino electorate in the years to come. Fortunately, the Election Eve Poll identifies both younger voters (eighteen to thirty-nine years old) and first-time voters, and thus, allows for the possibility of examining these two groups' preferences in isolation.

The preferences of younger Latino voters and first-time voters, perhaps not surprisingly, align closely with the overall Latino electorate in Colorado. Younger Latinos voted for Hillary Clinton at a rate of 78%, while first-time voters supported Clinton at a rate of 84%. Both are within common margins of error for the overall sample's 81% for Clinton. Support for Trump fell within a margin of error for the overall sample as well. Support for Democrats in Congressional races was high, at 81%, but both were lower than older voters or seasoned voters. Support for Democratic Senate candidate Bennet was in line with older voters, at around 80% for both groups. Overall, then, first-time voters and younger voters displayed strong partisan preferences benefitting Democratic candidates. While rates were slightly lower than for complementary groups, in no race did younger or first-time Latino voters support the Democratic candidate at a rate lower than 78%, or a margin of 62%.

The polling results also hint at an effect of the context of the 2016 elections regarding the centrality of immigration policy and a preference for policies championed in Democratic proposals rather than those proposed by Republicans and Donald Trump, in particular. For instance, 43% of younger voters and 49% of first-time voters identified immigration reform and deportations as an important issue to the Latino community, compared to 30% of older voters and 30% of seasoned voters. Support for DACA was also higher among younger and first-time voters (at 87% and 90%, respectively) than among older voters and seasoned voters, who both supported DACA at 76%. Similar differences emerged when respondents were asked about their opposition to Republican efforts to block DACA and DAPA implementation. In short, preferences of younger and first-time voters, the groups that will form the core of Latino voters over the next decade, are substantially oriented toward the Democratic Party; find immigration to be an important policy issue; and view Democratic immigration proposals as more favorable than Republican positions. Moreover, Donald Trump's high-profile positions on immigration solidified candidate preferences, as indicated by more than 50% of these two groups agreeing that the Republican Party has become so anti-immigrant that it would be hard to support it in the future. President Trump's January 2017 Executive Orders and February 2017 Department of Homeland Security policy memos regarding border security and immigration enforcement, while leaving DACA in place, likely cemented this orientation.

What, then, about the future partisan impact of Latino voters in Colorado? There is a clear benefit to the Democrats, and assuming the 2016 election underscored immigration differences between the parties, that benefit should be sizeable. At a margin of 62%, the lowest Democratic margin for the two groups for all three candidate levels, and at a low estimate of the Latino electorate a decade from now (10%), Latinos will account for a 6.2% margin for the Democrats. At a high estimate of Latinos' percentage of the future electorate (16.9%), that margin would almost double to 10.5%. If, however, the preferences for Democrats narrow, down to about 60–40, or a 20% margin, Latinos would still provide Democrats anywhere from a 2% to 3.3% electoral benefit. The latter scenario seems unlikely, given the preferences of younger and first-time voters in 2016. But even at that rate, Latinos can potentially flip elections in tight races. If the former estimates hold, then Latino voters will firmly place Colorado in the Democrats' camp, with only a remarkable election favoring Republicans being able to overcome the 6 to 10.5% statewide advantage.

Conclusion

Latino voters played a pivotal role in the 2016 election outcome in Colorado. By accounting for a statewide advantage of 6.5% to 9.4%, Colorado's Latino voters flipped the election to Clinton, who eventually beat Donald Trump in the state by a 4.9% margin. The pivot affected down-ballot races as well, enough to give incumbent Democratic Senator Michael Bennet a win over Republican challenger Darryl Glenn. Immigration remained one of the most important issues, and while enthusiasm relative to 2012 fell compared to a similar measure four years ago, the combination of a push away from GOP candidates and a somewhat lesser pull to the Democrats resulted in Latino voting decisions, from outcome to motivation, that closely reflected the last two presidential elections in Colorado.

The election of 2016 seems to have solidified, rather than altered, the

Democratic orientation of Latino voters and their role in Colorado's political landscape. Going forward, the degree to which this trend holds relies on the voting decisions of those who participated for the first time in 2016 as they continue their new level of participation and younger voters as their cohort replaces older voters. Most indicators suggest that these groups will continue and expand the solidly Democratic orientation of Latino voters in Colorado. In short, the significant impact of Latinos ensured Colorado remained a blue-leaning state. With continued expansion of the Latino electorate and the orientation of new and younger voters in 2016, Colorado ought to maintain that trajectory.

Postelection events provide a glimpse of the continued centrality of Latinos in electoral politics in Colorado as the Trump Administration's policies emerge and political actors and the Latino community respond to those policies statewide. Stepped-up immigration enforcement and threats of ending funding to local governments perceived to challenge those efforts led to a variety of responses throughout Colorado. For instance, Denver has become a high-profile example of the growing sanctuary movement as its area churches provide protection from deportation for two undocumented mothers of U.S.-born children, and other religious organizations explore the possibility across the state (Aguilar 2017). Prominent leaders of the Latino community also note an increase in general anxiety among the Latino community due to the Trump Administration's proposals (Lopez 2017).

State and local officials of both parties have responded to this concern in a nod to the electoral clout of the Latino community. Republican U.S. Representative Mike Coffman co-sponsored the BRIDGE Act, which would essentially maintain the DACA program in reaction to a perceived threat to repeal the program under Trump (Lopez 2017). Democratic Governor John Hickenlooper openly declared that mass deportations would not be allowed in Colorado, and local leaders across the state have argued against the imposition of penalties for sanctuary cities. Republican Senator Cory Gardner, who also serves as chairman of the National Republican Senatorial Committee, publicly displayed his apprehension about building a physical wall along the Mexican border while still arguing for the need for greater border security (Stokels 2017). In all, the Trump Administration and its policies regarding immigration seemingly solidified the Latino community, if only through fear, which in turn has led to responsiveness to their concerns from local and statewide officials. Coupled with the demographic trends and political preferences of the Latino community, this responsiveness of elected officials suggests a continued level of influence of the Latino electorate and the centrality of Latino voters' concerns on Colorado electoral politics in both the 2018 statewide elections and the 2020 national elections.

References

Aguilar, John. 2017. "Now That Trump's in Charge, Church Communities Across Colorado Explore Providing 'Sanctuary' for Unauthorized Immigrants." *Denver Post*, March 12.

CensusViewer. 2012. "Population of Colorado: Census 2010 and 2000." http:// censusviewer.com.

Colorado Secretary of State. 2012. "Presidential Electors." http://www.sos.state. co.us.

———. 2016. "Unofficial Results, November 8, 2016 General Election." http://results. enr.clarityelections.com.

Englebart, Drew. 2016. "Latino Voters Set to Have Major Impact in Colorado." *Fox 31 News Denver*, October 18. http://kdvr.com.

Gamboa, Suzanne. 2016. "Latino Voter Is 'Front and Center' in Colorado." *NBC News*, October 12.

Jacobson, Gary C. 2016. "The Obama Legacy and the Future of Partisan Conflict: Demographic Change and Generational Imprinting." *Annals of the American Academy of Political and Social Science* 667 (1): 72–91.

Latino Decisions. 2010. *Latino Decisions Election Eve Poll—State by State Results 11/02/2010.* http://www.latinodecisions.com.

———. 2012. *ImpreMedia/Latino Decisions 2012 Latino Election Eve Poll.* http://www. latinovote2012.com.

———. 2014. *Latino Decisions Election Eve Poll November 2014—by State.* http://www. latinodecisions.com.

Lopez, Paul. 2017. "A Bridge to Legal Status for the Undocumented Immigrants in Our Communities." *Denver Post*, February 28.

NALEO. 2016. 2016 "Primary Election Profile Colorado. National Association of

Latino Elected Officials Education Fund." https://d3n8a8pro7vhmx.cloudfront. net.

New York Times. 2016. "Election 2016: Exit Polls," November 8. https://www.nytimes. com.

Passel, Jeffrey S., and D'Vera Cohn. 2014. "Unauthorized Immigrant Totals Rise in 7 States, Fall in 14: Decline in Those from Mexico Fuels Most State Decreases." Washington, D.C. Pew Research Center's Hispanic Trends Project, November. http://www.pewhispanic.org.

Pew Center. 2014. "Demographic Profile of Hispanics in Colorado, 2014." http://www.pewhispanic.org.

———. 2016. "Mapping the Latino Electorate by State." January 19. http://www.pewhispanic.org.

Preuhs, Robert R. 2012. "Colorado's Latina/Latino Gender Gap." Latino Decisions Blog Post, September 13. http://www.latinodecisions.com.

———. 2015. "The 2012 Latino Vote in Colorado." In *Latinos and the 2012 Election: The New Face of the American Voter,* edited by Gabriel Sanchez, 61-75. East Lansing: Michigan State University Press.

Republican National Committee. 2013. *Growth and Opportunity Project: One Year Checkup.* Available at http://goproject.gop.com.

Rosenstone, Steven J., and John Mark Hansen. 1993. *Mobilization, Participation, and American Democracy.* New York: MacMillan.

Stein, Nat. 2016. "Colorado Latinos to the GOP: 'Intolerance Won't Win Our Voters.'" *Colorado Independent,* October 28.

Stokels, Eli. 2017. "GOP Campaign Chair Disses Trump's Wall: Colorado Sen. Cory Gardner Says 'A Wall Is Not the Right Way to Proceed.'" *Politico,* March 9.

U.S. Census. 2016. Population Estimates, American Community Survey, Census of Population and Housing, Current Population Survey, Small Area Health Insurance Estimates, Small Area Income and Poverty Estimates, State and County Housing Unit Estimates, County Business Patterns, Nonemployer Statistics, Economic Census, Survey of Business Owners, Building Permits. http://www.census.gov.

VanSickle-Ward, Rachel, and Adrian D. Pantoja. 2016. "Latina Voters Say Adiós to Trump." *Huffington Post,* October 4.

Calexit

California Moves Left as the Nation Moves Right

Ivy A. M. Cargile, Jason L. Morin, and Adrian D. Pantoja

THE TERM *BREXIT* ENTERED THE LEXICON IN 2016 WHEN, THROUGH A referendum, the United Kingdom withdrew from the European Union. In the aftermath of the 2016 presidential election, Californians began using the term *Calexit* as a signal that they, too, would consider leaving the United States, given the outcome of the election. Conservative sentiment and forces inspired the UK example, while liberal sentiment and forces drove the California example. This chapter explores how California politically moved to the left while the nation moved right in 2016. Although the future is not completely certain, the election of Donald Trump suggests that the country will take a turn to the right on a number of key policy issues, such as immigration, health care, the environment, and the economy. What is clear, however, is that Latinos and other groups have taken to the streets to protest the outcome of the election and the impending threat a Trump presidency may pose. California's political leadership, newly elected Senator Kamala Harris, Governor Jerry Brown, and President Pro Tempore of the State Senate Kevin De Leon, have made it clear that they would fight any efforts to roll back California's progressive politics, especially around un-documented immigrants.

California's move to the left is not surprising, given the demographic shifts in the state since the 1990s, and Latinos are the primary drivers leading that change. In 1990, about 7.7 million Latinos called California home. Today, that figure has doubled to 15 million, making California the state with the largest concentration of Latinos in the country. Los Angeles County, for example, is home to the largest population of Latinos in the country, with 4.9 million or 48% of the county's population. Latinos were a quarter of the state's population in 1990, while today they are 40%. Indeed, Latinos are more numerous than non-Hispanic Whites, who have become a demographic minority. Thus, it is no exaggeration to say that the epicenter of Latino politics can be found broadly in California and, specifically, in Los Angeles County and the City of Los Angeles.

Shifting demographics changed the political landscape of the state. In 1980, Latinos were 6.6% of California's eligible electorate. By 2000, the share had grown to 14%, and today, the share is at 28%. The Democratic Party in California benefited greatly from the rise of the Latino electorate. Latinos are not born Democrats; the disastrous anti-immigrant policies of Republicans in the mid-1990s caused Latinos and other voters to move away from the GOP (Damore and Pantoja 2013; Morin and Pantoja 2015). Currently, the state legislature in California is overwhelmingly Democratic. In the eighty-seat state assembly, Democrats occupy fifty-five seats. In the forty-member state senate, there are twenty-six seats occupied by Democrats. Latinos, once politically marginal, have come to occupy prominent political positions throughout the state. In short, the Golden State has turned into a solidly blue state as a result of demographic and political shifts in the last two decades.

With this backdrop in mind, we next turn to the 2016 general election. We rely on survey data from a number of sources to trace the political attitudes and behaviors of the Latino electorate in California and Los Angeles County.[1] Specifically, we examine Latinos' choices for president and U.S. Senate, as well as down-ballot candidates and propositions at the state and local level. We also examine Latino political participation in the 2016 election with particular attention to naturalization, registration, and voter turnout. Finally, we discuss the political implications of a Trump presidency in California.

Support for Clinton and Democratic Candidates

During the 2016 presidential election, it was unclear whether California Latino voters would show their support for the Democratic candidate as they had in 2008 and 2012. Both Donald Trump and Hillary Clinton were heralded as two of the most unpopular candidates to run for president in recent history. Leading up to the election, a Field/IGS Poll found that 53% of likely voters had an unfavorable view of Clinton, and 69% of likely voters indicated they had an unfavorable view of Trump (DiCamillo 2016). Moreover, there was some concern as to whether voters for Bernie Sanders would support Clinton in the general election. A *Los Angeles Times*/University of Southern California (USC) survey, for instance, found that 58% of younger Latinos had a favorable view of Bernie Sanders while only 31% said they had a favorable view of Clinton (Madrid 2016). Questions, therefore, surrounded Clinton's ability to court Latino voters heading into the general election.

Despite the apparent unpopularity of both candidates, the Election Eve poll indicated that Latino voters overwhelmingly preferred Hillary Clinton to Donald Trump. Eighty percent of likely Latino voters said they had already voted or intended to vote for Hillary Clinton while only 16% said they had already voted or intended to vote for her Republican challenger. Clinton's level of support in California was slightly higher than in the rest of the nation (79%) and on par with other non-battleground states in the Southwest, such as Texas (80%). Moreover, Latino voters showed greater support for Clinton than for her Democratic predecessor, Barack Obama. In fact, Hillary Clinton outperformed President Obama in California by 2 percentage points in 2012 (78%)—an election in which Barack Obama defeated Mitt Romney by a margin of 58%. Thus, Hillary Clinton's support among California Latino voters was considerably high even though she lost the general election.

The Pat Brown Institute/Latino Decisions survey also reveals a similar trend in Latino voting behavior at the local level. In Los Angeles County, 73% of Latino respondents said they intended to vote for Hillary Clinton while a mere 13% said they were voting for Donald Trump. Additionally, Hillary Clinton increased her support among Latino voters as the general election neared. While the Pat Brown Institute/Latino Decisions survey was conducted in mid-October, the Election Eve Poll was conducted just days before the November election. An earlier survey conducted by Latino Decisions and NALEO further confirms this point. Between the months of September and October 2016, Latino voters in California were asked about their preference for president if the election were held today. According to the poll, 78% said they would vote for Hillary Clinton and just 11% said they would vote for Donald Trump (National Association of Latino Elected and Appointed Officials [NALEO] 2016a).

Down-ballot, Latino voters played a key role in determining important statewide races, initiatives, and local measures. Perhaps one of the most important races in California was the Senate race between State Attorney General Kamala Harris (D) and Representative Loretta Sanchez (D). The presence of two Democrats facing off against each other was the result of California's "top-two" primary system that voters approved in 2010. Under this system, the top two vote getters in the primary, regardless of party affiliation, go on to compete in the general election. Both sought to fill the seat being vacated by Barbara Boxer (D). Each would be breaking important barriers if elected. In the case of Harris, she would be the second Black woman ever elected to the U.S. Senate. Sanchez would not be the first Latina ever elected to the Senate. As it turned out, that honor would go to Nevada's Catherine Cortez-Masto.

Latinos' support for Loretta Sanchez was evident from the June primary onward. An analysis of vote choice at the city level during the primary race shows that Sanchez was outperforming her opponent, Harris, in Latino-majority cities (Pantoja 2016). For example, in the city of South Gate, which is 66% Latino, Sanchez won 51% of the vote while Harris won a mere 20% of the vote—a gap of 46 points. The day before the election, both statewide and local polls indicated that Latino voters maintained their preference for

Loretta Sanchez. By November, the Latino Decisions 2016 Election Eve Poll indicated that 57% of Latino voters reported voting for Sanchez while only 37% reported voting for Kamala Harris. Loretta Sanchez gained most of her support from Latinas and Latinos with lower levels of income and education, first-generation Latinos, and Spanish-speaking Latinos. Additionally, Sanchez drew a great deal of support from first-time voters (70%). In Los Angeles, 50% of respondents reported their intention to vote for Sanchez while 27% selected Harris, a gap of 23 points. Even though both women were on the verge of being one of the few women of color in the U.S. Senate, the race was relatively low key. Perhaps this is one of the reasons why 23% of survey respondents said they were undecided. In the end, however, Kamala Harris won a lopsided victory over Sanchez (65.2% to 34.8%). Several factors contributed to Sanchez's defeat, including a few political missteps and a significantly smaller campaign war chest.

The Trump Effect and Immigration

What explains Clinton's 64-percentage-point margin of victory in the polls? We contend that Donald Trump's rhetoric and hard-line stance on immigration, which captures the so-called "Trump effect," pushed Latinos to vote for Hillary Clinton. Figure 1 shows Latinos' top policy priorities in California and Los Angeles. Statewide, a plurality of Latino voters (39%) indicated immigration to be the most important issue facing the Latino community, followed by the economy (30%), education (18%), health care (10%), and anti-Latino discrimination (10%). In Los Angeles County, Latinos demonstrated similar policy concerns. According to the figure, immigration and economic issues were tied as top priorities. The third issue listed is discrimination/race relations, followed by education and crime.

Latinos listing immigration and economic policies as top issues is not surprising. While Latinos consistently identify economic issues as top priorities, the salience of immigration was heightened by Trump's remarks during the presidential election. In the previous presidential election, for example, the 2012 ImpreMedia/Latino Decisions Election Eve Poll revealed

Figure 1. Top Issue Facing Latinos in California and Los Angeles

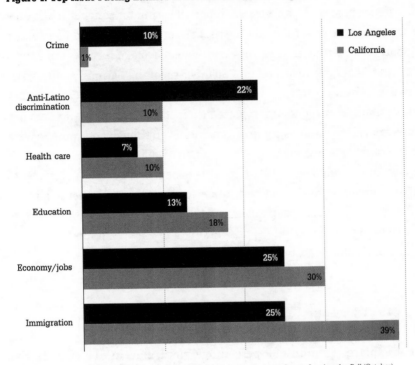

Source: Latino Decisions 2016 Election Eve Poll; Pat Brown Institute/Latino Decisions Survey, Los Angeles Poll (October).

that less than 25% of Latino voters had mentioned immigration as being a top priority. This makes sense, given that neither candidate during the 2012 election cycle attacked immigrants the way that candidate Trump blatantly did in 2016. Candidate Trump made several promises in his campaign that were particularly threatening to Latinos. Trump promised to build a wall between the United States and Mexico (and presumably have Mexico pay for it), repeal President Obama's executive order, Deferred Action for Childhood Arrivals (DACA), and develop a special task force to deport undocumented immigrants living in the United States. Moreover, he relied on xenophobic rhetoric to appeal to a more conservative base of voters, often referring to Mexican immigrants as "rapists," "criminals," and "drug dealers."

Californians, unfortunately, are very familiar with such political contexts. In the 1990s, Californians passed Proposition 187, a voter-led initiative that denied undocumented immigrants social services, denied undocumented children access to education, and required state employees to whistle-blow on undocumented immigrants. Governor Pete Wilson, who supported the proposition, blamed Mexican immigrants for taking jobs and putting a drain on the state's resources. As noted earlier, the anti-immigrant sentiment expressed by proponents of the proposition led to the "Prop 187 Effect" (see Damore and Pantoja 2013). In response to the hostile social and political environment, citizen and non-citizen Latinos alike became more engaged in their opposition to the proposition and the Republican Party (e.g., Pantoja, Ramírez, and Segura 2001; Barreto and Woods 2005). The fact that California became a solidly blue state from the mid-1990s onward is indicative of the political shifts that were driven by the Latino backlash.

Unsurprisingly, Donald Trump's policies failed to resonate with Latino voters in the Golden State. According to the Latino Decisions 2016 Election Eve Poll, 57% of Latino voters said Donald Trump is hostile toward Latinos and another 31% of Latino voters said Donald Trump does not care too much about Latinos. Moreover, Clinton drew considerable support from a wide variety of demographic groups. Table 1 shows Latinos' preference for president across selected demographic characteristics. Regardless of gender, nativity, national origin, and socioeconomic status, the table shows that Latino voters overwhelmingly preferred Hillary Clinton to Donald Trump. For example, foreign-born Latinos were more likely than U.S.-born Latinos to support Clinton, as the table shows a 10-percentage-point gap between the two groups. In Los Angeles County, the rate of the intended vote for Clinton among native-born Latinos is 69% while the vote choice rate among foreign-born Latinos is 10 points higher at 79%. Latinos of Mexican ancestry were also more likely to support Clinton than other national-origin groups. According to the table, 80% of Latinos who identified as Mexican said they voted for Clinton—a 5-percentage-point difference. Even a large percentage of younger Latinos (77%) preferred Clinton, despite some earlier concerns that millennial voters would fail to support her in November. This last finding suggests that younger Latino voters may have set aside their differences and voted for Clinton to prevent a Trump presidency. In all, Trump's

Table 1. Vote Choice for President by Key Demographic Characteristics, 2016

Gender	Clinton	Trump	National origin	Clinton	Trump	Income	Clinton	Trump
Female	89%	9%	Mexican	80%	16%	<$40K	87%	7%
Male	71%	23%	Non-Mexican	75%	22%	>$40K	74%	22%
Nativity			**Age**			**Education**		
U.S.-born	78%	19%	18–39	77%	15%	No college	83%	14%
Foreign-born	88%	10%	39+	82%	16%	College	76%	20%

Source: Latino Decisions 2016 Election Eve Poll.

comments alienated many Latinos during the election, but his comments pushed immigrants, Mexicans, and younger voters even closer to Clinton and the Democratic Party.

In Los Angeles, discrimination/race relations was the third most important issue facing Latinos, while in other areas of California, discrimination and health care tied as the fourth most important issue facing Latinos. It is not entirely clear why the issue of discrimination emerges as a higher priority in Los Angeles. One possibility relates to a difference in question wording. In the Pat Brown Institute/Latino Decisions survey, we ask respondents to list the top issue facing Latinos in the city/county. In the Latino Decisions Poll, though, we ask them to list the top issues facing Latinos more generally. The wording of the former leads Latinos to think about local concerns, while the wording of the latter does not steer Latinos to think about local or national politics specifically. Locally, such issues are not often found in political discourse. This, of course, is an inference, but it does require us to consider that the reasons for voting may vary when thinking about national, state, or local politics.

The Latino Gender Gap

If anything, this election demonstrated the power of the women's vote, particularly that of Latina women. As noted in table 1, 89% of women reported voting for Clinton --18-percentage points more than men who also supported Clinton. In Los Angeles County, the gender gap in vote choice is also striking. Among men, 65% were voting for Hillary Clinton, while 80% of women were voting for Clinton, a gap of 15 points. The gender gap in vote choice is also striking among native-born and foreign-born Latino respondents, which points to a 10-point difference with foreign-born Latinas being more supportive of Clinton. This is an early indication that even within the Latino community gender can now serve as an indicator for policy positions and, of course, candidate choice. This is a nascent phenomenon, given that as recently as 1998 Lien (1998) reported that there was no indicative distinction between the sexes for the Latino community because participation was low. Given the aforementioned 18-point gap, it is safe to say that Latinas' political views are quite distinct from their male counterparts.

Based on the results from the Latino Decisions 2016 Election Eve survey, Latinas and their male counterparts differed not just in their favoring of Clinton but also in regard to their support for the Democratic Party, which is in line with existing research that finds as much (Montoya 1996; Bejarano 2014). In the survey, Latinos were asked about their vote choice for member of the House of Representatives, and Latinas responded by favoring the Democratic candidate by 92%, resulting in a gender gap of 13 points. Similarly, respondents were also asked about their opinions regarding agreement with one party over the other; whether either party cared more for Latinos than the other; and whether Latinos felt that Republican nominee Trump cared for the community. In the answers to these questions, the pattern continues. Latinas' responses are in alignment with the modern gender gap, which indicates that women hold more liberal positions than do men (Ingelhart and Norris 2000). Specifically, the survey results reveal that Latino males agree more with the issue positions of Republicans than do Latinas (25% vs. 12%), and Latino males also perceive Republicans as truly caring about Latino voters (34% vs. 22%). Furthermore, this gender gap persists when respondents were asked about whether they thought Republican nominee Trump cared about the Latino community. Here, we see that 65% of Latinas overwhelmingly answered that he is hostile to the Latino community while only 48% of Latino males felt the same, thus, indicating that within-group differences exist in the Latino electorate.

Evidently, for Latinas the harsh rhetoric represented by Trump and the weak denunciation by the Republican Party led to more overwhelming support of Clinton and the Democrats. While the gap regarding political opinion between Latinas and their male counterparts is not surprising, this election demonstrated that the divide runs a bit deep. Latinas continue to engage in and understand politics differently than Latino males, which is what scholars like Hardy-Fanta (1993) have demonstrated. To some degree, Latinas are one of the newest subgroups to get involved in American politics. Regardless, they are unabashedly proving that they interpret politics in a manner where their support lies with those whom they perceive as buttressing their community. As such, we see that Latinas consider Trump and the Republican Party as political actors who are not to be trusted or supported. What they perceive as hostile treatment and framing of their community guides their evident antipathy. This is clearly in distinction from how their male counterparts view politics but very much in line with what is known about the modern gender gap (Bejarano et al. 2011).

Support for Liberal Policies

Besides the presidential election and election for U.S. Senate, California's down-ballot propositions, including Los Angeles County measures, sparked a lot of attention in 2016. On November 8, Californians voted on seventeen statewide propositions and more than 650 local measures, which contributed to the longest ballot in recent memory. The propositions focused on a range of issues, including education, health care, and criminal justice, just to name a few.

Propositions and measures offer a unique opportunity for voters to engage in direct democracy. However, they can often be complex and require voters to become informed about policy, which can take time and resources. To help alleviate some of the burden, the California Secretary of State provided a more than 200-page ballot guide to educate voters about the seventeen statewide propositions. However, the media criticized the guide for being too long; moreover, one reporter found the guide's word count to rival those of famous literary works, such as *The Grapes of Wrath* and *Crime and Punishment* (Reese 2016). Given the rather daunting task of reading through the voter guide, extant research suggests that voters are more likely to rely on informational shortcuts, such as endorsements by interest groups and representatives, to make decisions about policy (e.g., Lupia 1994). While some of these shortcuts may be found in the voter guides themselves, voters may also find informational shortcuts in television and radio programming and editorials.

Among the several propositions, our Latino Decisions 2016 Election Eve Poll asked Latino voters about their level of support for two key propositions in public education: Propositions 55 and 58. Proposition 55 is an extension of the 2012 Proposition 30, which increased taxes on individuals making $250,000 for funding public schools in higher education. Proposition 58, which was authored by former California Latino Legislative Caucus Chair and current State Senator Ricardo Lara, is a repeal of Proposition 227, a 1998 voter-led initiative that placed a ban on bilingual education in the state for more than fifteen years. In its place, Proposition 58 authorizes school districts to establish dual-language immersion programs for both native and nonnative English speakers and promotes community involvement in schools' language programs.

On November 8, the California electorate voted to pass both propositions with overwhelming support. According to the most recent vote tally, Propositions 55 and 58 received 63% and 73% of the vote, respectively (California Secretary of State 2016. While the passage of Proposition 55 meant that the state would continue its taxation strategy for funding public education, the repeal of Proposition 227 represents a significant shift in attitudes toward language and public education. Under the new law, English-speaking students and English language learners (ELLs) alike now have more opportunities to become fluent in multiple languages.

The Latino Decisions 2016 Election Eve Poll indicated that more than two-thirds of Latinos voted in favor of Propositions 55 (67%) and 58 (68%). Indeed, several factors shaped their decisions at the polls. Latinos, for instance, have long supported bilingual education programs and increases in social spending in education (e.g., Uhlaner 1991). While education can provide economic opportunities, such as jobs and higher salaries, bilingual education offers opportunities for Spanish-speaking Latinos to speak and learn in multiple languages.

Latino voters were also aided by the several key endorsements. Propositions 55 and 58 received disproportionate backing from a coalition of high-profile representatives, political parties, interest groups, and civic organizations. The list of endorsers included high-profile names, such as Governor Jerry Brown, the Democratic Party, the *Los Angeles Times*, and the California Teachers Association, to name a few. Both propositions also received support from key Latino representatives, including the Senate President Pro Tempore Kevin De Leon and Speaker of the Assembly Anthony Rendon; Latino civic organizations including the Mexican American Legal Defense and Education Fund; and Spanish newspapers such as *La Opinión*.

Finally, both propositions received major financial support from political action committees (PACs), which provided greater opportunities for Latinos to receive messages through commercial advertising. The PACs that supported Proposition 55 raised more than $58 million and spent more than $56 million during the election. Meanwhile, supporters of Proposition 58 raised more than $4.8 million (California Fair Political Practices Commission 2016). In both cases, the political opposition's efforts to raise funds paled in comparison to the PACs that supported the propositions. While opponents to Proposition 55 raised only $3 million, opponents to Proposition 58 failed to register any PACs to raise funds against it (California Fair Political Practices Commission 2016).

Aside from statewide initiatives, voters in Los Angeles County had the opportunity to decide the fate of two important measures: County Measure A, which raised property taxes to 1.5 cents per square foot to pay for buildings and maintain parks and other open spaces, and County Measure M, which added a half-cent sales tax to improve public transportation. Without significant Latino support, it is unlikely that these measures would have passed. In the survey, Latinos supported these measures by wide margins. For example, 64% favored Measure A (it passed with 73.5% of the vote), while 71% favored Measure M (it passed with 69.8% of the vote).

The Trump Effect, Enthusiasm, and Participation

While the so-called "Trump effect" caused Latinos from diverse backgrounds to vote for Hillary Clinton and Democratic candidates, Trump's vitriolic rhetoric toward Latinos and immigrants also pushed Latinos to participate politically. In this section, we explore Latino political participation across three indicators of political participation: voter turnout, voter registration, and naturalization. Then we examine two key explanations of political participation—psychological resources and mobilization efforts—to examine the extent to which Donald Trump, the candidate, pushed Latinos to participate and vote against him.

Leading up to the 2016 presidential election, researchers and pundits alike expected Latinos to vote in record numbers across the United States, including in electorally safe states, such as California. Although it is still too soon to tell the extent to which Latinos turned out to vote in the 2016 general election, the National Association for Latino Elected and Appointed Officials (NALEO) projected Latino voter turnout to surpass 3.8 million in California alone. The estimate represents a 22% increase from the previous presidential election and a 145% increase since 1996 (NALEO 2016b). In California's June primary election, the California Civic Engagement Project (CCEP) also found evidence of higher voter turnout. Among eligible voters, the CCEP (2016) found that Latino voter turnout had increased to 24.3%, 10 percentage points higher than the voter turnout rate in the previous presidential primary. While it is important to note that there is no discernable relationship between voter turnout in the primary and general elections, the pattern in this year's election suggests that Latinos were politically engaged and they were engaged early on.

Voter registration rates offer some additional insight into the extent to which Latinos participated in this year's election. Table 2 examines voter registration numbers across heavily populated Latino counties in 2012 and 2016. According to the table, voter registration increased by an average of 7.8% from the previous presidential election. Imperial County, which is home to the largest percentage of Latinos in all of California, experienced the greatest percentage increase in the number of registered voters statewide. Monterey,

Table 2. Voter Registration in Heavily Populated Latino Counties in 2016 and 2012

County	Percent Latino population	2016 Registered voters	2012 Registered voters	Change in registration (2016–2012)	Percent change in registration (2016–2012)
Imperial	82	70,189	61,086	9,103	+14.9
Tulare	63	154,000	145,348	8,652	+6.0
San Benito	58	28,224	26,580	1,644	+6.2
Colusa	58	8,638	7,765	873	+11.2
Merced	58	99,145	98,890	255	+0.2
Monterey	57	185,786	166,290	19,496	+11.7
Madera	56	58,086	53,779	4,307	+8.0
Kings	53	52,124	47,655	4,469	+9.4
Fresno	52	437,423	410,188	27,235	+6.6
San Bernardino	52	888,019	851,581	36,438	+4.3
Kern	52	370,804	332,864	37,940	+11.4
Los Angeles	48	5,253,427	4,758,437	494,990	+10.4
Riverside	47	1,019,130	943,405	75,725	+8.0
Santa Barbara	44	222,983	203,994	18,989	+9.3
Stanislaus	44	241,144	232,909	8,235	+3.5
Ventura	42	442,951	426,948	16,003	+3.7

Sources: California Secretary of State; U.S. Census Bureau population estimates, July 1, 2014. Heavily populated Latino counties are defined as counties with Latino populations of 40 percent or higher.

Colusa, Kern, and Los Angeles counties also made significant registration gains, as all four counties experienced an increase of 10 percentage points or higher. According to the Secretary of State, Monterey and Kern counties were ranked just behind Imperial as having the second- and third-largest registration increases in the state, respectively. Finally, Los Angeles and Riverside, as two of the most populous counties in the table, contributed heavily to California's registered voter population. Los Angeles County added nearly a half a million new registered voters and Riverside County added approximately 75,000 new registered voters over the four-year period.

Finally, Latino immigrants responded to the hostile political environment by applying for U.S. citizenship. For noncitizens, the naturalization process is an important first step towards voter eligibility. Moreover, research suggests that newly naturalized voters are more likely to participate when they are subject to hostile environments (Pantoja, Ramírez, and Segura 2001). Early in the Republican primary, it became clear that Donald

Figure 2. Number of Naturalization Applications in California (All Immigrants), 2015–2016

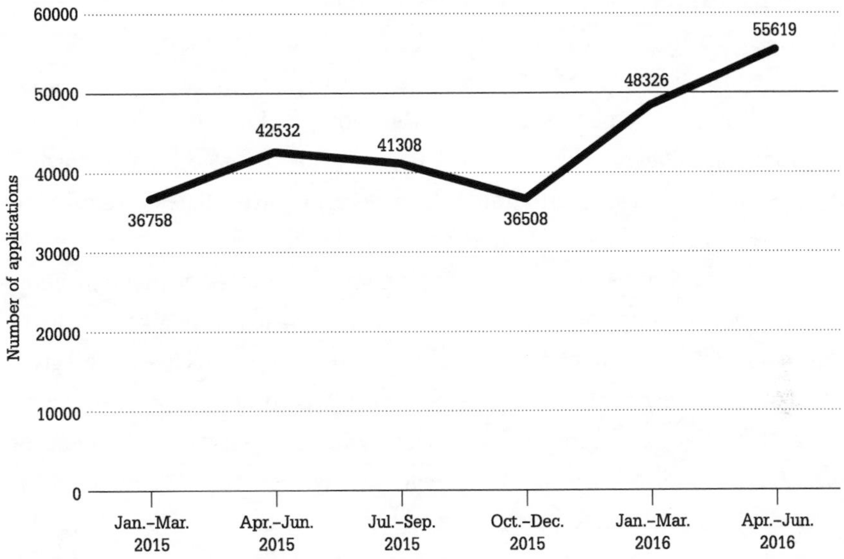

Source: U.S. Citizenship and Immigration Services.

Trump was going to become the nominee and go on to compete in the general election. As Trump's nomination became a growing reality, Latino immigrants engaged in what Ramírez (2013) refers to as "defensive naturalization" to protect themselves and their families from deportation in the event of a Trump presidency. Figure 2 reports the number of naturalization applications submitted by all immigrants in California for each quarter prior to November's election.[2] Overall, the table shows a surge in the number of noncitizens applying for U.S. citizenship. Between the last quarter of 2015 (October–December) and the first quarter of 2016 (January–March), the number of applications increased from 36,508 to 48,326—a 32% increase in applications. In the following quarter (April–July), the number of applications continued to increase by another 15% to 55,619 applications.

While Latino political participation increased, it is important to understand the psychological motivations for participating in this year's election. It has been well established that psychological factors can influence the decision to participate. Studies of anti-immigrant rhetoric and policies have shown that these events have a mobilizing effect on Latino voters (Merolla, Pantoja, Cargile, and Mora 2013; Pantoja, Ramírez, and Segura 2001). Given the divisive rhetoric of Donald Trump's campaign, we anticipated turnout among Latinos to dramatically increase. Leading up to the election, an October 2016 Latino Decisions poll asked Latino voters to compare their level of interest in the 2012 and 2016 elections. According to the NALEO Educational Fund/Latino Decisions Non-Battleground State Poll, 50% of Latino voters said they were more enthusiastic about this year's election, in comparison to 32% who said they were more enthusiastic about the election in 2012.[3] In Los Angeles County, Latinos were also politically interested and eager to turn out and vote. In the Pat Brown Institute/Latino Decisions Survey of the Los Angeles Latino Electorate, respondents were asked whether they were following closely the 2016 election. Eighty-seven percent of respondents said they were following the election "somewhat" to "very" closely. Respondents were asked how likely they were to vote in this election. Eighty-seven percent answered "absolutely certain" to "probably." The majority, 71%, said "absolutely certain."

One of the defining features of Trump's campaign was that his rhetoric and actions were particularly venomous toward immigrants and women. If this was the case, then we should observe some type of gender gap and immigrant gap when it comes to political participation. In other words, while Latinos overall are mobilized to turn out and vote, the desire to do so will be strongest among Latinas and immigrants. The Pat Brown Institute survey data confirm the presence of a gender and immigrant gap in Los Angeles County. Among men, 67% said they were absolutely certain about voting. For women, 75% said they were certain about voting, a gap of 8 points. While there were no differences between native- and foreign-born Latinos, we do observe differences between respondents who completed the survey in English and those who completed it in Spanish. Among the former 68% were absolutely certain about voting, while the latter group's voting rate was at 78%, a gap of 10 points.

Trump's comments may have also heightened a sense of group consciousness or group identity—a psychological resource that has been found

Figure 3. Reasons for Voting in the 2016 Presidential Election

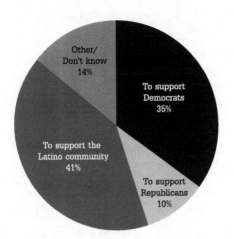

Source: Latino Decisions 2016 Election Eve Poll.

to be positively associated with various forms of participation, such as voting (Sanchez 2006). In the Latino Decisions 2016 Election Eve Poll, respondents were asked whether they were voting to support the Democratic Party, to support the Republican Party, or to represent and support the Latino community. According to figure 3, a plurality of Latinos (41%) said they planned on voting to represent and support the Latino community, followed by the Democratic Party (35%) and the Republican Party (10%), respectively.

Finally, political parties and civic groups facilitated Latino political participation by engaging in get out the vote (GOTV) drives. Mobilization efforts such as these are particularly important because they can help individuals with fewer resources overcome the costs of participating in politics (Rosenstone and Hansen 1993). In California as a solidly blue state, however, Latino voters were less likely to be contacted than Latino voters residing in swing states, such as Florida and Nevada. According to the Latino Decisions 2016 Election Eve Poll, 38% of Latino voters said they were contacted by a political party, campaign, or an organization and were asked to register or vote. At the same time, it is worth noting that the level of outreach in this year's election was comparatively higher than last year's election by 8 percentage points—an indication of the political stakes in this year's presidential election.

Democrats were more likely than Republicans to contact Latino voters. According to the Election Eve Poll, 65% of Latino voters reported being contacted by the Democratic Party, while just 31% reported being contacted by the Republican Party. Both political parties displayed similar strategies by attempting to mobilize their base. However, Democrats were more likely than Republicans to contact their political opposition (43% vs. 34%), as well as independents, third-party members, and undecided voters (80% vs. 34%). While Democrats' overall efforts to reach out to partisans and nonpartisans likely contributed to Clinton's vote share in California, the Republican Party's efforts to court Latino voters likely had little impact on Latinos' choice for president. Almost immediately following the 2012 election, the California Republican Party leadership declared it would change its electoral strategy by courting Latinos on the issues and engaging in more voter outreach activities (Castro 2013). However, Republicans seemingly failed to follow this strategy, and with Trump's victory, there is no indication that they will be adopting a new approach to Latino voters.

Lessons from Calexit

There is considerable debate at the moment over the factors motivating Trump's supporters. Some contend that the primary motivator was economic insecurity. The essence of this perspective is that working-class Whites have lost economic status over the years and voted for a candidate whom they believed could reestablish their status. White working-class voters had greater faith in Trump's "businessman" acumen than Clinton's political experience to alleviate their economic troubles. Others contend that sexism, homophobia, and racial prejudice were strong motivating factors. Certainly, Trump's campaign did not hold back on inflammatory rhetoric that emphasized divisions between in-groups (straight White men) and out-groups (ethnic and sexual minorities). On Election Day, however, the greatest divide between voting for Trump or Clinton was not between men and women or between blue- and white-collar workers. Rather, the divide was most pronounced between minorities (ethnic/racial) and Whites. A similar cleavage emerged in California in the mid-1990s when Whites overwhelmingly supported Propositions 187 (anti-immigrant initiative), 209 (ending affirmative action), and 227 (ending bilingual education). Yet the failure of these initiatives and Republican candidates to alleviate economic worries or turn the tide against ethnic and cultural change may have led White voters in California to abandon the GOP. Some contend that White voters turned away from the GOP because of its explicitly racialized campaigns that violated the norms of egalitarianism (Bowler, Nicholson, and Segura 2005; Mendelberg 2001). If California provides lessons for the Republican Party nationally, it is that racialized campaigns and quick-fix solutions will also alienate White voters. Thus, in the long run, Trump's presidency is likely to repel minority and nonminority voters from the Republican Party.

Regardless of the political behavior of White voters, the Republican Party still has a demographic problem on its hands. If Trump and the Republican-controlled Congress enact harsh policies, then it will create a Latino-Democratic firewall. In previous elections, we have seen Latino support for Republicans fluctuate dramatically. That variation will be gone for some time. This means that the road ahead for the GOP will be more challenging. In the next election cycle, Democrats need to double down on White voters. Undoubtedly, they will chip away at that Republican base for some of the reasons previously noted. Republicans, on the other hand, have no opportunity to chip African American and Latino voters away from the Democratic Party. This is especially evident with the results we see for how Latinas voted in this election cycle relative to Latino males. Their overwhelming support for the Democratic Party will be a challenge to pull from, given not just the rhetoric of this campaign cycle but that of previous ones as well. In addition to race and ethnicity being a factor in upcoming elections, gender will also continue to be an important differentiating characteristic; this scenario played itself out in California. In the Golden State, the Republican Party has been in a death spiral for the past two decades and will continue to be, given the continuous population changes in the state. In the 2016 election, Orange County (OC), a bastion of Republicanism in California, went blue. The last time OC went blue was in 1936.

Currently, the new administration is not helping matters for the Republican Party. In the aftermath of the of the Trump inauguration, we are learning that his campaign rhetoric was more than just promises. As executive orders pour out of the White House, the fear and resentment among California's Latinos increases. This is primarily because the administration has put immigration enforcement on the forefront of its agenda, resulting in anxiety and fear over racial profiling and deportation. Immigration and Customs Enforcement (ICE) agents are continuously undertaking enforcement sweeps where any Latino can be detained (De Francesco Soto 2017). This new approach is in contrast to that of the previous administration where ICE was more constrained on who it could detain and deport.

Additionally, California Latinos are paying close attention to the fact that those undocumented immigrants who were previously protected by the DACA executive order are no longer an exception to detention. As noted by scholars such as De Francesco Soto (2017), the anxiety is only getting worse due to the fact that the protections bestowed upon those covered by DACA are unofficially being rescinded. While Trump is not fully committing to repealing the current order, he also is not saying what will happen to it once it expires (Bennet and Memoli 2017). This allows ICE large discretion to detain and deport formerly protected classes of individuals.

California politicians, many of whom are of Latino descent, are fighting back against what they see as an attack on immigrants. One way they are doing so is through legislation, as is evidenced by California's Senate Bill 54, which would prevent law enforcement officials at the state and local level from using their resources to assist in federal immigration enforcement (Luna 2017). Colleges and cities throughout California have declared themselves to be places of sanctuary for undocumented persons. In essence, they have vowed not to cooperate with ICE in its enforcement of Trump's immigration agenda. Also, in order to ensure that California is able to legally and effectively resist the Trump agenda and what the leadership in the state legislature perceives as a rollback of the state's progressive policies and diversity, it has hired legal counsel led by former U.S. Attorney General Eric Holder. Steps such as these are evidence that the pervasive anti-Latino, anti-immigrant sentiment at the federal level will be challenged by the state.

Unfortunately for California Republicans, the actions of the administration are not boding well for them. In a recent article by Politico (Siders 2017), it is noted that California Republicans once again experienced the losses of various seats at the local and state level during the 2016 election, and, interestingly, the losses were to Latino Democratic candidates (Siders 2017). Moreover, the argument by Republican strategists that what is happening nationally is only making matters worse for them at the state level makes complete sense. Attempts at courting the Latino vote for future party building may continue to prove ineffective, given that the Trump agenda is perceived as continually attacking Latinos. This provides ample opportunities for the Democratic Party to maintain its hold as the viable political alternative for Latinos who feel that the Republican Party is tone deaf. As some scholars have argued, it appears that even today Latinos are not ripe for Republican conversion, given that the policy approaches of the party are not in line with the community's preferences (Barreto and Segura 2014; De La Garza and Cortina 2007).

This all begs the question of how Latino voters may feel in regard to the responsiveness of the state's Democrats to their new reality. We are beginning to see that, overall, the public response is on the side of the state's Democratic politicians. Particularly, this effect can be seen in a recent Berkeley Institute of Governmental Studies (IGS) Poll that was fielded in April 2017 and finds that public opinion is currently at a 57% approval rating for the California state legislature, which is dominated by the Democratic Party and led by two Latinos. This is the highest approval rating for the legislature since 1998 and is at odds with Congressional approval ratings, which are in the high twenties (DiCamillo 2017). While the Berkeley IGS Poll does not solely target Latinos, it is based on a representative sample and was also conducted in Spanish for those who are not English- dominant speakers (DiCamillo 2017). Furthermore, in general, Latinos in the state are in favor of and supportive of the steps being taken by their elected representatives. There appears to be a sense in the Latino community that the state's Democrats are being responsive to keeping them safe from federal interventions.

Trump's arrogance and dismissal of political facts suggest that the damage he will inflict on the GOP will be long-lasting, at least when it comes to Latino voters. A similar bravado guided the GOP in California in the mid-1990s. Latinos fought back to the point that California politics is now synonymous with Latino Democratic Party politics. If California is a roadmap for the GOP's future, then the road ahead is clear: Broaden the base, abandon racialized campaigns, and abandon anti-immigrant and antiminority policies, or face political extinction.

Notes

1. Throughout this chapter, we primarily rely on the Latino Decisions 2016 Election Eve Poll, which was administered on November 2–7, 2016, and has a subsample of 400 respondents. We also rely on a survey conducted by the Pat Brown Institute/Latino Decisions Survey, Los Angeles, which was administered in mid-October. The Pat Brown Institute (PBI)/Latino Decisions survey has a random sample of 600 Latinos residing in the city of Los Angeles and 900 outside of the city but with residency in Los Angeles County for a total sample of 1,500 respondents.

2. Due to data limitations, figure 2 includes all immigrants (Latinos and non-Latinos) applying for U.S. citizenship. See U.S. Citizenship and Immigration Services (n.d).

3. See NALEO Education Fund State Polls—September–October, 2016, www. latinodecisions.com.

References

Barreto, Matt A. and Gary M. Segura. 2014. *Latino America: How America's Most Dynamic Population Is Poised to Transform the Politics of the Nation.* New York: PublicAffairs.

Barreto, Matt A., and Nathan Woods. 2005. "The Anti-Latino Political Context and Its Impact on GOP Detachment and Increasing Latino Voter Turnout in Los Angeles County." In *Diversity in Democracy: Minority Representation in the United States,* edited by Gary Segura, and Shaun Bowler, 148–69. Charlottesville: University of Virginia Press.

Bennet, Brian, and Michael A. Memoli. 2017. "The White House Has Found Ways to End Protection for Dreamers' While Shielding Trump from Blowback." *Los Angeles Times.* https://www.latimes.com/politics/la-na-pol-trump-daca-20170216-story.html.

Bejarano, Christina E. 2014. *The Latino Gender Gap in U.S. Politics.* New York: Routledge Press.

Bejarano, Christina, Sylvia Manzano, and Celeste Montoya. 2011. "Tracking the Latino Gender Gap: Gender Attitudes Across Sex, Borders, and Generations." *Politics & Gender* 7 (4): 521–49.

Bowler, Shaun, Stephen P. Nicholson, and Gary M. Segura. 2006. "Earthquakes and Aftershocks: Race, Direct Democracy, and Partisan Change" *American Journal of Political Science* 50 (1): 146–59.

California Civic Engagement Project. 2016. "California's Latino and Asian-American Vote in the June 2016 Primary Election." *U.C. Davis Center for Regional Change.* Fact Sheet #8, October. http://regionalchange.ucdavis.edu/.

California Fair Political Practices Commission. 2016. "November 2016 General Election," November 23. http://www.fppc.ca.gov.

California Secretary of State. 2016. "Semi-Official Election Results." http://vote.sos.ca.gov.

Castro, Tony. 2013. "California Republicans Pin Their Hopes on Effort Led by Jim Brulte." *Huffington Post,* January 16.

Damore, David, and Adrian Pantoja. 2013. "Anti-Immigrant Politics and Lessons for the GOP from California." *Latino Decisions.* www.latinodecisions.com.

De Francesco Soto, Victoria. 2017. "On ICE Deportation Surges, Separating Facts from Speculation." *NBC News.* https://www.nbcnews.com/news/latino/opinion-ice-deportation-surges-separating-facts-speculation-n720086.

De la Garza, Rodolfo O., and Jeronimo Cortina. 2007. "Are Latinos Republicans but Just Don't Know It? The Latino Vote in the 2000 and 2004 Elections." *American Politics Research* 35(2): 202–23.

DiCamillo, Mark. 2016. "Release #2545: Clinton's Lead in California Slips as Her Image Among Voters Declines." *The Field Poll.* www.field.com.

DiCamillo, Mark. 2017. "Californians Remain Much More Optimistic about the Overall Direction of the State Than the Nation. Views of the Job Performance of the Governor and the State Legislature at Near Record Heights." UC Berkeley: Institute of Governmental Studies. //escholarship.org/uc/item/0j85w5pv.

Hardy-Fanta, Carol. 1993. *Latina Politics Latino Politics*. Philadelphia: Temple University Press.

U.S. Citizenship and Immigration Services. n.d. "Immigration and Citizenship Data." www.uscis.gov.

Inglehart, Ronald, and Pippa Norris. 2000. "The Developmental Theory of the Gender Gap: Women and Men's Voting Behavior in Global Perspectives." *International Political Science Review* 21 (October): 441-63.

Lien, Pei-Te. 1998. "Does the Gender Gap in Political Attitudes and Behavior Vary Across Racial Groups?" *Political Research Quarterly* 51 (December): 869-94.

Lupia, Arthur. 1994. "Shortcuts Versus Encyclopedias: Information and Voting Behavior in California Reform Elections." *American Political Science Review* 88 (1): 63-76.

Luna, Taryn. 2017. "What Happens When California Becomes a 'Sanctuary State.'" *The Sacramento Bee*. https://www.sacbee.com/news/politics-government/ capitol-alert/article169828172.html.

Madrid, Mike. 2016. "There's a Generational Divide in California's Latino Voting Bloc." *Los Angeles Times*, June 7.

Mendelberg, Tali. 2001. "The Race Card: Campaign Strategy, Implicit Messages, and the Norm of Equality." Princeton, NJ: Princeton University Press.

Merolla, Jennifer L., Adrian D. Pantoja, Ivy A. M. Cargile, and Juana Mora. 2013. "From Coverage to Action: The Immigration Debate and Its Effects on Participation." *Political Research Quarterly* 66(2): 322-35.

Montoya, Lisa J., 1996. "Latino Gender Difference in Public Opinion: Results from the Latino National Political Survey." *Hispanic Journal of Behavioral Science* 18 (May): 255-76.

Morin, Jason, and Adrian Pantoja. 2015. "The *Reconquista* of California: Latinos and the 2012 Election." In *Latinos and the 2012 Election: The New Face of the American Voter*, edited by Gabriel R. Sanchez. East Lansing: Michigan State University Press.

National Association of Latino Elected and Appointed Officials (NALEO). 2016a. "Latinos in Non-Battleground States of CA, TX, NY Reporting Much Lower Levels of Outreach." Latino Decisions. www.latinodecisions.com.

———. 2016b. "2016 Primary Election Profile, California." http://www.naleo.org.

Pantoja, Adrian. 2016. "Why Kamala Harris Can't Win California Without the Latino Vote." *Latino Decisions*. www.latinodecisions.com.

Pantoja, Adrian D., Ricardo Ramírez, and Gary M. Segura. 2001. "Citizens by Choice,

Voters by Necessity: Patterns in Political Mobilization by Naturalized Latinos." *Political Research Quarterly* 54 (4): 729–50.

Ramírez, Ricardo. 2013. *Mobilizing Opportunities: The Evolving Latino Electorate and the Future of American Politics.* Charlottesville: University of Virginia Press.

Reese, Phillip. 2016. "California's Voter Guide: Longer than 'Grapes of Wrath,' Shorter than 'Crime and Punishment.'" *Sacramento Bee,* October 28.

Rosenstone, Steven J., and John Mark Hansen. 1993. *Mobilization, Participation, and Democracy in America.* New York: Macmillan.

Sanchez, Gabriel. 2006. "The Role of Group Consciousness in Political Participation Among Latinos in the United States." *American Politics Research* 34 (4): 427–50.

Segura, Gary, and Shaun Bowler. 2005. *Diversity in Democracy: Minority Representation in the United States.* Charlottesville: University of Virginia Press.

Siders, David. 2017. "Why Californian Republicans Love Karen Handel." *Politico,* June 21.

Uhlaner, Carole Jean. 1991. "Perceived Discrimination and Prejudice and the Coalition Prospects of Blacks, Latinos, and Asian Americans." In, *Racial and Ethnic Politics in California,* edited by Bryan O. Jackson and Michael B. Preseton. Berkeley, CA: Institute for Governmental Studies Press.

Virginia's New Latino Voters

The Future of the *Nuevo South*

Xavier Medina Vidal and Zessna García Ríos

IN ARKANSAS IN 2016, A LATINO MAN IN HIS LATE SIXTIES, ACCOMPANIED by his twenty-year-old daughter, early-voted on the weekend before Election Day. Don José, a Mexican immigrant who was unable to finish his education in his home country, had been interested in voting but as a young man was never able to do so. Years after moving to the United States for work, Don José became a U.S. citizen and was able to vote in the 2016 election. After casting his vote for the first time, Don José reflected on his experience, commenting, "Lo hice por ellos" (I did it for them). "Ellos," in this case, refers to both his family and the Latino community. His is a common sentiment among Latino first-time voters, most of whom are intimately tied to family and community. In the 2016 election, such affinities contributed to a growing interest in voting and civic participation among eligible Latino voters, including many in the Southern states.

With a growing Latino population across the South and a new generation of U.S.-born Latinos coming of age, the pool of eligible Latino voters in the Southern states is increasing, though it remains small compared to the vast Latino electorates of California, New Mexico, and Texas. In 2016, 27.3

million Latinos nationwide were eligible to vote in the presidential election, making up 12 percent of all eligible voters (Krogstad 2016). (Eligible voters are U.S. citizens aged eighteen and older; they may or may not be registered to vote.) An estimated 8.6 million of these eligible Latino voters were in the South (Pew Research Center 2016). In Don José's Arkansas alone, the number increased from 51,000 in 2012 to roughly 60,000 in 2016 (López and Stepler 2016; Motel and Patten 2012). As the South's Latino population grows, we observe many more Latinos participating in formal and informal politics amid a changing political climate. Despite persistent racism and a surge of anti-immigrant measures in various states, the new Southern Latino electorate continues to expand its potential influence in the region.

While the nation as a whole has seen substantial Latino population increases since 2000, the increase in percentage terms has been greatest in the so-called "new destination states," many of which are in the South (table 1). Georgia and North Carolina are large Southern states with recent Latino population booms, driven mainly by strong economic growth (Marrow 2005), and are important new destinations for Mexican immigrants. Drawn to the metropolitan hubs of Atlanta and Charlotte, Latinos, mostly of Mexican origin, are changing the social and cultural landscapes of these Southern states. Yet their potential impact on electoral outcomes still depends on each state's political competitiveness and how Latino voters fit into its political landscape. North Carolina Latino voters, for instance, were influential in the 2012 presidential election largely because of their favorable location in a competitive battleground state (Wilkinson 2015). Though Georgia has been a solidly red state overall and is considered noncompetitive, the state's 290,000 Latino voters are likely to be key to making the state more competitive in future election cycles.

Latinos' diverse experiences with and opportunities to shape Southern politics are also reflected in their demographics. Although the Latino populations in most Southern states are majority-Mexican (78% in Arkansas, 62% in Georgia, 60% in North Carolina), certain states are more heterogeneous with respect to national origin. In Louisiana, 43% of Latinos are of Mexican origin, as are 25% in the battleground state of Virginia (Pew Research 2014).

Table 1. Latino Population Growth and New Latino Voters in the South, 2016

	Latino Population Growth in Selected Southern States: 2000–2014			New Southern Latino Voters in 2016	
	Population, 2000	Population, 2014	Percent change	Population of eligible Latino voters	Percent all voters
Georgia	853,689	923,000	8.1	290,000	4.1
North Carolina	377,000	890,000	136.1	248,000	3.4
Virginia	333,000	732,000	119.8	277,000	4.6
Tennessee	117,000	322,000	175.2	92,000	1.9
South Carolina	95,000	258,000	171.6	88,000	2.4
Arkansas	85,000	205,000	141.2	60,000	2.7
Alabama	72,000	190,000	163.9	67,000	1.8
Kentucky	57,000	145,000	154.4	49,000	1.5

Source: Pew Research (Stepler and López 2016). Per terms and conditions: http://www.pewhispanic.org/2016/09/08/4-ranking-the-latino-population-in-the-states.

We contend that Virginia's recent electoral competitiveness and its highly diverse Latino population, with a range of life and migration experiences, is an ideal laboratory in which to examine new Southern Latino voters. Therefore, in this chapter, we look to Virginia as a case study of the new Southern Latino electorate, a collectivity of active and vocal participants in U.S. democracy who are changing the region's and the nation's political landscape.

In 2013, Virginia voters learned that dealing with immigrants is like dealing with rats—or that was one Republican politician's opinion, at any rate. During his Tea Party-backed campaign to become Virginia's governor, the state's attorney general Ken Cuccinelli declared, "If you don't move an animal at least 25 miles, it'll come back … It is worse than our immigration policy—you can't break up rat families" (Kessler 2013). That year, Virginia's Latino voters helped defeat Cuccinelli and elect Democrat Terry McAuliffe governor of the commonwealth. They did so in a charged political climate where heated controversies over immigration policy placed Latinos in the South and elsewhere in the crosshairs. Though no one knew it then, Cuccinelli's words and the political climate of which they were part would contribute to establishing Virginia as a bellwether of Southern politics. The continued salience of immigration politics in the state, along with the rapid growth of a diverse Latino electorate, suggests that the preferences of Virginia's Latino voters can advance understanding of Latino political behavior and of U.S. electoral politics more broadly.

In this chapter, we analyze the growing influence of Latino voters on the Virginia electorate and on political outcomes across the changing U.S. South. We build on analysis of Hispanic voters in the 2012 presidential race in Virginia and the 2013 Virginia gubernatorial race, as well as on research exploring the effects of immigration politics in motivating group-conscious voting behavior in Virginia (Medina Vidal 2015). We argue that the characteristics of Virginia's population and electorate, both national and state immigration politics, and group-conscious voting among the state's Latino voters are important to understanding the changing landscape of U.S. politics and the role of Latino newcomers to Southern politics in shaping national election outcomes in the long term.

As in the 2012 presidential contest, Virginia was a key battleground state in 2016, and again Latinos played a meaningful role in the election results at the state level. Figure 1, which reports data from the Latino Decisions 2016 Election Eve Poll and the Virginia Department of Elections (2016), illustrates the margin of Hillary Clinton's victory over Donald Trump in Virginia and Latinos' level of support for the candidates. According to the Election Eve Poll, taken in the final days before the November 8 election, Virginia Latinos' 81% support for Clinton was significantly stronger than their 66% support for President Obama's reelection in 2012. In 2012, Republican Mitt Romney did better than twice as well among Virginia Latinos than Donald Trump did in 2016; Romney earned 31% support while only 15% supported Trump.

According to the U.S. Census Bureau, the Latino population in Virginia grew by 120% between 2000 and 2014, when Latinos made up 8.8% of the commonwealth's population and 4.6% of its electorate (Pew Research Center 2014). By 2020, Hispanics are projected to be 11.1% of Virginia's population (Weldon Cooper Center for Public Service 2013). By examining election returns from the areas of Virginia's significant Latino concentrations, we can see more clearly how Latino support for Clinton contributed to her 5.4% margin of victory over Trump in the state. Much of Virginia's Hispanic population is concentrated in the northern part of the state, in the suburbs

Figure 1. Vote for President in 2016 in Virginia

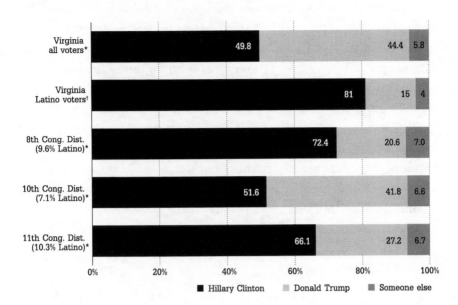

Source: *Virginia Department of Elections, †Latino Decisions 2016 Election Eve Poll; 2010 Census Files, Virginia Summary File.

of Washington, DC. We can observe in figure 1 that in three northern congressional districts where Latinos make up more than 7% of eligible voters, Clinton did significantly better than she did statewide. Clinton's best performance was in the 8th Congressional District, where Latinos are 9.6% of eligible voters and she won 72.4% of the vote. It is worth noting that the 8th District's congressional race included a Latino candidate; Independent Julio Gracia, a retired FBI special agent, earned 4.1% of the total vote in the 8th District congressional contest, which was won by incumbent Democrat Don Beyer with 68.4%. In the 10th Congressional District, where Latinos are 7.1% of the electorate, Clinton's margin was 9.8 percentage points over Trump. In the 11th Congressional District, where Latinos are 10.3% of the electorate, Clinton beat Trump by 38.9 percentage points.

A characteristic of the Virginia Latino electorate that helps make the state a potential bellwether is its heterogeneity. No single national-origin group of Latinos forms a majority of the state's Hispanic population. Though nearly one-third (32.7%) of Virginia Latinos are of Central American origin, this is far from a majority. The 2016 Election Eve Poll in Virginia showed a similar distribution among likely Latino voters, with those of South American and Central American origin most numerous in the sample, but no national group was a majority. Voter mobilization in the state, thus, depends on tapping into a pan-ethnic, Hispanic/Latino identity, rather than highlighting specific national-origin identities.

Before exploring in more detail how the demographic characteristics and behavior of Virginia's Latino voters in 2016 contribute to our understanding of Latino politics, Southern politics, and U.S. politics at large, we examine the significance to Latinos of Hillary Clinton's selection of Virginia Senator Tim Kaine as her running mate.

The Kaine Choice

Secretary Clinton's selection of Senator Kaine as the vice-presidential candidate on the Democratic ticket made an important statement about the value her campaign placed on the Latino community. In 2012, when Kaine ran for the U.S. Senate, Latinos gave him 70% of their support in a race he won with just under 53% of the total vote (Latino Decisions 2012; Virginia Department of Elections 2016). Kaine's triumphant declaration in his victory speech, "¡Todos somos virginianos!" (We are all Virginians!), signaled that he held the Latino community in great esteem. While many Latinos were disappointed with the lack of ethnoracial diversity on the 2016 Democratic ticket—indeed, there was more diversity among presidential hopefuls on the Republican side—Clinton's strategic selection of Kaine indicated that she viewed the Southern battleground state of Virginia and Latino voters as critical to her path to the presidency.

In results from the NALEO/Telemundo/Latino Decisions September 2016 tracking poll, which included 418 Virginia Latino voters in its sample, Latino approval of Clinton's choice of running mate was apparent (figure 2). Nationally, the Latino electorate agreed with Clinton that Kaine was a good pick, with 71.7% of likely Latino voters holding a favorable opinion of

Figure 2. Hillary Clinton and Tim Kaine Favorability among Virginia Latinos

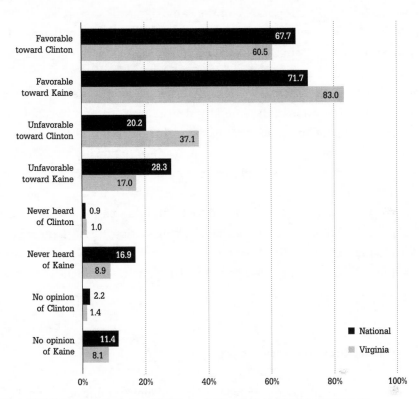

Source: NALEO/Telemundo/Latino Decisions 2016 September Tracking Poll. Virginia Latino/Hispanic likely voters.

the senator. Indeed, Latinos nationally expressed higher favorability toward Kaine than toward Clinton herself (67.6%). On the other hand, Latinos nationally also gave higher unfavorable ratings to Kaine (28.3%) than to Clinton (20.2%). Nationally, 28.3% of Latinos had never heard of or had no opinion of Kaine, which suggests that, in September 2016, many Latinos outside Virginia still needed time to get to know the candidate. In Kaine's home state of Virginia, Latino opinion of the senator was even more favorable than nationally, at 83%, and his unfavorable ratings were lower (17%). With 81% of their vote going to the Clinton-Kaine ticket by Election Day, Virginia Latinos were slightly more supportive of the Democrats than were Latinos nationally (79%).

While the Clinton-Kaine campaign was not the first to use personal anecdotes and Spanish phrases on the campaign trail, research suggests that Spanish-language appeals are indeed important in mobilizing the Latino vote, especially in the case of low-propensity Latino voters (Abrajano and Panagopoulos 2011; DeFrancesco Soto and Merolla 2008; García Bedolla and Michelson 2012). Though we lack conclusive evidence of a strong "Kaine effect" on the outcome of the 2016 presidential race, it is fair to conclude, given Kaine's popularity among Virginia Latinos in 2012 and the Clinton-Kaine ticket's strong performance among Latinos nationally, that Kaine's direct appeals to Latino voters played a meaningful role in attracting Latino support in the 2016 race.

The Clinton-Kaine ticket indeed took Virginia's battleground status and its Latino voters seriously. In the following section, we further explore the importance of Virginia's Latino electorate by examining what its demographic characteristics tell us about how Hispanic/Latino identity relates to voting behavior.

Latino Group-Conscious Voting

An important phenomenon related to Hispanic demographic heterogeneity in Virginia is the extent to which pan-ethnic identity as Hispanic/Latino motivates the state's Latino electorate to turn out to vote. Group-conscious voting, in this case voting to advance the interests of the Hispanic/Latino community, is a behavioral expression of group consciousness. The extent to which ethnic group consciousness shapes individual opinion and behavior is often governed by the structural conditions, producing social constraint and individual agency (Junn 2006), and also a sociopsychological endorsement of the "system" implicit in group-conscious participation (Miller et al. 1981). For Latinos in Virginia and other new immigrant destinations in the South, those structural conditions include the salience of immigration politics and policy, both nationally and locally, as well as the fact that Latinos have less historical presence in the Southern states than in, for example, Illinois or New Mexico. In Virginia, identifying as a

Figure 3. Virginia Latinas/os' Primary Motivations to Turn Out to Vote

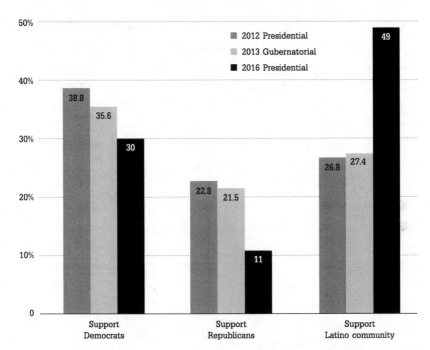

Source: ImpreMedia/Latino Decisions Election Eve Poll; Latino Decisions 2013 Virginia Election Eve Poll; Latino Decisions 2016 Election Eve Poll. Virginia Latino/Hispanic likely voters.

Salvadoran (or other nationality) generally confers less power than identifying as Hispanic/Latino.

Together, Virginia Latinos' heterogeneity and the state's political context lead us to examine the importance of group consciousness to political behavior. Figure 3 illustrates the behavioral dimension of group consciousness, that is, group-conscious voting, in the 2012 presidential, 2013 gubernatorial, and 2016 presidential elections. In 2012, Virginia Latinos' strongest vote motivator was to support Democrats (38.8%), followed by group-conscious voting (voting to support the Latino community) (26.8%) and voting to support Republicans (22.8%).

In the 2013 gubernatorial race, voting to support Democrats was again an important motivator, cited by 35.6% of Virginia's Latino voters. Yet 27.4% of the respondents reported that their primary reason for voting in that election was to support the Latino community (Latino Decisions 2013). This Latino group-conscious vote in Virginia was largely a function of Spanish-language media consumption and salience of immigration issues among Latino voters, and it had a profound effect on the likelihood of supporting Democrat Terry McAuliffe in 2013 (Medina Vidal 2016). To be sure, the Republican gubernatorial candidate Ken Cuccinelli, who compared immigrants to rats, did his part to foment strong feelings among Latino voters that Democrats, not Republicans, were the party that best represented the Hispanic/Latino community's interests. The response from Latino group-conscious voters in 2013 was that they were 30% more likely to vote for Democrat Terry McAuliffe (Medina Vidal 2016).

Cuccinelli was far from the last Republican to "inspire" the Latino vote. As figure 3 illustrates, by the 2016 presidential race Virginia's Latino voters were even more likely to link group consciousness to their voting behavior. Nearly half (49%) said their reason for voting in 2016 was to support and represent the Latino community, far above the rates of group-conscious voting in previous elections. Latino voters in 2016 were much less motivated than they were in the 2012 presidential and 2013 gubernatorial elections to vote for the purpose of supporting either Democrats (30%) or Republicans (11%).

What explains the group-conscious voting phenomenon and its sharp increase in 2016? For Virginia Latinos, immigration politics play a significant role in predicting group-conscious voting; those with intense interest in immigration issues are three times more likely to cast group-conscious votes than those for whom immigration politics are not important (Medina Vidal 2016). From its inception, Donald Trump's vitriolic anti-Mexican, anti-Latino, and anti-immigrant campaign ensured that immigration politics would play a meaningful role in the 2016 election. The 2016 Election Eve Poll reveals that immigration was the top issue of concern to Latinos nationally (39% ranked it most important) and was more important still to Virginia Latinos (49%).

Many analysts would agree that Trump played a key role in Virginia Latinos' tendency to link immigration politics to voting in support of the Hispanic/Latino community. The fact that Virginia Latinos had already established a strong connection between supporting their community and voting Democratic solidified their support for Clinton. In the next section, we build on the discussion of group-conscious voting by examining the principal voting motivations of two subgroups of Virginia Latino voters, namely, previous voters and first-time voters.

The Newest Newcomers

Having established Virginia Latinos as political newcomers to Southern U.S. politics, we now examine the differences in group-conscious voting between Latinos who had voted in prior elections and the 13% of Virginia Latinos who voted for the first time in 2016—the newest political newcomers. In figure 4, we immediately note that in 2016, the group-conscious voting phenomenon is especially pronounced among Hispanic first-time voters in the commonwealth. Among those casting a ballot for the first time that year, 70.3% reported casting a group-conscious vote, while 14% said their motivation for voting was to support Republican candidates and only 10.3% said they voted in order to support Democrats.

The significant differences in principal vote motivation among previous and first-time voters suggest important qualities of the changing electorates in Virginia and other Southern states. First-time voters, whether millennials aging into the electorate or older Latinos recently naturalized, are entering electoral politics in a climate in which the lives and futures of immigrants are hotly contested. These debates likely will shape their political preferences and patterns of participation for years to come. For these new voters, formative "psychohistorical experiences" (Alvarez 1973) include California's Proposition 187, a Republican anti-immigrant ballot measure in 1994 that had lasting effects on the strength of Latino Democratic partisanship and on Latino patterns of participation (Ramírez 2013). More recently, passage of anti-immigrant legislation in various states, such as Arizona's SB 1070 (2010) and Alabama's HB 56 (2011), has impacted new voters. And the Obama-era legislation known as DACA (Deferred Action for Childhood Arrivals), which has benefited many Latino youth, is at risk from Republicans in Congress who want to repeal it. The preferences of first-time

Virginia Latino voters in 2016 suggest that the new Southern Latino electorate is motivated to vote primarily by their community's interests—which many see as threatened—and only secondarily by a desire to support the Democratic Party and its candidates.

But is this motivation somehow a function of mobilization outreach by the major political parties and by community organizations? Figure 4 also shows that Virginia Latino voters who were contacted by a political party or community organization in the months leading up to the general election were more likely (58.6%) to be motivated to vote based on supporting the Latino community compared to voters not contacted (41.1%). Contacted voters also expressed a weaker motivation to vote for the sake of supporting Democrats (26.9%) compared to voters not contacted (33.1%), even though the Democratic Party in Virginia reached out to Latino voters at higher rates than either the Republican Party or community organizations. Among Latino voters reporting contact, 64% were contacted by Democrats, 45.9% by community organizations, and only 28.8% by Republicans. (Note: Voters could report contact by more than one source.)

The evidence presented here suggests that for Virginia Latinos, most notably for first-time voters, supporting the Latino community is critical to engagement in electoral politics. Nonetheless, an important question to consider in preparation for future elections is whether Latino voters in Virginia and throughout the country will remain reliably loyal to the Democratic Party should Trump and the Republican Party soften their views toward Latinos and immigrants. In the following section, we explore the conditions that might predict just how solidly Democratic we can anticipate Latino voters to be in the near future.

Southern Divide on Issues Important to Latinos

Spurred by the strongest rates of population growth among Latinos anywhere in the United States, Latinos in the South are poised to transform the region's political landscape in the coming years. Nonetheless, the 2013 Virginia gubernatorial race and the 2016 presidential contest illustrate that

Figure 4. Primary Vote Motivation Among Virginia Hispanic Voters in 2016

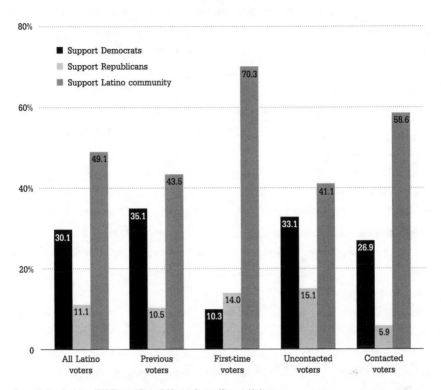

Source: Latino Decisions 2016 Election Eve poll. Virginia Latino/Hispanic likely voters.

the political transition in Virginia and in the South generally is taking place in a context of deep divisions on key issues, making the pace of this transformation uncertain. The Latino Decisions 2016 Election Eve Poll finds that among all issues that Latinos believe politicians should address, immigration reform/deportations is of greatest importance to Latinos nationally (39%) and in the new Southern destination states of Virginia (61%) and North Carolina (50%). This is an issue where deep fissures are evident in the South and throughout the nation.

To explore how different groups feel about immigration politics and policy, a separate 2016 postelection survey polled a national sample of 3,668 respondents, approximately half of them in the South (Medina Vidal 2018). The sample included Latinos (*n* = 1,021), African Americans (*n* = 915), and non-Hispanic White Americans (n = 1,732). Conducted by the Diane D. Blair Center of Southern Politics and Society, the poll asked respondents whether a wall should be built along the southern U.S. border with Mexico and whether undocumented immigrants living in the United States should be able to become citizens after meeting certain requirements over time. The degree to which opinion is divided on these issues between Latinos and Whites, and Southern Whites in particular, suggests that Latino newcomers and the growing Latino electorate in the South stand to challenge the region's status quo.

In the 2016 Blair Center Poll, 38.7% of all Whites and 35% of Southern Whites disagree that a wall should be built along the border with Mexico, while 68.9% of all Latinos and 64.5% of Southern Latinos oppose such a wall. While Southern Latinos are marginally more supportive of a border wall than Latinos in other regions, their support is far below that of Southern Whites, who are the group most in favor of a border wall. An even greater Southern divide exists on opinion regarding a pathway to citizenship for undocumented immigrants. This is significant, because unlike a border wall, a pathway to citizenship is a policy proposal that has long been debated in Congress. Support for it among Southern Latinos (76.2%) is the highest among all subgroups, and support among Southern Whites (44.6%) is the lowest. This nearly 32-percentage-point gap provides important evidence that Latino newcomers to Southern U.S. politics are strongly motivated by immigration policy and face significant challenges as they incorporate politically into new immigration destination states in the South.

Conclusion

Although it proved nonessential to Trump's Electoral College victory in 2016, Virginia continues to be a key battleground state, in part because of its growing Latino population. The Clinton-Kaine campaign's attention to Latinos along with Latino voters' strong support for the Democrats in 2016 suggests the future role that this expanding Latino electorate may play. Together, the demographic characteristics of the Latino electorate in Virginia, our understanding of Virginia Latino voter preferences and motivations, and the attitudes of non-Latinos in the South and nationally on the issues most important to Latinos lead us to several valuable conclusions.

First, the Latino electorate across the U.S. South is diverse, but the politics of immigration are important and unifying. Second, the development among Virginia Latinos of a strong tendency toward group-conscious voting suggests that new Latino voters entering the electorate in the coming years will be less likely to view electoral politics as a strictly partisan enterprise than did older generations of Latino voters. Third, even though Latinos are increasingly influential voters in new destination states, the Democrats' reliance on demographic shifts and on Latinos' distaste for politicians like Trump will not be an effective long-term strategy. The characteristics of the Virginia Latino electorate suggest that voter outreach and mobilization will need to be more nuanced than in the past.

Finally, for Latinos in Virginia and throughout the South, there are many challenges ahead. These exist not only in the realm of political organization and voter mobilization but also at the policy and legal levels. Virginia is one of the states, prior to 2013, covered by the preclearance provision of the Voting Rights Act. This provision effectively protected African Americans, Latinos, and other minority groups by prohibiting localities with histories of racial discrimination in voting—mostly Southern states—from implementing any change to their voting laws without federal preapproval. However, in 2013, the Supreme Court struck down this provision in *Shelby County v. Holder*. This important action by the Supreme Court, combined with the proliferation of anti-immigrant measures and restrictive voting laws at the state level, means that new Latino voters are entering a climate both politically and legally more hostile toward their interests than in decades past.

In this context, stories of first-time voters like Don José from Arkansas, who cast his vote "for them," for his family and the Latino community, take on added resonance. With U.S. public opinion sharply divided on the immigration policies of concern to the Latino community and politicians taking sides as well, voting becomes an act that transcends individual interests. Like Don José, Latino newcomers to Southern politics are making it known that they will continue to engage an often hostile political system at the polls in order to move the Latino community forward.

References

Abrajano, Marisa, and Costast Panagopoulos. 2011. "Does Language Matter? The Impact of Spanish-Versus English-Language GOTV Efforts on Latino Turnout." *American Politics Research* 39 (4): 643-63.

Álvarez, Rodolfo. 1973. "The Psychohistorical and Socioeconomic Development of the Chicano Community in the United States." *Social Science Quarterly* 53 (4): 920-42.

DeFrancesco Soto, Victoria, and Jennifer Merolla. 2008. "Spanish Language Political Advertising and Latino Voters. In *New Race Politics: Understanding Minority and Immigrant Voting*, edited by K. Haynie and J. Junn, 114-29. New York: Cambridge University Press.

García Bedolla, Lisa, and Melissa R. Michelson. 2012. *Mobilizing Inclusion: Transforming the Electorate through Get-Out-the-Vote Campaigns.* New Haven, CT: Yale University Press.

Junn, Jane. 2006. "Mobilizing Group Consciousness: When Does Ethnicity Have Political Consequences?" In *Transforming Politics, Transforming America: The Political and Civic Incorporation of Immigrants in the United States*, edited by S. Lee Taeku, Karthick Ramakrishnan, and Ricardo Ramírez, 32-47. Charlottesville: University of Virginia Press.

Kessler, Glenn. 2013. "Did Cuccinelli Compare Immigration Policy to Exterminating Rats?" *Washington Post*, October 14.

Krogstad, Jens. 2016. "Key Facts About the Latino Vote in 2016." Pew Research Center. http://www.pewresearch.org.

Latino Decisions. 2012. "ImpreMedia/Latino Decisions 2012 Election Eve Poll." http://www.latinodecisions.com.

———. 2013. "America's Voice/People for the American Way Virginia Gubernatorial 2013 Election Eve Poll." http://www.latinodecisions.com.

———. 2016a. "NALEO Educational Fund/Noticias Telemundo/Latino Decisions Weekly Tracking Poll—September-November 2016." http://www.latinodecisions.com.

———. 2016b. "2016 Election Eve Poll." http://www.latinodecisions.com.

López, Gustavo, and Renee Stepler. 2016. "Latinos in the 2016 Election: Arkansas." Hispanic Trends, Pew Research Center, January 19. Available at www.

pewhispanic.org.

Marrow, Helen B. 2005. "New Destinations and Immigrant Incorporation." *Perspectives on Politics* 3 (4): 781–99.

Medina Vidal, Xavier. 2015. "The New Virginiano Electorate and the Politics of Immigration in Virginia." In *Latinos and the 2012 Election: The New Face of the American Voter*, edited by Gabriel R. Sánchez, 129–48. East Lansing: Michigan State University Press.

——. 2017. "Immigration Politics and Group Consciousness for Newcomers to Southern US Politics." *Politics, Groups, and Identities* 5 (4): 679–706.

——. 2018. "Immigration Politics in the 2016 Election." *PS: Political Science and Politics* 51 (2): 304–8.

Miller, Arthur H., Patricia Gurin, Gerald Gurin, and Oksana Malanchuk. 1981. "Group Consciousness and Political Participation." *American Journal of Political Science* 25: 494–511.

Motel, Seth, and Eileen Patten. 2012. "Latinos in the 2012 Election: Arkansas." Hispanic Trends, Pew Research Center, October 1. www.pewhispanic.org.

Pew Research Center. 2014. "Demographic and Economic Profiles of Hispanics by State and County, 2014." http://www.pewhispanic.org.

——. 2016. "Mapping the Latino Electorate by State." Hispanic Trends, Pew Research Center, January 19. http://www.pewhispanic.org.

Ramírez, Ricardo. 2013. *Mobilizing Opportunities: The Evolving Latino Electorate and the Future of American Politics*. Charlottesville: University of Virginia Press.

Stepler, Renee, and Mark Hugo Lopez. 2016. *U.S. Latino Population Growth and Dispersion Has Slowed Since Onset of the Great Recession*. Washington, DC: Pew Research Center.

Virginia Department of Elections. 2016. "2016 November General: Official Results." http://results.elections.virginia.gov.

Weldon Cooper Center for Public Service. 2013. "Virginia Population Projections." University of Virginia, Charlottesville. http://demographics.coopercenter.org.

Wilkinson, Betina. 2015. "North Carolina Latinos: An Emerging, Influential Electorate in the South." In *Latinos in the 2012 Election: The New Face of the American Voter*, edited by Gabriel R. Sanchez, 149–66. East Lansing: Michigan State University Press.

North Carolina Latinos and the 2016 Election

Betina Cutaia Wilkinson

IN 2015, THE NATIONAL LATINO[1] VOTE WAS PLACED IN THE SPOTLIGHT ON the day when Donald Trump announced his run for the presidency along with his hostile immigration policy pronouncements. A specific group that obtained national recognition throughout the 2016 electoral campaign was the millennial Latino electorate in North Carolina. While most Latinos are not eligible to vote in North Carolina (only 27.8% of the Latino population is eligible), approximately 38% of Latinos of ages eighteen to twenty-nine years were eligible to vote in 2014. The share of eligible Latinos in this age range was in fact higher than that of Latinos voters of any other age category. What is more, the percentage of eligible Latino voters aged eighteen to twenty-nine is strikingly larger than the percentage of Whites (18.8), Blacks (24.4), and Asian Americans (24.5) of the same age category (López and Stepler 2016). Thus, the face of the North Carolina Latino voter is younger, more potent than that of other racial/ethnic groups. Future electoral results in North Carolina will be greatly shaped by these voters.

The Demographic Profile of North Carolina Latinos

The demographic characteristics of Latino residents in the Tar Heel State somewhat parallel those of the national Latino population as reflected by the Census Bureau's 2010 data. Though most Latinos in North Carolina are native born (52%), comparable to the national population (63%), the foreign-born presence in the state is significant at 48%. Like the U.S. Latino population, the most dominant national origin of Latinos in the state is Mexican at 61%. Latinos in North Carolina are also quite young, slightly younger than the national Latino population, with a median age of twenty-four years. The median personal earnings of Latinos sixteen years and older in the state is $17,500, slightly lower than the median earnings of U.S. Latinos, $20,000. Also, similar to the national average earnings of all workers including those who are full-time, year-round workers, native-born Latinos earn slightly more than foreign-born Latinos in North Carolina (U.S. Census Bureau 2010; Pew Research Hispanic Center 2011). Based on the latest U.S. Census data, the city of Winston-Salem, located in Forsyth County, has the largest Latino population, with Latinos making up 14.7% of the city's populace. Durham (14.2%), Charlotte (13%), and Raleigh (11.4%) trail Winston-Salem in the size of the Latino population (Chesser 2012; U.S. Census Bureau 2010).

In regard to North Carolina Latinos' religious background and partisan identification, there are a few facts that must be noted. While data on North Carolina Latinos' religious affiliation and behavior is limited, we know that more than two-thirds of Latinos in the United States identify as Roman Catholic and 15% identify as born-again/Evangelical Protestants (Pew Hispanic Project and the Pew Forum on Religion & Public Life 2007). At the national level, Latinos are twice as religious as other U.S. residents, with 46% attending church weekly in comparison to 23% of the others. Nonetheless, most Latino voters say that religion does not impact their presidential vote and an overwhelming majority of Latinos strongly prefer separation of church and state, with 82% of Latino voters and 75% of born-again Latinos preferring that pastors abstain from discussing politics with their congregations (Barreto 2012). In terms of partisan identification, the majority of

Latino voters in North Carolina are supporters of Democratic candidates, with 71.5% of Latinos voting for President Obama in the last presidential election (Wilkinson 2015).

The North Carolina Latino Electorate

Latinos in North Carolina are a small yet powerful, young electorate whose extensive growth in numbers and political clout have granted them national recognition. The size of the Latino population in the Tar Heel state has skyrocketed from 1.2% of the state's total population in 1990 to 9.1% in 2014, making Latinos in this state the eleventh largest Latino population in the U.S. (U.S. Census Bureau 2001; 2014). Similar to the Latino population in the state of Virginia, the emerging Latino presence in North Carolina has amplified the size and influence of its Latino electorate. The number of Latinos registered to vote increased considerably from 2004 (10,000) to 2016 (135,000). Further, the share of Latino registered voters in North Carolina has risen these last few years, from 0.2% in 2004 to 2.1% in 2016. These surges are greatly due to Latinos' aging and increasing eligibility to vote.

North Carolina Latinos and the 2016 Election

Next, I provide an in-depth discussion of North Carolina Latinos' voting behavior in the 2016 election using Latino Decisions 2016 Election Eve poll data.[2] In my analyses, I place an emphasis on the vote of young Latinos, in addition to the difference in voting preference and behavior between first-time voters and experienced voters.[3]

North Carolina has recently become a swing[4] state in U.S. electoral politics. President Obama won in this state by a very narrow margin in 2008, and in 2012 Mitt Romney narrowly won the Tar Heel state with only 51% of the vote and approximately 97,000 more votes than Obama ("North Carolina Election 2012 Results" 2012). While North Carolina remained in favor of the Republican Party for most of the second half of the twentieth century, the increasing presence of non-Southern migrants (mostly identifying as independents) in the state has recently contributed to the decreasing predictability of election outcomes and power of the GOP in the state. President Obama's win in 2008 can be attributed partly to the growing presence of Northern migrants to the state (Hood and McKee 2010).

Latinos have greatly contributed to North Carolina's swing state status. In 2012, North Carolina Latinos played a pivotal role in the election results. President Obama chose to hold the 2012 Democratic National Convention in Charlotte, North Carolina. The convention spotlighted Latinos with Los Angeles Mayor Antonio Villaraigosa as the convention's chairman and numerous Latino political and community leaders, including an undocumented immigrant, Benita Veliz, and San Antonio mayor Julian Castro as the convention's key note speaker (Becerra 2012; Foley 2012; Miles 2012). While some may have been surprised by the 2012 presidential results in North Carolina, Latino voters in the swing state strongly revealed their electoral strength and commitment to the Democratic Party. Latinos, the fastest growing electorate in the state, were vital to the success of the Democratic Party in 2012. More than 70% of Latinos voted for President Obama while less than 28% favored Mitt Romney. Latinos strongly perceived that Democrats cared for and reached them more than Republicans. Young immigrant Latinos participated in get-out-the-vote initiatives and advocated in favor of Democratic candidates whom they perceived were more favorable toward their concerns about immigration and civil rights. A combination of Latinos' consistent support of Democrats in state and national elections with their growth (from 0.2% of the registered voters in 2004 to 1.7% in 2012 according to the Pew Research Hispanic Center) and their commitment to the Democratic Party regardless of religious background strongly illustrates that Latinos are a key constituent for Democrats' success in North Carolina (Wilkinson 2015).

In 2016, North Carolina was regarded as a swing state as well as a battleground[5] state, probably even more so than in previous elections. Since 2013, North Carolina has been in the news, given its heated policy debates that parallel several debates that occur at the national level. House Bill 589, one of several controversial voting ID laws passed throughout the country, called for substantial changes to how North Carolinians vote. In efforts to combat voter fraud, the law required voters to show a voter ID before voting, shortened the early voting period, and eliminated the one-stop registration and voting opportunity as well as straight-ticket voting. In late July 2016, a U.S. Fourth Circuit panel deemed the law unconstitutional, given that the law's provisions disproportionally harm Blacks, who overwhelmingly vote in favor of Democratic candidates. Further, the court stated that the justifications for passing the law do not conceal the state's exact motivations (Barnes and Marimow 2016). As of the 2016 presidential election, most of the components of HB 589 were dismantled. In addition to voting rights, North Carolina has been in the national spotlight for HB2, a law signed by Governor Pat McCrory in March 2016 that requires transgender people in government facilities to use the bathrooms that match the gender on their birth certificates instead of the gender with which they identify. Further, the law prevents North Carolina cities and counties from imposing protections of members of the LGBT (lesbian, gay, bisexual, transgender) community (Jarvis 2016). In response to this controversial law, the state suffered economically by losing the NCAA Basketball Championship from Charlotte, the NBA All-Star game, and numerous national lacrosse, tennis, soccer, and golf championships for men and women throughout the state (Carter 2016). Like the voting rights law, HB2 highlights North Carolina's swing-state status by promoting and capturing a significant portion of the political views and divisions that exist among the national electorate. Thus, it comes as no surprise that the top 2016 presidential candidates' campaigns apportioned vast mobilization efforts in the state.

Another reason for North Carolina's solid reputation as a swing state is the top Democratic and Republican nominees' tight grasp on their respective electorates in the state. According to Politico's battleground states polling average obtained approximately one month before the November election, Hillary Clinton and Donald Trump, the Democratic and Republican nominees, respectively, were nearly tied in support (42.6% for Clinton, 42% for Trump) (Politico 2016).[6] This deep competition at the polls continued until Election Day. Thus, after winning their respective primaries in North Carolina and before and after the National Conventions, the Clinton and Trump teams' mobilization efforts were quite forceful ("North Carolina Primary Results" 2016).

Trump and Clinton recognized the importance of the North Carolina electorate and, thus, established a solid presence in the Tar Heel State throughout the elections. Trump set up eleven field offices in the state, and Clinton established thirty-eight offices, mostly in Democratic strongholds (Darr 2016). After June 2016, both candidates made numerous visits to the state. Hillary Clinton visited the state more than ten times. Donald Trump visited North Carolina more than twelve times in the last few months leading up to the election (Glassberg 2016).

Though Hillary Clinton did not win North Carolina's popular vote in the 2016 presidential election, North Carolina Latinos were firmly committed to Hillary Clinton. Donald Trump won 50% of the popular vote compared to Hillary Clinton's 46% (North Carolina State Board of Elections 2016). Still, as figure 1 reveals, 82% of Latinos favored Clinton while only 15% favored Trump. Experienced voters supported Clinton (77%), and first-time voters overwhelmingly favored her (90%). When juxtaposing young Latinos' presidential vote with older Latinos, I find that young Latinos (ages eighteen to thirty-nine) fervently supported Clinton, with 86% favoring her, as well as 78% of individuals forty years and above. When examining Latinos' presidential choice by nativity, I find that native-born and foreign-born Latinos did not differ in their support for Clinton since more than 80% of both groups supported the former Secretary of State. National origin, particularly Mexican origin, is a significant factor to consider when analyzing North Carolina Latinos' presidential vote choice. Donald Trump's reference to Mexicans as rapists, drug dealers, and criminals in the beginning of his campaign placed Mexicans in the spotlight. Not surprisingly 87% of North Carolina Mexicans favored Clinton over Trump, as well as 78% of non-Mexicans. Thus, Latinos in the Tar Heel State were firmly committed to Hillary Clinton in 2016.

Throughout North Carolina, Clinton also won in counties with emerging Latino electorates. In Forsyth County including Winston-Salem, the city with the largest Latino population in the state, Hillary Clinton won with 53.6% of the vote. In Mecklenburg County containing Charlotte, Clinton

Figure 1. North Carolina Vote for President

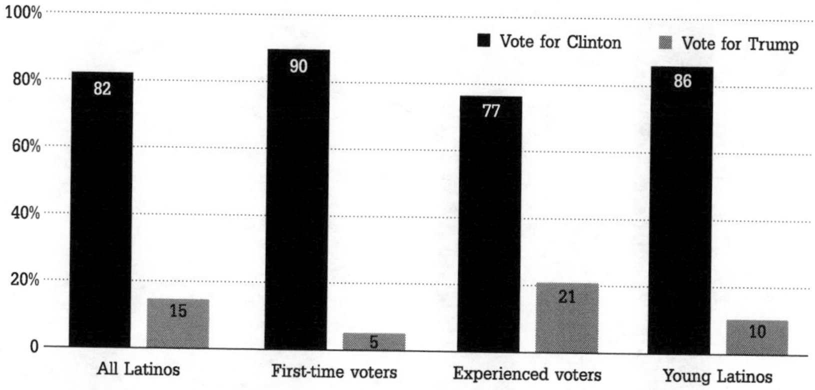

Source: Latino Decisions 2016 Election Eve Poll.

obtained 63.3% of the vote. Further, in Durham County, with one of the highest percentages of Latinos, Clinton won with 78.9% of the vote ("North Carolina Presidential Results" 2016). Interestingly, Clinton obtained greater electoral support from North Carolinians in these counties than Obama did in 2012 (Wilkinson 2015).

Immigration has been a policy concern of Latinos in the last few presidential campaigns, and it continued to be a deep concern in the 2016 election (Damore 2016a; Damore 2016b). Figure 2 presents North Carolina Latinos' answers to the question examining the most important issue facing their community. Immigration was the issue that most concerned them (50%). The economy/jobs was also deemed critical to their community (32%), followed by education (15%) and health care (11%). When comparing first-time voters with experienced voters, there are some differences in the importance that they place on issues. While immigration is most important for both groups, the importance placed on immigration by experienced voters is less (39%) than that placed by first-time voters (59%). This does not come as a surprise since within-group differences in immigration attitudes exist for Latinos. For instance, foreign-born Latinos tend to have more positive attitudes toward immigration than second- and third-generation Latinos (Rouse, Wilkinson, and Garand 2010). Still, I also find that immigration

Figure 2. Most Important Issue Facing the Latino Community in North Carolina

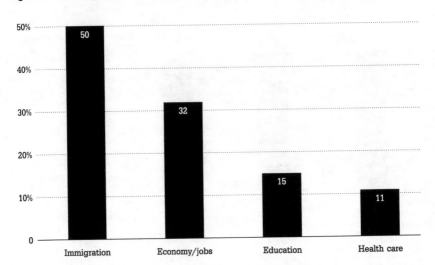

Source: Latino Decisions 2016 Election Eve Poll.

was the most critical issue (56%) for Latinos eighteen to thirty-nine years of age. Hence, the issue of immigration may have mobilized young, first-time voters to turn out to cast their vote in favor of a candidate whose immigration stance was not hostile compared to theirs.

Immigration played a prominent role in Trump's and Clinton's presidential campaigns. While Donald Trump led a racialized campaign with hostile rhetoric toward immigrants, Hillary Clinton adopted a much less restrictive stance on immigration, favoring comprehensive immigration reform with a path to full and equal citizenship (Lee 2015; www.hillary-clinton.com). Clinton's campaign reached out to Latino voters considerably more than Trump's. Among various appearances and tactics to mobilize Latino voters, Clinton launched a church-based voter mobilization drive in Latino churches in at least nine states and was the first presidential candidate to appear on a prominent Univision talk show, "El Gordo y La Flaca" (Goodwin 2016; Ramirez 2016). Thus, it comes as no surprise that the Election Eve poll indicates that 80% of North Carolina Latinos made a decision about the presidential election months before the election (24% said over the summer, 56% said more than six months ago), and Latinos

Figure 3. Candidate Latino Outreach in North Carolina

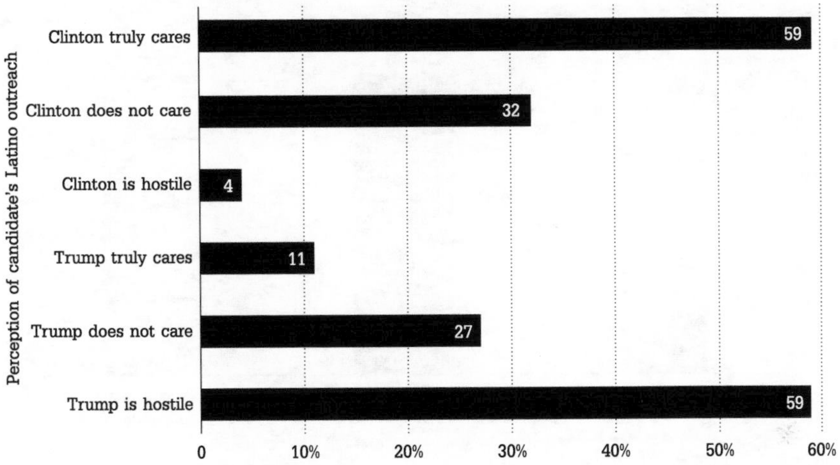

Source: Latino Decisions 2016 Election Eve Poll.

strongly felt that Clinton, and not Trump, cares about Latinos. Figure 3 presents Latinos' perception of candidates' outreach, noting that 59% of North Carolina Latinos believe that Clinton truly cares about Latinos, relative to 11% of Latinos who believe that Trump truly cares about Latinos. Merely 4% of Latinos believe that Clinton was hostile toward Latinos, relative to 59% of Latinos who believe that Trump was hostile toward them. Notably, the same percentage of individuals who believed that Clinton truly cared about them believed that Trump was hostile to them. What is also striking is that 84% of Latinos who stated that they were voting to help the Latino community affirmed that they voted or will vote for Hillary Clinton. Clearly, Latinos in North Carolina perceived that Clinton had the interests of their ethnic group in mind. What is more, the issue of immigration and Democrats' outreach played key roles in shaping Clinton's success among North Carolina Latinos.[7] In terms of vote history, some differences exist between first-time Latino voters and experienced voters. While 68% of experienced voters perceived that Clinton truly cares for Latinos, 44% of first-time voters believed the same. As to views about Trump, 99% of first-time voters believed that Trump does not care about Latinos or is hostile toward them,

Figure 4. Voter Favorability toward GOP in Future in North Carolina

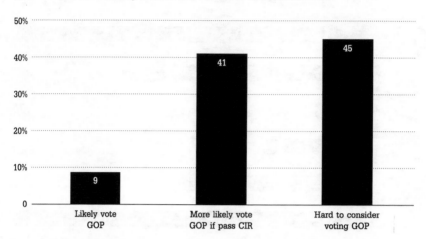

Source: Latino Decisions 2016 Election Eve Poll.

as did 82% of experienced voters. Among young Latinos, 95% believed that Trump does not care about them or is hostile to them, whereas 39% of young Latinos believed the same about Clinton.

Given that immigration is of great importance to North Carolina Latinos, does their immigration policy stance translate to solid loyalty to the Democratic Party? Figure 4 presents Latinos' answers to a question regarding their likely support of the GOP in the future. Interestingly, while 45% of North Carolina Latinos stated that they find it hard to consider voting for the Republican Party in the future, 41% stated that they are more likely to vote in favor of the GOP if it passes immigration reform with a path to citizenship. Among young Latinos and first-time voters, the majority expressed that they are more likely to support the GOP if it passes immigration reform. Thus, North Carolina Latinos' support for Democrats is not solid. This is not that surprising since 42% of Latinos said that they voted in order to support the Latino community (while 37% voted in order to support Democratic candidates and 9% voted to support Republican candidates). Republicans have the opportunity to win over North Carolina Latino voters but only to the extent that they present policies that Latinos perceive as favorable to them and their co-ethnics.

I now focus on the extent to which North Carolina Latinos felt and were mobilized and the factors that may have prompted them to turn out on Election Day. As the North Carolina polls revealed that Clinton and Trump were practically tied in the Tar Heel State for months and weeks leading up to the election, a significant focus of mobilization efforts centered on Latinos. Voto Latino, a civic media organization designed to empower Latino millennials, was quite active throughout the 2016 campaign cycle, and a significant portion of its efforts was placed in mobilizing Latinos in North Carolina. The group registered 7,107 Latino voters, the fourth highest total in the United States, following California, Texas, and Florida—states with much larger Latino populations (Bernal 2016). Hillary Clinton's campaign is also responsible for mobilizing Latino voters in North Carolina. As mentioned previously, she visited the state more than ten times throughout her campaign and campaigned in predominantly urban areas with large numbers of Latinos. She chose to end her campaign with a midnight rally in Wake County, whose Latino population makes up 10% of the population and is home to the capital city of Raleigh ("WakeGOV: Census, Demographics and Population Data" 2016; Heye 2016).

While immigrant youth advocacy groups such as El Cambio NC and NC Dream Team were very active in mobilizing Latino voters in 2012, their mobilization efforts in 2016 were nearly nonexistent. There are several reasons for this; one possible explanation for the limited power of these groups is Latinos' increasing frustration with the U.S. government and loss of hope that all immigrants will have the opportunity for a better life in this country. In June 2016, the Supreme Court of the United States ruled to leave in place an appeals court ruling that blocked President Obama's Deferred Action for Childhood Arrivals (DACA) and Deferred Action for the Parents of Americans and Lawful Permanent Residents (DAPA) programs. These programs would have protected as many as five million unauthorized immigrants from deportation and would have allowed them to remain in the United States and work (Liptak and Shear 2016). With the dismantling of these programs, the future of many unauthorized immigrants in this country is not secure.

While Voto Latino and Clinton's campaign attempted to mobilize Latinos, the amount of mobilization that actually occurred in the state is debatable. According to the America's Voice/Latino Decisions 2016 poll conducted in September, only 33% of Latinos said that they were contacted by a campaign, political party, or community organization asking them to vote or register to vote. Further, the 2016 Latino Decisions Election Eve Poll data indicates that only 50% of North Carolina Latinos were mobilized, with 49% stating that they were not mobilized. Still, Latinos in the Tar Heel State felt that it was important to vote in the 2016 election, and Donald Trump's comments about Mexicans at the start of his campaign may be a reason for this. According to the America's Voice/Latino Decisions September 2016 poll, more Latinos were enthusiastic about voting in 2016 (49%) than were enthusiastic about voting in 2012 (38%). Further, this poll indicates that 61% of Latinos think that it is important to vote in the 2016 election in order to stop Trump.

The aftermath of North Carolina's voter ID law (HB 589) and the dismantling of the Voting Rights Act may have also contributed to Latinos' desire and ability to vote in North Carolina. As mentioned previously, much of North Carolina's Voter ID law was deemed unconstitutional by a federal court in the summer of 2016, yet not all of the components of the law were removed by the November 2016 election. Straight-ticket voting, a voting option quite popular with African Americans and Latinos, was no longer an option at the voting booths. Furthermore, while the length of the early voting period increased slightly from 2012, some counties reduced the number of polling sites or shortened the hours of sites, especially during the first week of the early voting period. Forsyth, Guilford, and Mecklenburg, three large counties with a considerable number of Latinos, set restrictive early voting schedules during the first week of voting (U.S. Census Quickfacts n.d.). No straight-ticket voting and restrictive early voting schedules resulted in longer lines at the polls (Roth 2016a). The *Shelby County v. Holder* U.S. Supreme Court ruling in 2013 dismantled Section 5 of the Voting Rights Act, resulting in the closing of 868 polling sites throughout the United States; twenty-seven polling sites were closed in North Carolina. These polling sites were in locations with a long history of racial discrimination and, with that, voter suppression, which were present throughout many cities and towns in North Carolina. Three days before Election Day, a federal judge ruled that North Carolina allowed three counties to purge voters from the rolls illegally (most of them were African Americans and Democratic) and ordered that the disenfranchised voters be allowed to cast ballots. There were also numerous reports of individuals not feeling safe to vote due to verbal and physical intimidation at or near voting sites. For instance, in Henderson County, there were reports of individuals driving around yelling at people in predominantly Black neighborhoods. Residents did not feel safe being out and some worried about losing their jobs. In Lee County, an election worker was seen carrying a baseball bat with a "Trump" sign on it, and in Forsyth County (a county with a large Latino population), some voters reported feeling intimidated after seeing a military vehicle with Trump signs parked across from a polling site (Roth 2016b). Still, these efforts did not seem to considerably deter many Latinos from voting, and some Latinos may actually have been mobilized by these efforts.

Conclusion

While some may have been surprised by the 2016 presidential results in North Carolina, Latino voters in the swing state strongly revealed their electoral strength and commitment to Hillary Clinton. Latinos, the fastest growing electorate in the state, were vital to the success of the Democratic Party. Regardless of whether they voted for the first time or not, Latinos perceived that Clinton reached out and cared for them much more than Donald Trump did. Latino voters advocated in favor of Democratic candidates whom they perceived as more favorable toward their concerns about immigration and civil rights. A combination of Latinos' consistent support of Hillary Clinton along with their growth (from 0.2% of the registered voters in 2004 to 1.7% in 2012, according to the Pew Research Hispanic Center) strongly illustrates their commitment to policies that favor their ethnic group, such as nonrestrictive immigration. While some North Carolina Latinos would consider voting for a GOP candidate in the future, the candidate's policy stances and campaign play a significant role in the amount of Latino support that the candidate earns. Thus, as long as Republican candidates adopt restrictive immigration stances and run hostile campaigns against an expanding Latino electorate, the North Carolina vote that currently leans slightly to the right will change.

Appendix: Description of Variables

Clinton Presidential vote choice, 0 = other, 1 = Hillary Clinton

Trump Presidential vote choice, 0 = other, 1 = Donald Trump

Most important issues facing the Latino community, 1 = create more jobs/fix the economy, 2 = immigration reform/deportations, 3 = education reform/schools, 4 = health care, 5 = terrorism/ISIS/national security, 6 = college cost/affordability, 7 = protecting reproductive rights/women's rights, 8 = housing affordability/mortgages, 9 = money in politics/Wall Street influence, 10 = climate change/global warming/environment, 11 = anti-immigrant/Latino discrimination, 12 = taxes/government spending, 13 = criminal justice reform/mass incarceration, 14 = protecting Social Security, 15 = income inequality/poverty, 16 = hard to get ahead/make ends meet, 17 = politicians are dishonest/broken system, 18 = stop Trump/make sure Trump is not president, 19 = something else, 88 = don't know, 99 = refused.

Clinton's Latino outreach, 0 = Clinton truly cares about the Latino community; 1 = didn't care too much; 2 = was being hostile; 8 = don't know; 9 = refused

Trump's Latino outreach, 0 = Trump truly cares about the Latino community; 1 = didn't care too much; 2 = was being hostile; 8 = don't know; 9 = refused

Voter favorability toward GOP in future, 1 = I generally agree with the Republican Party on most issues and am likely to vote for them in future elections, 2 = I disagree with the Republican Party on many issues, but I would consider voting for them in the future if they help pass immigration reform with a path to citizenship, 3 = the Republican Party has now become so anti-[Hispanic/Latino] and anti-immigrant that it would be hard for me to ever consider supporting them in the future, 5 = none of these, 88 = don't know, 99 = refused.

Notes

1. The term "Latino" is used here as a gender-inclusive term.
2. The coding of the variables used in these analyses is provided in the appendix.

3. In the 2016 Latino Decisions Election Eve poll, 19% identify as first-time voters, 81% as individuals who voted before, and 27% range in age from eighteen-to thirty-nine years.

4. A swing state is a state in which both political parties have a strong chance of winning, given that the electorate in the state is evenly divided between the two parties (Democratic, Republican).

5. A battleground state is a state with an electorate that is not dominated by one political party in presidential voting. Parties "battle" to win over the electorate (Gimpel, Kaufmann, and Pearson-Merkowitz 2007).

6. Politico's battleground-state average includes results from the five most recent polls from each state (in this case, Bloomberg Politics, Quinnipiac, High Point University, Meredith College, and Fox News). These polls not only contact landlines but also cell phone numbers. The results are weighted according to the state's Electoral College vote count.

7. This statement is supported by results from estimated ordered logistical model with a dependent variable of presidential vote choice (1 = Clinton as the presidential vote choice, 1 = Trump as the presidential vote choice) controlling for the effects of how much Clinton cares about Latinos, Trump cares about Latinos, gender, education, income, and partisan identification.

References

Barnes, Robert, and Ann E. Marimow. 2016. "Appeals Court Strikes Down North Carolina's Voter-ID Law." *Washington Post*, July 29.

Barreto, Matt A. 2012. "Moral Values Not a Defining Issue for Latino Voters." *Latino Decisions*, May 16. http://www.latinodecisions.com.

Becerra, Hector. 2012. "Illegal Immigrant Makes History, Addresses Democratic Convention." *Los Angeles Times*, September 5.

Bernal, Rafael. 2016. "Latino Voter Registrations Spike in North Carolina." *The Hill*, October 6.

Carter, Andrew. 2016. "NCAA Pulls Championship Events from North Carolina over HB2." *Charlotte Observer*, September 12.

Chesser, John. 2012. "Hispanics in N.C.: Big Numbers in Small Towns." August 15. http://ui.uncc.edu.

Damore, David. 2016a. "10 Reasons Why Immigration Politics Will Affect the Latino Vote." *Latino Decisions*. www.latinodecisions.com.

———. 2016b. "Translating Trump: When He Talks Immigration, What Latino

Voters Hear." *Latino Decisions.* www.latinodecisions.com.

Darr, Joshua. 2016. "Where Clinton Is Setting Up Field Offices—and Where Trump Isn't." *FiveThirtyEight,* October 7. Available at www.fivethirtyeight.com.

Foley, Elise. 2012. "Democratic National Convention Draws Record Number of Latino Delegates." *Huffington Post,* September 3.

Gimpel, James G., Karen M. Kaufmann, and Shanna Pearson-Merkowitz. 2007. "Battleground States Versus Blackout States: The Behavioral Implications of Modern Presidential Campaigns." *Journal of Politics* 69 (3):786–97.

Glassberg, Ronnie. 2016. "How Many Times Have Clinton and Trump Been to North Carolina? Here's Your Answer." *Charlotte Observer,* November 2. www.charlotteobserver.com.

Goodwin, Liz. 2016. "Clinton Campaign Launches Early Voting Drive in Latino Churches." *Yahoo News,* September 25.

Heye, Doug. 2016. "Hispanic Turnout, N.C. Demographics and Other Key Election Day Indicators." *Wall Street Journal,* November 8. www.blogs.wsj.com.

Hillary Clinton Website. n.d. "Issues: Immigration Reform." www.hillaryclinton. com.

Hood, M. V., and Seth C. McKee. 2010. "What Made Carolina Blue? In-Migration and the 2008 North Carolina Presidential Vote." *American Politics Research* 38 (2): 266–302.

Jarvis, Craig. 2016. "Gov. McCrory Defends NC's HB2 on 'Meet the Press.'" *The Charlotte Observer,* April 17. www.charlotteobserver.com.

Lee, Michelle Ye Hee. 2015. "Donald Trump's False Comments Connecting Mexican Immigrants and Crime." *Washington Post,* July 8.

Liptak, Adam, and Michael D. Shear. 2016. "Supreme Court Tie Blocks Obama Immigration Plan." *New York Times,* June 23.

López, Gustavo, and Renee Stepler. 2016. "Latinos in the 2016 Election: North Carolina." *Pew Research Center Hispanic Trends,* January 19. http://www. pewhispanic.org.

Miles, Kathleen. 2012. "Antonio Villaraigosa, DNC Chairman 2012, Says GOP Platform 'Looks Like the Platform of 1812' (VIDEO)." *The Huffington Post,* September 4.

NC Dream Team. n.d. http://ncdreamteam.org/take-action.

"North Carolina Election 2012 Results." 2012. *New York Times.* www.nytimes.com.

"North Carolina Presidential Results." 2016. NPR. Election 2016. November 8. www.

npr.org.

"North Carolina Primary Results." 2016. *New York Times.* September 29. http://www. nytimes.com.

North Carolina State Board of Elections. "11/08/2016 Unofficial General Election Results-Statewide." www.ncsbe.gov.

Pew Hispanic Project and the Pew Forum on Religion & Public Life. 2007. "Changing Faiths: Latinos and the Transformation of American Religion." Pew Research Center. www.pewforum.org.

Pew Research Hispanic Center. 2011. "Demographic Profile of Hispanics in North Carolina, 2010." http://www.pewhispanic.org.

Politico. 2016. "The Battleground States Project." www.politico.com.

Ramirez, Tanisha Love. 2016. "Hillary Clinton Dances on 'El Gordo Y La Flaca' Ahead of Birthday." *The Huffington Post,* October 26.

Rouse, Stella M., Betina Cutaia Wilkinson, and James C. Garand. 2010. "Divided Loyalties? Understanding Variation in Latino Attitudes toward Immigration." *Social Science Quarterly* 91 (3): 856-82.

Roth, Zachary. 2016a. "Black Turnout Down in North Carolina After Cuts to Early Voting." *NBC News,* November 7.

———. 2016b. "Election 2016: Tracking Reports of Voting Problems Across the United States." *NBC News,* November 7.

U.S. Census Bureau. n.d. "QuickFacts." www.census.gov/quickfacts.

———. 2001. "The Hispanic Population: Census 2000 Brief." May. http://www. census.gov.

———. 2010. "American Fact Finder." http://factfinder2.census.gov.

———. 2014. "American FactFinder." http://factfinder.census.gov.

"WakeGOV: Census, Demographics and Population Data." 2016. www.wakegov.com.

Wilkinson, Betina Cutaia. 2015. "North Carolina Latinos: An Emerging, Influential Electorate in the South." In *The Pivotal Role of the Latino Electorate in the 2012 Election,* edited by Gabriel R. Sanchez, 149-66. East Lansing: Michigan State University Press.

Ecological Inference Meets the Texas Two-Step

Francisco I. Pedraza and Bryan Wilcox-Archuleta

LATINO VOTERS ARE PART AND PARCEL OF THE CULTURE OF MODERN ELEC-toral politics, including the election-night reports on vote returns that captivate audiences. Pundits, scholars, journalists, and other citizens benefit from advances in modern day polling, which typically offer an accurate appraisal of the overall estimates provided by exit polls. One staple of election-night reporting and analysis, the National Election Poll Survey (which we refer to here as the Exit Poll) by Edison Research, typically squares with the overall final reports provided by election officials. However, when it comes to the accuracy of voting patterns of subgroups, including Latinos, exit polls leave much to be desired.

Sorting votes by various demographic groups the national Exit Poll found that Hillary Clinton picked up 66% of Latino votes, and Donald Trump earned 28%, much higher than scholars expected and pollsters found. Could it be that scholarly accounts and other researchers missed a pending shift in Latino voting preferences? Is it the case that in 2016, Latinos thought twice about lending their muscle to the Democratic Party?

We argue that the answer is no. The primary reason that the Exit Poll does not provide an accurate appraisal of Latino voting is because it was never designed for that task. A credible polling of Latino voting requires that both English- and Spanish-language interviews are available to participants and that a careful consideration of sampling ensures that the diversity of immigrant generation, socioeconomic status, and language proficiency—all of which are related to partisan affiliation—is representative of the overall Latino voting population. However, the principal investigators of the Exit Poll provide no such details about the sampling strategy or protocols for interviewing Latino participants in their accompanying methodology reports. Contrary to the recommendations of the American Association of Public Opinion Polling, the Exit Poll survey methodology is not transparent. Without complete transparency, the scientific credibility of the Exit Poll's estimates of Latino voting remains an open question.

However, even setting aside the concern about the transparency of sampling methodology, the results of the Exit Poll run counter to a major trend that scholars have documented in American partisan dynamics. Since the 1990s, Latinos have increasingly distanced themselves from the Republican Party and offered their votes to Democrats (Barreto and Segura 2014; De La Garza, DeSipio, and Leal 2010; Sanchez 2014). In general, scholars agree that the reason why Latinos generally lean Democrat is because the GOP is increasingly perceived as anti-immigrant and anti-Latino. Thus, it comes as a surprise that after a year of Trump slighting Latinos—claiming a judge could not be impartial because of his Mexican heritage, insulting the famous Latino reporter Jorge Ramos, fat-shaming Miss Universe winner Alicia Machado, and labeling Mexican immigrants as rapists and "bad hombres" and promising to build a border wall to keep them out—the Exit Poll figures report Trump still had a better showing than Romney in 2012, by 1 percentage point.

Ramírez and Solano (2017) dissect the 1% difference between Trump and Romney at the national level. They critique the explanation that Trump bested Romney's performance as a result of a combined decline in overall White support and increase in overall minority support for the GOP. However, Ramírez and Solano show that in states where ethnic and racial minorities are most concentrated, support for Trump generally declined, whereas Trump did, in fact, best Romney in states with the smallest shares of minorities.

In the rest of the chapter, we offer evidence complimentary to the Ramírez and Solano analysis by examining actual vote returns. Specifically, we show that Trump did much worse among Latinos than the Exit Poll suggests through a focus on the state of Texas. Texas is the place where we should expect to find strong support for Trump if it existed. Unlike California or New York—liberal bastions driven by the two largest urban areas in the country—Texas's political culture, history of conservative and republican politics, and urban/rural divide suggest that is where we are the most likely to find evidence contrary to our claim. In the conclusion, we reflect on why it is critical for democracy that Latino voters are accurately represented in future accounts of election results.

The Lone Star State as Case Study of Latino Support for GOP Candidates

For several reasons, Texas is an ideal case study for close inspection of Latino voting patterns in 2012 and 2016. First, Texas is home to approximately 10,405,000 Latinos, which accounts for 39% of the overall state population (Pew Research Center 2016). After California, more Latinos live in Texas than in any other state in the United States. Second, Texas also reflects the diversity in the rural and urban divide of America, a division in Texas that breaks down similarly for Latinos and for non-Latino voters.

Research suggests that Texas Latinos are willing to back Republican candidates at levels that are higher than Latinos in other states. For example, Collingwood, Gross, and Pedraza (2014) note that Latino voters in Texas offered 29% of their vote to the Republican Mitt Romney in the 2012 presidential election, surpassed only by the 40% of Latino voters in Florida and the 31% in Virginia who backed Romney in 2012. This level of Latino support for the GOP candidate in Texas follows a longer historical pattern that DeSipio (1996) links to the importance of Anglos providing limited political opportunities for mass Latino civic engagement and leadership positions. Complimenting this interpretation, Garcia and Sanchez (2008) suggest that in such a context, prominent Latino political leaders without support from the Latino community can rise, like Republican Ted Cruz, the junior senator of Texas. In the lead-up to the 2016 presidential election, Latino Decisions estimated that 24% of Latino voters in a national sample would likely vote for Senator Cruz as early as October 2014. That was about 10 points less than the level of support Latinos indicated for other GOP candidates Jeb Bush (32%), Chris Christie (33%), and Marco Rubio (35%), the other prominent Latino candidate of the 2016 presidential election. Although these specific figures are not of Latino Texas voters, the figures for candidates who polled better than Ted Cruz among Latinos suggest that any GOP candidate who is not Ted Cruz has a chance to collect about one in three Latino votes.

Nevertheless, whether the urban and rural division in voting preferences underpins the Latino vote remains without close examination. We highlight the analytical value of Texas rurality because there is literature that suggests rural voters, all else being equal, tend to be more conservative and supportive of Republican candidates than their urban counterparts (Gimpel and Karnes 2006, McKee and Tiegen 2009). If rurality structures Latino voting, then one place where we should observe such a link is in Texas.

According to 2010 U.S. Census figures compiled by the Pew Research Center (2016), a majority 55% of Texas Latinos live in the six most populous counties of the state. Table 1 lists these details for the counties of Harris (Houston) 18%, Bexar (San Antonio) 11%, Dallas (Dallas) 10%, Tarrant (Fort Worth) 5%, Travis (Austin) 4%, and El Paso (El Paso) 7%. However, about 25% of Texas Latinos live in counties that have less than 250,000 people, providing some indication that a fair number of Lone Star Latinos live in rural areas (about 12% of Texas Latinos live in counties with less than 100,000 people). Webb County along the Rio Grande Valley, for example, has a population density of 74 people per square mile, but Latinos account for 96% of all Webb County residents as of 2010. Related to this point, some Latinos in Texas live in counties where more than 95% of the county is Latinos whereas others live in counties where more than 95% of the county is White. As we will explain , we leverage this variation as part of our strategy for assessing the

Table 1. Select Texas Counties, Demographic Statistics, and U.S. Presidential Election Results in 2012 and 2016

County	Total population[*]	% Latino population[*]	Population per square mile[†]	Share of Texas Latinos[‡]	Obama 2012[d]	Romney 2012[§]	Clinton 2016[§]	Trump 2016[§]
Bexar	1,714,773	58.7	1,383	10.6	52	47	54	41
Cameron	406,220	88.1	456	3.8	66	33	65	32
Collin	782,341	14.7	1,053	1.2	33	65	39	56
Dallas	2,368,139	38.3	2,950	9.5	57	42	61	35
El Paso	800,647	82.2	791	6.9	66	33	69	26
Fort Bend	585,375	23.7	697	1.5	46	53	51	45
Harris	4,092,459	40.8	2,608	17.6	49	49	54	42
Hidalgo	283,246	81%	493	7.4	70	29	69	28
Jim Hogg	5,300	92.6	5	<0.1	78	21	77	20
Lubbock	278,831	31.9	332	0.9	29	70	28	66
Potter	121,073	35.3	133	0.5	27	72	27	69
Presidio	7,818	83.4	2	<0.1	70	28	66	30
Randall	120,725	16.4	132	0.2	15	83	15	80
Tarrant	1,809,034	26.7	2,095	5.1	41	57	43	52
Travis	419,576	33.5	1,163	3.6	60	36	66	27
Webb	250,304	95.7	74	2.5	77	23	74	23
Zapata	14,018	93.3	14	0.1	71	28	66	33

Source:
* From the compilation of U.S. Census 2010 data by the Pew Research Center, available at http://www.pewhispanic.org/states.
† Population density data available at: https://www.census.gov/2010census.
‡ Calculated by authors using the U.S. Census 2010 data compiled by the Pew Research Center
§ From the State of Texas, Office of the Secretary of State, available at http://elections.sos.state.tx.us/index.htm.

accuracy of the exit polls. This rich demographic and geographic diversity means that Texas provides the appropriate setting for comparing Latino voting in 2012 and 2016.

Given what we know about Texas, if upward of 28% of Latinos supported Trump, we should expect to find some evidence of it here. In fact, the 2016 Exit Poll reports that 34% of Latinos supported Trump in Texas. Yet in an Election Eve survey released by the polling firm Latino Decisions, Trump's support among Latino voters was 16%, more than 50% lower than the Exit Poll finding. We leave the details that explain why these two polling firms came to such different results for others to unpack (see Barreto, Reny, and Wilcox-Archuleta [2017] for a full discussion, as well as Ramirez and Solano [2017]); however, we do acknowledge a common challenge.

In the context of a democratic republic, the secret ballot means we must rely on indirect evidence to assess how individual Latinos voted. The strength of public opinion polling methods is that they provide valuable evidence at the individual level. What we cannot know with certainty from survey evidence is whether an individual cast a vote for a particular contest or which candidate they selected. Our approach is to provide a companion analysis that relies on the actual election return results as reported by officials at the smallest electoral jurisdiction, the local voting precinct.

Ecological Inference Meets the Texas Two-Step

We two-step around the challenge to voting analysis posed by the secret ballot using statistical tools and actual vote returns. Specifically, we make use of advancements to the approach of ecological inference to assess the extent to which Latinos in the Lone Star State backed Trump. Our process begins by systematically gathering precinct-level vote returns for various counties in Texas, as well as demographic information for corresponding precincts. We then examine these data in two ways. First, we compare the vote share for Trump with the Latino citizen voting-age population (CVAP). While this particular strategy for comparison is informative, it excludes a key strength of statistical regression analysis, which can provide more precise, complimentary information about the average support for Trump among Latinos. We also want to know exact estimates of how different group members voted, not just generalized patterns. To accomplish this, we turn to an analysis utilizing ecological inference, a statistical tool specifically designed to determine how certain group members behave when the only available data are aggregate election results.

Precinct Analysis

We begin by gathering precinct-level vote returns for selected counties across the state. Precinct-level vote returns represent the official tallies

Figure 1. Map of the Texas Counties Selected for Precinct-Level Analysis of Presidential Voting in 2012 and 2016.

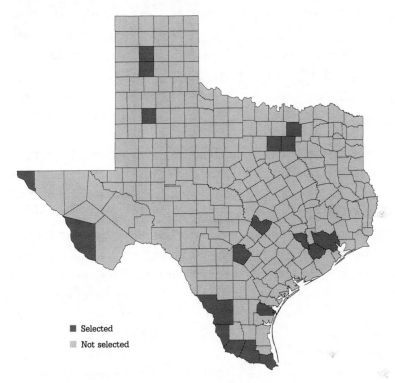

■ Selected
▨ Not selected

as reported by local election officials, data subsequently approved for final reporting by the Texas Secretary of State. In sorting the precinct-level returns for counties that we collected, we included a wide range of factors that cover the heterogeneity in urban and rural areas, heavily Latino areas, and some geographic variation across the state. In total, our data represent 75% of the Latino community in Texas. The full list of counties is in table 1, and a map of the counties is presented in figure 1. The map corroborates our aforementioned discussion about how Texas is experiencing the overall contemporary demographic growth of Latinos, while simultaneously striking a balance with key features of where Latinos live in terms of population density and demographic composition. Next, we leverage this excellent cross section of counties and sort the voting district precincts within each county according to Latino composition and the population density that approximates the rural and urban divide in the state.

We merge precinct-level vote returns with 2010 U.S. Census redistricting demographics calculated for each precinct by the Texas Legislative Services. These demographics allow us to calculate the Latino CVAP for each precinct in the selected counties. Since the voting precinct is not a Census-measured geographic unit, we rely on the data compiled by the Texas Legislative Service. Unfortunately, we cannot use more recent Census Bureau estimates.

With these data in hand, we start with a simple scatter plot, which plots the share of the vote for each candidate against the proportion of Latino registered voters in the precinct. These results are displayed in figure 2. We then add a locally weighted regression curve (loess) for each candidate to highlight the trend for Clinton and Trump. This line helps to capture the relationship between the proportion of Latinos in the precinct and the overall vote share for each candidate. The simple illustration demonstrates a clear finding: As the proportion of Latinos in the precinct increases, the two-party vote share for Clinton increases and the two-party vote share for Trump decreases. What is particularly striking is that the regression curve remains near 50% for both candidates for precincts that range between 0% and 50% Latino. However, in precincts where the Latino CVAP exceeds 75%, the regression curve and corresponding scatterplot points are increasingly separate and undermine the Latino vote estimates as reported by the Exit Poll.

Ecological Inference

Next, we use the ecological inference (EI) statistical method developed and advanced by Harvard political scientist Gary King (1997). While there are inherent issues in estimating individual-level behavior from aggregate data (for a discussion see King, Rosen, and Tanner 2004), EI has been the gold standard in academic applications and used extensively in voting rights court cases (Grofman and Merrill 2004; King 1997). Given that we have secret ballots in the United States, EI is the most relied-upon method

Figure 2. Texas Presidental Vote Among Latinos

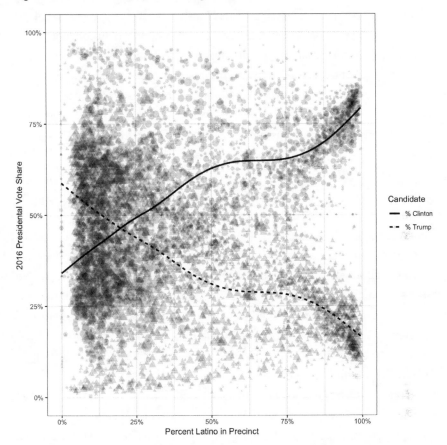

Notes: The triangles represent Trump's precinct level vote share, and the circles represent Clinton's precinct level vote share. The dashed line is a smoothed average of Trump's precinct level vote share given the percent Latino in the precinct. The solid line is a smoothed average of Clinton's precinct level vote share given the percent Latino in the precinct.

for determining how different groups voted. One of the benefits of this methods is that it provides exact estimates of how groups voted. The level of precision that EI analysis provides allows us to make statements that go beyond the general patterns highlighted in figure 2 regarding the relationship between a precinct's ethnic composition and candidate support.

Table 2 shows the EI estimates for Texas using the all-sampled counties' precinct-level returns and CVAP demographics. Using these data, we estimate that 77% of Latinos supported Clinton in 2016, and only 18% of Latinos voted for Trump. These numbers are vastly different than the 61% for Clinton and 34% for Trump reported by the Exit Poll. By our account, nearly half of the support from Latinos that the Exit Poll credits to Trump is simply not there.

Perhaps our estimates overlook important differences across Texas that precinct-level votes and the ethnic composition of a precinct, however detailed, do not capture. One possible difference relevant to the 2016 election is the rural and urban divide. A prominent narrative of the campaign (Alcantara, Uhrmacher, and Guskin 2016; Williams 2016), and certainly a motif of various post-election accounts from both left-of-center and right-of-center outlets (Bottemiller Evich 2016; Kurtzleben 2016; Sarlin 2016), was the remarkable support that Donald Trump captured in rural parts of America. In general, these accounts emphasize that rural voters feel like cities get everything and the rural parts of America are neglected (Kurtzleben 2016). However, a central feature of this line of reasoning is that rurality also correlates highly with ethnic composition; nearly all rural parts of the United States are majority non-Hispanic Whites. One outstanding question about the importance of the urban and rural divide that pundits use to characterize Whites is whether it also extends to Latinos. Do Latinos who live in rural areas cast voting decisions that are distinct from their counterparts who live in metropolitan locales?

Historian Geraldo Cadava, in his postelection analysis, championed the notion that Latino rural voters helped to secure Trump's victory. Using data on county-level vote returns, he argued that rural Hispanic voters shifted toward Trump in comparison to their voting preferences in 2012. Why? Like White rural voters, Latinos in rural settings, explains Cadava (2016), "have suffered some of the same tough economic circumstances as did some of the Midwestern counties that handed Trump the election." As part of the evidence he marshals to advance this claim, Cadava samples several rural counties in Texas, including Duval and Starr counties. Although the population density in each of those counties is 6.6 and 50 persons per square mile, respectively, the average population density in the entire state of Texas is 103 persons per square mile. According to proponents of explanations rooted in the urban and rural divide, these geographic differences map onto economic assessments and, by extension, candidate preferences. To

Table 2. King's Ecological Inference Estimates of Latino Vote in Texas

Geography	Candidate	Estimate	Standard Error
Entire sample	Clinton	0.7674	0.0028
	Trump	0.1768	0.0029
Large population	Clinton	0.8014	0.0052
	Trump	0.1374	0.0033
Medium population	Clinton	0.7288	0.0091
	Trump	0.1879	0.0099
Small/rural population	Clinton	0.7655	0.0010
	Trump	0.1872	0.0018

Notes: Counties included (n = 4,868 precincts). Large: Harris, Bexar, El Paso, Dallas, Tarrant, Austin; Medium: Collin, Lubbock, Nueces, Fort Bend, Randall; Small: Webb, Starr, Hidalgo, Cameron, Presidio, Potter.

the extent that Latinos formulate their candidate preferences using similar issues, this means that Latinos in rural parts of Texas are expected to have backed Trump to a greater degree than Latinos from large cities like Houston, San Antonio, Dallas, and El Paso.

It is possible that our estimates of Latino support for Trump are too low because we simply include too many densely populated and urban counties in our sample and not enough rural counties. However, as we noted earlier, our sample of precincts includes seventeen Texas counties and covers a broad territorial range, as shown in figure 1. Nevertheless, it is also possible that the rural and urban divide that Cadava observes at the county level also appears in other rural counties in Texas. If this is the case, we should see some evidence of this at the precinct level. If the more rural precincts we sampled showed strong support for Trump, then the increased vote tallies in the counties must come from a greater share of individual voters who back Trump. In the next section, we sort our sampled precincts by population size to test this possibility.

The Rural Urban Divide

We want to ensure that counties that strongly supported Clinton are not driving our overall estimate. Earlier we noted that the urban and rural divide could be a large factor in how Latinos voted in 2016, with more rural residents supporting Republican candidates at higher levels. We begin by examining figure 3, which plots the precinct-level vote share for each candidate on the *y*-axis against the percent of Latino CVAP on the *x*-axis. It consists of three panels that correspond to large population, medium population, and small population counties. If the rural and urban divide operates for Latinos in the same manner that pundits claim for non-Hispanic Whites, then we should see a positive relationship between Latino composition and support for Trump in the small-population counties, and perhaps in the medium-population counties as well, but not in the large-population counties.

As we saw in figure 2, the results in figure 3 show a clear relationship between percent Latino CVAP in the precinct and support for Clinton across the three different county types. In large-population counties, which include cities such as Houston, Dallas, San Antonio, Fort Worth, and Austin, Trump consistently garners the least support in the precincts that are the most heavily populated with Latinos. In the second panel of figure 3, we show medium-population counties. Overall, medium-population counties tended to support Trump more on average than Clinton, but when we look at the heavily Latino precincts, support for Trump drops profoundly. In the last panel, we show small-population counties, which include Webb, Presidio, Starr, Hidalgo, Cameron, Zapata, and Potter. In the precincts where very few Latinos live, support for Trump was quite high. However, contrary to the argument emphasizing the distinctive voting preferences of the rural electorate, even in these more rural counties—which are precisely the places that tend to support Republican and conservative candidates more than the urban population centers—support for Trump is quite low in the precincts with many Latino voters.

Our goal is to leverage as much evidence as we can to understand how Latinos voted in 2016. As mentioned earlier, using ecological inference tools can complement what we learn from the general patterns in figure 3. Next, we turn to the EI results to get exact estimates for the three different county types. The EI results are shown in the lower rows of table 2. Looking at large-population, medium-population, and small-population counties,

Figure 3. Texas Presidential Vote Among Latinos by County Type

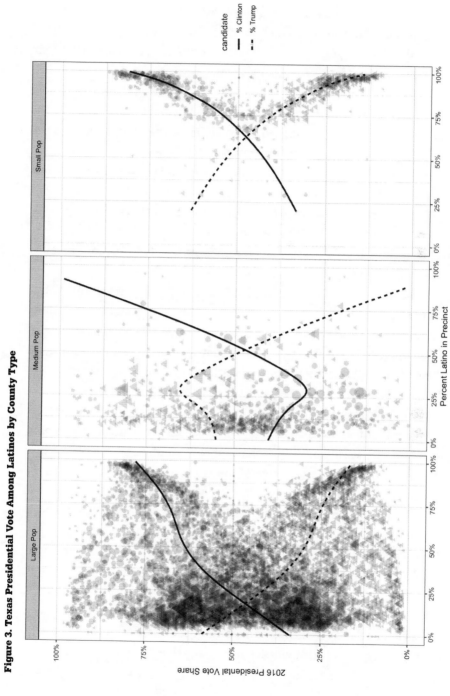

we see that the estimates are consistent across the different areas. In the large-population counties, which include the major cities Houston (Harris), Dallas (Dallas), San Antonio (Bexar), Fort Worth (Tarrant), and Austin (Travis), support for Trump among Latinos was 14%, the lowest out of all the regions, which lends some credibility to the notion that urban voters, *ceteris paribus,* tend to support Democratic candidates at higher levels. In the medium-population counties, our estimates show that Trump received 19% of the Latino vote. In the smallest counties, the place we could expect to see more support for Trump, he received 19% of the Latino vote. None of these numbers comes close to the estimated 34% promulgated by the Exit Poll, nor do these support Cadava's claims that rural Latinos strongly supported Trump. Regardless of how we cut the data or the analysis, we are unable to recover any estimates where support for Trump is as high as the Exit Poll or Cadava claimed.

In one additional test, we break down the EI even further. The results from the preceding show the average support for Clinton and Trump among Latinos given the various geographies. However, EI also provides estimates for each precinct within the counties that were analyzed. In figure 4, we show the distribution of each precinct from the entire state sample. We illustrate the distribution because it is possible that the average does not capture the full range of variation in support for Trump, which is precisely the point that motivates analysis by the urban and rural divide. A standard lesson of statistical analysis is that a mean, and by extension a regression estimate, can be indicative of multiple, different distributions. In other words, it could be the case that precinct-level estimates are almost uniformly distributed or cover a wide range of support for Trump, both producing the same average. It is easy to imagine that in a state as large and diverse as Texas, there could be lots of precincts where Latinos supported Trump and many precincts where Latinos supported Clinton. If this were the case, the resulting distribution could be nearly flat with very wide tails, or it could be bimodal. In contrast, if the results are unimodal and narrowly distributed around the mean estimate from above, then we would be confident that there is little evidence to support that Trump did well among Latinos in any Texas precincts.

Figure 4. Distribution of Precinct-Level Support for Clinton

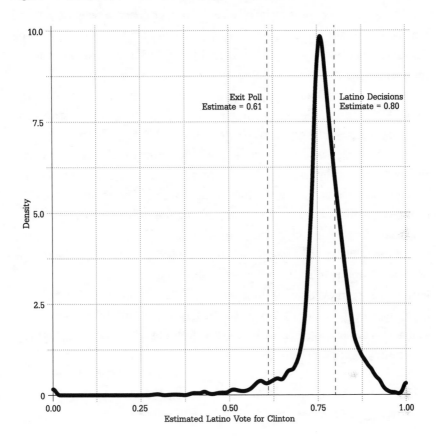

In figure 4, we show support for Hillary among Latinos on the x-axis. According to this data-rich summary, we see no evidence that there is a wide distribution in support for Clinton. In fact, the density of support for Clinton is distributed narrowly around the 77% estimate from above, meaning that in the majority of precincts, the results were very similar to the average. We designed this final test specifically to avoid the misstep of reporting an average that mischaracterizes a more complex portrayal of the Latino vote in 2016. To add further context to this finding, we also plot the estimates culled from the Latino Decision Election Eve (LDEE) survey data and the Exit Poll for points of comparison. It turns out that the LDEE estimate is in the densest part of the distribution, suggesting that it is much more likely to occur, given the evidence from actual vote tallies. The Exit Poll estimate, on the other hand, is located at the narrow part of the distribution tail, indicating that it is highly unlikely given the much fewer number of precincts with a similar breakdown in the two-party vote. When it comes to evaluating the extent of Latino support for Trump, the evidence from official vote tallies at the precinct level suggests a simple story: The estimate that 34% of Texas Latino voters supported Trump is too high.

The findings we show cast serious doubt on the election result estimates reported by the Exit Poll. In Texas, a place where we could have expected to see greater support for Trump, our analyses using official election returns from 4,372 precincts suggest a quite different story. Arguably, Texas could be an anomaly this year and the polling—both the Exit and the Latino Decision Election Eve polls—could be off. After all, we did see the pre-election polls miss the outcome of the presidential election. Recently Barreto, Reny, and Wilcox-Archuleta (2017) did a similar analysis across ten different states, including Texas. In the authors' EI analysis, they report that across almost 40,000 precincts, only 14.8% of Latinos supported Trump. This number is hardly close to the 28% reported by the Exit Poll.

What Is at Stake?

What distinguishes democracies and democratic republics from alternative forms of government is the role of ordinary citizens. Elections are the mechanism by which people hold public officials accountable and demonstrate their preferences for how government ought to operate. Although we looked specifically at the vote of Latinos in Texas in this analysis, our aim was to make a broader statement about how the Exit Poll characterized the Latino vote in general. Our main concluding point is a note of caution: How we generalize the sources of support for a candidate has consequences for the specific policy agenda that officials craft and the laws they eventually enact.

In the context of explaining election results, accurate descriptions and understandings of electoral outcomes are required and the news media and press have a duty to report those outcomes accurately as possible. In our view, the continued reliance on exit poll figures by major media outlets is alarming. Our investigations, along with evidence from other scholars and analysts, show the exit poll estimates for Latinos are inflated. Journalists and news outlets should draw on multiple sources and weigh the quality of the evidence they cite in their reporting, instead of exclusively using the very survey that they fund as the truth. Of course, we as citizens cannot hold members of the press responsible for inaccuracy when we know they did their best. However, the case of the Exit Poll is different. Published research since at least 2006 highlights how the Exit Poll estimates of Latino preferences were unlikely to be accurate (Barreto, Guerra, Marks, Nuño, and Woods, 2006; Pedraza and Barreto 2008). Over the years, the methods to determine how various groups have voted in a society that privileges the secret ballot have improved considerably, yet the estimates have not changed very much. The Exit Poll consistently misses how the Latino community voted, and the press continues to hire Edison Research to conduct it. If this were only about poll accuracy, then perhaps this issue would not be a big deal. However, it is about more than that.

When Trump declared to supporters in Phoenix, Arizona, "I will win the Latino vote" and "They love me. I love them" (Gomez, 2016), such declarations are problematic for at least two reasons. First, it is an unfounded assurance that betrays decades of Latino election behavior patterns. Second, these statements are difficult to square with the numerous slights that Trump aimed at Latinos in general, and those of Mexican heritage in particular, throughout the campaign, many of which were deployed as part of his pitch on immigration policy. The problem, then, with the Exit Poll estimates of the Latino vote is that it creates an illusion of broad support among Latinos for the kinds of restrictive immigration policies that Trump champions. For instance, the real-world implications include the deployment of mass deportation forces that systematically target Latinos and a false impression that Latinos back such a course of action. If the 2016 election taught us only one thing, it is that accurate and reliable information is not necessary to operate in politics. On the other hand, democracy demands honest numbers.

References

Alcantara, Chris, Kevin Uhrmacher, and Emily Guskin. 2016. "Clinton and Trump's Demographic Tug of War." *Washington Post*, October 16.

Barreto, Matt, Fernando Guerra, Mara Marks, Stephen A. Nuño, and Nathan D. Woods. 2006. "Controversies in Exit Polling: Implementing a Racially Stratified Homogenous Precinct Approach." *PS: Political Science* 39 (3): 477–83.

Barreto, Matt, Tyler Reny, and Bryan Wilcox-Archuleta. 2017. "Survey Methodology and the Latina/o Vote: Why a Bilingual, Bicultural, Latino-Centered Approach Matters." *Aztlán: A Journal of Chicano Studies* 42 (2): 211–27.

Barreto, Matt, and Gary M. Segura. 2014. *Latino America: How America's Most Dynamic Population Is Poised to Transform the Politics of the Nation.* New York: PublicAffairs.

Bottemiller Evich, Helena. 2016. "Revenge of the Rural Voter." *Politico*, November 13.

Cadava, Geraldo L. 2016. "Rural Hispanic Voters—Like White Rural Voters—Shifted Toward Trump. Here's Why." *Washington Post*, November 17.

Collingwood, Loren, Justin Gross, and Francisco I. Pedraza. 2014. "A 'Decisive Voting Bloc' in 2012." In *Latino America: How America's Most Dynamic Population is Poised to Transform the Politics of the Nation,* edited by Matt Barreto and Gary M. Segura, 145–70. New York: Public Affairs.

De la Garza, Rodolfo O., Louis DeSipio, and David Leal. 2010. *Beyond the Barrio: Latinos in the 2004 Elections.* Notre Dame, IN: University of Notre Dame Press.

DeSipio, Louis. 1996. *Counting on the Latino Vote: Latinos as a New Electorate.* Charlottesville: University of Virginia Press.

Garcia, F. Chris, and Gabriel R. Sanchez. 2008. *Hispanics and the U.S. Political System.* Upper Saddle River, NJ: Pearson Prentice Hall.

Gimpel, James G., and Kimberley A. Karnes. 2006. "The Rural Side of the Urban-Rural Gap." *PS: Political Science and Politics* 39 (3): 467–72.

Gomez, Alan. 2016. "Another Election Surprise: Many Hispanics Backed Trump." *USA Today*, November 9.

Grofman, Bernard, and Samuel Merrill. 2004. "Ecological Regression and Ecological Inference." In *Ecological Inference: New Methodological Strategies,* edited by Gary King, Ori Rosen, and Martin Tanner, 123–43. New York: Cambridge University Press.

King, Gary. 1997. *A Solution to the Ecological Inference Problem: Reconstructing Individual Behavior from Aggregate Data.* Princeton: Princeton University Press.

King, Gary, Ori Rosen, and Martin Tanner. 2004. "Information in Ecological Inference: An Introduction." In *Ecological Inference: New Methodological Strategies*, edited by Gary King, Ori Rosen, and Martin Tanner, 1-12. New York: Cambridge University Press.

Kurtzleben, Danielle. 2016. "Rural Voters Played a Big Part in Helping Trump Defeat Clinton." *NPR*, November 14.

McKee, Seth C., and Jeremy M. Tiegen. 2009. "Probing the Reds and Blues: Sectionalism and Voter Location in the 2000 and 2004 U.S. Presidential Elections." *Political Geography* 28(8): 484-95.

Pedraza, Francisco I., and Matt Barreto. 2008. "Exit Polls and Ethnic Diversity: How to Improve Estimates and Reduce Bias Among Minority Voters." In *Election and Exit Polling*, edited by Wendy Alvey and Fritz Scheuren, 194-202. Hoboken, NJ: Wiley and Sons, Inc.

Pew Research Center. 2016. "Hispanic Population Growth and Dispersion Across U.S. Counties, 1980-2014." *Hispanic Trends*. http://www.pewhispanic.org.

Ramírez, Ricardo, and Romelia Solano. 2017. "How Geography Trumps Alternative Facts: Using State Context and Demography to Explain Presidential Vote Choice in 2017." *Aztlán: A Journal of Chicano Studies* 42 (2): 181-92.

Sanchez, Gabriel R. 2014. *Latinos and the 2012 Election: The New Face of the American Voter*. East Lansing: Michigan State University Press.

Sarlin, Benjy. 2016. "United States of Trump: An Inside Look at the Voters Who Took Over the Republican Party." *NBC News*, June 20.

Williams, Joseph P. 2016. "Penthouse Populist: Why the Rural Poor Love Donald Trump." *US News*, September 22.

Florida's Latino Electorate in the 2016 Election

Benjamin G. Bishin and Casey A. Klofstad

IN MANY WAYS FLORIDA MAY BE PERCEIVED AS AN OUTLIER IN THIS VOL-
ume. The state is isolated geographically from the U.S. border with Mexico,
arguably the "front line" of the immigration reform debate. Additionally,
Florida's Latino community is more conservative and identifies more
strongly with the Republican Party compared to Latinos in other states,
due mostly to the large number of Cuban Americans living there. This all
said, data from Latino Decisions, among other sources, show that the policy
concerns and vote preferences of Latinos in Florida were relatively similar
to those of Latinos living in other states in 2016.

The Changing Hispanic Population

There are few places where the power of the Hispanic voter has received
as much attention in the last two decades as in Florida.[1] The spectacle of
George Bush's razor-thin 537-vote victory in the state over Al Gore in 2000
combined with a large population of Republican-leaning Cuban American

voters has underscored the importance of the Hispanic vote in Florida. Like other places, however, Florida and its Hispanic population is undergoing dramatic demographic changes. The Hispanic population in Florida more than doubled between 2000 and 2015, growing from 2,297,944 to 4,962,905. Making this growth even more striking is that its rate was nearly double that of the state, which grew from 15,982,378 to 20,271,272 over this same period. Perhaps most staggering, the growth in the Hispanic population accounts for 62.2% of the state's population increases between 2000 and 2015 (U.S. Census Bureau 2000; U.S. Census Bureau 2015).

Given the group's large size and rapid growth, it is no surprise that Latinos once again played a major role in the outcome of the 2016 election. The 2016 campaign saw record Latino turnout and support for the Democratic candidate, Hillary Clinton (Leary 2016). Indeed, the increases in the early vote were so massive that initial projections were that Donald Trump would need record turnout among White voters in order to win. Despite losing the national popular vote, Trump set record gains among Republican suburban and rural voters, garnering 454,769 more votes in Florida than did Mitt Romney in 2012 and offsetting the votes the Clinton campaign banked in the heavily Latino southern and central urban centers of the state (Musgrave and Stucka 2016).

Florida politics is perhaps best known for the political power of its Cuban American community. Emigration following the Cuban Revolution on January 1, 1959, transformed the state, and in many ways is responsible for the creation of modern-day South Florida. In 1950, Dade County had 495,084 residents, but by 1970 the population had over doubled to 1,267,792 (U.S. Census 1950; Metropolitan Center 2007). While less pronounced in other parts of the state, these changes were broadly felt as Cuban immigrants exercised disproportionate power owing to their size and ideological homogeneity. By 2000, Cubans made up 4.9% of state residents, almost double any other Hispanic group, and just over one-third of Hispanics in the state (U.S. Census 2000).

Politically, Cubans Americans' disproportionate political power stems from several sources. Unlike immigrants from most other countries, Cubans only have to wait one year to obtain permanent residency in the

United States, and are not subject to quotas. According to the "wet foot, dry foot" policy, Cubans who make land in the United States are allowed to stay. Moreover, the bulk of early Cuban immigrants—those arriving prior to 1980—were political refugees who tended to be of higher socioeconomic status and ideologically homogeneous relative to other Hispanic immigrants, giving them greater influence (Bishin and Klofstad 2012). Finally, scholars have noted that many of these early Cubans who arrived in the United States at a time when the social welfare state was still well funded were able to take full advantage of a wide range of government programs designed to help those in need of assistance, whether with housing or with obtaining loans to start businesses (Eckstein 2009).

The size and influence of Florida's Cuban population continue even today. While the relative rate of growth of the Cuban population lags other Hispanic groups in the state, their population is still growing. In fact, more than half of Cubans in Florida today either came themselves or come from families who immigrated after the Mariel Boatlift of 1980, an important cultural marker scholars use to differentiate the more recent economic refugees from the earlier political refugees (Bishin and Klofstad 2012). By 2015, the Cuban population increased from 4.9% to 7.0% of a much larger state. Today, Cubans remain the single largest Hispanic group in the state and still hold disproportionate political power that, at times, has engendered antipathy from other Hispanic groups (Bishin, Kaufmann, and Stevens 2011).

In part because of the nature of the Cuban American diaspora, the politics of the group are complex. For decades, Cuban Americans have long been the Hispanic Republican voting bloc, owing to the GOP's staunch opposition to communism and Democrats' accommodations toward Fidel Castro's government. The growth in the Cuban population from post-Mariel economic refugees, who now significantly outnumber the pre-Mariel cohort, are much more liberal, and are more likely to identify with the Democratic Party, has led to a voting bloc whose votes are increasingly up for grabs (Bishin and Klofstad 2012; Klofstad 2015). Despite this growth, the Cuban American electorate has not fully reflected the power of the population primarily because obtaining citizenship can be expensive, and until just recently, U.S. immigration policy has not required them to obtain citizenship in order to live and work in the United States. Moreover, even those who are citizens may be harder to mobilize and less likely to vote, owing to their relatively lower socioeconomic status. On balance, the result of these trends is an electorate that is increasingly up for grabs. In 2012, the vote was sufficiently close that significant debate ensued about whether Barack Obama was the first Democrat to win the "Cuban vote" in Florida (Bishin 2012).

While the story of the Cuban diaspora is largely seen as the story of Hispanics in Florida, the last several elections have seen a small but growing recognition of a new challenge to Cuban hegemony. The size and proportion of the Puerto Rican population in Florida has grown dramatically, increasing from 409,953 in 2000 to 1,069,446 in 2015. Puerto Ricans now make up 5.3% of the state's population, a proportion greater than that of Cubans in 2000 (U.S. Census 2000; U.S. Census 2015). While the Puerto Rican population lags behind that of Cuban Americans, Puerto Ricans who migrate to the United States are already citizens and immediately eligible to vote. Therefore, they have the potential for political influence that outstrips their size (Klofstad 2015). By early 2015, the number of Puerto Ricans citizens of voting age was only about 10,000 fewer than the number of Cubans citizens of voting age (U.S. Census 2015). Consequently, with respect to the size of the population of eligible voters, the groups are on roughly equal terms numerically.[2]

This population growth has potentially profound political consequences for two reasons. First, unlike the Cuban American population that for years was ideologically conservative and Republican, the political preferences of these newer Puerto Rican migrants are less well-studied and seem, like so many other (im)migrants, to be less well developed and less hardened. The central implication is that both parties believe they can compete for these votes. Indeed, some political operatives credited Florida's Puerto Rican population as being crucial to George Bush's expanded vote share between 2000 and 2004 (e.g., Bishin and Klofstad 2009). Second, their size, rapid growth rate, and geographic concentration in the center of the state—as opposed to Cubans who are concentrated in the South—means

Figure 1. Percent of State Population by Group, 2000–2015.

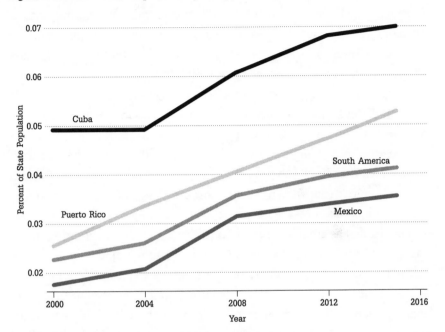

that politicians must increasingly tailor unique appeals to their interests. Despite this political impact, Puerto Ricans are seldom identified in many political surveys, including in the 2016 National Election Pool Exit Poll of Voters reported by CNN (see http://www.cnn.com/election/results/exit-polls/florida/president).

While politicians and a few scholars have begun to recognize the dramatic change and political implications of the growth of the Puerto Rican population, less well recognized is the dramatic growth of other Hispanic populations. In particular, the South American (836,208) and Mexican (723,190) populations in 2015 were larger than and comparable to, respectively, the size of the Cuban population (786,977) that was so crucial to George Bush's victory in 2000 (U.S. Census 2000; U.S. Census 2015). In figure 1, we plot the size of each of five key Hispanic subgroups as a percent of the state population from 2000 to 2015, the latest year for which data are available. These percentages are based on data from the U.S. Census American Community Survey in 2000, 2004, 2008, 2012, and 2015.

Several trends are apparent in figure 1. First, and most dramatically, the rise in the Hispanic share of the state population is staggering. In 2000, Hispanics were about one in seven Floridians. Today, they are about one in four. The increase is even more dramatic considering the large increase in the overall population of the state, which has grown by about 4 million during this period (e.g., based on the 2010 Census, Florida gained two seats in the U.S. House due to reapportionment). Simply put, Hispanics today are a larger share of a substantially larger population in Florida.

The second striking finding is the relative uniformity of the growth of the various Hispanics subgroups in the state. Excepting only those from Central America (not shown), the proportion of each of the major the Hispanic groups has increased across the board. The rates of increase vary somewhat across groups, however. In particular, we see a flattening in the rate of increase in the Cuban population and a more rapid increase in the size of the Puerto Rican and, to a lesser extent, Mexican populations.

Historically, changes in the Hispanic population have been slow to manifest politically. The population tends to have high levels of noncitizens who cannot participate at the polls. Earning citizenship takes time and money. In the case of more recent Cuban immigrants, for instance, their privileged immigration status expedites obtaining permanent residency, but does nothing to relieve the costs of citizenship (e.g., legal fees). Consequently, poorer and, as such, likely more liberal-leaning members of this group may not immediately apply for citizenship. These factors serve to delay or deny Hispanics the political power that typically comes with population increases.

We examine the changes in the distribution of registered voters in Florida between 2000 and 2016 using the race and ethnicity data made available by the Florida Division of Elections (http://dos.myflorida.com). Because the state did not collect data on the number of Hispanics prior to 2006, Hispanic registrants were forced to select from the categories of "other" or "unknown." Consequently, we impute the Hispanic voting population in these years.[3] The changing makeup of the state's electorate is depicted in figure 2.

The rapid growth of Florida's electorate is accompanied by a concomitant increase in its diversity. Figure 2 illustrates the size of the Black and

Figure 2. Percent of State Electorate by Group, 2000–2016.

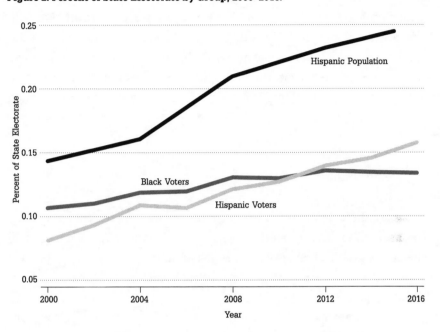

Hispanic electorates, as well as the Hispanic population that is included for reference. While Hispanics' (15.7%) share of the electorate lags behind their share of the population (24.5%), the rate of growth in the electorate may indicate that the gap between the population and the electorate is slightly increasing over time. While the gap grew from about 6 percentage points to 9 percentage points between 2000 and 2015, the rate of increase seems to be slowing as the Hispanic electorate is a larger percentage of the Hispanic population today (64.1%) than it was in 2000 (56.3%).

What are we to make of these dramatic increases in Florida's Hispanic population? To what extent do people from different ethnic backgrounds hold different political preferences? How has the changing constellation of Hispanics from different countries affected the overall political outlook of the state? To the extent that these differences foreshadow changing political preferences of the population, the changes can be quite important. As we noted in our discussion of the Cuban population, even changes in the makeup of members of a single ethnic group can lead to dramatic shifts in the opinions and behavior of group members (e.g., pre- vs. post-Mariel Cuban immigrants). Consequently, there is good reason to think that both the large increases in the overall population, and the changing distribution of the population of Hispanics with different ethnic origins, may lead to dramatic differences in the preferences and power of the community. Examining the political implications of these changes is the task to which we now turn.

Partisanship

What are the political implications of these demographic changes in the composition and size of Florida's Hispanic population? To what extent do the demographic changes we see translate to the electorate? As we have seen, one impediment to Hispanic political influence in the past has been the slippage between Hispanics' share of the population and their share of the electorate. As just one example, research shows that some subconstituencies, like post-Mariel Cuban immigrants, are less likely to apply for and obtain citizenship and, instead, maintain permanent resident status, thereby diminishing the political clout of their community (e.g., Bishin and Klofstad 2012). Similarly, Florida's Mexican community tends to be young with a median age of twenty-five, as compared with the Cuban community with a median age of 41.8, for instance, suggesting that some of the gap may decrease as these residents naturalize and age into the voting eligible population (U.S. Census 2012).

We begin to address this question by examining the partisanship of the electorate. Partisanship is perhaps the most fundamental political identity, but one that may take time to acquire (Cain, Kiewiet, and Uhlaner 1991). Consequently, the influx of immigrants to Florida suggests that for many, these partisan identities may be less strongly held or still developing. Nationally, Hispanics have become among the most staunchly and consistently Democratic constituencies, a trend that is only likely to increase, given the xenophobic and racist campaign platform espoused by the GOP 2016 nominee, Donald Trump. To examine the political consequences of Florida's

Table 1. Percent of Florida Hispanics Who Identify as Democratic by Origin or Heritage

Origin or heritage	Florida	Non-Florida	Difference
Cuba	36.5	50.1	13.6
Puerto Rico	72.7	78.7	16
Mexico	78.5	81	2.5
Central America	63.3	79.7	16.4
South America	73.6	70.7	−2.9
All	61.4	78.4	17

Source: Latino Decisions 2016 Election Eve Poll.

demographic shifts we estimate the percent of each group that identifies as Democratic by country of identification for Hispanic citizens residing in Florida, over eighteen, who responded to the Latino Decisions' 2016 National Latino Election Eve Poll. These results are presented in table 1.[4]

The data presented in table 1 evince several interesting results. First, consistent with the findings nationally, we see that, excepting Cubans, a majority of Florida Hispanic's identify as Democrats. We also see, however, that by a 17-percentage-point difference, Florida's Hispanics are less likely to identify as Democrats than are those from outside of Florida. This gap is likely driven by the large number of Cuban Americans in Florida and the lower rates of Democratic identification among Florida's Puerto Ricans and Central Americans. Indeed, we find that, excepting South Americans, the degree to which respondents identify as Democrats is lower for those members who reside in Florida than for those who reside elsewhere among every major group.

Given their recent growth, patterns among Puerto Ricans are particularly interesting. While a strong majority of Puerto Ricans identify as Democrats, they do so at a rate lower than those who reside outside of Florida. While Puerto Ricans in the northeastern United States have a reputation for being among the most liberal and steadfastly Democratic groups, Puerto Ricans in Florida, as we saw in figure 1, tend to be more recent immigrants. As a consequence, we might expect them to show lower levels of affiliation with the Democratic Party relative to those outside the state who have lived in the United States much longer (Cain, Kiewiet, and Uhlaner

1991). Closer examination of the Latino Decisions Election Eve data shows that only about 2.7% of Puerto Ricans in Florida identify as Independents. Taken together, these factors illustrate the increased power Puerto Ricans hold. With a voting-eligible population that now rivals the size of Cubans and affiliation with the Democratic Party that exceeds those seen among Cubans to the Republican Party, this group is transforming the landscape of Florida politics and gradually helping to turn it blue.

Cuban Americans' declining commitment to the Republican Party in Florida has been widely reported by journalists and pundits. While studies of the 2012 election debate whether a majority of Florida's Cubans voted to re-elect Barack Obama, all agreed the community was closely split (Caputo 2012). While growing, the proportion of the Cuban American electorate that identifies as Democratic remains relatively small. The Latino Decisions Election Eve data, however, raise a flag of caution, as about 58.9% of Cubans in Florida still identify as Republicans while only about 4% identify as Independent (table 1). How can we reconcile the data with the demographic trends and 2012 election results?

It is important to keep in mind that Cubans' move toward the Democratic Party is driven by the influx of more recent, post-Mariel immigrants and their children who tend to come from lower socioeconomic status backgrounds than those from families who have been in the United States longer. As a consequence, they are somewhat underrepresented in the electorate, relative to the population as a whole, where they now constitute a majority (Bishin and Klofstad 2012). This implies that, to the extent that Cubans are increasingly voting Democratic, at least some are crossing traditional party lines to do so.

Perhaps the most striking result is the strength of attachment South Americans and Mexican Americans have with the Democratic Party. While Mexicans living in Florida show much lower levels of attachment to Democrats than do those living outside the state, their absolute levels of support are still very high. Moreover, when one considers that these groups, along with Puerto Ricans, represent the fastest-growing Hispanic groups in the state, they portend a rapidly growing, Democratic influence on Florida politics. Further, the evolution of the Cuban community from solidly red to purple, combined with its lower rates of growth relative to these other groups, further buttresses this transition.

Policy Preferences

Perhaps no bromide is more widely espoused in American politics than "It's the economy stupid." Behind every cliché, however, is at least some grain of truth, and so it is with respect to Florida Hispanics' view of which issues are most important. Similar to the results seen in 2012 (Klofstad 2015), the 2016 Latino Decisions Election Eve Poll shows that almost one in three (30.9%) Hispanics in Florida named the economy as the most important issue facing the Hispanic/Latino community that the Congress and the President should address. The next most important issues was immigration (26.1%), after which there was a significant drop-off to stopping Donald Trump (5.1%), followed by terrorism (4.2%) and discrimination against immigrants and Latinos (4.2%).

These findings nicely reflect contemporary political cleavages. At first glance, the importance placed on the economy might be seen as surprising, given that at the time of the poll (early November 2016), the U.S. economy was coming out of a record-setting seventy-second consecutive month of job growth (September 2016), leading to an unemployment rate of 4.9%, identical to that in the state of Florida, with improving wage growth and labor participation rates (Mitchell 2016; Bureau of Labor Statistics 2017). On the other hand, the primary campaigns and the Republican National Convention emphasized the weakness in the U.S. economy, a view that was not unfounded, as studies show that the economic gains disproportionately went to the well-educated and those living in one of several dozen metropolitan areas across the United States (Mitchell 2016). And while four of the twenty most rapidly growing counties for new company formation in the United States were in Florida, only one of these (Miami-Dade County) rated among the fastest-growing counties for employment growth (Economic Innovation Group 2016). In short, smaller cities and especially rural areas are still struggling following the Great Recession.

Table 2. Percent of Hispanics Identifying the Issue as Most Important

Issue	Origin or heritage				Party identification	
	Cuba	Puerto Rico	South America	Mexico	Democrat	Republican
Economy	36.9	32.3	18.8	27.9	26.4	36.9
Immigration	22.2	20.8	38.1	36.6	31	20.8
Stopping Trump	2.2	5.4	5.5	10.8	8.6	0.3
Terrorism	5.5	2.9	3	4.4	1.7	8.3

Source: Latino Decisions 2016 Election Eve Poll.

At the same time, the importance placed on the issues of immigration seems especially apt, given the changing background of Florida's Hispanic population. Immigration is especially interesting in Florida since the issue affects the two largest Hispanic groups, Cuban Americans and Puerto Ricans, to a much lesser degree than it does Mexicans and Central and South Americans. Cubans enjoy a privileged status, enjoying an expedited path to permanent residency, and are not subject to immigration quotas in the same way that other immigrant groups are. Similarly, Puerto Ricans hold American citizenship and thus are not subject to restrictions on immigration. Despite this, Cubans have historically been more progressive on questions of immigration than on other issues, perhaps because of the recency of the immigrant experience for so many of them (Bishin and Klofstad 2012). For other groups, however, questions of immigration affect themselves and their family members.

To what extent do these ethnic backgrounds affect how members of these groups view which issues are most important? In table 2, we present the proportion of each group that identifies each of the four issues most frequently mentioned as "most important."

The results of table 2 allow for comparison of group attitudes across Florida's Hispanic groups. By a substantial margin, Cubans (36.9%) identify the economy as the most important issue relative to other groups. In contrast, fewer South Americans rate it as highly, at 18.8%, while Puerto Ricans and Mexicans rate it roughly in between. These results are somewhat puzzling in that the Cuban population is concentrated in the southern part of the state, which has seen by far the most growth, whereas Puerto Ricans and Mexicans tend to be concentrated in the central part of the state where growth has been more tepid.

One explanation for this might lie in the partisan cues received by these groups. Decades of research on public opinion show that voters typically take political cues from prominent party elites both on which positions to take and on how important those issues are (Zaller 1992). Consequently, these differences might be a function of partisanship. Specifically, if the importance placed on the economy is driven by party elites, then we should see a disproportionate emphasis of this issue by Republicans, rather than Democrats. Such an expectation would be consistent with the presentation of group preferences described earlier since Cubans are the most Republican group.

To investigate this possibility, we tabulated the responses to the most important issue question by respondent's partisan identification. The results, presented in the rightmost columns of table 2, are consistent with this elite-driven view. Republican respondents were 10 percentage points more likely than Democrats to identify the economy as the most important issue. Interestingly, they were also 10 percentage points less likely to mention immigration as most important. Consistent with the notion that Hispanics saw the issues through partisan cues, hardly any Republicans saw stopping Trump as important (0.3%), instead placing emphasis on stopping terrorism (8.6%). Conversely, Democrats placed substantial importance on stopping Trump (8.3%) and little emphasis on stopping terrorism (1.7%).

Campaign Outreach to Florida's Latino Community

How did the campaigns respond to this changing community in Florida in 2016? In 2012, both Democrats and Republicans made extensive outreach efforts to Latinos in Florida, including heavy use of Spanish-language advertising (Klofstad 2015). Arguably one of the more memorable of these advertisements was actually a Republican spot titled "Nosotros" ("Us"), a Spanish-language television advertisement narrated by GOP Governor Mitt

Romney's son, Craig, who became fluent in Spanish during his time as a Mormon missionary in Chile (Killingsworth 2012; Llorente 2012).

In 2016, however, the GOP appeared to have made mobilizing Latino voters in Florida a lower priority. Data from the Latino Decisions Election Eve Poll show that 43% of Latinos in Florida were contacted by a campaign, political party, or community organization to vote or to register to vote, higher than the national average of 35%, and an increase from 37% in the 2012 Latino Decisions Election Eve Survey. This said, among those 43% who were contacted during the 2016 election, 63% were contacted by Democratic candidates or the Democratic Party, while only 46% reported having been contacted by Republican candidates or the Republican Party, a sizeable gap of 17 percentage points. In contrast, the 2012 Latino Decisions Election Eve Poll showed that 53% of Latinos in Florida were contacted by Democrats compared to 51% by Republicans, a much smaller gap of only 2 percentage points. In line with this increasing gap in outreach between the Democratic and Republican Parties to Florida's Latino voters, the Trump campaign did not release any Spanish-language advertising anywhere in the United States until two weeks before Election Day (Fox News Latino 2016). The advertisement depicted Secretary Clinton as a dog (Fox News Latino 2016).

How were these outreach efforts by both sides of the presidential campaign perceived by Florida's Latino community in 2016, and how do these perceptions compare to how the campaigns were viewed in 2012? As seen in table 3, the efforts of the Obama campaign were perceived far more favorably than those of the Romney campaign in 2012 (also see Klofstad 2015). In total, 62% of respondents reported that Obama "truly cares" about Latinos, compared to only 27% saying the same about Romney. Given GOP presidential candidate Trump's strong anti-immigrant and racist rhetoric during the campaign, we anticipated that this perception gap between the parties would increase in 2016. Our expectations were reflected in our comparison of the 2012 and 2016 Latino Decisions Election Eve Survey data (table 3). Looking first at perceptions of the Romney and Trump campaigns, the results in table 3 show that Trump was perceived far less favorably than Romney, with half of respondents reporting that Trump was "hostile" toward Latinos/Hispanics. The Clinton camp was perceived far more favorably, with 58% of

Table 3. Florida Latinos' Opinions on the 2012 and 2016 Presidential Campaigns.

View on campaign	Republican candidates		Democratic candidates	
	Romney (2012)	Trump (2016)	Obama (2012)	Clinton (2016)
"Truly cares"	27%	20%	62%	58%
"Didn't care too much"	57%	26%	35%	33%
"Was hostile"	16%	49%	3%	6%

Source: Latino Decisions 2016 Election Eve Poll; ImpreMedia/Latino Decisions 2012 Election Eve Poll.

respondents reporting that Secretary Clinton "truly cares" about Latinos, and only 6% reporting that she was "hostile" to Florida's Latino community. In comparing the results in the last two columns of table 3, Clinton's numbers were comparable to the perceptions of the Obama campaign in 2012, though Clinton was perceived somewhat less favorably.

Vote Choice

How did Florida's Latino community cast their ballots for president in 2016, and how do these figures compare to the results of the 2012 election? Given Trump's strong anti-immigrant and racist rhetoric during the campaign, we anticipated that the community would be more supportive of Secretary Clinton in 2016 than they were of President Obama in 2012 in response to this overt threat. Data from the 2012 Latino Decisions Election Eve Poll show that 58% of Latinos in Florida cast their vote to re-elect President Obama (also see Klofstad 2015). In line with our expectation, the 2016 Latino Decisions Election Eve Poll shows that 67% of Florida's Latinos cast their ballot for Secretary Clinton, an increase of 9 percentage points over Obama's performance in 2012. It is important to note, however, that these findings contradict exit poll results. Consistent with the work of others in this volume, we find that the exit poll had numbers much different than ours in Florida. For example, citing data from the 2016 National Election Pool Exit Poll, the Pew Research Center claims that the Latino vote in Florida decreased from 71% for Obama in 2012 to 65% for Clinton in 2016 (Krogstad and Lopez 2016).

Table 4. Presidential Vote Choice by Origin or Heritage and State

Vote choice	Origin or heritage of Latinos in Florida			State	
	Cuba	Puerto Rico	Other	Florida Vote	National Vote
Clinton	47%	72%	76%	67%	79%
Trump	52%	26%	21%	31%	18%

Source: Latino Decisions 2016 Election Eve Poll.

In addition to comparing Florida's Latino vote across time we also wanted to examine how the Latino vote in Florida in 2016 varied by country of origin/heritage and how it compared to that of Latinos in other states (table 4). Looking first at country of origin/heritage in the left-hand side of table 4, data from the 2016 Latino Decisions Election Eve Poll show that Cuban American support for GOP candidate Donald Trump was much higher compared to his support among Latino voters with roots in Puerto Rico or other countries in line with findings presented earlier on partisan identification (table 1). This said, however, their support for Trump in 2016 at 52% was much lower than their support for Romney in 2012 at 64% (as measured in the 2012 Latino Decisions election eve poll), in line with our earlier discussion how the Cuban American voter base in Florida is evolving over time to the benefit of the Democratic Party.

With regard to comparing Florida's Latino vote to the national Latino vote, the right-hand side of table 4 shows that support for Secretary Clinton was weaker in Florida. This is due, no doubt, as we mentioned earlier, to the sizeable and more Republican-leaning Cuban American population in the state. That said, a sizeable majority of Florida's Latino voters cast their ballot for Clinton, in line with Latinos in the rest of the nation.

The Future of Presidential Politics in Florida

The outcome of the 2016 presidential election shocked the world, and the state of Florida was arguably at the epicenter of Mr. Trump's unexpected victory, but what does the future portend for presidential politics in the state, and what role will the growing Latino electorate play in that future? If Latinos continue to increase their presence at the polls in Florida, data from the 2016 Latino Decisions Election Eve Poll paint a bleak picture for the GOP in the state. In total, 39% of Latinos in Florida reported that the "Republican Party has now become so anti-Latino and anti-immigrant that it would be hard for me to ever consider supporting them in the future." A comparable number, 33%, said they would consider supporting GOP candidates in the future if the party would "help pass immigration reform with a path to citizenship." Given the rhetoric of the 2016 campaign, GOP support for this type of comprehensive immigration reform seems very unlikely, if not impossible. As such, taken together, the 2016 Latino Decisions Election Eve data show that a massive majority of Latinos in Florida (72%) have written off the Republican Party. This is the case even if we account for the sizeable right-leaning, Cuban American population in the state.

Conclusion

In words and in actions, the Republican Party appears to have abandoned any desire to persuade or mobilize Latino voters in Florida in 2016. As evidenced by the outcome of the historic 2016 election, Mr. Trump did not need the support of Florida's Latino community to win the state's twenty-nine electoral votes and the presidency. Given the demographic and attitudinal changes we described in this chapter, however, we expect that this will no longer be the case in future presidential elections. To wit, our analysis suggests that the Republican Party needs to make legitimate inroads with Latino voters in Florida, and the rest of the nation as well, in order to remain viable.

Notes

1. We recognize the important differences between the terms Hispanic and Latino. For semantic ease, we use the term Hispanic and Latino interchangeably throughout while recognizing that surveys conducted in Florida by Latino Decisions show that respondents in Florida prefer the term Hispanic.

2. We also note that after Hurricane Katrina in 2005, migration from Puerto Rico increased by 12%. The disaster of Hurricane Maria in 2017 may lead to even more migration from the island to the United States (see Matthews 2017).

3. We do this by calculating the percentage of Hispanics in those years for which the state collected data on Hispanics, "other," and "unknown" categories, and then extrapolate from the trend in percentages seen in those years as the Hispanic population was growing during this period. More specifically, we estimate that Hispanics were 70% of the population of Hispanics, other, and unknown during this period. We use a similar process to estimate the "other" category for 2006.

4. We note that the table does not reflect the views of all Hispanics in Florida, as it omits those from countries not included in these regions (e.g., Dominican Republic and Spain and those who do not identify with a particular country). We code those who answer independent but see themselves as closer to one party with members of that party. All analyses from this survey employ weights provided by Latino Decisions.

References

Bishin, Benjamin G. 2012. "Did Little Havana Just Go Blue?" *Monkey Cage* (blog), *Washington Post*, November 11. http://themonkeycage.org.

Bishin, Benjamin G., Karen M. Kaufmann, and Daniel P. Stevens. 2011. "Turf Wars: Local Context and Latino Political Development." *Urban Affairs Review* 48 (1): 111-37.

Bishin, Benjamin G., and Casey A. Klofstad. 2009. "Deceit, Diversity, or Mobilization: Intra-ethnic Diversity and Changing Patterns Florida's Hispanic Vote." *Social Science Journal* 46: 571-83.

———. 2012. "The Political Incorporation of Cuban Americans: Why Won't Little Havana Turn Blue?" *Political Research Quarterly* 65: 588-601.

Bureau of Labor Statistics. 2017. "Local Area Unemployment Statistics." September 2016. https://data.bls.gov.

Cain, Bruce E., D. Roderick Kiewiet, and Carole J. Uhlaner. 1991. "The Acquisition of Partisanship by Latinos and Asian Americans." *American Journal of Political Science* 35: 390-422.

Caputo, Marc. 2012. "Obama Got Big Share of Cuban American Vote, Won Among Other Hispanics in Florida." *Miami Herald*, November 8.

Carpenter, Alan, and Carl Provorse. 1996. *The World Almanac of the U.S.A.* Mahwah,

NJ: World Almanac Books.

Economic Innovation Group. 2016. "The New Map of Economic Growth and Recovery." https://eig.org/recoverymap.

Eckstein, Susan Eva. 2009. *The Immigrant Divide: How Cuban Americans Changed the US and Their Homeland.* New York: Routledge.

Fox News Latino. 2016. "Pro Donald Trump PAC Releases Candidate's First Spanish-Language Ads." http://latino.foxnews.com/latino.

Killingsworth, Sylvia. 2012. "Can Romney Speak Spanish?" *New Yorker,* January 14.

Klofstad, Casey A. 2015. "Florida's Latino Electorate in the 2012 Election." In *Latinos and the 2012 Election: The New Face of the American Voter,* edited by G. R. Sanchez, 167–80. East Lansing: Michigan State University Press.

Krogstad, J. M., and M. H. Lopez. 2016. "Hillary Clinton Wins Latino Vote, But Falls Below 2012 Support for Obama." http://www.pewresearch.org.

Leary, Alex. 2016. "Hispanics Voting in Record Numbers in Florida, Other States, Boosting Hillary Clinton." *Tampa Bay Times,* November 6. http://www.miamiherald.com.

Llorente, Elizabeth. 2012. "New Romney Ad in Florida Kicks Race for Latino Vote into High Gear." *Fox News Latino,* January 11. latino.foxnews.com.

Matthews, Dylan. 2017. "What the Hurricane Maria Migration Will Do to Puerto Rico—and the US." *Vox.com,* October 5.

Metropolitan Center. 2007. "Thirty Year Retrospective: The Status of the Black Community in Miami Dade County." https://www.miamidade.gov.

Mitchell, Josh. 2016. "Modest U.S. Jobs Growth Keeps Labor Market Steady." *Wall Street Journal,* October 7.

Musgrave, Jane, and Mike Stucka. 2016. "Trump's Rick Scott Strategy Beat Clinton's Obama Strategy in Florida." *Palm Beach Post,* November 9.

U.S. Census Bureau. 1950. Number of Inhabitants; Florida. Table 4. Population of Urban Places of 10,000 or More from Earliest Census to 1950. https://www2.census.gov/prod2/decennial/documents/23761117v1ch05.pdf.

———. American Community Survey, 2000 Public Use Micro Sample Data American Community Survey 1-Year Estimates.

———. 2008. American Community Survey, 2008 American Community Survey 1-Year Estimates, Table B03001 https://factfinder.census.gov.

———. 2012. American Community Survey, 2012 American Community Survey 1-Year Estimates, Table B03001 https://factfinder.census.gov.

————. 2015. American Community Survey, 2015 American Community Survey 1-Year Estimates, Table B03001 https://factfinder.census.gov.

Zaller, John R. 1992. *The Nature and Origins of Mass Opinion*. Cambridge: Cambridge University Press.

Demography Realized?

The 2016 Latino Vote in Nevada

David F. Damore

ON ELECTION NIGHT, AS IT BECAME CLEAR THAT DONALD TRUMP WOULD be elected the next president of the United States and that the Republicans would maintain control of both chambers of Congress, Nevada was perhaps the lone Democratic bright spot. Not only did Hillary Clinton win the Silver State's six Electoral College votes, but also Democrat Catherine Cortez Masto was elected to replace retiring Senate Minority Leader Harry Reid to become the first Latina to serve in that body. Further down the ballot, in a cycle when the Democrats gained just six House seats nationally, two of those were in Nevada, including the election of the state's first Latino House member, Ruben Kihuen. Democrats also regained majority control of both houses of the Nevada Legislature.

As I argue here, the success of Nevada Democrats in what was an otherwise disappointing cycle for the party resulted from contextual and organizational factors that are in many ways unique to Nevada. Nevada's highly diverse and concentrated population facilitated coordination among the state's politically engaged labor unions, its budding progressive infrastructure, and the "Reid Machine" (the nickname for the Nevada Democratic

Party and allied interests) to register and turn out voters in the urban core of Clark County in southern Nevada. Indeed, it was the Democrats' outsized margins in the Latino-heavy precincts of East Las Vegas that ensured many of the party's victories.

Nevada's Growth and Its Political Consequence

In the last thirty years Nevada has undergone an unprecedented transformation. Once demographically homogeneous and rurally oriented, domestic and foreign migration have reshaped Nevada into the fourth most urbanized state in the country, and the state is now majority minority. During the 1990s and the 2000s, no state grew faster. Nevada's population increased from 1.22 million in 1990 to 2.02 million in 2000 to 2.71 million in 2010. After the 2000 and 2010 Censuses Nevada gained House seats and Electoral College votes. By 2016, more than 2.9 million people called Nevada home.

Today, nearly nine out of ten Nevadans live in just two counties: Washoe County in northern Nevada, where Reno is located, is home to roughly 16% of the state's population, while nearly three out of four Nevada residents live in Clark County in southern Nevada. Clark County also contains three of the state's four most populous cities—Las Vegas, Henderson, and North Las Vegas. By comparison, the state's fifteen sparsely populated counties have a combined population of less than 320,000 people.

Both demographically and politically, Clark County is distinct from the rest of Nevada. The U.S. Census reports that Clark's population is home to 80% of the state's Latino population (Latinos constitute 28.1% of all Nevadans), 93% of the African American population (who comprise 9.3% of Nevada's population), and 87% of the state's Asian American population (who constitute 8.5% of Nevada's population). While more than one-fifth of the residents in Washoe and the rural counties are Latino, there are very few African Americans and Asian Americans living in these spaces, and as a consequence, outside of Clark County, the rest of Nevada is predominantly White.

Given the outsized support for Democrats from minority voters, Clark

County is the only county in Nevada where Democrats have a registration advantage. At the close of registration for the 2016 election, the Democrats' statewide registration advantage over the GOP was around 89,0000, but in Clark it was more than 140,000. In contrast, the Republicans have the registration advantage in every other county, and nonpartisans and those registering with minor parties constitute more than a quarter of all registered voters in Nevada.

Yet despite Clark County's demographic might, it underperforms relative to the rest of the state in terms of voter registration and turnout. As a consequence, Washoe and rural voters typically exert greater electoral influence relative to their populations owing to their higher registration and turnout rates. The implications of these regional demographic and political differences are at least threefold.

First, Nevada's electorate tends to be much less diverse, more conservative, and more Republican than the state's demographics might suggest. This difference was particularly evident in the 2014 midterm elections. Turnout in Clark County among registered voters declined from 81% in 2012 to 41%, resulting in rural voters accounting for 17% of the electorate despite constituting 11% of the population. As a consequence, the GOP swept the state's six constitutional offices and Republicans took control of both chambers of the statehouse. It was the first time the Republicans had unified control of state government since 1929.

Second, Republicans' outsized support in the rural counties means that the GOP begins statewide races with a reliable base from which to build. From there, Republican candidates attempt to cut into the Democrats' margins in Clark County by targeting voters in the inner and outer suburbs ringing the Las Vegas Valley, winning the nonpartisan voter, and carrying Washoe County by a significant margin. In 2000 and 2004 George W. Bush successfully implemented this strategy on his way to a pair of 30,000-vote victories. For Democrats the strategy is the opposite. Democrats seek to run up large margins in Clark County to offset the party's weaknesses in the rural counties and keep it close or even eke out a win in Washoe. President Obama was able to do this in 2008 and 2012, as was Harry Reid in his 2010 reelection to the U.S. Senate.

Third, although Nevada's changing demography and population growth comprise the primary reason why the state leans Democratic, the party has yet to fully realize its demographic advantages, in large part because Nevadans tends to participate in elections at a rate below the national average (see Damore 2017). As a consequence, Nevada continues to be a battleground that has been targeted by both parties in recent presidential elections. Analyzing data from the November Current Population Survey for the 1994-2014 elections, Damore and Gill (2015) find that relative to the age eligible voting population, on average, Latinos under vote by 3.6 percentage points; Asian Americans under vote by 1.5 percentage points; and African Americans under vote by 1 percentage point.[1] In contrast, Whites over vote relative to the White age-eligible population by more than 6 percentage points. Put differently, given the partisan voting patterns of these different racial and ethnic groups, if non-White voters in Nevada voted at the same level as Whites, Nevada would no longer be a swing state.

Front and Center in 2016

Nevada was prominently featured throughout the 2016 election cycle. In the spring of 2015, Hillary Clinton used a roundtable discussion at a Las Vegas high school with local immigrant activists to establish her immigration priorities. President Obama also used a Las Vegas high school as the backdrop for his 2012 DACA (Deferred Action for Childhood Arrivals) and 2014 DAPA (Deferred Action for Parents of Americans and Lawful Permanent Residents) announcements. In the fall of 2015, both parties' presidential candidates held debates in Las Vegas, and in early February the Nevada caucuses were some of the first presidential delegate allocating events of the cycle. The University of Nevada, Las Vegas (UNLV) hosted the last general election debate between Hillary Clinton and Donald Trump.

In addition to being a presidential battleground, Nevada featured one of the country's most competitive U.S. Senate elections, between Democrat Catherine Cortez Masto and Republican Joe Heck to replace Harry Reid, and two of the state's four House races (the Third and Fourth Districts) were hotly contested. According to OpenSecrets, the Third District was the top targeted race by outside groups ($16.7 million in total outside spending) and the Fourth was not far behind, ranking seventh ($11.2 million). However, these totals pale in comparison to the $91 million in outside spending in the Senate election. In addition, the House and Senate candidates spent an additional $38 million on their campaigns.

In short, while the campaign between Clinton and Trump dominated the state's political landscape, there was plenty at stake in Nevada for both parties, and as a consequence, Nevada received significant national and international media attention. Much of this coverage focused on two storylines: how issues such as health care, jobs and the economy, and immigration were playing in a competitive electoral environment, and how the state's diversifying electorate was likely to affect electoral outcomes. The media crush also provided opportunities for savvy political operators to garner significant attention.

No entity did a more effective job capturing media attention than Culinary Workers United 226, an affiliate of UNITE HERE. A long-time force in Nevada politics, the private-sector union represents around 57,000 workers in the state's gaming and hospitality sector. The union is heavily female and more than half of its members are Latino (Barry 2016). During the cycle the union worked with other progressive organizations to promote citizenship among the state's large immigrant population (one in five Nevadans is foreign born and the state has the largest share of undocumented immigrants in the country). In the fall, the union partnered with Democratic and progressive groups to coordinate voter registration drives that then gave way to get out the vote (GOTV) efforts targeting voters in the core of Las Vegas who were either newly registered or sat out the 2014 election (Damore 2017).

Although the union often works to elect Democrats, Culinary's support and its accompanying political muscle are not a given. In the 2008, Culinary endorsed Barack Obama, but in 2016 Culinary did not endorse either Clinton or Bernie Sanders despite significant lobbying by both candidates (Nagourney 2016), preferring instead to save its resources for the general election and to concentrate on contract negotiations.[2] The union was also a vocal critic of the Affordable Care Act's "Cadillac tax," an excise tax assessed on premium employer-provided health care plans that the union's members would be subject to starting in 2020. During the 2014 cycle, the union was quiet after helping to elect former Culinary Training Academy (a training facility for hospitality workers supported by the union and Las Vegas Strip properties) executive Steven Horsford to the then newly created Fourth House District. Horsford would lose the seat in 2014 despite a substantial Democratic registration advantage in the district.

Still, any differences that Culinary had with the Democrats were mild in comparison to its ongoing fight with Republican presidential nominee Donald Trump. After workers at Trump International Hotel in Las Vegas had voted to unionize, the property's management refused to negotiate a contract with the Culinary Union. In response, the union members staged protests in front of the hotel whenever a major political event occurred in the city that invariably received ample coverage by visiting journalists. At a rally before the October 2015 Democratic presidential candidate debate in Las Vegas, Hillary Clinton made an appearance and spoke briefly to the crowd.

But perhaps the union's greatest media coup occurred during the week of the last presidential debate, held at UNLV, when more than 5,000 journalists descended on the city. Playing off of a Trump surrogate's claim that expanding Latino culture would result in "a taco truck on every corner," the union, along with a host of progressive and immigration advocacy groups including American Bridge, America's Voice, Latino Victory Project, Next Gen Climate Nevada, the Nevada State AFL-CIO, the Progressive Leadership Alliance of Nevada Action Fund, and Mi Familia Vota, registered voters at taco trucks throughout the Las Vegas Valley (Latimer 2016). The union also staged a wall of taco trucks in front of Trump's Las Vegas property to protest the GOP nominee's refusal to negotiate with the union and to put a human face on the communities that Trump was quick to vilify and that had the most to lose if Trump's policies were implemented.

When it came to the presidential election, the union's signage and T-shirts focused on defeating Trump as opposed to electing Clinton. In contrast, Culinary gave full-throttle support for electing the first Latina to the U.S. Senate, Democrat Catherine Cortez Masto, and electing Nevada's first Latino member of the House of Representatives, Democrat Ruben Kihuen (Kihuen's mother is a housekeeper at the MGM Grand and a longtime Culinary member). After Kihuen's victory, the Culinary Union's political director, Yvanna Cancela, was appointed to fill the remainder of Kihuen's term in the Nevada State Senate.

The galvanizing presence of organized labor and the emergence of a progressive political infrastructure are made possible by the nature of the Nevada's economy and its dense and diverse population. These features of the state's political landscape provide the grist underlying the state's Democrats potential. However, the entity most responsible for realizing this potential is the "Reid Machine"—the personal political organization of the state's dominant political figure, Harry Reid. Over the last dozen years, under the guidance of Rebecca Lambe, Reid built the state Democratic Party into a political force just at the moment that Nevada's electorate began diversifying and the state was emerging as a presidential battleground in both the general and primary elections. Keys to the Reid Machine's success are mobilizing the previously untapped Latino electorate, recruiting Latino candidates for state legislative offices, and using Reid's clout in the U.S. Senate and his close relationship with President Obama to make comprehensive immigration reform a party priority.

At the start of the 2000s, Nevada was evenly divided in terms of voter registration, but the Republicans won most, if not all, of the competitive statewide races. Ever since the 2008 Nevada Democratic caucuses, the Democrats maintained a substantial organizational and registration advantage that was critical to Reid's 2010 reelection and Obama's 2008 and 2012 victories in the state. Yet even in those cycles, the Democrats' wins were limited. The GOP won the governorship in 2010, the U.S. Senate election in 2012, and the competitive Third House District in 2010 and 2012 (see Damore 2011a, 2011b, 2015). Moreover, with Reid's retirement, it is unclear what will become of the state party organization. To wit, the primary election for the Fourth District was the first seriously contested Democratic primary in the state in a decade or more. To ensure Kihuen's victory over Lucy Flores, a former Assemblywoman, lieutenant gubernatorial candidate, and vocal Bernie Sanders supporter, necessitated intervention by Reid and Culinary.

There was also concern that there was much less enthusiasm in Nevada for Clinton as compared to for Obama in 2008 and 2012 and that this, in turn, would lead to a decline in participation. To compensate, the Democrats and allied groups not only poured resources into voter registration and GOTV efforts, but also blitzed the state with an onslaught of English- and Spanish-language radio, television, and digital advertisements, and organized a series of high-profile rallies in Las Vegas and Reno featuring entertainers such as Katy Perry and Los Tigres del Norte and national Democratic figures including President Obama, Bernie Sanders, Elizabeth Warren, and Cory Booker.

The party's organizational advantage also allowed it to refine its outreach efforts over the course of Nevada's two weeks of early voting to ensure that its voters got to the polls. On the last night of early voting, polling locations in the heavily Latino precincts of East Las Vegas were kept open for hours after their scheduled closing time to accommodate the flood of voters. On Election Day, mariachi bands escorted voters to polling locations. Consistent with the Democrats' need to motivate strong turnout among Latinos, the Latino Decisions 2016 Election Eve Poll for Nevada reported that 71% of Latino voters reported being contacted by Democratic operatives and 45% reported being contacted by representatives from community organizations. In contrast, just 31% reported similar outreach efforts by the GOP.

Thus, while the Democrats did everything possible to position the party for victory, the same could not be said for the GOP. Once again, the dysfunctional Nevada Republican Party (Damore 2011b, 2015) was plagued by infighting between its activist and establishment wings, which was further heightened by Trump's presence (see Damore 2017). Moreover, the Republican presidential nominee's decision to eschew investing in GOTV and the inability of the state party to pick up the slack hurt not only Trump's prospects in Nevada, but those of down-ticket Republicans who were forced to rely on the Koch-brothers-backed Americans for Prosperity for canvassing. Just prior to Election Day, long-time Trump confidant Roger Stone offered a candid assessment of the GOP's effort in Nevada by stating that "Nevada is problematic ... Frankly, Trump has run one of the worst campaigns in political history in the state" (Concha 2016). In the end, both the presidential and the U.S. Senate elections were decided by fewer than 30,000 votes.

Figure 1. Issue Priorities of Latino Voters in Nevada, 2016

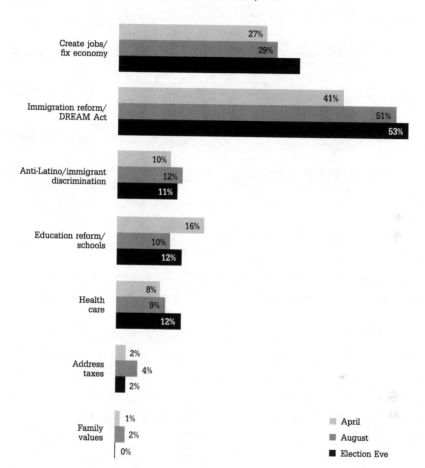

Source: America's Voice/Latino Decisions 2016 3-State Battleground (April) and National Battleground State Polls (August); Latino Decisions 2016 Election Eve Poll.

Contours of the Latino Vote in Nevada

Throughout 2016 the issue priorities of Latino voters in Nevada were quite stable. Figure 1 summarizes the responses to an open-ended question from the America's Voice/Latino Decisions 2016 National and Battleground State Poll (August), the America's Voice/Latino Decisions 2016 3-State Battleground Survey (April), and the Latino Decisions 2016 Election Eve Poll

Figure 2. Perceptions of Presidential Candidates and Political Parties Toward the Latino Community, 2016

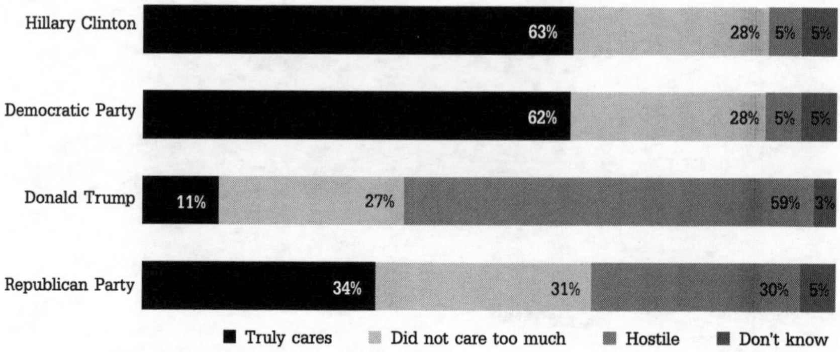

	Truly cares	Did not care too much	Hostile	Don't know
Hillary Clinton	63%	28%	5%	5%
Democratic Party	62%	28%	5%	5%
Donald Trump	11%	27%	59%	3%
Republican Party	34%	31%	30%	5%

Source: Latino Decisions 2016 Election Eve Poll.

asking respondents what they thought was the most important issue facing the Latino community that should be addressed by Congress and the president.

As the figure makes clear, immigration was the top-ranked priority, followed by jobs and the economy, in all three surveys. Also ranking highly were education reform and health care—two perennial issues in Nevada, given the state's underperforming educational institutions and its limited health care infrastructure. Republican staples such as tax reform and family values had little to no resonance. Interestingly, all three surveys found significant numbers of respondents offering anti-Latino and immigrant discrimination as an issue priority, and as the Election Eve data in figure 2 indicate, there was little doubt among the state's Latino voters who was responsible for these perceptions.

Specifically, the data in figure 2 summarize the degree to which the presidential candidates and the parties were perceived as caring about the Latino community. While Hillary Clinton and the Democrats were perceived as truly caring by more than 60% of respondents, only 11% perceived Trump as caring about their community. In contrast, nearly three out of five Latino voters felt that Trump was hostile: nearly double the number of respondents ascribing that position to the Republican Party.

Figure 3. Vote Choice Among Latino Voters in Nevada, 2016

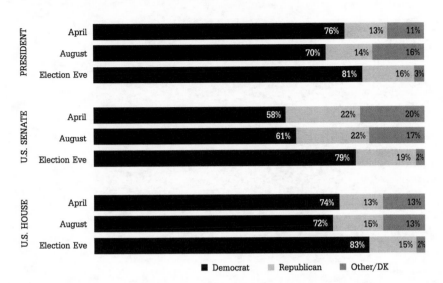

Source: America's Voice/Latino Decisions 2016 3-State Battleground (April) and National Battleground State Polls (August); Latino Decisions 2016 Election Eve Poll.

Given these perceptions and the saliency of immigration among Nevada's Latino electorate (69% of Election Eve respondents reporting knowing a family member, friend, coworker, or other acquaintance who is undocumented), immigration provided Democrats with a significant advantage. The Latino Decisions 2016 Election Eve Poll found that better than four out of five Latino voters supported President Obama's DACA action and more than two-thirds opposed the Republican efforts to stop President Obama's 2012 (DACA) and 2014 (DAPA) executive orders. More generally, 71% reported that immigration was the top or one of the most important issues affecting the decision to vote and who to vote for. At the same time, there was much less certainty about where the U.S. Senate candidates stood on immigration. Just 36% knew that Catherine Cortez Masto supported President Obama's executive actions and immigration reform, including a pathway to citizenship, and only 39% knew that Joe Heck opposed these policies.

Still, as the data in figure 3 suggest, throughout 2016 Democratic candidates were the preferred choices of Nevada's Latinos. The figure summarizes

Figure 4. Precinct-Level Vote Choice and Share of Latino Registered Voters, 2016

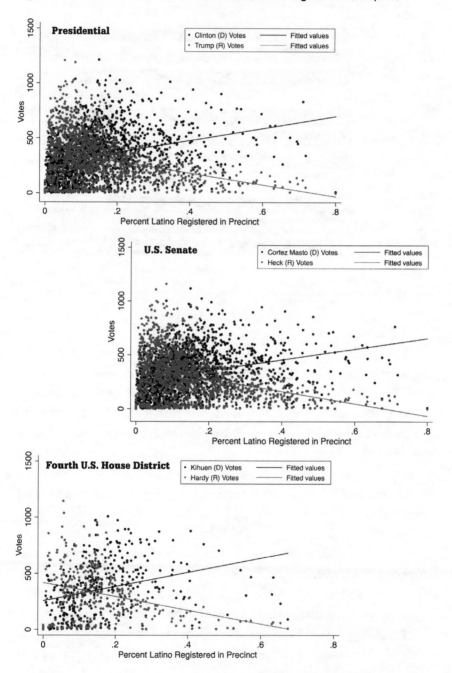

Source: Data from Nevada Secretary of State and Pedraza and Wilcox-Archuleta (2017).

candidate preferences from the April and August 2016 America's Voice/ Latino Decisions Battleground Surveys and the 2016 Latino Decisions Election Eve Poll for the presidential, U.S. Senate, and U.S. House of Representatives. In all three surveys, Hillary Clinton was the overwhelming favorite, and according to the Election Eve Poll, 80% of Latino voters decided whom to vote for as president before the fall campaign even began. In contrast, support for Cortez Masto solidified over the fall. Although she had served as the Attorney General from 2007 to 2015, Cortez Masto was not particularly well known in southern Nevada at the start of the campaign, particularly compared to her opponent Joe Heck, who represented southern Nevada in the House. However, as the campaign progressed and Cortez Masto became more comfortable highlighting her family's immigrant history (her grandfather had emigrated from Mexico) and embracing the symbolic importance of being the first Latina to serve in the U.S. Senate, the state's Latino voters responded.

Given the closeness of the 2016 outcomes in Nevada, the Democrats' victories in the presidential, U.S. Senate, and Fourth House District elections were dependent upon outsized support among the state's Latino voters. The data in figure 4 indicate just how critical the support of these voters was to the Democrats' success. Specifically, the figure presents precinct-level scatterplots and fitted values summarizing the relationship between the raw precinct vote and the share of Latino registered voters in each precinct using data from the Nevada Secretary of State and Pedraza and Wilcox-Archuleta (2017) for the presidential, U.S. Senate, and Fourth House District races.

For all three elections, the trend lines indicate that the greater the share of Latino registered voters was in a precinct, the greater was the support for Democratic candidates. Parsing the data more finely, in the eighty-two precincts where Latinos constituted 40% or more of registered voters, Clinton's margin was 24,000 votes or 90% of her total margin of victory in the state. For Cortez Masto, her margin in these precincts was 23,000 votes, which equates to 86% of her total margin of victory. In the nineteen precincts in the Fourth House District where Latinos constituted 40% or more of registered voters, Kihuen's margin was 5,000 votes or roughly half of his total margin of victory.

Figure 5. Contours of Latino Vote in Nevada, 2016

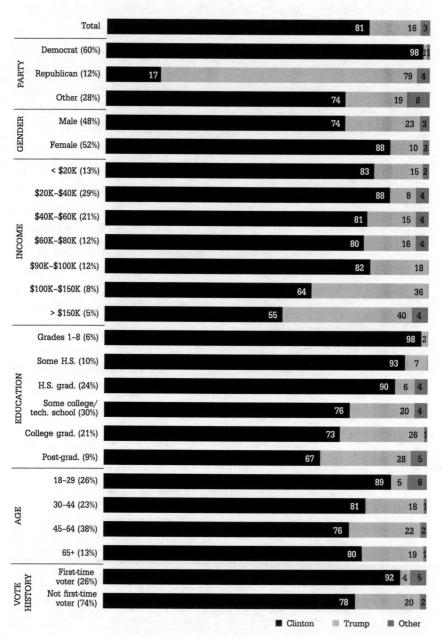

Source: Latino Decisions 2016 Election Eve Poll.

More generally, as the data presented in figure 5 detail, in the presidential election, except for registered Republicans, Hillary Clinton carried every subgroup of Latino voters on her way to securing 81% of the Latino vote. In contrast, Donald Trump won just 16% of the Latino vote, with 17% of Republicans defecting to Clinton. Although Trump did somewhat better with males, it was not enough to offset the overwhelming support for Clinton among Latinas. Even among higher income Latinos, Trump failed to win a majority of the highest earning voters, as Clinton carried every income category.

Figure 5 also suggests long-term problems for the GOP in Nevada. Among Latinos twenty-nine years old or younger, Trump won just 5% of the vote. Not only did this cohort account for over a quarter of the Latino electorate, these voters were the least likely of an age group to identify themselves as Republicans. Among first-time voters, the patterns are even more lopsided. More than 90% of first-time voters cast their votes for Clinton and less than 5% identify as Republicans. Thus, to the degree to which Trump and his anti-immigrant rhetoric and policy priorities define the Republicans moving forward, it is unlikely that Nevada's Electoral College votes will be in the GOP's column any time soon. Indeed, 2016 marked the third straight victory for the Democrats in Nevada, and 2016 is only the second instance since 1912 that Nevada's Electoral College votes did not go to the winner of the presidential election.

Conclusion

Between 2012 and 2016, the Nevada electorate increased by more than 200,000 voters and the 2016 election resulted in the most ballots cast in any election in the state's history. However, data from the Nevada Secretary of State report that turnout among registered voters decreased from 81% to 77% compared to 2012 and Hillary Clinton's margin was less than half of Obama's. Donald Trump's vote total increased in every county relative to Mitt Romney's 2012 performance, and none of the four big Democratic winners, Clinton, Cortez Masto, Kihuen, and Jackie Rosen, the Democratic candidate in the Third House District, won a majority of the vote.

Yet unlike in prior elections cycles, the Democrats' victories extended all the way down the ballot. In addition to Cortez Masto's election to the U.S. Senate and Kihuen's victory in the Fourth District, the Democrats' carried the Nevada Third District for only the second time since the district was created after the 2000 Census (the Democrats also won the Third Distract in 2008, when Obama won Nevada by more than 12 points). The Democrats also regained majority control of both chambers of the Nevada Legislature, and the state passed initiatives requiring background checks on private gun sales, legalizing recreational use of marijuana, and deregulating the state's utility market to encourage competition from renewable energy.

Within Nevada, it was majority-minority Clark County that was the difference maker. While Clinton narrowly won Washoe County, the only county where Cortez Masto and the background checks ballot initiative received a majority was Clark. In the state's rural counties, both Clinton and Cortez Masto lost by a combined 82,000 votes. In the Nevada Legislature, just five of the thirty-nine Democrats represent a district outside of Clark County.

Thus, taken collectively, these data suggest a bit of a conundrum. The Democrats fared worse at the top of the ticket, but the party had its strongest overall electoral performance since 2008. The ebbs and flows of the state's political demography can explain much of this. As Bowler and Segura (2012) argue, Democrats' success is dependent upon significant turnout and dramatic pro-Democratic voting by minorities. Underlying their thesis is the notion of coalitional voting among minority voters. However, these blocs often underperform at the ballot box relative to their population shares but have the potential for increased participation in response to short-term influences.

The data in table 1 put these dynamics in context. Using data from the November 2012 and 2016 Current Population Survey, the table summarizes the shares of the Nevada age-eligible voting populations that are African American, Asian American, Latino, and White, the age-eligible share of each racial and ethnic group that registered to vote, the age-eligible share of

Table 1. Ethnic and Racial Composition of the Nevada Electorate, 2012 and 2016

	Age-eligible		Age-eligible registered		Age-eligible voted		Share of the electorate	
	2012	2016	2012	2016	2012	2016	2012	2016
African Americans	9.1%	8.6%	65.2%	72.2%	61.6%	65.1%	9.6%	9.2%
Asian Americans	6.4%	8.3%	71.3%	55.8%	58.3%	44.2%	6.4%	6.0%
Latinos	16.7%	17.5%	59.9%	67.6%	52.0%	56.6%	15.0%	16.4%
Whites	64.5%	62.6%	67.3%	71.1%	60.3%	63.2%	67.2%	65.4%

Source: Data from the 2012 and 2016 November Current Population Survey. Values for African American, Asian American, Latino, and White rows calculated using "Black alone," "Asian alone," "Hispanic (of any race)," and "White non-Hispanic alone" U.S. Census designations, respectively.

each racial and ethnic group that voted, and each group's share of the total electorate.[3]

Compared to 2012, the Latino share of the Nevada electorate increased by 1.4 percentage points, and this increase was driven by growth in the age-eligible Latino population share, as well as higher registration and turnout rates. Yet even with these increases, Latinos underperformed relative to the age-eligible Latino population share. Perhaps more telling of the pace at which Nevada's political demography is changing is the row for Whites. In 2016, the White share of the Nevada electorate decreased by 1.8 percentage points compared to 2012, even though White registration and turnout increased and the difference between the age-eligible White share and the White share of the electorate increased slightly. As was the case in 2012 (and 2008 as well), African American participation exceeded African American population share owing to the fact that Nevadan African Americans have the highest registration and turnout rates of any ethnic or racial bloc. However, as a share of the overall electorate, African Americans decreased from 9.6% in 2012 to 9.2% largely because of the growth in the Latino electorate. The table also indicates that Asian American participation decreased compared to 2012.

Unlike in swing states such as Florida and North Carolina where the increase in White participation was likely the key factor in Trump's victories, the increase in White participation in Nevada was not detrimental to the Democrats because of the diversity within Nevada's minority population. Instead, increased participation among Whites resulted in narrower margins for Clinton and Cortez Masto and helps to explain why Kihuen won by 4 points in a district with an 11-point Democratic registration advantage, but a district that encompasses many of the state's rural counties. It also demonstrates how prescient the Democrats and allied interests were to engage the Latino community throughout the cycle by sponsoring citizenship fairs and voter registration drives and canvassing Latino neighborhoods with a sophisticated and relentless GOTV effort.

Certainly, Trump's candidacy motivated many Latinos to have their voices heard. However, equally as important was having attractive and passionate Latino candidates like Cortez Masto and Kihuen on the ballot. Indeed, when asked in the Election Eve Poll why they were voting, 45% responded they were voting to support and represent the Latino community: a 5-point increase from 2012 and 11 points greater than the share of respondents who indicated that they were voting to support Democratic candidates.

At least in the short term, then, it appears that the potential of the Latino electorate in Nevada is being realized. Without outsized support from Latino voters, Clinton, Cortez Masto, or Kihuen would not have been victorious. From 2016, it appears that the real test comes in 2018. Reid's retirement brings uncertainty about the future of the state Democratic Party and its ability to command the resources and discipline that swung Nevada from Republican to Democratic leaning. The new party leadership will need to solve the party's midterm drop-off problems: a concern of particular urgency given that in 2018 all six of the state's constitutional offices, including an open governor's seat, and Nevada's other U.S. Senate seat will be on the ballot. The Democrats will be defending three of the state's four seats in the House of Representatives and majorities in both of houses of the Nevada Legislature.

Clearly, the ingredients for Democrats' success in Nevada are in place: a diverse and concentrated population that will undoubtedly bear the brunt of the Trump administration's immigration, health care, and educational policies; a robust political infrastructure anchored by organized labor and a cadre of progressive interests; and an opposition that is likely to be internally divided and on the defensive. But as they say, without the Latino vote, there is no hope. This was certainly true in 2016 and will continue to be in future election cycles in the Silver State.

Notes

1. These differences are larger in midterm elections as compared to presidential elections. For instance, in midterm elections the average Latino under vote is 4.8 percentage points, as compared to 2.2 percentage points in presidential elections. Similarly, the White over vote averages 3.4 percentage points in presidential elections and 8.47 points in midterm elections.

2. In the aftermath of the caucuses, working off a story broken by the *New York Times*, Nevada political reporter Jon Ralston (Ralston 2016) reported that prior to the caucuses Harry Reid asked the union's leadership to encourage its members to participate, particularly at the at-large caucus sites that were held at various Las Vegas Strip properties to accommodate participation by hotel and casino employees. Hillary Clinton would go on to dominate the Strip caucuses on her way to a closer than expected victory over Bernie Sanders. The following week, Reid endorsed Clinton, and Culinary followed suit in July. Still, many in the union remained angry with the Clintons because of the Clintons' treatment of the union during the 2008 Democratic caucuses. Clinton surrogates took the union to court to challenge its voting procedures, and Bill Clinton urged union workers to support his wife despite Culinary's endorsement of Obama (Nagourney 2016).

3. Although these data do have large error margins, particularly for smaller voting blocs, they do provide one of the few reliable over time estimates of voter participation. The results for Nevada are largely consistent with analyses of voter files conducted by commercial firms such as Catalist (2016).

References

Barry, Dan. 2016. "Latina Hotel Workers Harness Force of Labor and Politics in Las Vegas." *New York Times*, November 6.

Bowler, Shaun, and Gary M. Segura. 2012. *The Future Is Ours*. Los Angeles: SAGE/CQ Press.

Catalist. 2016. "2016 Turnout and Presidential Support Analysis: Nevada." February 16. https://www.catalist.us/

Concha, Joe. 2016. "Roger Stone: Trump Has Run One of Worst Campaigns in Nevada History." *The Hill*, November 8. http://thehill.com.

Damore, David F. 2011a. "Reid vs. Angle in Nevada's Senate Race: Harry Houdini

Escapes the Wave." In *Cases in Congressional Campaigns: Storming the Hill*, 2nd ed., edited by David Dulio and Randall Adkins, 32-53. New York: Routledge.

——. 2011b. "The Tea Party Angle in the Nevada Senate Race." In *Tea Party Effects on 2010 Senate Elections*, edited by Will Miller and Jeremy Walling, 47-66. Lanham, MD: Lexington Books.

——. 2015. "It's the Economy Stupid? Not So Fast: The Impact of the Latino Vote on the 2012 Presidential Election in Nevada." In *Latinos and the 2012 Election: The New Face of the American Voter*, edited by Gabriel R. Sanchez, 181-98. East Lansing: Michigan State University.

——. 2017. "'The Reid Machine's' Last Stand." In *The Roads to Congress 2016*, edited by Sean D. Foreman and Marcia Godwin, 305-20. New York: Palgrave Macmillan.

Damore, David F., and Rebecca D. Gill. 2015. "Swing-State Politics in the Silver State." In *Presidential Swing States: Why Ten Only Matter*, edited by David Schultz and Stacy Hunter Hecht., 195-222. Lanham, MD: Lexington Books.

Latimer, Brian. 2016. "'Wall' of Taco Trucks to Line Up at Trump's Las Vegas Hotel in Protest." *NBC News*, October 18.

Nagourney, Adam. 2016. "Culinary Workers Won't Take Sides in Nevada Democratic Caucuses." *New York Times*, February 18.

Pedraza, Francisco I., and Bryan Wilcox-Archuleta. 2017. "Precinct Returns Prove Exit Polls Wrong on Latino Vote." *The Nevada Independent*, January 21.

Ralston, Jon. 2016. "'Reid-Culinary Bond' Won Nevada for Clinton." *Reno Gazette Journal*, February 20.

A Mirage in the Desert

Arizona and Latinos in the 2016 Presidential Election

Lisa M. Sanchez and Stephen A. Nuño-Pérez

IN A NIGHT OF SHOCKING SURPRISES, THE FACT THAT A REPUBLICAN PRES-
idential candidate won in Arizona hardly registers. With 3 million fewer
votes than Hillary Clinton, however, Donald Trump pulled off a historic
Electoral College victory with consequences that will reverberate for decades. Much has already been written about the underlying systemic factors driving President Trump's victory. From gerrymandering to the debate
between economic anxiety and racial animosity, academics have found
themselves with a fascinating natural experiment in democracy.

But while Arizona did not bring any surprises to the forefront of the
news, the steady drumbeat of progress for Latinos continued apace in the
Grand Canyon State. While Hillary Clinton lost to Donald Trump roughly
49% to 46%, Mitt Romney had won Arizona by 54% to 44% in 2012 (Motel and
Patten 2012). However, buried in the 2% gain by the Democrats and the loss
of 5% by the Republicans in the presidential race is a harbinger of a state
in transition, and many point to Latinos as the reason. When looking at
the raw numbers, Democrats gained more than 135,000 voters from 2012 to
2016, while Republicans gained only 19,000 voters (Arizona Secretary of State

2018). With the continued growth in the population, and with much of that coming from Latinos, political pundits have been predicting that Arizona will move into "purple" status sooner rather than later (Arkin 2018). Data support this assertion. According to the Arizona Office of Economic Opportunity, Latinos currently (2018) make up 32.5% of the population in the state of Arizona. By 2050, Latinos are projected to grow to 42.2% of the state's population. As early as 2029, the state will shift to a majority-minority population.

Background

The Sonoran Desert spans a 100,000-square-mile region reaching from Hermosillo, Mexico, up to Prescott, Arizona, where groups of the Hohokam culture lived among the towering Saguaro along the Gila River more than 2,000 years ago. Today, Tucson and Phoenix make up the largest cities of the Sonoran Desert (Goth 2017), where land and bounty transferred from Native tribes to the Spanish, then to the Mexicans, then briefly as a prize of war to the Confederacy during the Civil War. Arizona was the last of the contiguous states to be admitted into the Union.

The economics of modern Arizona is dominated by the "five Cs": copper, cattle, cotton, citrus, and climate. The Southwest has always held a mythical place in the nation's heart for adventure and opportunity. From the Grand Canyon to the Yuma Desert, pioneers and prospectors have traveled through "la zona arida," the arid zone, looking for a better quality of life. That has not changed much, and neither has the politics that is associated with newcomers and old anxieties over past quarrels. Phoenix is now one of the fastest growing cities in the country, recently surpassing Philadelphia as the fifth largest city in the United States. With these population surges has come increased attention to Arizona politics. Arizona's congressional delegation has almost doubled in size since the 1980s, going from five members in 1983 to nine members in the 2013.

Though Republicans will miss the stronghold status that has accrued to Arizona for decades, Arizona is once again a player in national politics with presidential candidate, Hillary Clinton, making an eleventh-hour campaign stop in Arizona during the 2016 electoral cycle.

Today, Mexican immigration resonates throughout the political landscape in Arizona, particularly through tough economic times, and the 2016 Presidential election was the culmination of a particularly tumultuous era for the state of Arizona. From a historical perspective, White Arizonans have always had anxiety over Mexicans. Arizona was once a part of the New Mexican Territory and evolved through a series of negotiations largely influenced over the controversies of the day, namely, slavery. The differing cultures between the White-dominated (and Mormon) territory that is now Arizona and the Mexican traditions of New Mexico reflect much of the anxiety we see today.

This anxiety reached a fever pitch in 2010, two years into the Obama Administration and well into the rise of the Tea Party, which emerged during the debate over President Obama's overhaul of the health care system. Arizona is famous for its "snowbird" population, retirement-aged residents who stay in Arizona during the winter months. Arizona's climate has been a draw for older Americans, but Whites have been in steady decline as a percentage of the population for decades. Since 2000, the non-Latino White population has been steadily declining. According to the 2000 Census, non-Latino Whites made up 64% of Arizona's state population.

In 2018, they account for 54% of the state population and are projected to fall to nearly 43% by 2050. With minorities making up a majority of the population under eighteen years, projections are not difficult to assess on the impact Latinos will have in the immediate future.

Demographics

Arizona, long considered a solidly "red" state, took center stage in the political debates of the 2016 electoral cycle—and for good reason. With its close proximity to the border, decades of rapid population increase, and large Latino population, the long-time Republican stronghold became a national test for the power of mobilization of Latino populations when salient issues take center stage in a presidential campaign.

Despite its red-state history, the changing demographic makeup of Arizona has caused many to question whether Arizona is, and will continue to be, a "safe" Republican state. Much of this speculation hinges on the state's population increases in recent years, in particular, the simultaneous increase in Latino populations and decline in White non-Hispanic populations in the state of Arizona. The U.S. Census estimates a population increase of 8.4% between Census 2010 and July 1, 2016. This puts Arizona in the top ten states for population growth since the 2010 census. A look at Arizona population trends over time reveals that the state is well on its way to becoming a majority-minority state, with only 55.8% of the population identifying as non-Hispanic White. This number has been in steady decline: dropping from 64% in 2000 to 57.8% in 2010, a net decline of 6.2% in the space of just ten years. By far, the largest racial/ethnic group in the state is comprised of Latinos at 30.7% of the population as of July 2015, followed by 4.8% African American, 5.3% American Indian, and 3.4% Asian (U.S. Census Bureau 2015). When asked to identify their country of origin, Arizona Latinos overwhelmingly identify themselves as Mexican American. At nearly 31% of the Arizona population, Latinos comprised almost double their national percentage of 17.6 % in the same year. Many mistakenly assume that close proximity to the border ensures that the Arizona Latino population is predominately comprised of recent, foreign-born arrivals, but according the 2015 American Community Survey, foreign-born individuals only comprised 13.5% of the Arizona population. Nationally, this number was 13.2%. This means that a supermajority of 86.5% of Arizona residents are native-born citizens.

Perhaps more telling are the statistics surrounding the date of entrance for foreign-born individuals in the state of Arizona. Sixty-three percent arrived in the United States and settled in Arizona prior to the year 2000. Only 9.4% of foreign-born arrivals into the state of Arizona entered in 2010 or later. This means that 90% of foreign-born arrivals in the state of Arizona have resided in the state for at least six years or longer. Arizona demographics diverge from national rates in a few key areas, such as home language use and the ethnic diversity of children under eighteen years of age. Among the population over five years old, roughly 27% of Arizona residents speak a language other than English at home. Moreover, 43.3% of Arizona children under age eighteen identify themselves as Hispanic/Latino. By comparison, non-Latino White children under eighteen comprise only 40.7% of this population. Their political pressure, if properly focused, could be felt for years to come, given that 96.6% of children in Arizona are native born, and thus immediately armed with the ability to engage politically upon reaching adulthood. Though these demographics help to paint a picture of the Arizona population, they are most important when viewed in light of their impacts on political engagement and mobilization efforts within the state. The demographic makeup of Arizona creates unique challenges for politicians and interest groups seeking to engage this population in the political process.

The year 2010 was a watershed moment for Latino politics in Arizona. With the combination of the Tea Party movement and the economic recession, Governor Jan Brewer was headed into an election campaign with low approval ratings. In March 2010, polls had Brewer's approval ratings in the mid-30s against Terry Goddard. But the Tea Party activists had shifted their focus away from health care after the Affordable Care Act was signed, and their attention turned to immigration. The result was a concentrated campaign by Brewer on SB 1070, a bill that largely reflected a similar referendum in California almost fifteen years earlier, Proposition 187. SB 1070 was a strict anti-immigrant measure that many argued would result in racial profiling of Hispanics. The bill became a referendum divided along racial lines, but that mobilized White voters in support of Governor Brewer. Brewer won the election by over 200,000 votes. Senator John McCain won his Senate seat with more than 1 million votes.

By 2016, former Governor of Arizona Jan Brewer raised the ire of Latinos by dismissing the notion that they could propel Hillary Clinton to victory in a state that has been one of the most reliable sources of electoral votes in the nation for the GOP. Brewer served as governor from 2009 to 2015, a tumultuous period for a state where the economy relied heavily on housing construction, tourism, agriculture, and thus cheap labor from Mexico, for its growth during the housing boom of the 2000s. "Nah," she said, "They don't get out and vote. They don't vote." Academics who study Latino politics are keenly aware of the sentiment expressed by Brewer. Much of the literature on Latino politics has been focused on participation and turnout precisely because turnout rates have been so low for so long (see, e.g., Hero and Campbell 1996; Leighley and Vedlitz 1999).

Unsurprisingly, political scientists see voter participation in more complicated terms than the former governor. The SB 1070 bill, which codified racial profiling against Latinos, was a wakeup call to the minority community, but without any substantial infrastructure in place to recruit Latinos, there has been a difficult path to realizing the power of the Latino vote.

Political Engagement and Mobilization Efforts

At 30% of Arizona's population, Latinos appeared to be uniquely situated to sway electoral politics within the state during the 2016 presidential election cycle. However, a close inspection of Latino political behavior in the state reveals that the ability of Latino voters to deliver a "blue" victory to the Clinton campaign hinged on several important and often difficult-to-achieve factors. Chief among these factors is voter eligibility. Only 47.2% of the total Latino population in Arizona meets the basic citizenship and age requirements to vote in U.S. elections. This means that less than half of the 30% Arizona Latino population is eligible to vote when the most basic requirements are taken into account. Moreover, when voter registration status is taken into account, this number is further reduced to 40.5% of Arizona Latinos who are both eligible and registered to vote (ACS November 2015).

To put this number in perspective, Latino registered voters made up 20.8% of all registered voters in Arizona. The bright spot in these numbers is that 83% of Latinos who registered to vote reported actually voting in the 2016 election. Interestingly, these were similar to national trends for Latinos as well. Therefore, Latino voters made up 19.6% of all voters in the 2016 Arizona presidential election. Where these numbers become most interesting is in the exit polling data that estimate Latino vote choice for each of the

Table 1. Party Affiliation in Arizona

	Frequency	Percent	Cumulative percent
Republican	44.87	10.76	10.76
Democrat	254.31	60.99	71.75
Independent	95.24	22.84	94.59
Other party	11.30	2.71	97.29
Don't know	9.89	2.37	99.67
Refused	1.39	0.33	100.00
Total	417	100.00	

Note: Survey weights used for analysis. Survey text read: "Generally speaking, do you think of yourself as a Republican, a Democrat, an independent, or something else?"

Source: Latino Decisions 2016 Election Eve Poll.

presidential candidates. National exit polls estimate that in Arizona, 31% of Latinos voted for Donald Trump in the 2016 presidential election. However, methodologically appropriate estimates from Latino Decisions find a more realistic Trump vote share to be about 12% in the state of Arizona (Nuño and Archuleta-Wilcox 2016). Therefore, roughly 16.5% of the Arizona electorate was made up of Latinos who voted for the Democratic candidate, Hillary Clinton, whereas an estimated 2.4% of the Arizona electorate was made up of Latinos voting for the Republican candidate, Donald Trump. Moreover, the difference between the vote shares of the candidates was a mere 3.4%, or 91,234 votes, of the total vote share in Arizona (State of Arizona 2016). In such a close race, Latinos did make a difference but not necessarily in the desired direction. Multiple scenarios involving Latinos could have borne a drastically different electoral outcome. If Latinos had registered and voted in higher numbers, the outcome would have favored the Democratic candidate, given the strong Democratic lean among Latinos in both party identification and vote choice. Election-eve data from Latino Decisions support this assertion. Table 1 depicts the partisan affiliation of Arizona Latinos on the eve of the election. With the growing population and growing Democratic partisanship of Latinos, the purple status of the state seems highly dependent on the continuing growth and political integration of Latinos.

Clearly, Arizona Latinos strongly affiliate with the Democratic Party at nearly 61%. Moreover, the second highest category is not Republican

Table 2. Party Mobilization of Latinos in Arizona, 2016

	Frequency	Percent	Cumulative percent
Yes	171.38	41.10	41.10
No	241.46	57.90	99.00
Don't know	3.53	0.85	99.85
Refused	0.62	0.15	100.00
Total	*417*	*100.00*	

Note: Survey weights used for analysis. Survey text read: "Over the past few months, did anyone from a campaign, political party, or a community organization anyone else ask you to vote, or register to vote?"

Source: Latino Decisions 2016 Election Eve Poll.

partisan affiliation, but rather part of a growing national trend among Latinos who choose to affiliate as Independent at nearly 23%. In a second scenario, 4% fewer Latinos voting for Trump would have clinched the election for Hillary Clinton. According to the Pew Research Center, the eligible voter population grew from 824,000 Hispanics in 2010 to 992,000 Hispanics in 2014 (López and Stepler 2016). Despite efforts on behalf of the Clinton campaign, mobilization still remained low among Arizonans. Table 2 highlights that nearly 58% of Arizona Latinos were not mobilized through contact from a campaign, a political party, or a community organization.

Those who closely followed the election, however, would not find this statistic surprising, given the late hour at which Arizona became a supposed "battleground" state. Given the large percentage of Arizona Latinos who were not mobilized, it is reasonable to argue that stronger mobilization efforts could have had an impact on the close electoral outcome in the state of Arizona. However, the important questions to ask are: What explains the variation in Latino partisan identification and voting patterns? Which issue preferences came to bear on the voting decisions of Latinos during the 2016 general election?

The 2016 Election

Although immigration was not the number one issue among voters nationwide, it was the top issue among Arizona Latinos during the 2016 election.

Table 3. Most Important Issues Facing the Latino/Hispanic Community

	Frequency	Percent	Cumulative percent
Fixing economy/jobs/unemployment	114.74	27.52	27.52
Immigration reform/deportations	124.78	29.92	57.44
Education reform/schools	24.90	5.97	63.41
Health care	10.53	2.53	65.93
Terrorism/ISIS/national security	8.24	1.98	67.91
College cost/affordability	6.17	1.48	69.39
Protecting reproductive rights/women's rights	5.53	1.33	70.72
Housing affordability/mortgages	1.00	0.24	70.95
Climate change/global warming/environment	0.59	0.14	71.10
Anti-immigrant/Latino discrimination	20.43	4.90	76.00
Taxes/government spending	5.34	1.28	77.28
Criminal justice reform/mass incarceration	1.54	0.37	77.65
Protecting Social Security	2.06	0.49	78.14
Income inequality/poverty	6.48	1.55	79.69
Hard to get ahead/make ends meet	5.10	1.22	80.92
Politicians are dishonest/broken system	6.69	1.60	82.52
Stop Trump/make sure Trump is not president	24.76	5.94	88.46
Something else	21.92	5.26	93.72
Don't know	24.27	5.82	99.54
Refused to answer	1.93	0.46	100.00
Total	*417*	*100.00*	

Note: Analyzed using survey weights. Survey text read "Thinking about the 2016 election, what are the most important issues facing the [Latino/Hispanic] community that our politicians should address?" First choice.

Source: Latino Decisions 2016 Election Eve Poll.

Table 3 shows the top issues that Arizona Latinos deemed the most important issue facing the Latino community.

Arizona Latinos pointed to immigration reform and deportations as a top issue facing the Latino community at 29.92%, and rightly so. Among Arizona Latinos polled, roughly 61% personally knew someone who was of undocumented status. Therefore, it is unsurprising that Arizona Latinos would place this issue at the top of community concerns.

Following closely were concerns regarding the economy, jobs, and unemployment at 27.82%. Trailing far behind in third place was educational reform, at a mere 5.97%. Though anti-Trump sentiment was discussed widely at the national level, those suggesting it was the most important issue facing the Latino community amounted to only 5.94%.

With a perceptibly tight race for Senate that left Senator John McCain's image tattered with his refusal to denounce Donald Trump—combined with a strong moderate Democrat in Ann Kirkpatrick challenging him— many pundits viewed the state as ripe for the picking. In the month before the election, the campaign sent crowd favorites to Arizona in Vermont Senator Bernie Sanders and First Lady Michelle Obama, with a Chelsea Clinton rally sandwiched between the two megastars. Bernie Sanders made waves in Arizona during the primary battle against Hillary Clinton earlier in 2016. Anchored by two "bluish" cities in Flagstaff to the north and Tucson in the south, Sanders garnered more than 40% of the Democratic vote. But the strength of White voters in Arizona has also long been bolstered by a system designed to minimize their impact on Election Day.

Hillary Clinton also made an appearance in the Grand Canyon state just before the election, hoping to capitalize on Latino outrage toward the racial and ethnic comments made about the Latino community by Donald Trump. She hoped to capitalize on the fact that though Arizona is a stalwart Republican state, it has always been made up of a testy electorate. Indeed, the last time a Democrat won the Presidential vote in Arizona was in 1996 with Bill Clinton, but that required a tumultuous campaign and a third-party candidate in Ross Perot, who siphoned off about 8% of the voters. Clinton won the state with less than half the vote in Arizona, and not since Harry Truman in 1948 has a Democrat surpassed that mark of almost 54%. Clinton lost the 1992 election to George H. W. Bush, with Perot slamming Arizona's two-party system with more than 23% of the vote.

Latinos are faced with a plethora of systemic barriers that contribute to historically low turnout rates. In 2004, Arizona adopted Proposition 200, a ballot initiative that required proof of citizenship and identification in order to register and vote in the state of Arizona. Though the law was struck down in 2013 by the U.S. Supreme Court, the impact on Latino voter registration and voting is still being documented. However, in states such as Indiana, New Mexico, Washington, and California, scholars have shown that certain populations (racial and ethnic minorities, low-income populations, the elderly, and immigrants) are less likely to have access to mandated forms of ID and are therefore less likely to register and vote (Barreto,

Table 4. Vote Choice Arizona Latinos

	Frequency	Percent	Cumulative percent
Presidential election			
Hillary Clinton	326.11	78.20	78.20
Donald Trump	45.11	10.82	89.02
Someone else	14.86	3.56	92.59
Undecided/don't know	16.59	3.98	96.57
Refused to answer	14.32	3.43	100.00
Total	*417.00*	*100.00*	
Congressional election			
Did/will vote Democrat	319.23	76.55	76.55
Did/will vote Republican	45.26	10.85	94.65
Did not/will not vote for Congress	7.84	1.88	96.54
Undecided/don't know	30.22	7.25	83.80
Refused to answer	14.45	3.46	100.00
Total	*417.00*	*100.00*	
Maricopa County Sheriff election			
Vote for Penzone	172.17	84.40	84.40
Vote for Arpaio	17.24	8.45	92.85
Undecided/don't know	11.02	5.40	98.25
Refused to answer	3.57	1.75	100.00
Total	*204.00*	*100.00*	

Note: Survey weights used for analysis. Survey text read (in order of appearance in table): (1) "In the election for President, did/will you vote for the [ROTATE: Democratic candidate Hillary Clinton, Republican candidate Donald Trump], or someone else?" (2) "In the election for U.S. House of Representatives, did/will you vote for the [ROTATE: Democratic candidate or the Republican candidate] in your district?" (3) "In the election for Maricopa County Sheriff, did/will you vote for . . ."

Source: Latino Decisions 2016 Election Eve Poll.

Sanchez, and Nuno 2009). Arizona has long been seen as an innovator in voter suppression (Wang and Nittoli 2012). It was in Arizona that former Chief Justice William Rehnquist was accused of actively working to challenge minority voters during the 1960s: Operation Eagle Eye, a Republican program designed to fan out poll watchers for the purposes of intimidating Black and Hispanic voters on Election Day. He famously walked by voting lines asking "suspicious" voters questions about the Constitution. "Caging" was another popular tactic employed by Republicans, where letters would be sent out to predominantly Black neighborhoods and any discrepancies or undelivered mail would be used to place voters on a list that would be used to challenge their eligibility to vote, purging them from the voter rolls (Wang and Nittoli 2012).

Given the alignment of the Democratic Party with expansive immigrant policies, it is unsurprising that Arizona Latinos supported democratic candidates in the 2016 election. Finally, table 4 describes the vote choices among Arizona Latino Decisions 2016 Election Eve survey respondents.

Overwhelming majorities of Latino Decisions 2016 Election Eve survey respondents voted for Hillary Clinton (78.2%), the Democratic Congressional candidate (76.55%), and Democratic candidate Paul Penzone for Maricopa County Sherriff (84.4%). Tom O'Halleran defeated former Sheriff Paul Babeu by more than 7 percentage points for the seat in the First Congressional District, a traditional swing district in Arizona often targeted by both Republicans and Democrats. However, Babeu's campaign was beset with controversy over rumors of his affair with an undocumented immigrant (Alonzo 2012). Paul Babeu rose to prominence in Arizona politics because of his strong anti-immigrant stance, proposing to build a "double wall" along the border. Tom O'Halleran is considered to be a more centrist Democrat; he was a former Republican who grew frustrated with the lack of attention by the GOP to education. That he is considered to be a more conservative Democrat and was still only winning by 7 percentage points should give Democrats pause in their thinking that the movement from red to purple is a done affair.

Latinos are also disproportionately young and poor compared to their White counterparts, making them more difficult to reach via the system; 43% of Hispanics in Arizona are millennials, compared to 28% of non-Hispanic Whites. About 80% of non-Hispanic White Arizonans were not born in Arizona, giving it the fourth highest nonnativity rate in the country, behind Washington, DC, Nevada, and Florida. The resulting relationship has always been a tumultuous one, and Latinos have made their presence increasingly felt throughout he years.

Language barriers have also created problems in the past. Counties in Arizona have been known to print the wrong information on Spanish-language ballots, and candidates have tried all sorts of tricks to confuse Latino voters. For instance, Russell Pearce, a powerful state senator who came under attack by moderate Republicans for his role in crafting SB 1070, was accused of putting a "sham" candidate named Olivia Cortes on the ballot in the hopes that her name would split the Latino vote.

The tricks employed against Hispanics are legend in Arizona. One Republican candidate not only changed his party affiliation to Democrat, but legally changed his name to Cesar Chavez, the farm workers movement civil rights activist. His website contained stock photos of crowds holding "Chavez" signs, which turned out to be rallies for Hugo Chavez, the former President of Venezuela.

The response to Brewer's statement that Latinos don't vote was swift; local media and organizations moved to capitalize on Brewer's provocation. With two weeks to go before the election and with ballots already being cast in Arizona, the Clinton campaign seemed to show interest in the potential presented by a young voting bloc that makes up over 30% of the population and 20% of the voters in this election. Laurie Roberts, a columnist for the largest paper in Arizona, wondered if the "sleeping giant" long talked about might be snoring no longer. Of course, those who study Latino politics hate this term, but we hear it every four years. However, if Brewer's statement woke anyone up, they'd be out of luck if they were not already registered: The deadline for this presidential election, October 10, passed a full month before the election date.

Conclusion

The median age of Latinos in Arizona is twenty-six years, while the median age of non-Hispanic Whites is forty-six years. Of particular importance, among Hispanics, the foreign-born population is much older than the U.S.-born Hispanic population. The median age for foreign-born Hispanics in Arizona is forty-one years and the median age for U.S.-born Hispanics in Arizona is just twenty years. Any notion among Republicans that the future of Arizona as a purple state can be mitigated through immigration is a false god, and similar trends across the country are starkly reflected in the Grand Canyon State.

In a state with a history of disenfranchisement of Latinos, it is perhaps a sign of the times that in the same election that saw an aging and frail Sheriff Joe Arpaio voted out of office in Maricopa County, a Latino was elected as the new Maricopa County recorder. Adrian Fontes defeated a long-time incumbent, Helen Purcell, who had been criticized throughout her career for implementing policies that hurt Latino turnout. Purcell had been county recorder for seven terms and generally went unchallenged on election day. Now responsible for the conduct of elections in Maricopa, Fontes has pledged protection for voters from the history of purges from voter rolls, an end to confusion during elections, and to restore trust in the electoral system.

With almost one-third of Phoenix identifying as Latino, and a growing cadre of Democrat or moderate city council members, the traditional center of power in Arizona is already changing the political landscape. The next election in Arizona will largely reflect much of the same currents that were illustrated in 2016: rising anxiety in response to a growing Latino population, attempts by the Republican Party to hold the line through legislative means, and a finicky population that will remain sensitive to the tide of Arizona's economic fortune.

However, the purple status of the state should not be a foregone conclusion. The Democrats still need to invest heavily in their outreach and manage the transition of Arizona's demographics by building the infrastructure needed to capture the demographic changes. Republicans have also been keen to target Latinos though Koch-funded organizations like the Libre Initiative, a libertarian group tailored to the Latino community that has all the appeal of the Republican rhetoric of a pro-business message that emphasizes low taxes, small government, and school choice, without the historical racial baggage of the Republican Party.

While the numbers favor a shift in Arizona politics toward a more competitive state, the institutional forces that created the state are still very present. Despite its libertarian leanings, Arizona is still a very religious state, supported by a strong Mormon population that dominates the region in nearby Utah and Nevada. Interestingly enough, Latinos now make up one of the most rapidly growing groups in the Latter-Day Saints Church (Reyes 2016). The future of Arizona is still very much in play, and the demographic growth of Latinos in and of itself will not write the future chapters of Arizona politics.

References

Alonzo, Monica. 2012. "Paul Babeu's Mexican Ex-Lover Says Sheriff's Attorney Threatened Him with Deportation." *Phoenix New Times*, February 16.

American Community Survey. 2015. "2015 Data Profiles." https://www.census.gov.

Arizona Secretary of State. 2018. "Voter Registration & Historical Election Data." https://www.azsos.gov.

Arkin, James. 2018. "Can Democrats Turn Arizona Blue?" *RealClearPolitics*, January 12. https://www.realclearpolitics.com.

Barreto, Matt, Gabriel Sanchez, and Stephen Nuno. 2009. "The Disproportionate Impact of Voter-ID Requirements on the Electorate—New Evidence from Indiana." *PS: Political Science & Politics* 42 (1): 111-16.

Goth, Brenna. 2017. "Phoenix Is the Nation's 5th Largest—but Is It a 'Real' City?" *AZCentral*, June 11. https://www.azcentral.com.

Hero, Rodney E., and Anne G. Campbell. 1996. "Understanding Latino Political Participation: Exploring the Evidence from the Latino National Political Survey." *Hispanic Journal of Behavioral Sciences* 18 (2): 129-41.

Leighley, Jan E., and Arnold Vedlitz. 1999. "Race, Ethnicity, and Political Participation: Competing Models and Contrasting Explanations." *Journal of Politics* 61 (4): 1092-114.

López, Gustavo, and Renee Stepler. 2016. "Latinos in the 2016 Election: Arizona." *Pew Research Center's Hispanic Trends Project* (blog), January 19. http://www.pewhispanic.org.

Motel, Seth, and Eileen Patten. 2012. "Latinos in the 2012 Election: Arizona." *Pew Research Center's Hispanic Trends Project* (blog), October 1. http://www.pewhispanic.org.

Nuño, Stephen, and Bryan Archuleta-Cox. 2016. "Viewpoints: Why Exit Polls Are Wrong about Latino Voters in Arizona." *AZCentral*, November 26. https://www.azcentral.com.

Reyes, Raul. 2016. "The Future of the Mormon Church? It's Latino." *NBC News*, August 22.

State of Arizona. 2016. "Elections | Arizona Secretary of State." https://azsos.gov/elections.

Wang, Tova Andrea, and Janice Nittoli. 2012. *The Politics of Voter Suppression: Defending and Expanding Americans' Right to Vote.* Ithaca, NY: Cornell University Press.

U.S. Census Bureau, 2015 "Annual Estimates of the Resident Population." https://factfinder.census.gov.

——. 2016 "Voting and Registration in the Election of November 2016." https://www.census.gov.

Mobilizing the Latino Vote?

Partisan and Nonpartisan Selective Outreach of Latino Voters in the 2016 Election

Ricardo Ramírez and Juan Angel Valdez

SINCE THE 1988 PRESIDENTIAL ELECTION, PUNDITS, ACTIVISTS, AND scholars have developed two overarching narratives about the role of Latinos in elections. They largely vacillate between overly optimistic pre-election predictions of Latinos being determinative of election outcomes (Damore 2013; McArthur 2014; Scherer 2012) and overly pessimistic views that Latino turnout fails to meet lofty expectations (Cillizza 2013; Schecter 2012) or is largely inconsequential to election outcomes (De la Garza and DeSipio 1996; De la Garza and DeSipio 1999; De la Garza and DeSipio 2004).[1] These narratives are driven by considerations of the presence and growth of the Latino electorate and whether they were the pivotal voters that impacted the outcome of elections.

The perception of Latinos' perpetual potential in American elections relies too heavily on the continuing growth of the Latino population, which is expected to translate into political power (Bowler and Segura 2011). This "demography is destiny" narrative inherently sets up Latino voters with expectations that are unlikely to be met in one, two, or three election cycles because the average Latino is more likely than non-Latinos to be younger, more proximate to the immigration experience, and from lower socioeconomic backgrounds. These are persistent barriers to full engagement in electoral politics for Latinos in the United States. Even as the number of registered Latino voters and those who vote increases, the inability to match the growth of the population often casts a shadow of doubt on the outlook for political incorporation after each presidential election. The better-than-normal Latino voter turnout in the 2008 election raised expectations that the established "rinse, recycle, and reuse" optimistic to pessimistic media narratives would no longer apply. However, the slight drop in turnout percentages in 2012 and 2016 led pundits to revert to simplistic accounts of voter turnout rather than more nuanced assessments of the role of Latinos in presidential elections.

In this chapter, we consciously avoid narratives about Latinos that focus on electoral participation or whether they were the pivotal vote in presidential elections and, instead, focus on the role of mobilization. That is, rather than focus on whether Latinos voted at higher rates nationally or in particular states, we focus on the patterns of Latino mobilization by political parties, campaigns, and nonpartisan organizations. We make a concerted effort to be as specific as possible, given that "Latino mobilization" is a broad term that the extant literature discusses and measures in a variety of ways. It can, for example, include electoral and nonelectoral reactive mobilization, which increases Latino engagement in the political system in response to perceived or real political threats (Ramírez 2013; Zepeda-Millán 2017) or symbolic mobilization evident in presidential campaign outreach that "plays the Latino card" (Fraga and Leal 2004). It can also include the possible mobilizing effect of increased interest in politics and voting due to the presence of co-ethnic candidates (Barreto 2010), ethnic media use, or media coverage about Latino immigrants (Abrajano 2010; Medina Vidal 2018; Merolla et al. 2013). Most intuitively, the extant literature has attempted to identify the effect of real-world, get-out-the-vote efforts of nonpartisan organizations (García Bedolla and Michelson 2012; Ramírez 2007; Ramírez 2005; Ramírez 2013; Michelson 2005). Finally, research on Latino mobilization can focus on the extent to which there are measurable patterns of Latinos being strategically targeted or neglected by focusing on the behavior of national campaigns (Hersh 2015), county party chairs (Leighley 2001), or Latino and non-Latino self-reported contact (Ramírez et. al. 2015; Ramírez, Solano, and Wilcox-Archuleta 2018; Stevens and Bishin 2011).

We focus on the mobilization strategies utilized by partisan campaigns and nonpartisan organizations in the 2016 election and the consequences for Latino voter mobilization. We examine the types of voters contacted by either partisan campaigns and/or nonpartisan organizations for the 2016 election. Using the Latino Decisions 2016 Election Eve Poll and appended Catalist data that included public voter registration records, we find that partisan campaigns and nonpartisan organizations engaged in strategic— yet distinct—mobilization strategies. In particular, partisan campaigns rely more on an individual's political information (party registration, length of registration status, and battleground state residence), while nonpartisan campaigns appear to rely more on an individual's social information (age and marital status) in forming contact strategies. However, it is not necessarily the case that partisan campaigns exclusively rely on political variables while nonpartisan on social variables. National origin, for example, distinctly influences the tactical outreach of partisan mobilizers compared to nonpartisan mobilizers. The behavior of partisan campaigns regarding Latino voters largely confirms Hersh's (2015) assertion that political parties don't necessarily microtarget using vast amounts of consumer data. However, we find that a necessary caveat to the discussion about the prevalence of information that allows for microtargeting should be considered given that nonpartisan organizations have longer term goals of growing the electorate. It is, therefore, necessary to review traditional explanations of voter turnout to explore the possible consequences for mobilization strategies targeting Latino voters. Our multivariate results of the Latino Decisions 2016 Election Eve Poll and appended Catalist data demonstrate that strategic mobilization strategies often leave certain segments of the Latino electorate not contacted. Indeed, mobilization strategies have consequences for American democracy and are dependent on who is doing the mobilizing.

Understanding the Relationship of Latino Turnout and Mobilization

One of the reasons for the pessimistic narrative about the role of Latino voters in presidential elections, as stated earlier, has to do with the Latino electoral participation (or lack thereof). Indeed, while the number of Latino voters increased, the rate of Latino voter turnout decreased in 2016; some attribute this to Donald Trump's presidential campaign, which is often described as outwardly and unabashedly hostile to Latino communities across the nation. It was assumed that the vitriolic comments about Mexican immigrants in the Trump campaign would lead to "reactive mobilization" among all Latino voters, as had been the case in California in the 1990s with similar anti-immigrant rhetoric during its 1994 gubernatorial election (Pantoja et al. 2001; Ramírez 2013). If reactive mobilization occurred, we should have witnessed greater rates of voting in 2016. According to Krogstad and Lopez (2017), 12.7 million Latinos cast a vote in the 2016 election, an increase of 1.5 million when compared to the 11.2 million Latino voters in 2012. However, the number of Latino nonvoters—those eligible voters who did not vote—exceeded the number of Latino voters by 1.3 million. As is evident in figure 1, the gap between Latino nonvoters (i.e., U.S. citizens of voting age) and Latino voters has steadily widened since 1988. Plainly stated, while there have been record numbers of Latinos turning out to vote in each election, the number of eligible Latino voters who are not turning out to vote is higher. This facile conclusion leads many to assume a lack of interest in politics or voting among Latinos. However, it should be noted that the primary driver of this growing gap is the initial hurdle of voter registration. Once people are registered to vote, the "gap" is significantly reduced and not too different from what is evident among other racial and ethnic groups.

Gaps in turnout among racial and ethnic minorities have been a long-standing feature in American politics (Abrajano et al. 2008; Pantoja, Ramírez, and Segura 2001; Ramírez 2007; Stevens and Bishin 2011). Resource-based models of participation contend that differences in socioeconomic resources can explain differences in turnout (Verba, Schlozman, and Brady 1995). That is, people may want to participate, but the limited number of resources individuals possess (i.e., time, skills, money) may keep them from

Figure 1. Latino Citizen Voting-Age Population, Voter Registration, and Turnout, 1988–2016

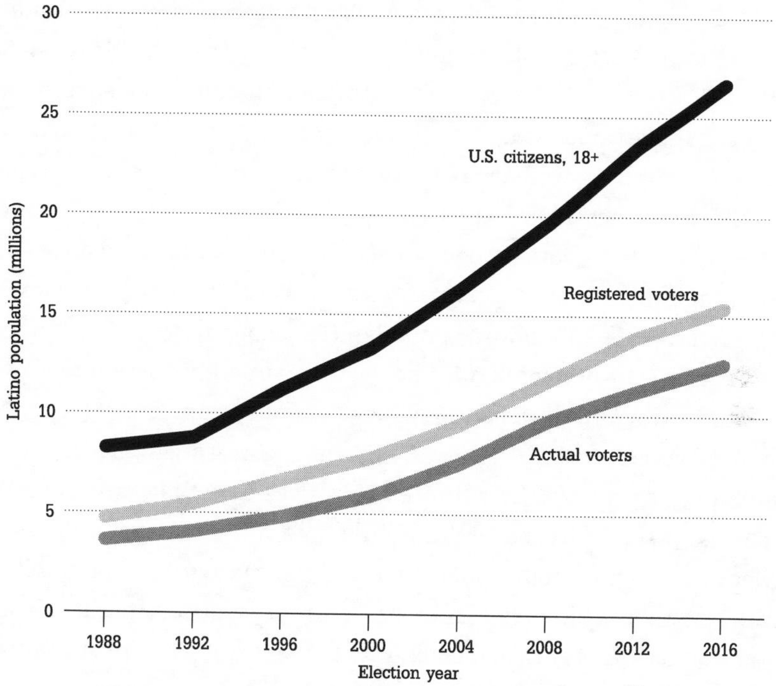

Source: U.S. Census Bureau, Voting and Registration in the November Elections: 1988–2016.

participating or voting (Rosenstone and Hansen 1993; Verba and Nie 1972; Verba, Schlozman, and Brady 1995). Resource-based explanations, therefore, provide a compelling, though partial, explanation for lower turnout levels among Latino voters.

Other studies rightly signal that the other key determinant of voting is mobilization and demonstrate that it positively and significantly affects turnout (Gerber et al. 2003; Gerber and Green 2000; Gershtenson 2003; Nickerson 2007; Rosenstone and Hansen 1993). In particular, modern campaigns and mobilization methods often attempt to maximize efficiency with their limited resources and consequently focus on media campaigns, even though personal contact has greater effects (Gerber and Green 2000). The need to be selective in the use of resources has led national campaigns to use segmented voter mobilization strategies that often focus on campaign resources in battleground states (Enos and Fowler 2016).

This finding conforms to previous analyses of partisanship and tactical mobilization strategies used by political campaigns. For instance, Gershtenson (2003) demonstrates how temporal, spatial, and racial considerations affect voter mobilization by partisan campaigns. Gershtenson (2003) finds that Black voters were less likely to report Republican contact during the Civil Rights Era, while Southern Whites were less likely to report Democratic contact during the same era. At the turn of the millennium, Black voters were less likely than non-Blacks to be targeted by the Republican campaign (Panagopoulos and Wielhouwer 2008). Patterns of noncontact, or neglect, are an enduring and defining characteristic of American politics where partisan campaigns privilege the voice of their base and easily accessible groups. Unsurprisingly, campaigns and politicians utilize their limited resources to contact and mobilize those whom they perceive are more likely to turnout to vote (Enos and Fowler 2016; Leighley 2001; Rosenstone and Hansen 1993). We purposefully emphasize that strategies can be based on perceptions, because there are several assumptions made about who votes and the effect of direct mobilization. It is difficult to determine fully whether campaigns target those who vote or whether people vote because campaigns contact them. According to Jan Leighley (2001, 161), "It is virtually impossible to estimate the effects of mobilization on participation while giving sufficient consideration to the extent to which they are interrelated. Individuals and institutions are likely to mobilize those who are likely to participate and mobilization always predicts participation successfully." Even though there is evidence that mobilization can increase Latino turnout (García Bedolla and Michelson 2012; Ramírez 2007; Ramírez 2005; Ramírez 2013), campaigns and candidates often are excused for investing less in mobilizing Latinos and other new electorates because of the strategic nature of campaigns. This is not a new phenomenon. In their analysis of the 1992 election, De la Garza and DeSipio (1996) take it as a given that political campaigns' low rates of Latino mobilization are attributable to low turnout rates among Latino voters. They state:

Candidates, campaigns, and political professionals are knowledgeable about Latino turnout rates. While they may not understand or care about the reasons, they understand the bottom line: investment in traditional voter mobilization in Latino neighborhoods generates relatively few votes because it will reach large numbers of citizens who are less likely to vote. (De la Garza and DeSipio 1996, 5)

As evidenced in figure 1, Latino mobilization will not automatically yield less votes relative to other racial and ethnic communities. The narrative should more appropriately be framed as one where there is a large untapped pool of eligible Latino voters who have not been engaged sufficiently by political parties, candidates, and organizations to feel compelled to overcome the first hurdle of voter registration. Once they are registered to vote, their rate of voting significantly improves and the differences that remain can largely be explained by socioeconomic status, differential rates of mobilization, and other factors. Ramírez, Solano, and Wilcox-Archuleta (2018) demonstrate that race is a key factor accounting for patterns of unequal mobilization as it influences strategic considerations of who is contacted. In particular, White mobilizers are less likely to outreach to minority groups, especially those living in diverse or nonswing states. The conventional wisdom regarding low Latino turnout rates and the concomitant excuses for why campaigns neglect them should thus be revised to account for the fact that campaign strategies often result in neglect of registered Latino voters relative to White voters even when we account for characteristics that make some Latino voters likely to vote.

Differences in resources aside, minorities exhibit a number of unique factors that affect the mobilization calculus that political campaigns and nonpartisan organizations follow. For instance, African Americans and Latinos often reside in residentially segregated communities (Iceland and Weinberg 2002) and have higher residential mobility rates (Ramírez 2008), while Asian Americans and Latinos have larger foreign-born populations in their communities (Lee, Ramakrishnan, and Ramírez 2006; U.S. Census Bureau 2017a). These factors require campaigns to dedicate more time to minority communities than they are willing to invest and may reinforce preexisting perceptions of the difficulties associated with minority voter outreach. Low turnout among minorities, therefore, can be attributed to lower rates of contact in partisan campaign strategies (Ramírez 2008; Stevens and Bishin 2011. If voter turnout is driven by recruitment into politics (Rosenstone and Hansen 1993) and voter mobilization strategies are inherently unequal (Phillips 2016), then Latinos are consequently subject to systematic neglect by partisan campaigns. The tactical mobilization strategies in 2012, which led partisan campaigns to neglect recruiting immigrants and Spanish speakers, should not be surprising. Within the Democratic Party, racial minorities are often deemed as captured groups, and consequently, this perception influences campaign strategies to target high-propensity voters while only symbolically reaching out to minority groups (Fraga and Leal 2004; Frymer 1999; Ramírez 2013; Wong 2006).

In addition to determining whether political campaigns targeted Latinos as much as other racial and ethnic groups, it is also important to determine whether certain characteristics make some Latino voters more likely than others to be contacted by civic organizations, political parties, or campaigns. Among the many changes that took place in 2008 and 2012, the Obama campaign was lauded for its strategic efforts in reaching out to many voters who were previously excluded from presidential campaign strategies (e.g., young voters, LGBT, Latinos, Asians, and blacks). The expectation was that more Latinos would report being contacted to vote. Based on the Latino Decisions 2012 Election Eve Poll, Ramírez and his colleagues (2015) find that context mattered for patterns of mobilization. Of the 11.2 million Latinos who voted in the 2012 election, only 20.7% lived in battleground states (Ramírez et al. 2015). Registered Latino voters residing in battleground states turned out at a higher rate (87%) than Latinos residing in nonbattleground states (80.4%). However, by focusing on the survey variables that are similar to the type of characteristics that may be available for political campaigns to purchase from data vendors, they find that political campaigns' Latino outreach varied considerably (Ramírez et al. 2015). For instance, 65% of registered Latino voters in nonbattleground states reported contact from a partisan campaign, compared to 71% of those residing in battleground states. Moreover, native-born and English-dominant Latinos were more likely to report partisan contact. The disparity in Latino turnout between battleground and nonbattleground states and among demographic subgroups makes it clear that political campaigns in 2012 engaged in tactical mobilization—or short-term voter-engagement efforts focused on increasing Latino turnout (Ramírez et al. 2015).

A closer inspection of the 2012 election reveals that partisan campaigns only selectively mobilized those subgroups with the highest propensity to turnout, even among Latinos. The 2012 Obama campaign targeted native-born and English-dominant Latinos, whereas Spanish-speaking and foreign-born Latinos were left out of the strategic calculus (Ramírez et al. 2015). Nonpartisan organizations filled the void and engaged in their own strategic efforts to mobilize naturalized and Spanish-dominant Latinos. Partisan campaigns' modern mobilization strategies, therefore, inherently favor certain groups while neglecting others.

Patterns of Latino Mobilization in 2016

Despite the preponderance of enthusiastic media outlets parading the caliber of increased identification strategies campaigns utilized in 2012, media outlets have been mostly silent on the topic of partisan mobilization strategies in 2016. Given the distinct patterns of microtargeting strategies that implemented in 2012, it would make sense that similar patterns continued in 2016. Indeed, during the 2016 election, campaigns prioritized White voters over Latino voters, and regardless of race, voters living in battleground states were more likely to report contact (Ramírez, Solano, and Wilcox-Archuleta 2018). The results of the 2016 election, in combination with new insights generated from 2012 election, indicate that the media may have overstated campaigns' capacity to microtarget voters. Rather than appending existing voter data files with private consumer data, Hersh (2015) contends that political campaigns often utilize easily accessible public voter files when developing their mobilization strategies. To date, no study has determined whether political characteristics found in voter files can largely explain the pattern of Latino mobilization, or whether partisan and nonpartisan mobilizers engage in similar microtargeting, explaining variations in self-reported contact within the Latino electorate. To that end, we use only the three questions in the Latino Decisions 2016 Election Eve Poll that ask whether the respondents were contacted, and if so, whether they were contacted by partisan campaigns or nonpartisan organizations. The remainder of our independent variables are exclusively those that came from voter files and other variables provided by Catalist. Our goal is to determine whether information of voter files is sufficient to explain the patterns of mobilization, or whether other information made available by data vendors sheds more light on who is targeted and/or neglected. We contend that the more proximate contact of nonpartisan organizations to the growing segments of the Latino electorate means that for them it is not just the political variables that matter, but rather the personal. This then helps explains the patterns of outreach and neglect due to the differential goals exhibited by partisan and nonpartisan organizations.

Table 1 illustrates the rate of self-reported contact by partisan and nonpartisan organizations for registered Latino voters by national origin. It is important to consider that a majority of Latino voters do not report contact. As such, throughout the text, we reference this mobilization outcome as "neglect." Of the four largest national-origin groups, Cubans report the lowest rate of contact mobilization neglect (69.8%), while Dominicans report the lowest rate of total mobilization contact (11.9%), making them the most neglected (88.1%). While it may be an artifact of smaller numbers, those for whom the data vendors either could not identify by national origin or were not in one of the largest groups appear to be less neglected than any other national origin group (64% and 63.3%, respectively). Not only is it important to note that Latino national origin appears to matter for overall patterns of neglect, but it also seems to matter for the distribution of the type of contact because there are very different patterns for the types of contact each of the national origin groups report. There is no single pattern of contact type reported. For example, Cuban- and Mexican-registered voters report "only partisan" contact at a greater rate than "both partisan and nonpartisan" and then "only nonpartisan" contact. Puerto Ricans, on the other hand, report that they were more likely to be contacted

Table 1. 2016 Mobilization Type by National Origin Among Latino Registered Voters Contacted (Row Percent)

Mobilization by type	Neglect	Only partisan	Only nonpartisan	Partisan and nonpartisan
Cuban	69.8%	15.1%	3.5%	11.6%
Dominican	88.1%	3.4%	3.4%	5.1%
Mexican	72.5%	12.3%	5.2%	10.1%
Puerto Rican	72.1%	13.2%	8.5%	6.3%
Other Latino	63.3%	16.7%	6.7%	13.3%
Unknown	64%	14.6%	5.9%	15.5%

Source: Latino Decisions 2016 Election Eve Poll. Analyses presented are weighted.

Table 2. 2016 Mobilization Type by Selected Individual Characteristics Among Latino Registered Voters Contacted (Row Percent)

	Neglect	Only partisan	Only nonpartisan	Partisan and nonpartisan
Age (years)				
<30	64.4%	13.6%	8.3%	13.8%
30–39	72.6%	13.8%	4.0%	9.6%
40–49	72.3%	10.8%	8.1%	8.8%
50–59	67.5%	13.8%	4.4%	14.3%
60–69	76.1%	9.7%	4.1%	10.1%
>70	78.0%	15.0%	1.8%	5.1%
Gender				
Female	70.60%	13.20%	5.80%	10.40%
Male	71.30%	12.50%	5.00%	11.30%
Marital status				
Married	73.20%	11.00%	4.80%	11.10%
Single	68.90%	14.50%	6.20%	10.50%
Unknown	72.10%	12.40%	4.30%	11.20%
Religious affiliation				
Catholic	72.60%	12.30%	5.10%	9.90%
Non-Catholic	79.50%	15.40%	0.00%	5.10%
Unknown	63.20%	14.70%	7.10%	15.00%
Income				
<$20K	75.0%	13.5%	2.4%	9.1%
$20K–$50K	71.7%	14.9%	4.9%	8.5%
$50K–$100K	71.9%	10.9%	6.3%	10.9%
Over $100K	74.5%	11.9%	2.9%	10.7%
Unknown	64.4%	13.2%	7.4%	14.9%

Source: Latino Decisions 2016 Election Eve Poll. Analyses presented are weighted.

exclusively by partisan sources most frequently, followed by exclusively nonpartisan sources, and then both partisan and nonpartisan outreach. Dominicans were more likely to report contact from both sources, and they were equally as likely to report contact from exclusively nonpartisan and partisan contact.

In table 2, we provide self-reported contact rates based on individual characteristics among registered Latino voters. To maximize readability, we parse out the data into five additional key characteristics that are readily available in data purchased from data vendors like Catalist: age, gender, marital status, religious affiliation, and income.

AGE

Overall, there is no clear, linear pattern for how age structures partisan and nonpartisan contact. The youngest cohort reports the lowest rate of neglect (64.4%), followed by the fifty- to fifty-nine-year-old cohort (67.5%). For all other cohorts, closer to three-quarters of respondents are neglected by both partisan and nonpartisan campaigns. The distribution of type of mobilization contact is interesting in that registered voters under the age of fifty are more likely to report exclusive partisan contact than exclusively nonpartisan or both types of contact. However, Latino voters between fifty and sixty-nine are more likely to be targets of both partisan and nonpartisan campaigns. The age cohorts that report more even distribution of the type of mobilization contact were those under thirty and Latino voters aged forty to forty-nine. In the former, 13.6% reported exclusive partisan contact, 8.3% reported exclusive nonpartisan contact, and 13.8% reported contact from both. In the latter cohort, the type of contact was more evenly distributed because 10.8% reported exclusive partisan contact, 8.1% reported exclusive nonpartisan contact, and 8.8% reported both types of contact. While the rate of overall contact should not be celebrated, it is promising that the youngest cohort does appear to be contacted more. The more even distribution in the type of contact could be seen in a positive light because this is where most of the growth in Latino voters will occur. If partisan and nonpartisan campaigns continue to target this growth segment, it is possible that the established pattern of the neglected Latino voter could begin to change.

GENDER AND MARITAL STATUS

There were very few differences in rates of contact, neglect, or type of contact for registered Latino and Latina voters. Both Latina and Latino respondents were more likely to report that political parties contacted them (13.2% and 12.5%). One of the surprising emergent patterns is that those voters who identified as single in the Catalist data were less likely to be neglected (68.9%) than those who identified as married (73.2%) or those who could not be identified as either (72.1%). Not only are single Latino voters more likely to report any contact, but the type of contact that they report is more likely to come from exclusively partisan campaigns (14.5%).

RELIGIOUS AFFILIATION

When discussing the role of religion regarding the political behavior of Latino voters, the focus tends to be on vote propensity or vote choice. That is, researchers will ask, "To what extent do Catholics (or other religious affiliation) vote and which party do they support?" We know very little about whether partisan or nonpartisan mobilizers distinctly target Latinos based on their religious affiliation. While the proportion of Latinos who identify as Catholic is diminishing, they are still the largest group. Given their large presence, we may expect that voters who identified as Catholic would be the most likely target of mobilization efforts. Interestingly, while those who identified as Catholic were less likely to be neglected (72.6%) than non-Catholic Latino voters (79.5%), those voters who did not identify as a member of a particular religion reported the lowest rate of neglect (63.2%). This should not be read as nonreligious Latinos being contacted more, but rather, those for whom data vendors cannot readily identify a particular religion are more likely to be contacted. It could very well be that many of these voters do identify with a religion, but the personal nature of religion makes it a variable unconducive to categorization to data vendors. It is still curious that this group reported more overall recruitment to the polls than those who identified as either Catholic or non-Catholic. Even more interesting is that our data indicated that non-Catholics did not report contact from exclusively nonpartisan mobilizers. Partisan and nonpartisan sources contacted them, as well as contact exclusively by partisan sources.

INCOME

According to the participation and mobilization literature, we should expect a linear and positive relationship between income and both participation and mobilization. While respondents earning less than $20,000 reported the highest rate of mobilization neglect (75%), those respondents earning more than $100,000 reported almost the same level of neglect (74.5%). Respondents with incomes falling between $20,000 and $100,000 reported slightly less neglect at a rate of less than 72%. Interestingly, respondents with unknown income earnings reported the lowest rate of neglect (64.4%); they were the only income category that reported higher rates of contact from both partisan and nonpartisan sources at a greater rate than exclusively partisan or nonpartisan contact. Quite unexpectedly, the pattern of reported mobilization suggests that not being easily classified into a particular income category yields more interest by both partisan and nonpartisan contact. In the following section, we move from personal characteristics to those considered political and accessible from voter file.

If, as Hersh (2015) suggests, characteristics found in voter files can largely explain mobilization, then distinct patterns of contact should be evident when considering "political variables." In table 3, we report the rate of self-reported partisan contact for registered Latino voters, where some interesting patterns emerge. First, Latino Democrats reported the highest rate of contact overall (30% contact, 70% neglect). What was more interesting is these voters had contact rates very similar to those of registered nonpartisans, which is comprised of those with "unknown" partisanship (UNK), those who indicated "decline to state" (DTS), "independent" (IND), or "no party affiliation" (NPA). There were some differences among registered Democrats, registered Republicans, and nonpartisan voters based on the

Table 3. 2016 Mobilization Type by Selected Political Variables Among Latino Registered Voters Contacted (Row Percent)

	Neglect	Only partisan	Only nonpartisan	Partisan and nonpartisan
Party registration				
Democrat	70.0%	14.7%	5.2%	10.1%
Republican	78.0%	10.6%	2.3%	9.1%
UNK/DTS/IND/NPA*	70.2%	11.0%	6.8%	12.0%
Registration date				
New registered voter	64.6%	13.1%	7.5%	14.8%
Registered before 2015	72.5%	12.7%	5.0%	9.9%
Battleground state				
Nonbattleground	74.5%	10.2%	5.2%	10.0%
Battleground	62.3%	19.0%	6.0%	12.7%

*Unknown/Decline to State/Independent/No Party Affiliation.

type of contact received. Latino Democrats reported the highest rate of contact (14.7%) by only partisan mobilizers, while Latino Republicans reported the lowest rate (10.6%). As should be expected, Latino nonpartisans were more likely to report "only nonpartisan" mobilizers (6.8%) or a combination of nonpartisan and partisan mobilizers (12%), while 5.2% of Democrats reported "only nonpartisan" contact and 10.1% reported contact from a combination of partisan and nonpartisan mobilizers. In each of the three types of contact, Republicans reported the lowest rate of contact. Another way to view this is that Latino Republicans reported the highest rate of neglect or lack of contact (78%) of anyone.

As this table demonstrates, it is not just about whether individual voters are registered with a political party, but it is also important to consider whether they were existing or newly registered voters. On the one hand, there is more information about existing voters with respect to vote history; on the other hand, new voters' contact information is more likely to be current. Quite surprisingly, voters for whom this was the first presidential election were more likely to report each of the three types of contact (partisan, nonpartisan, or both). In other words, Latinos registered to vote before 2015 were more likely to be neglected by mobilizers, with 72.5% of existing voters compared to 64.6% of those newly registered. The final political variable we considered was whether these registered voters live in a battle-ground state. As expected, Latinos living in battleground states reported the highest rate of contact, irrespective of type of contact. Latinos living in battleground states reported the lowest rate of neglect than Latinos living in nonbattleground states (62.3% vs 74.5%).

While the above differences in reported contact by partisan or nonpartisan sources are interesting, it is important to consider the significance of these variables in multivariate regressions. Our dependent variables are self-reported, mobilization items taken from the 2016 Latino Decisions 2016 Election Eve Poll. The self-reported items indicate contact by partisan campaigns, nonpartisan organizations, and/or contact by both partisan campaigns and nonpartisan organizations during the 2016 election cycle. We use logit models, given the dichotomous nature of the dependent variables in each model, while controlling for individual personal characteristics, such as age, national origin, gender, and income. Political characteristics here are operationalized as recency of voter registration, party registration, and whether an individual lives in a battleground state or not. One approach considers linear effects of ordinal variables, such as age and income, but we allowed for a nonlinear relationship of these variables and self-reported contact. When the variables are in dichotomous groups, the reference category is listed next to the first variable. For example, the reference category for age is voters under thirty years old, whereas the reference category for income is those who make less than $20,000. The remaining variables were either dichotomous with only two possibilities or were categorical in nature and therefore required us to separate them into multiple dichotomous variables. The respective reference categories include "Married," "Catholic," "Mexican," and "Democrat." This allows us to understand better how certain groups are more or less likely to be targets for mobilization by partisan campaigns or nonpartisan groups based on the personal and political characteristics of the respondent. Table 4 presents the results for the first four logit regression models that highlight partisan contact.

The dependent variable for Model I is contact by any partisan campaign, including contact from both Democratic and Republican campaigns.

It should be noted that this model allows for respondents who were also contacted by nonpartisan organizations. Registered Republicans were less likely to report contact from partisan campaigns. Some of this may be attributable to strategic decisions by partisan campaigns that make Latino Republicans less essential to election outcomes. As was the case in 2012, all else being equal, Latino respondents living in battleground states were more likely to report contact from a partisan campaign. Less expected was that resource-based variables that make someone likely to vote did not appear to affect the likelihood of partisan contact. In particular, income does not impact who gets contacted by partisan campaigns. There were less consistent patterns for other individual-level variables. Respondents between the ages of forty and forty-nine and over the age of sixty were less likely to report contact from any partisan campaign. Respondents identified as Dominican in the Catalist data were less likely to report contact from a partisan campaign. We were not necessarily expecting, a priori, certain national origin groups to report differential rates of contact. However, this became an interesting characteristic evident in the patterns of partisan mobilization.

Although the first model did not exclude from consideration those respondents who were contacted nonpartisan sources, the dependent variable for Model II is reported contact by only partisan campaigns. Age is no longer a statistically significant determinant of contact. Dominicans remain less likely to report contact than voters of Mexican origin. It is not clear why single voters are more likely than married voters to report only partisan contact. With respect to political variables, Republicans were still less likely to report contact by exclusively partisan campaigns, while voters in battleground states were more likely to report only partisan contact.

The dependent variable for Model III is reported contact only from a Democratic source. Relative to young voters under thirty, voters between the ages of forty and forty-nine were less likely to report Democratic contact, while respondents between the ages of fifty and fifty-nine were more likely to report contact by Democrats. All else being equal, respondents identified as either Dominican or Puerto Rican were less likely to report Democratic contact relative to Mexican-origin respondents. Not surprisingly, registered

Table 4. Predictors of Self-Reported Mobilization of Latinos, by Source of Mobilization

	Model I, partisan	Model II, only partisan	Model III, Democrat	Model IV, Republican
Age 30–39 (<30)	−0.093	0.15	−0.031	−0.022
	(0.144)	(0.180)	(0.149)	(0.210)
Age 40–49	−0.317*	−0.11	−0.308*	0.072
	(0.149)	(0.191)	(0.157)	(0.204)
Age 50–59	0.184	0.146	0.27[†]	0.353[†]
	(0.137)	(0.176)	(0.142)	(0.191)
Age 60–69	−0.261[†]	−0.224	−0.193	0.09
	(0.147)	(0.193)	(0.153)	(0.202)
Age 70+	−0.305[†]	0.23	−0.175	−0.209
	(0.163)	(0.196)	(0.171)	(0.230)
Male	0.004	−0.048	−0.095	0.128
	(0.082)	(0.105)	(0.085)	(0.112)
Income $20K–50K (<$20K)	0.005	0.286	0.256	−0.188
	(0.189)	(0.233)	(0.206)	(0.258)
Income $50K–100K	−0.166	−0.033	0.117	−0.189
	(0.203)	(0.254)	(0.220)	(0.272)
Income $100K+	−0.068	0.215	0.28	−0.447
	(0.234)	(0.297)	(0.252)	(0.316)
Unknown income	−0.323	−0.194	−0.223	−0.748
	(0.345)	(0.440)	(0.367)	(0.458)
Single (married)	−0.006	0.237[†]	0.084	−0.248[†]
	(0.099)	(0.126)	(0.103)	(0.132)
Unknown marital status	−0.284	0.262	−0.144	−0.644[†]
	(0.217)	(0.283)	(0.225)	(0.336)
Other religion (Catholic)	−0.312	0.113	−0.378	0.497
	(0.438)	(0.487)	(0.476)	(0.490)

Republicans were less likely to report Democratic contact and Latino voters living in battleground were more likely to be targeted by Democrats.

The dependent variable in Model IV is reported contact by a Republican campaign only, excluding contact from Democratic campaigns and nonpartisan organizations. Respondents between the ages of fifty and fifty-nine were more likely to report contact by a Republican campaign. Respondents with an unknown national origin were more likely to report Republican contact. Respondents who registered as Republicans were more

	Model I, partisan	Model II, only partisan	Model III, Democrat	Model IV, Republican
Unknown religion	0.285	0.395	0.32	0.361
	(0.203)	(0.254)	(0.213)	(0.269)
Cuban (**Mexican**)	−0.045	−0.208	−0.123	0.269
	(0.196)	(0.242)	(0.211)	(0.233)
Dominican	−0.86[†]	−1.107[†]	−0.767[†]	−1.08
	(0.448)	(0.666)	(0.449)	(0.834)
Puerto Rican	−0.245	−0.026	−0.294[†]	0.08
	(0.166)	(0.196)	(0.174)	(0.216)
Other Latino	0.316	0.021	0.214	0.015
	(0.442)	(0.565)	(0.475)	(0.557)
Unknown Latino	0.059	−0.193	0.023	0.167
	(0.186)	(0.236)	(0.194)	(0.248)
Registered GOP (**DEM**)	−0.431[‡]	−0.495*	−0.803[‡]	0.437*
	(0.148)	(0.189)	(0.169)	(0.171)
Declined to state	−0.053	−0.222	−0.088	0.246*
	(0.088)	(0.113)	(0.091)	(0.124)
Registered other	0.46	0.658	−0.015	1.039[‡]
	(0.308)	(0.356)	(0.349)	(0.365)
Battleground state	0.571[‡]	0.768[‡]	0.53[‡]	0.585[‡]
	(0.095)	(0.117)	(0.099)	(0.129)
New voter	0.184	−0.023	0.304	0.169
	(0.266)	(0.344)	(0.278)	(0.341)
Constant	−1.169[‡]	−2.33[‡]	−1.556[‡]	−2.345[‡]
	(0.232)	(0.293)	(0.251)	(0.316)
N	4602	4602	4602	4602

*$p < 0.1$, [†]$p < 0.05$, [‡]$p < 0.01$

Note: Reference categories are bold and in parentheses.

likely to report contact. Respondents who did not register as Republicans or Democrats were more likely to report contact. Finally, respondents living in battleground states were more likely to report contact.

Table 5 presents the results for the next four logit regression models. It reports the coefficients of the models with standard errors in parentheses. The dependent variable in Model V is reported contact by any source, including both partisan and nonpartisan contact. Respondents over the age of sixty were less likely report to report any kind of contact. Respondents

Table 5. Predictors of Self-Reported Mobilization of Latinos, by Source of Mobilization

	Model V, any	Model VI, nonpartisan	Model VII, only nonpartisan	Model VIII, partisan + nonpartisan
Age 30–39 (<30)	−0.144	−0.541*	−0.775*	−0.344[†]
	(0.131)	(0.169)	(0.282)	(0.200)
Age 40–49	−0.106	−0.31[†]	−0.02	−0.474[‡]
	(0.132)	(0.162)	(0.239)	(0.204)
Age 50–59	0.054	−0.103	−0.615[‡]	0.155
	(0.127)	(0.155)*	(0.266)	(0.180)
Age 60–69	−0.211	−0.456	−0.758*	−0.241
	(0.132)	(0.166)*	(0.279)	(0.195)
Age 70+	−0.424*	−1.25	−1.451*	−1.042*
	(0.15)	(0.222)	(0.401)	(0.260)
Male	0.027	−0.002	−0.102	0.059
	(0.074)	(0.094)	(0.154)	(0.112)
Income 20K–50K (<$20K)	−0.059	−0.108	0.486	−0.376
	(0.173)	(0.244)	(0.476)	(0.275)
Income 50K–100K	−0.057	−0.003	0.65	−0.325
	(0.184)	(0.252)	(0.488)	(0.286)
Income 100K+	−0.252	−0.347	−0.275	−0.409
	(0.215)	(0.29)	(0.574)	(0.325)
Unknown income	−0.243	−0.183	0.444	−0.456
	(0.315)	(0.399)	(0.699)	(0.463)
Single (married)	0.004	−0.222[‡]	−0.061	−0.29[‡]
	(0.089)	(0.115)	(0.188)	(0.136)
Unknown marital status	−0.395[‡]	−0.779*	−0.568	−0.775*
	(0.198)	(0.247)	(0.424)	(0.285)
Other religion (Catholic)	−0.414	−1.260[†]	−1.682	−1.024
	(0.402)	(0.739)	(1.609)	(0.821)

indicating Dominican national origin were less likely to report any kind of contact. Income does not impact who gets contacted in Model V. Respondents who registered as Republicans were also less likely to report contact of any kind. Finally, respondents living in a battleground state were more likely to report contact of any kind.

The dependent variable in Model VI is reported contact by a nonpartisan organization. It is important to note that some of these respondents may also have been contacted by partisan sources. Respondents between

	Model V, any	Model VI, nonpartisan	Model VII, only nonpartisan	Model VIII, partisan + nonpartisan
Unknown religion	0.284	0.244	0.477	0.066
	(0.187)	(0.232)	(0.352)	(0.276)
Cuban (Mexican)	−0.107	−0.003	−0.445	0.189
	(0.183)	(0.244)	(0.472)	(0.273)
Dominican	−0.969‡	−0.54	−0.606	−0.473
	(0.394)	(0.486)	(0.836)	(0.578)
Puerto Rican	−0.121	0.008	0.635‡	−0.502†
	(0.145)	(0.187)	(0.251)	(0.265)
Other Latino	0.353	0.683	0.591	0.591
	(0.41)	(0.489)	(0.744)	(0.572)
Unknown Latino	0.016	0.03	−0.576†	0.342
	(0.171)	(0.215)	(0.349)	(0.249)
Registered GOP (DEM)	−0.54*	−0.336	−0.617	−0.224
	(0.136)	(0.182)	(0.366)	(0.204)
Declined to state	0.004	0.240‡	0.339‡	0.152
	(0.079)	(0.1)	(0.162)	(0.120)
Registered other	0.078	−0.328	−18.068	0.044
	(0.305)	(0.445)	(5439)	(0.449)
Battleground state	0.571*	0.185	0.192	0.143
	(0.088)	(0.113)	(0.180)	(0.135)
New voter	0.232	0.319	0.157	0.355
	(0.244)	(0.295)	(0.482)	(0.346)
Constant	−0.742*	−1.324*	−3.019*	−1.624*
	(0.212)	(0.283)	(0.532)	(0.322)
N	4602	4602	4602	4602

$*p < 0.01$, $†p < 0.1$, $‡p < 0.05$.

the ages of thirty and forty-nine and respondents over the age of sixty were less likely to report contact. Respondents who declined to state their registration affiliation were more likely to report contact. Respondents who indicated not being married and those with an unknown marital status were less likely to report contact. Similarly, respondents who indicated not being Catholic were less likely to report contact. It is important to consider whether nonpartisan organizations strategically target registered Latino voters in ways that are distinct. To that end, the dependent variable in

Model VII is reported contact only by nonpartisan organizations. Respondents between the ages of thirty and thirty-nine and respondents over the age of fifty were less likely to report contact. In both Model VI and Model VII, living in a battleground state did not lead to more reported contact. One of the more interesting changes when we focus exclusively on nonpartisan contact is that respondents of Puerto Rican national origin were more likely to report contact relative to those of Mexican national origin, while controlling for all other personal and political characteristics. Given the statistically significant change, this gives support to the notion that the identity of the mobilizers matters regarding who is neglected and targeted, and it is not simply a matter of voter characteristics from the voter file.

Conclusion

A retrospective look at the media coverage of past presidential elections reveals two now-familiar narratives about the Latino vote: (1) Latino voters are poised to determine the election outcome and (2) there will be an election "surprise" regarding some aspect of Latino voter turnout. In 2008 and 2012, the unexpectedly high Latino turnout for the Democratic candidate gained attention. In 2016, attention focused more on exit poll results indicating higher-than-expected turnout for the Republican candidate. In the 2008 and 2012 elections, the higher-than-expected Latino turnout was attributed to enhanced microtargeting strategies that the Obama campaign utilized. The narratives surrounding the 2016 election were markedly less cohesive due to the confusion as to what happened with the Latino vote. Latching on to exit poll results, media outlets were quick to report that Clinton won the Latino vote (66%) but were unable to match 2012 Latino support (71%) for Obama (Krogstad and Lopez 2016). However, upon closer inspection of the data, Latino Decisions estimates that Latinos gave 79% of their votes to Clinton, far surpassing the 2012 Latino vote (71%) for Obama. Additionally, overall minority voter turnout declined between 2012 and 2016, with Black turnout having the largest drop (U.S. Census Bureau 2017b). What is particularly puzzling regarding narratives surrounding the

2016 Latino vote is the relative absence of campaign- and partisan-related explanations that were prevalent during the 2008 and 2012 narratives. Although partisan campaigns were credited for increased Latino turnout in 2008 and 2012, mobilization-type explanations have been largely absent in 2016.

We contend that in order to fully understand why Latino voters participate or who they vote for, one must fully consider whether Latino voters are included in actual voter mobilization efforts as well as the extent to which segments of the Latino electorate are neglected. Our analyses of how personal and political variables matter for mobilization efforts suggest that it is not simply about whether Latinos are likely voters or whether they may be key segments of the electorate in battleground states. Instead, it is important to distinguish between partisan and nonpartisan mobilizers. The patterns that emerge contrast claims that mobilization strategies can be explained largely by variables in the voter files. We find that national origin, marital status, and even religion can help shape who either partisan or nonpartisan mobilizers contact. Even more interesting is the fact that, sometimes, those registered Latino voters for whom there is less information or certainty of partisan preferences, religious affiliation, or marital status were more likely to report contact from various sources. Perhaps the case perceptions do matter, and mobilizers' certain established perceptions about likelihood of voting or likely vote-choice preferences lead to certain patterns of contact. Conversely, it may mean that they also hedge their bets with outreach to those voters for whom they have less information. Those patterns aside, it is important to point out that the rates of partisan outreach to Latino voters need to change perceptions of Latinos as an unmotivated electorate. When Latino voters are motivated by the political context or when they are actively incorporated into mobilization strategies, they can affect election outcomes and be consequential.

Notes

This material is based upon work partially supported by the National Science Foundation under grant number DGE-1313583. Any opinions, findings, conclusions, or recommendations expressed in this material are those of the author(s) and do not necessarily reflect those of the National Science Foundation.

1. For considerably different and more nuanced views, see Gross and Barreto (2015).

References

Abrajano, Marisa A. 2010. *Campaigning to the New American Electorate: Advertising to Latino Voters.* Stanford: Stanford University Press.

Abrajano, Marisa A., R. Michael Alvarez, and Jonathan Nagler. 2008. "The Hispanic Vote in the 2004 Presidential Election: Insecurity and Moral Concerns." *Journal of Politics* 70 (2): 368–82.

Barreto, Matt A. 2005. "Latino Immigrants at the Polls: Foreign-Born Voter Turnout in the 2002 Election." *Political Research Quarterly* 58 (1): 79–86.

———. 2010. *Ethnic Cues: The Role of Shared Ethnicity in Latino Political Participation.* Ann Arbor: University of Michigan Press.

Bowler, Shaun, and Gary Segura. 2011. *The Future Is Ours: Minority Politics, Political Behavior, and the Multiracial Era of American Politics.* Washington, DC: Congressional Quarterly Press.

Cillizza, Chris. 2013. "The Hispanic Vote Is a Sleeping Political Giant. It Might Never Wake Up." *Washington Post.* June 4.

Damore, David. 2013. "How Latino Voters May Decide Control of the U.S. House of Representatives." *Latino Decisions,* July 9.

De la Garza, Rodolfo O., and Louis DeSipio, eds. 1996. *Ethnic Ironies: Latino Politics in the 1992 Elections.* Boulder, CO: Westview Press.

———, eds. 1999. *Awash in the Mainstream: Latino Politics in the 1996 Elections.* Boulder, CO: Westview Press.

———, eds. 2004. *Muted Voices: Latinos and the 2000 Elections.* Lanham, MD: Rowman and Littlefield.

Enos, Ryan D., and Anthony Fowler. 2016. "Aggregate Effects of Large-Scale Campaigns on Voter Turnout." *Political Science Research and Methods* 4 (2): 1–19.

Fraga, Luis R., and David L. Leal. 2004. "Playing the 'Latino Card': Race, Ethnicity, and National Party Politics." *DuBois Review: Social Science Research on Race* 1 (2): 297–317.

Frymer, Paul. 1999. *Uneasy Alliances: Race and Party Competition in America.* Princeton, NJ: Princeton University Press.

García Bedolla, Lisa, and Melissa R. Michelson. 2012. *Mobilizing Inclusion.* New Haven, CT: Yale University Press.

Gerber, Alan, and Donald Green. 2000. "The Effects of Canvassing, Direct Mail, and Telephone Contact on Voter Turnout: A Field Experiment." *American Political Science Review* 94 (3): 653–63.

Gerber, Alan S., Donald P. Green, and Matthew Green. 2003. "Partisan Mail and Voter Turnout: Results from Randomized Field Experiments." *Electoral Studies* 22 (4): 563–79.

Gershtenson, Joseph. 2003. "Mobilization Strategies of the Democrats and Republicans, 1956–2000." *Political Research Quarterly* 56 (3): 293–308.

Gross, Justin H., and Matt Barreto. 2015. "Latino Influence and the Electoral College: Assessing the Probability of Group Relevance." In *Latinos and the 2012 Election: The New Face of the American Voter,* edited by Gabriel R. Sanchez, 1–18. East Lansing: Michigan State University Press.

Hersh, Eitan. 2015. *Hacking the Electorate: How Campaigns Perceive Voters.* New York: Cambridge University Press.

Iceland, John, and Daniel H. Weinberg. 2002. *Racial and Ethnic Residential Segregation in the United States: 1980–2000.* Census 2000 Special Report, Washington, DC.

Krogstad, Jens Manuel, and Mark Hugo Lopez. 2016. "Hillary Clinton Won Latino Vote but Fell Below 2012 Support for Obama." Pew Research Center. https://www.pewresearch.org/fact-tank/2016/11/29/hillary-clinton-wins-latino-vote-but-falls-below-2012-support-for-obama/.

———. 2017. "Black Voter Turnout Fell in 2016, Even as a Record Number of Americans Cast Ballots." Pew Research Center. http://www.pewresearch.org/fact-tank/2017/05/12/black-voter-turnout-fell-in-2016-even-as-a-record-number-of-americans-cast-ballots/.

Lee, Taeku, S. K. Ramakrishnan, and Ricardo Ramírez. 2006. *Transforming Politics, Transforming America: The Political and Civic Incorporation of Immigrants in the United States.* Charlottesville: University of Virginia Press.

Leighley, Jan E. 2001. *Strength in Numbers? The Political Mobilization of Racial and Ethnic Minorities.* Princeton, NJ: Princeton University Press.

McArthur, Loren. 2014. "The Latino Vote Can Make a Difference in the 2014 Elections." *Huffington Post,* January 23.

Medina Vidal, Xavier. 2018. "Latino Immigrant Home-Country Media Use and Participation in US Politics." *Hispanic Journal of Behavioral Sciences* 40 (1): 37–56.

Merolla, Jennifer L., Adrian D. Pantoja, Ivy A. M. Cargile, and Juana Mora. 2013.

"From Coverage to Action: The Immigration Debate and Its Effects on Participation." *Political Research Quarterly* 66 (2): 322–35.

Michelson, Melissa R. 2005. "Meeting the Challenge of Latino Voter Mobilization." *Annals of Political and Social Science* 601 (1): 85–101.

Nickerson, David W. 2007. "Quality Is Job One: Professional and Volunteer Voter Mobilization Calls." *American Journal of Political Science* 51 (2): 269–82.

Panagopoulos, Costas, and Peter W. Wielhouwer. 2008. "Polls and Elections the Ground War 2000-2004: Strategic Targeting in Grassroots Campaigns." *Presidential Studies Quarterly* 38 (2): 347–62.

Pantoja, Adrian D., Ricardo Ramírez, and Gary M. Segura. 2001. "Citizens by Choice, Voters by Necessity: Patterns in Political Mobilization by Naturalized Latinos." *Political Research Quarterly* 54 (4): 729–50.

Phillips, Steve. 2016. *Brown Is the New White: How the Demographic Revolution Has Created a New American Majority.* New York: New Press.

Ramírez, Ricardo. 2005. "Giving Voice to Latino Voters: A Field Experiment on the Effectiveness of a National Nonpartisan Mobilization Effort." *Annals of the American Academy of Political and Social Science* 601 (1): 66–84.

———. 2007. "Segmented Mobilization: Latino Nonpartisan Get-Out-the-Vote Efforts in the 2000 General Election." *American Politics Research* 35 (2): 155–75.

———. 2008. "Residential Mobility and the Political Mobilization of Latinos in Houston." In *Latino Politics: Identity, Mobilization, and Representation,* edited by R. Espino, D. Leal, and K. Meier, 90–103. Charlottesville: University of Virginia Press.

———. 2013. *Mobilizing Opportunities the Evolving Latino Electorate and the Future of American Politics.* Charlottesville: University of Press.

Ramírez, Ricardo, Evan Bacalao, Edelmira P. Garcia, Rani Narula-Woods, and Clayton Rosa. 2015. "Proactive, Reactive, and Tactical: Mobilizing the Latino Vote in 2012." In *Latinos and the 2012 Election: The New Face of the American Voter,* edited by Gabriel R. Sanchez, 29–45. East Lansing: Michigan State University Press.

Ramírez, Ricardo, Romelia Solano, and Bryan Wilcox-Archuleta. 2018. "Selective Recruitment or Voter Neglect? Race, Place, and Voter Mobilization in 2016." *Journal of Race, Ethnicity and Politics* 3(1): 156–84.

Rosenstone, Steven J., and John Hansen. 1993. *Mobilization, Participation, and Democracy in America.* New York: Macmillan Press.

Schechter, Dave. 2012. "'Sleeping Giant' Latino Vote Yet to Awaken." *CNN.com,* May 30.

Scherer, Michael. 2012. "Yo Decido: Why Latino Voters Will Pick the Next President." *Time Magazine*, March 5.

Stevens, Daniel, and Benjamin Bishin. 2011. "Getting Out the Vote: Minority Mobilization in a Presidential Election." *Political Behavior* 33 (1): 113-38.

U.S. Census Bureau. 2017a. "American Community Survey, 2011-2015: Voting Age Population by Citizenship and Race." https://www.census.gov/rdo/data/ voting_age_population_by_citizenship_and_race_cvap.html.

———. 2017b. "Voting and Registration in the Election of November 2016 (Table 4b: Reported Voting and Registration by Sex, Race and Hispanic Origin, for States) (Nov. 2016)." https://www.census.gov/data/tables/timeseries/demo/voting-and-registration/p20-580.html.

Verba, Sidney, and Norman H. Nie. 1972. *Participation in America: Political Democracy and Social Equality.* New York: Harper & Row.

Verba, Sidney, Kay Lehman Schlozman, and Henry E. Brady. 1995. *Voice and Equality: Civic Voluntarism in American Politics.* Cambridge, MA: Harvard University Press.

Wong, Janelle. 2006. *Democracy's Promise Immigrants & American Civic Institutions.* Ann Arbor: University of Michigan Press.

Zepeda-Millán, Chris. 2017. *Latino Mass Mobilization: Immigration, Racialization, and Activism.* New York: Cambridge University Press.

The Puerto Rican Diaspora in the 2016 Elections

Aileen Cardona-Arroyo

THIS CHAPTER FOCUSES ON A GROUP OF LATINO VOTERS COMPRISED ENtirely of native-born citizens in the United States: Puerto Ricans. Despite their citizenship status at birth, in many ways Puerto Ricans undergo similar experiences to other national-origin Latinos upon arrival to the U.S. mainland (DeSipio and Pantoja 2007). Indeed, Puerto Ricans do have a distinct sense of nationhood independent to the United States (Duany 2003). Thus, when island Puerto Ricans migrate to the mainland, the political contexts to which they arrive shape their political socialization and participation (Cámara-Fuertes 2004; Vargas-Ramos 2016)—the importance of which is accentuated by the fact that stateside Puerto Ricans have grown to outnumber Puerto Ricans in the island.

The ongoing, fast-paced migration from the island to the mainland makes it difficult to calculate the exact number of stateside Puerto Ricans. However, U.S. Census estimates suggest that by 2016 the number of stateside Puerto Ricans rose to approximately 5.5 million compared to a steadily declining population of 3.4 million on the island. This means that if current trends continue, the population of stateside Puerto Ricans will eventually double that of their island counterparts. This represents a massive population shift. Indeed, as recently as the early to mid-2000s, the number of Puerto Ricans in the island remained larger than that of those on the mainland. Thus, understanding the relationship between the political contexts of migration and the electoral behavior of Puerto Ricans is now more important than ever.

This chapter provides a comparative analysis of the contexts of migration during two periods of peak exodus from the island to the mainland: (1) "The Great Migration" of the 1950s to New York City and the Northeast and (2) the present (and ongoing) migration to central Florida and other Southern states. Specifically, I examine how these distinct environments of political socialization shape the electoral behavior and political attitudes of old- and new-destination Puerto Ricans in the 2016 presidential elections. While the analysis in this chapter centers on the reality of stateside Puerto Ricans during the most recent presidential election cycle, it should be noted that the migration of Puerto Ricans to the mainland massively intensified after the devastating effects of Hurricane Maria in September of 2017 (Hinojosa et al. 2018). Considering that many of those Puerto Ricans are making the swing state of Florida their new home, any conclusions emerging from the present analysis should be of particular interest to scholars and political analysts alike as they consider the growing importance of the (new) Puerto Rican electorate in the United States.

The Origins of Puerto Ricans in the United States

The relationship between Puerto Rico and the United States is both long and complicated. In the aftermath of the Spanish-American War and the signing of the Treaty of Paris on December 10, 1898, the United States took over the former Spanish colonies of Puerto Rico, Cuba, Guam, and the Philippines. Since that time, the United States has embarked on a path to define and redefine repeatedly the place of the island—and its inhabitants—within the larger American nation. Through a series of legal decisions after the Spanish-American War commonly referred to as the "insular cases," the courts established the nature of the relationship between the United States and its dependencies, including Puerto Rico. Most notably, the decisions of the Supreme Court created the precedent that the U.S. Constitution does not apply in its entirety in the territories (Román and Simmons 2002). Thus, when the U.S. Congress extended citizenship to Puerto Ricans under the Jones Act of 1917, it did not automatically extend full political rights to Puerto Ricans on the island.

Unlike for their counterparts in the states, the Fourteenth Amendment does not ground the political rights of citizens in U.S. territories, but rather this is done by the Territorial Clause, which bestows on Congress complete authority to decide the administration of the territories. As a result, Puerto Ricans are the only Latino subgroup in the United States solely comprised of native-born citizens. However, unlike other Latino citizens on the mainland, both native-born and naturalized, the extent of the group's political rights is subject to a geographic caveat. Only those who reside in one of the fifty states—but not on the island—are eligible to vote in U.S. national elections (Cámara Fuertes 2004).

STATESIDE PUERTO RICANS IN OLD NORTHEAST ENCLAVES AND NEW SOUTHERN SETTLEMENTS

During the first half of the twentieth century, the duality of Puerto Rican citizenship—one type of citizenship for those who reside on the island and a second for those who move to the mainland—was not materialized on a large scale in practice. Indeed, while many Puerto Ricans fought (and died) as second-class citizens in World War I and World War II, there was very little movement from Puerto Ricans to the U.S. states during the first fifty years of Puerto Rico as a territory of the United States.

As figure 1 illustrates, that all changed in the 1950s with the beginning of what Puerto Rican historians refer to as the period of "the Great Migration." Between 1950 and 1960, the net migration of Puerto Ricans leaving the island in search of jobs and economic opportunities in the United States rose to a striking 430,000. The great majority made New York City and the broader Northeast region their home. Many of those original Puerto Rican

Figure 1. Net Migration from Puerto Rico to United States Mainland, 1900–1970

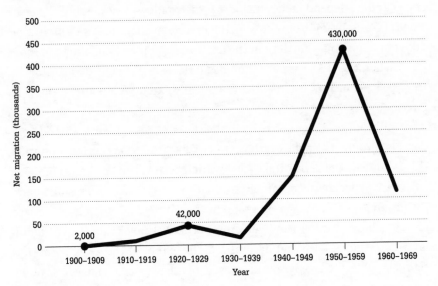

Source: Vázquez Calzada (1988).

Figure 2. Net Migration from Puerto Rico to United States Mainland, 2005–2014

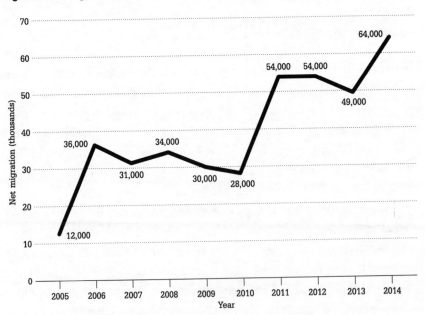

Source: Velázquez-Estrada (2016).

Figure 3. Puerto Rican Migration to United States Mainland by Region

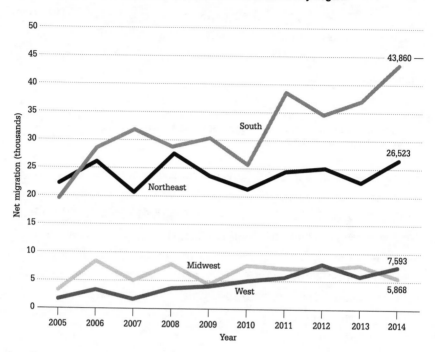

Source: Velázquez-Estrada (2016).

communities in the Northeast remain vibrant, with Puerto Rican Day parades in cities like New York City, as well as the creation of new identities, such as "Nuyorican," depicting the importance of Puerto Rican heritage within new cultural contexts.

Today, migration from the island to the mainland once again is experiencing an all-time high, with numbers surpassing the previous migration of the 1950s. As shown in figure 2, Puerto Rico to U.S. states net migration is close to 400,000 between 2005 and 2014, shrinking the population from approximately 4 million in 2005 to 3.4 million after 2014. Net migration particularly spikes after 2010. Indeed, in the four years between 2010 and 2014 alone, net migration surpassed that of the first five years of the 1950s.

Like Puerto Ricans who moved to the mainland during the Great Migration, Puerto Ricans today are also moving in search of jobs and better economic prospects (and most recently as a result of environmental displacement). However, unlike their predecessors, the bulk of Puerto Rico-United States migration is increasingly shifting away from the Northeast of the United States toward the South—particularly Orlando and the central corridor of Florida (see figure 3).

THE CONTEXT OF POLITICAL SOCIALIZATION FOR PUERTO RICANS IN OLD AND NEW DESTINATIONS

Beyond a mere geographic shift, this positions new, stateside Puerto Ricans in a different political socialization process. In the following comparison, I outline some of the key differences between these two political contexts. These variations include the following: (1) the degree of coordination of mass migration by the Puerto Rican government; (2) the demographics of Puerto Rican migrants; (3) the strength of local Puerto Rican networks; (4) Puerto Rican integration within mainland political parties; and (5) the ideological context of the state.

Old destinations	New destinations
Peak of migration: 1950s	Peak of migration: 2005–present
Puerto Rican government-encouraged and -organized migration	Non-government-orchestrated migration
Lower socioeconomic status	Higher socioeconomic status, more likely to identify as White
Established Puerto Rican networks, and history of activism and social movements	Emerging Puerto Rican organizations and associations
Longer history of Puerto Rican (Democratic) elected officials	Less incorporated within the Democratic Party
Ideologically liberal context	Ideologically moderate/conservative context

The first important distinction between the two periods of migration pertains to the level of government coordination. The exodus of Puerto Ricans to New York City and other areas in the Northeast followed the U.S. government's implementation of Operation Bootstrap on the island, which promoted the industrialization of the Puerto Rican economy (Aranda 2007). As the island transitioned from an agricultural to an industrialized economy, Puerto Ricans abandoned their rural towns in search of jobs in the overcrowded capital of San Juan and surrounding areas. Faced with too many people and not enough jobs, the Puerto Rican government encouraged its residents to venture north and find work in the growing factories of New York City and other cities on the mainland. For many of these migrants, the Puerto Rican government arranged for their air transportation to New York City—a phenomenon that has been depicted in popular culture and in the film *La Guagua Aérea* (The Flying Bus).[1]

Unlike the Great Migration of the 1950s, the current migration to the Southern destination of Florida occurs independently from any government coordination. While migration to Florida picked up during the early 2000s, it particularly intensified after the Puerto Rican government failed to recover from the financial crisis of 2007 and, most recently, in the aftermath of Hurricanes Irma and Maria. Puerto Ricans who leave the island in search of better economic prospects do so at their own expense and without coordinated efforts from the Puerto Rican government.

In contrast to the 1950s, the present exodus of Puerto Ricans is an issue for the government, as many migrants potentially leave gaps in important industries, such as the medical profession (Meléndez and Vargas-Ramos 2017). Certainly, the socioeconomic profile of the present Puerto Rican migration benefits from higher levels of education and economic resources than for their Northeast counterparts in the 1950s (Cruz 2011) or even today (Duany 2010). The differences in resources could be an important consideration in terms of political socialization. While the dynamics of partisanship acquisition among Latinos are still not well understood (see, however, Hajnal and Lee 2011; Alvarez and García-Bedolla 2003), Alvarez and García-Bedolla (2003) find evidence that more years of education correlate to a higher likelihood of affiliating with the Republican Party.

Further complicating the different demographic profiles of Puerto Ricans in older destinations and Florida is the fact that Puerto Ricans in Florida are more likely than those in the Northeast to identify as White in the U.S. Census (Duany 2010). Certainly, any analysis of Puerto Rican racial identification in the Census must accompany an important caveat: Similar to the situation for other national-origin Latinos (Wilkinson and Earle 2013; Mora 2014), traditional U.S. racial categories do not fully capture

Puerto Ricans' sense of identity (Oropesa et al. 2008). However, scholars have argued that racial identity is an important consideration when evaluating the partisan identification and political attitudes of Latinos (Stokes-Brown 2012), as well as their perceived commonality with other racial and ethnic groups (Wilkinson and Earle 2013). Thus, these regional differences in the racial identification are important to consider when evaluating the political behavior of stateside Puerto Ricans.

In addition to demographic considerations, Puerto Ricans in older destinations enjoy a longer history of social networks, activism, and Puerto Rican organizations. During the 1950s, the Puerto Rican government had a vested interest in retaining connections with the diaspora and saw remittances as an important part of the government's economic plan. Thus, the Puerto Rican government created a branch dedicated to migration issues within the Department of Labor to facilitate the integration of Puerto Rican migrants while, at the same time, retaining their connection to the island (and its economy) (Cruz 2011). In the 1960s, Puerto Rican activists, inspired by the Black Panthers, created organizations like the Young Lords with the goal of advocating for the Puerto Rican community both in the states and on the island (Beltrán 2010). Furthermore, these collective efforts led to the creation of spaces like the Museo del Barrio and the annual Puerto Rican Day Parade in New York City (Oropesa et al. 2008). While anecdotal evidence would suggest that Puerto Rican organizations are emerging and even joining forces all over central Florida,[2] they have undoubtedly had less time to develop. Moreover, the lack of central coordination by the Puerto Rican government could make the establishment of networks between these independent efforts much more difficult.

Finally, one of the most notable differences between Puerto Ricans in older and newer destinations pertains to their varying levels of integration within the major political parties and the ideological contexts of the states they reside in. When it comes to political integration, Puerto Ricans in older destinations have a longer history of integration within the Democratic Party with visible national-level figures, such as Representatives Nydia Velázquez and Jose Serrano from New York. Most recently, Puerto Rican congressional candidate Alexandria Ocasio-Cortez gained national attention after defeating New York long-time incumbent Representative Joe Crowley in the 2018 Democratic primary. There are no political figures in either political party with the same weight or political capital in Florida. Thus, we should expect Puerto Ricans in older destinations to be more affiliated with the Democratic Party than their counterparts in Florida. Given the importance of political integration and social networks for mobilization (Rosenstone and Hansen 1993), this is an important difference to consider when comparing regional differences among stateside Puerto Ricans.

When it comes to the ideological contexts of the Northeast and Florida, the impact of political socialization in the more ideologically liberal context of the Northeast, vis-à-vis the moderate to conservative context of a swing state like Florida, could be consequential. This is particularly the case for political socialization that occurs during childhood (Campbell et al. 1960; Converse 1969). However, political contexts could also shape adult political socialization (Brown 1981; 1988)—a process that could prove even more powerful for adult Puerto Rican migrants from the island to the mainland as they encounter a different political context with different political parties and electoral issues (Cámara-Fuertes 2004).

Today, we have two distinct sets of stateside Puerto Ricans: (1) new migrant communities in the South and (2) well-established Puerto Rican communities in the Northeast. Together, they represent old and new stateside Puerto Ricans. Given important differences in the contexts of migration I have discussed, scholars and political analysts should be careful not to draw predictions about the electoral behavior of new Puerto Rican migrants based on the political behavior of Puerto Ricans in older destinations. In the remaining pages of this chapter, I use data from the Latino Decisions 2016 Election Eve Poll of registered Latino voters to examine the political and electoral behavior of stateside Puerto Ricans. My goal is to highlight important differences in the political attitudes of Puerto Ricans in the new Southern destination of Florida vis-à-vis older destinations in the Northeast.

Puerto Rican Partisanship and Political Attitudes in 2016

I begin the analysis by comparing the partisan affiliation of Puerto Ricans by region and place of birth. Respondents in the 2016 Latino Decisions Election Eve Poll were asked: "Generally speaking, do you think of yourself as a Republican, a Democrat, an independent, or something else?" Figure 4 shows the weighted distribution of responses for partisan identification for Northeast and Florida Puerto Ricans, as well as partisan attachments among island-born and mainland-born Puerto Ricans and all Latinos.

In 2016, the majority of stateside Puerto Ricans across all categories self-identified as Democrats. Island-born and mainland-born Puerto Ricans self-identified as Democrats at comparable rates, with 63% and 61% identifying with the Democratic Party, respectively. A slightly higher percentage (11%) of island-born Puerto Ricans in the sample self-identified with the Republican Party than of those born stateside (7%). Overall, however, the partisan affiliations of island- and mainland-born Puerto Ricans are comparable. Moreover, these percentages are also similar to overall identification with the Democratic Party among all Latinos in the sample.

More notable differences emerge between Puerto Ricans in older Northeastern destinations and Puerto Ricans in Florida. While Florida Puerto Ricans had the lowest percentage of affiliation with the Democratic Party (51%), Puerto Ricans in older destinations in the Northeast reported the highest percentage of Democratic affiliation (72%). Similarly, only 4% of Northeast Puerto Ricans in the sample self-identified as Republican, while Florida Puerto Ricans had the highest percentage of Republicans (15%). Thus, for Puerto Rican respondents in the sample, regional differences appear to be more consequential than being born on the island or the mainland.

In addition to partisanship differences, Puerto Ricans in the Northeast also reported different motivations to vote than their counterparts in Florida. Figure 5 illustrates what motivated Puerto Rican voters in the 2016 election by region and place of birth. Consistent with their higher levels of Democratic affiliation, Puerto Ricans in the Northeast were the most likely out of all groups to indicate that supporting Democrats was their most

Figure 4. Puerto Rican Party ID by Region and Place of Birth

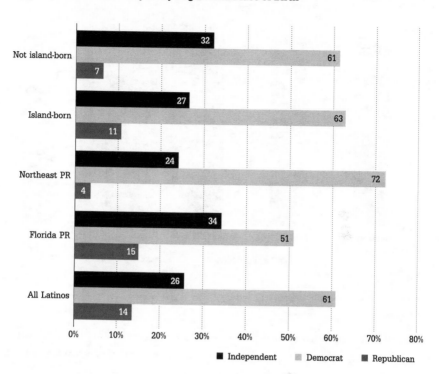

Source: Latino Decisions (2016).

important motivation to vote (56%). In contrast, Florida Puerto Ricans were the least likely to do so (24%). The higher relative strength of Democratic identity among Puerto Ricans in the Northeast is perhaps not surprising, given the longer history of Puerto Rican political integration within the Democratic Party in the region.

Interestingly, the majority of Florida Puerto Ricans (51%) chose "supporting Latinos" as their most important motivation to vote, with the other half evenly divided between supporting Democrats and supporting Republicans. In contrast, only 43% of Northeast Puerto Ricans indicated that their motivation to vote in 2016 was to show support for Latinos. There are, of course, limits to extracting meaning from descriptive data. However, these results are consistent with overall lower levels of partisan attachments

Figure 5. Puerto Rican Motivation to Vote by Region and Place of Birth

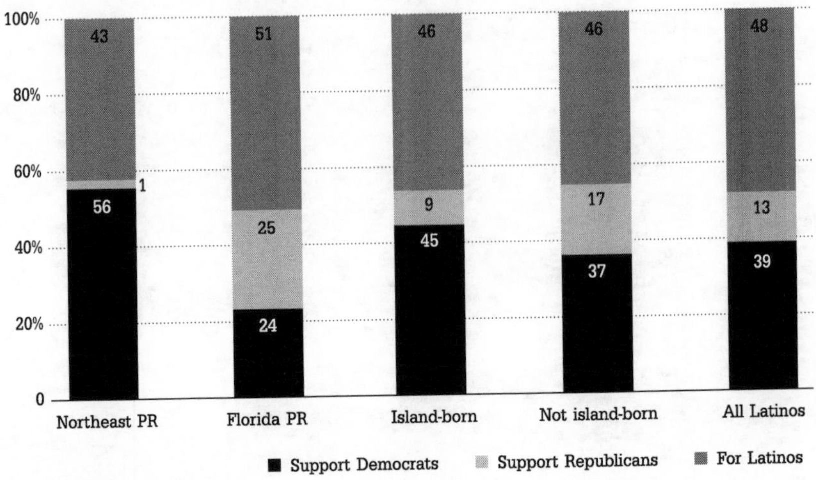

Source: Latino Decisions (2016).

among Florida Puerto Ricans, as well as their shorter history of integration within the Democratic Party (relative to Northeast Puerto Ricans). A higher interest in supporting the Democratic Party than supporting Latinos in the Northeast does not necessarily mean that Northeast Puerto Ricans care less about Latino interests than their Florida counterparts. It is possible, for example, that the stronger networks between the Democratic Party and Puerto Ricans in the Northeast have cemented the notion that Latino interests are best served by the Democratic Party.

Regardless of their partisan attachments or motivation to vote, Puerto Ricans, like most Latino subgroups, overwhelmingly supported the presidential candidacy of Secretary Clinton over that of now President Trump. In the Election Eve Poll, participants were asked to report for whom they were planning to vote. Figure 6 shows that, among those surveyed in the sample, 78% of island-born Puerto Ricans and 79% of mainland-born Puerto Ricans supported Hillary Clinton. That said, while support for Clinton does not seem to vary by place of birth, regional differences emerge once again between Northeast and Florida Puerto Ricans. Among Puerto Ricans in

Figure 6. Puerto Rican Vote Choice by Region and Place of Birth

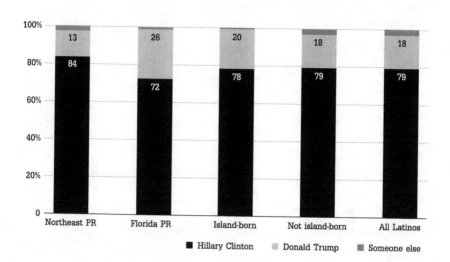

Source: Latino Decisions (2016).

the sample, Northeast Puerto Ricans supported Clinton the most (84%), while only 72% of Florida Puerto Ricans supported her candidacy. Similarly, support for Trump was the lowest in the Northeast (13%) and highest in Florida (26%). This regional difference in vote choice among Puerto Ricans is important to highlight, given mounting speculations about the effect of the growing Puerto Rican electorate in Florida. While Puerto Ricans in Florida overwhelmingly favored Clinton over Trump, they did so at a lower rate than their counterparts in the Northeast. Scholars and political strategists alike should exercise caution when predicting the political and electoral behavior of Florida Puerto Ricans based on historical trends among Northeast Puerto Ricans.

To explore the different dynamics of the Puerto Rican vote by region further, I move on to examine these regional differences by gender. The gender gap for Latinas/os in American elections (Bedolla, Monforti, and Pantoja 2007; Bejarano 2014; Montoya, Hardy-Fanta, and Garcia 2000) is well documented. However, we have yet to understand fully how gender plays a role within different political contexts. Thus, in table 1, I list the

Table 1. Puerto Rican Support for Clinton by Region and Gender

Group	Men	Women
Northeast Puerto Ricans	81%	86%
Florida Puerto Ricans	61%	82%
All Latinas/os	71%	86%

Source: Latino Decisions (2016).

weighted percentages of Puerto Rican men and women in the Northeast and Florida who supported Democratic presidential nominee Hillary Clinton in 2016. I also list percentages for all Latinos and Latinas in order to draw a comparison.

The data reveal interesting descriptive differences between the Puerto Rican gender gap in the Northeast and Florida. While the percentage of Northeast Puerto Rican women in the sample who supported Clinton was 5% higher than for their male counterparts, the gender gap is much larger in Florida. In fact, support for Hillary Clinton among Florida Puerto Rican women in the sample was a staggering 20% higher than for their male counterparts. While these data are descriptive and limited by sample size, scholars should explore potential differences in the political socialization of Puerto Rican men and women in Florida. These results would suggest that any regional differences in the electoral behavior of Puerto Ricans are primarily driven by men, not women.

Next, given the overall high percentage of Puerto Rican voters in the sample who did not identify with any political party and the important regional differences in both partisanship and vote choice, I move on to consider the likelihood that Puerto Ricans will consider voting for Republicans. In figure 7, I present the weighted distribution of Puerto Rican respondents who would likely (or not) vote for Republican candidates. Participants in the sample were asked to choose which of the following three statements they agreed with the most: (1) "I generally agree with the Republican Party on most issues and am likely to vote for them in future elections"; (2) "I disagree with the Republican Party on many issues, but I would consider voting for them in the future if they help pass immigration reform with a path to citizenship"; or (3) "The Republican Party has now become so

Figure 7. Likelihood of Puerto Ricans Voting Republican

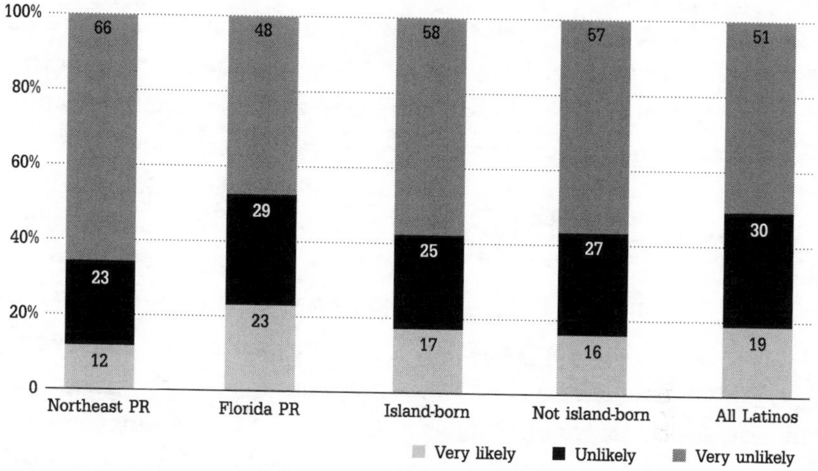

Source: Latino Decisions (2016).

anti-[Hispanic/Latino] and anti-immigrant that it would be hard for me to ever consider supporting them in the future."

The vast majority of island-born (83%) and mainland-born (84%) Puerto Ricans consider it very unlikely or unlikely that they would vote for Republicans in the future. These numbers are equally comparable to 81% of all Latinos in the sample. The biggest difference emerges between Northeast and Florida Puerto Ricans. Northeast Puerto Ricans are particularly unlikely to consider voting for a Republican in the future, with a combined percentage of 89% of Northeast Puerto Ricans indicating it is very unlikely or unlikely they would consider voting for Republicans. In contrast, Florida Puerto Ricans report the highest likelihood of voting for a Republican—with 23% indicating it is very likely they would vote for a Republican. These results are consistent with overall higher rate of Democratic affiliation among Puerto Ricans in the Northeast, as well as overall history of political integration within the Democratic Party in the region. Once again, the results indicate important differences in the political socialization of Puerto Ricans in the Northeast and the southern state of Florida.

Finally, I examine Puerto Rican attitudes on immigration. A growing amount of scholarship documents the racialization of immigration as a distinctively Latino issue (Chavez 2001; Massey 2009; Masuoka and Junn 2013; Santa Ana 2002). Given this process of racialization, Latinos as a group perceive attacks on immigration as attacks on themselves. Puerto Ricans certainly present an interesting challenge to this relationship, given that they represent the only Latino subgroup comprised entirely of native-born citizens. Thus, it would be reasonable to expect that Puerto Ricans are less invested in immigration relative to other subgroups with more direct ties to the issue.

As figure 8 illustrates, the results are consistent with this expectation. Puerto Ricans in the Northeast were less likely than Latinos as a group to report immigration as the most important issue or one of the most important issues. A combined total of 54% of Northeast Puerto Ricans—the most Democratic group within the subgroups—selected immigration as at least one of the most important issues, compared with a total of 65% of all Latinos. Given their longer history of integration within the Democratic Party, Puerto Rican affiliation with the Democratic Party predates the growing importance of immigration as a racialized Latino issue in the United States. Thus, it is likely that their Democratic affinity is rooted on other policy preferences.

Interestingly, 65% of island-born Puerto Ricans reported immigration as at least one of the most important issues, compared to only 55% of Puerto Ricans born outside of the island. These results are consistent with existing research suggesting that Puerto Ricans, like other national-origin groups, are more likely to hold welcoming attitudes on immigration when they have stronger ties to their country of origin (Branton 2007; Fraga et al. 2011). While Puerto Rico is not an independent country, scholars have argued that it has a distinct sense of nationhood outside of the United States (Duany 2003), and that Puerto Ricans who move to the mainland have experiences similar to those of other noncitizen migrants (Cámara-Fuertes 2004; De-Sipio and Pantoja 2007).

It is important to highlight that despite the fact that Florida Puerto Ricans hold the lowest levels of partisan attachment to the Democratic Party, 66% of them indicated that immigration is at least one of the most

Figure 8. Importance of Immigration for Puerto Ricans

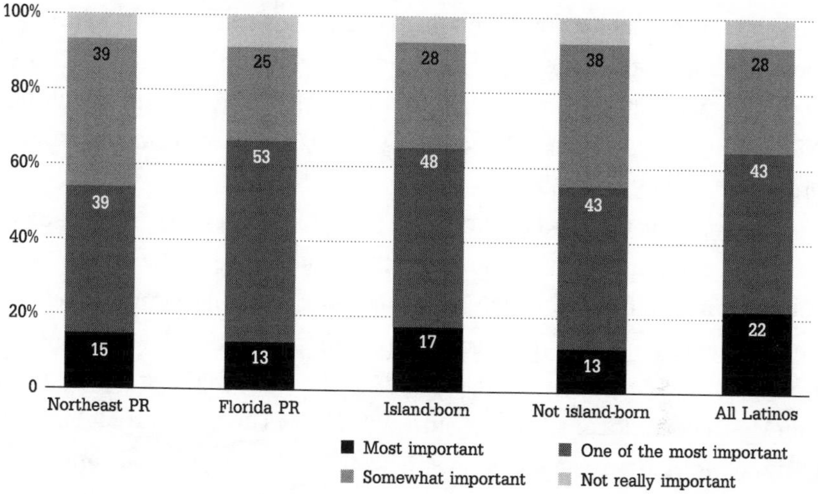

Source: Latino Decisions (2016).

important issues for them, making them the likeliest to choose immigration as an important issue among Puerto Rican voters in the analysis. Scholars should explore whether concerns about immigration among Florida Puerto Ricans correlate with welcoming or restrictive views on immigration.

Discussion and Conclusion

During the 2016 election cycle, major candidates from both parties actively courted island and stateside Puerto Rican voters. During the Democratic primary battle between Secretary Clinton and Senator Sanders, both candidates held events in Puerto Rico and released op-eds in Puerto Rico's top circulation newspaper, *El Nuevo Día,* in the hopes of securing the electoral support of Puerto Rican voters on the island and in Florida. On the Republican side, Puerto Rico was also important for what was quickly becoming the unlikely candidacy of Senator Marco Rubio. As Trump continued to dominate the electoral map during the primaries, securing the Puerto Rican vote on the island and in the key state of Florida was a matter of survival for the Rubio campaign. Ultimately, Rubio lost the Florida primary along with his bid for the Republican nomination. While Secretary Clinton outperformed Senator Sanders in both the Florida primary and the nationwide popular vote, she lost the state of Florida (and the presidency) to now President Trump.

Throughout the 2016 electoral cycle and its aftermath, many speculated and continue to speculate about the importance of the Puerto Rican vote in 2016 and beyond. As Puerto Ricans continue their journey south in unprecedented numbers, they could represent an advantage for Democrats. However, the analysis in this chapter would caution against the assumption that Puerto Ricans in the South will follow the electoral footsteps of their counterparts in the Northeast. The distinct sociopolitical contexts of migration between old- and new-destination Puerto Ricans have produced important differences in the political behavior of new- and old-destination Puerto Ricans.

As the 2016 results indicate, Puerto Ricans in Florida remain less attached to the Democratic Party. Specifically, the results of the Latino Decisions Election Eve Poll reveal that Puerto Ricans in Florida are less affiliated with the Democratic Party and more likely to consider voting for Republicans than Puerto Ricans in the Northeast. Moreover, a descriptive analysis of the data suggest that these regional differences could have an important gender component. Support for Clinton among Puerto Rican men in Florida was 20% lower than for Puerto Rican women in the state, while the gender gap between Puerto Rican men and women in the Northeast was only 5%. Taken together, these results suggest that a Democratic advantage with Puerto Rican voters in Florida is not an automatic mirror image of the long-standing Democratic advantage with Puerto Rican voters in the Northeast.

Since 2016, there have been events on and off the island that have increased both the number of Puerto Ricans on the mainland and their feelings of resentment against President Trump. In 2017, Puerto Rico suffered the devastating effects of two major hurricanes (Hurricane Irma and

Hurricane Maria), which left the entire island of Puerto Rico without power and access to clean water and food. In the immediate aftermath of the hurricanes, cellular communication was practically nonexistent. Many lost their homes and property; thousands lost their lives. In fact, a 2018 study from George Washington University estimates the number of hurricane-related deaths from Hurricane Maria on the island at 2,975 (Santos-Burgoa et al. 2018).[3] The dire conditions forced hundreds of thousands of Puerto Ricans into environmental displacement. Following recent trends of migration, the vast majority of them landed in the swing state of Florida.

During the months after Hurricane Maria, the relationship between the Puerto Rican community and Trump turned increasingly contentious. While the vast majority of Puerto Ricans in 2016 were not fans of then presidential candidate Trump, his response to the devastation in Puerto Rico could possibly further cement their negative opinions of him as well as the Republican Party by association. In a series of tweets and public statements, the president pointed to the government's debt and corruption to blame Puerto Ricans for their own suffering, personally attacked the mayor of San Juan, Carmen Yulín Cruz, and accused Puerto Ricans of wanting everything handed to them. During a visit to Puerto Rico, the president flew over the island to assess damages from the air and held a press event in the affluent town of Guaynabo, where he threw paper towels at a crowd of Puerto Ricans. Moreover, despite dire reports coming from the island about the loss of life, the president refused to accept any allegations of wrongdoing. Instead, he boasted that his administration was doing a "great" job.

Regional differences notwithstanding, the president's negative rhetoric about Puerto Rico—coupled with allegations that his administration did not do enough to help the island after the hurricanes—presents a political opportunity for Democrats to bring Puerto Ricans into a winning coalition in 2020 and beyond. Whether Puerto Ricans in Florida ultimately find a home in the future Democratic coalition will largely depend on how much time (and money) the Democratic Party is willing to invest in mobilizing this promising, but complicated, new electorate.

Notes

1. *La Guagua Aérea* was a 1993 film, directed by Luis Molina Casanova, that depicted the story of Puerto Ricans traveling to New York City during the holiday season of 1960.

2. Some anecdotal reports (Bernal 2018) observe the growth of Puerto Rican networks in Florida as displaced Puerto Ricans continue arriving in large numbers after Hurricane Maria.

3. An earlier widely cited Harvard study (Kishore et al. 2018) offers a much higher estimate of 4,645.

References

Alvarez, R. M., and L. García-Bedolla. 2003. "The Foundations of Latino Voter Partisanship: Evidence from the 2000 Election." *Journal of Politics* 65 (1): 31–49.

Aranda, E. M. 2007. *Emotional Bridges to Puerto Rico: Migration, Return Migration, and the Struggles of Incorporation.* Lanham, MD: Rowman & Littlefield.

Bedolla, L. G., J. L. L. Monforti, and A. D. Pantoja. 2007. "A Second Look: Is There a Latina/o Gender Gap?" *Journal of Women, Politics & Policy* 28 (3–4): 147–71.

Bejarano, C. E. 2014. *The Latino Gender Gap in US Politics.* New York: Routledge Press.

Beltrán, C. 2010. *The Trouble with Unity: Latino Politics and the Creation of Identity.* New York: Oxford University Press on Demand.

Bernal, R. 2018. "New coalition seeks to help Puerto Ricans adapt to life in Florida." *The Hill.* https://thehill.com/latino/384894-new-coalition-seeks-to-help-puerto-ricans-adapt-to-life-in-florida.

Branton, R. 2007. "Latino Attitudes Toward Various Areas of Public Policy and the Importance of Acculturation." *Political Research Quarterly* 60(2): 293–303.

Brown, Thad. 1981. "On Contextual Change and Partisan Attributes." *British Journal of Political Science.* 11 (4): 427–47.

———. 1988. *Migration and Politics: The Impact of Population Mobility on American Voting Behavior.* Chapel Hill: University of North Carolina Press.

Cámara Fuertes, L. R. 2004. *The Phenomenon of Puerto Rican Voting.* Gainesville: University Press of Florida.

Campbell, A., P. E. Converse, W. E. Miller, and D. E. Stokes. 1960. *The American Voter.* New York: Wiley.

Chavez, Leo R. 2001. *Covering Immigration: Popular Images and the Politics of the Nation.* Berkeley: University of California Press.

Converse, Philip E. 1969. "Of Time and Partisan Stability." *Comparative Political Studies* 2: 139–71.

Cruz, J. E. 2011. "Puerto Rican Politics in New York City During the 1960s: Structural Ideation, Contingency, and Power." In *The Politics of Inclusion and Exclusion: Identity Politics in Twenty-First Century America*, edited by David F Ericson, 79–102. New York: Routledge.

DeSipio, L., and A. D. Pantoja. 2007. "Puerto Rican Exceptionalism? A Comparative Analysis of Puerto Rican, Mexican, Salvadoran, and Dominican Transnational Civic and Political Ties." In *Latino Politics: Identity, Mobilization, and Representation*, edited by Rodolfo Espino, David L. Leal, and Kenneth J. Meier, 104–22. Charlottesville: University Press of Virginia.

Duany, J. 2003. "Nation, Migration, Identity: The Case of Puerto Ricans." *Latino Studies* 1 (3): 424–44.

———. 2010. "The Orlando Ricans: Overlapping Identity Discourses Among Middle-Class Puerto Rican Immigrants." *Centro Journal* 22 (1): 85–115.

Fraga, L. R., J. A. Garcia, R. E. Hero, M. Jones-Correa, V. Martinez-Ebers, and G. M. Segura. 2011. *Latinos in the New Millennium: An Almanac of Opinion, Behavior, and Policy Preferences.* Cambridge: Cambridge University Press.

Hajnal, Z. L., and T. Lee. 2011. *Why Americans Don't Join the Party: Race, Immigration, and the Failure (of Political Parties) to Engage the Electorate.* Princeton, NJ: Princeton University Press.

Hinojosa, J., N. Román, and Edwin Meléndez. 2018. "Puerto Rican Post-Maria Relocation by States." Centro RB2018-03. https://centropr.hunter.cuny.edu/sites/default/files/PDF/Schoolenroll-v4-27-2018.pdf.

Kishore, N., et al. 2018. "Mortality in Puerto Rico after Hurricane Maria." *The New England Journal of Medicine* 379 (2): 162–70.

Latino Decisions. 2016. "Latino Decisions 2016 Election Eve Poll." *Latino Decisions.* http://www.latinodecisions.

Massey, D. S. 2009. "Racial Formation in Theory and Practice: The Case of Mexicans in the United States." *Race and Social Problems,* 1 (1): 12–26.

Masuoka, N., and J. Junn. 2013. *The Politics of Belonging: Race, Public Opinion, and Immigration.* Chicago: University of Chicago Press.

Meléndez, E., and C. Vargas-Ramos, eds. 2017. *The State of Puerto Ricans 2017.* New York: Centro Press, Center for Puerto Rican Studies.

Montoya, L. J., C. Hardy-Fanta, and S. Garcia, 2000. "Latina Politics: Gender, Participation, and Leadership." *PS: Political Science & Politics* 33 (3): 555–62.

Mora, G. C. 2014. *Making Hispanics: How Activists, Bureaucrats, and Media Constructed a New American.* Chicago: University of Chicago Press.

Oropesa, R. S., N. S. Landale, and M. J. Greif. 2008. "From Puerto Rican to Pan-Ethnic in New York City." *Ethnic and Racial Studies* 31 (7): 1315–39.

Rosenstone, S. J., and J. Hansen. 1993. *Mobilization, Participation, and Democracy in America.* New York: Macmillan.

Román, E., and T. Simmons. 2002. "Membership Denied: Subordination and Subjugation Under United States Expansionism." *San Diego Law Review* 39: 437.

Santa Ana, Otto. 2002. *Brown Tide Rising: Metaphors of Latinos in Contemporary American Public Discourse.* Austin: University of Texas Press.

Santos-Burgoa, C., A. Goldman, E. Andrade, N. Barrett, U. Colon-Ramos, M. Edberg, A. Garcia Meza, L. Goldman, A. Roess, J. Sandberg, and S. Zeger. 2018. "Ascertainment of the Estimated Excess Mortality from Hurricane Maria in Puerto Rico." Himmelfarb Health Sciences Library. https://hsrc.himmelfarb. gwu.edu.

Stokes-Brown, A. K. 2012. *The Politics of Race in Latino Communities: Walking the Color Line.* New York: Routledge.

Vargas-Ramos, C. 2016. *Recent Trends in Puerto Rican Electoral and Civic Engagement in the United States.* Centro—Center for Puerto Rican Studies, Research Brief, https://centropr.hunter.cuny.edu.

Vázquez Calzada, J. L. 1988. *La Población de Puerto Rico y su Trayectoria Histórica.* Rio Piedras, Puerto Rico: Escuela Graduada de Salud Pública, Universidad de Puerto Rico, Recinto de Ciencias Médicas.

Velázquez-Estrada, A. 2016. "Perfil del Migrante 2014." Instituto de Estadísticas de Puerto Rico. Estado Libre Asociado de Puerto Rico, May.

Wilkinson, B. C., and E. Earle. 2013. "Taking a New Perspective to Latino Racial Attitudes: Examining the Impact of Skin Tone on Latino Perceptions of Commonality with Whites and Blacks." *American Politics Research* 41 (5): 783–818.

Latinos in National Politics

2016 and Beyond

Luis Ricardo Fraga

PERHAPS THE MOST IMPORTANT QUESTION THAT THE AUTHORS OF THE essays in this volume push us to consider is: How did this happen? Almost no pundits or scholars predicted that Donald Trump would win the 2016 presidential election and no one anticipated that attacking Latino communities and issues important to many Latino communities, like immigration, would serve as a major pillar of the successful presidential candidate's campaign. The most consistent prediction was that Latino voters would serve as critical contributors to the margins of victory for Hillary Clinton in key states like California, Florida, Colorado, and Nevada. Moreover, it was predicted that the growth in Latino registered and mobilized voters would continue their evolving influence in many parts of the nation, even in consistently red states like Texas and Arizona. So what role did Latinos play in the 2016 presidential election? What does that role tell us about the future of Latinos in American national politics?

There are four central findings about the role of Latinos in the 2016 election that appear in the essays in this volume. First, Latino voters, by overwhelming margins, preferred Hillary Clinton over Donald Trump. The data reported from the Latino Decisions Election Eve poll found that 80% of Latino voters preferred Clinton and only a historically low 16% supported Trump. The trend since 1960 of Latino voters preferring Democratic candidates over Republican candidates was maintained. Even in Florida, the state where Cuban American voters have provided among the greatest support for Republican candidates over the last five decades, the Latino Decisions poll indicated that 67% of Latino voters supported Clinton, and this included 52% of Cuban American voters. Although during the Presidential campaigns of George W. Bush many Latino voters were comfortable supporting his candidacy at noticeably high levels, this was clearly a George W. Bush-specific phenomenon, which has not been replicated in any subsequent presidential campaign. Second, there seemed to be heightened interest among Latino voters in this election as compared to others, and this was reflected in higher voter registration and turnout rates in 2016. Among the most fascinating relatively new pieces of information provided by the Latino Decisions poll was the response to the question "Why are you voting in 2016?" The answer cited most frequently by respondents was that they were voting "to support the Latino community." Whether due to concern generated by the Trump campaign's criticisms of Latino communities or due to the mobilization generated largely by the Clinton campaign and by nonpartisan civic engagement groups, the sense of the need to work on behalf of Latino communities was the most cited driver of Latino participation in the election.

Third, immigration was the primary issue that concerned Latino voters throughout the country. Although there were also concerns related to jobs and the economy, as well as education, it was immigration that was of greatest interest to Latino voters in 2016. Too often the only issue associated with Latino interests is immigration, and that this provides a narrow, one-dimensional understanding of Latino interests, but immigration was the most frequently stated issue of importance to Latinos across states and national origin groups. Lastly, a number of the authors in this volume note some differences among Latinos by gender and country of origin. For example, Latinas supported Clinton at a rate of 87%, but Latino men supported her at 76%. As stated earlier, Cuban American voters only supported

Clinton at 52%. What may be most significant about these differences, however, is how much more similarity there was across regions, national origin groups, genders, and even generations than there were differences. Latinos, on the whole, spoke with a clear voice in 2016: They supported Hillary Clinton by overwhelming margins, and even by a slight majority among Cuban Americans. Clinton's Latino advantage is consistent with the Democratic advantage that has developed over the last several presidential election cycles. In sum, Latino voters and communities generally were engaged in this election, registered and turned out in substantial numbers, were motivated to participate out of concern with immigration and the Latino community generally, and, across differences, had a clear and consistent set of preferences for the Democratic candidate. So why did none of this make a sufficient difference in determining who won the presidential election in 2016?

It is important to understand that the growth in the Latino electorate, partly driven by unquestioned demographic growth in the Latino citizen population, and the greater interest Latinos displayed in national politics, as well as the clear block voting that Latinos gave to the Democratic candidate, are clear signs of greater political inclusion in American national elections. One can see this greater inclusion as an unquestioned good. No doubt it is. However, the 2016 election allows us to consider that inclusion is no guarantee of increasing the probability that the candidate preferred by Latinos will be successful. I suggest that 2016 allows us to consider, more seriously than ever before, whether the demographic growth, higher participation, and greater strategic targeting of Latino voters may lead to a paradox filled with risks that jeopardize the role that Latino communities will play in national politics in the future. I refer to this counterintuitive reality as the paradox of inclusion.

One of the strategic challenges facing Latino communities is that as they continue to vote consistently and overwhelmingly for Democratic candidates they take the risk of "electoral capture" (Frymer 1999). This argument was made with regard to African American communities with their clear and consistent support for Democrats. As the Republican Party gained its national strategic strength in many parts of South as part of its Southern

Strategy, and as it simultaneously increased its support among some White ethnic and rural White voters, African Americans had little reason to consider supporting Republican candidates. Moreover, the Southern strategy pushed many Republican candidates to do nothing to reach out to African American voters and even less to mobilize them. As a result, the predictability of African American support for Democrats has the paradoxical consequence of allowing Democratic candidates and especially elected Democratic officials to take African American voters and, even more importantly, take African American communities for granted in terms of public policy benefits. African American voters are taken for granted when their votes are only sought on election eve but there is no systematic effort to build infrastructures of long-term voter and other civic engagement among those voters. They are celebrated and visited, sometimes often, just before primaries and the general election, but they are not provided the organizational and financial resources to remain engaged in politics between elections. It is between these elections that community-based, long-term engagement can be nurtured to make sure that participation rates are high during election time. Most paradoxically, capture places African American communities as a whole at even great risk when those Democrats are elected to office and do little to enact policies that directly benefit those segments of African American communities that still face overwhelming challenges related to employment, housing, education, health care, and, perhaps most tragically, police violence. Although no doubt some policies have been essential to the advancement of many members of African American communities into the middle and sometimes even upper class, this has coexisted with the continued severe life challenges faced by other segments of the same communities. One figure perhaps captures these challenges more than any other: 39% of all African American children under the age of eighteen live in poverty. This is a devastating reminder of how many in the next generation of African American communities have not benefited from any of the policies that have been enacted to promote racial justice.

One can make an argument that Latino voters and communities place themselves at the same risks from their potential electoral capture by the Democratic Party and its candidates. Some recent examples should cause one to pause and reflect on the meaning of the growth in the Latino electorate and its influence in national elections. Although the absolute number of Latino voters continues to grow, and nonpartisan groups and some Democratic campaigns increasingly reach out to potential Latino voters, the gap between the eligible, that is, citizen and older than eighteen, Latinos and actual Latino voters participating in elections has grown at the same time (Fraga 2015). The gap in Latino participation has increased as the eligible Latino population has grown. Stated differently, whatever the election-specific outreach and related engagement strategies of Latino voters, the strategies still seem to display a clear systemic failure in their lack of success at reversing the trend of a growing Latino participation gap. Relatedly, the Obama campaigns of 2008 and 2012 did more to engage Latino and other low-propensity voters than any other major Democratic campaign in the past, with some success; however, it was also under this administration that the policy decision was made and pursued to deport more undocumented residents, overwhelmingly Latinos, than had ever occurred in the nation's history. The current Trump administration may change who the first-place winner is in the deportation tragedy; however, that the current winner is a Democrat, whatever the strategic motives, is an unquestionable indicator of how greater Latino support of the Democrat led to a policy that directly harmed hundreds of thousands of Latino immigrants, and, because of the growing presence of mixed-status families, Latino U.S. citizens, many of them children, as well. The Deferred Action for Childhood Arrival Program of the Obama Administration did seek to resolve some elements of the harm of deportation; however, at present we see the limits of the strategy of using executive authority to provide that relief. Executive orders, however important in the moment, are no substitute for legislative enactment and the hard strategizing and politicking that such enactment requires. The Obama Administration, it can be argued, was not willing to use its political capital to work for the long- rather than short-term policy benefit of Latino communities.

A second paradox of greater Latino inclusion is "symbolic mainstreaming" (Fraga and Leal 2004). This paradox of greater Latino inclusion was perfected by George W. Bush in his presidential campaigns and has been tried, with very limited success, by other Republican candidates. In this paradox the growing demographic and electoral presence of Latinos provides the basis for candidates to embrace elements of perceived Latino values as fully aligned with many traditional American values. Among those values are hard work, sacrifice, family, patriotism, and commitment to the future. The candidate not only notes these values but argues that because these values are so consistent with "conservative" values, Latinos should be seen not as a community to be marginalized but as one that should be invited and embraced within the conservative values of the Republican Party. This builds on the earlier statement attributed to Ronald Reagan that "Latinos are Republicans ... they just don't know it yet." Interestingly, George W. Bush aligned this mainstreaming of Latino communities to further bolster his effort to distinguish himself from other Republican candidates as a "compassionate conservative." It is the case that Bush was the first national candidate of a major party who wanted all voters to see and understand his respect and admiration for the values that were present in this interpretation of Latino communities. He did not speak of Latinos as having values consistent with mainstream America just to potential Latino voters—he wanted all voters to see that his understanding of this community was an unambiguous indicator of his type of compassionate conservatism. It certainly was the case that he received more support from Latino voters than most other Republican candidates. National exit polls estimated that he received as much as 35% of the Latino vote in 2000 and perhaps as much as 40% in his 2004 reelection.

The symbolic part of this mainstreaming is that it rarely, if ever, leads to meaningful policy gains on behalf of Latino communities. The symbolism, in other words, does not also lead to substance. Bush did appoint substantial numbers of Latino and Latinas to his cabinet and other administrative positions. He also worked for comprehensive immigration reform in early 2004. However, Republican partisan strategizing in both the House and Senate did not allow for his efforts to result in policy changes that benefited many Latino families and their communities. Comprehensive immigration reform was never enacted. The paradox of inclusion is that the narrative of Latino communities changes to one of respect and admiration, but, similar to the risks of capture, does not lead to governmental action that works to the long-term benefit of those segments of Latino communities who still struggle to gain a more secure foothold in American society.

The third paradox of inclusion is the assumption of inevitable influence and gain. This reality is based upon an extremely favorable view of the growth in the influence of the Latino vote. As a number of the authors in this volume note, some with great analytical precision, Latino voters continue to exercise their electoral power in many regions of the country. Moreover, the increased presence of the second-generation, U.S.-born among Latinos makes this continued growth present in the foreseeable future. As but one example, it is often stated that 800,000 Latinos turn eighteen years of age every year. According to the American Community Survey conducted by the Census Bureau in 2014, a full 93.9% of Latinos under the age of eighteen are born in the United States. The pool of Latino voters continues to grow and their influence, if properly mobilized, will only increase as well. What 2016 allows us to see, however, is that, as hopeful and favorable as this demography is destiny view can be, it fails to take into account that any comprehensive analysis of Latino voter influence must be seen within the context of the preferences and rate of voter turnout of other major segments of the electorate. Latino influence in affecting the outcome of the 2016 election was limited by marginally higher White voter turnout in favor of Donald Trump, especially in rural, predominantly White areas of some parts of the country, and relative to the 2012 election, significantly lower levels of voter turnout among African American voters in support of Hillary Clinton. This significant lower African American turnout was especially the case in states like Florida where Latinos have a major presence, and in states where Latinos do not have a major presence, like Pennsylvania, Michigan, Wisconsin, and Ohio. The growth in Latino voter influence must always be understood within the context of the turnout rates and candidate preferences of White and African American voters who are significantly greater segments of the electorate in key states. Although Latino voters are likely to have been key players in the Clinton victories in Nevada and New Mexico, and, as we all know, there is no Democratic strategy to win the White House that is not grounded in winning California, where Latino voters continue to vote in coalition with others to keep the state solidly blue, this does not compensate for patterns of opposition to Latino preferences among Whites and patterns of lower voter turnout among African Americans. These two patterns of voter preferences can limit the extent to which Latinos see their preferences realized in who sits in the White House.

The fourth and final paradox of greater Latino electoral inclusion is that Latinos become the targets of vitriolic, negative campaigning and subsequent hostile policy action. Prior to the election of Donald Trump, one could argue that this paradox was only a possibility. His election proves that this paradox can be the driving force of much of our national politics. Several of the authors in this volume note how severely the Trump campaign, and especially Donald Trump himself, demonized, criminalized, and otherwise marginalized Latino communities. Moreover, the Trump campaign in 2016 simply built upon the anti-immigrant and anti-Latino rhetoric and policies of many state gubernatorial and legislative leaders in the areas of voting rights, educational access, cultural threats, and propensity to crime. At state levels, these arguments have been present since at least 1994, when Republican Governor Pete Wilson campaigned on behalf of one the first major state-based, anti-immigrant and anti-Latino statewide propositions, Proposition 187, the Save Our State Initiative. These severe critiques of Latino communities have become prevalent across many states. The anti-immigrant and anti-Latino language of Donald Trump and his campaign set a new standard in our nation for the ease and acceptance by many Americans of hostility toward immigrant and Latino communities. Stated differently, this final paradox of inclusion suggests that greater Latino electoral influence can lead to a severity of backlash and open, accepted hostility that places all Latinos vulnerable to being tagged as "perpetual foreigners" at best at the margins of American national identity. The risk that this paradox imposes on Latino communities is that such hostile marginalization becomes normalized and accepted in our politics and policymaking.

How might the elements of these paradoxes that are detrimental to the role of Latinos in national elections beyond 2016 be minimized? This certainly will not occur through great efforts by scholars to refine their analytical capacities to engage as political pundits. Predicting who the winner will be is fascinating and can put any data set, analytical design, and interpretive capacity to extreme tests. In the end, however, it risks succumbing to all of the paradoxes of inclusion noted earlier. Nonetheless, it can be exciting, but the impact in benefiting Latino communities as national political actors is uneven and is always vulnerable to unpredictable elements of turnout and quality of candidates. A much safer strategy is to remain engaged within the confines of the academy. We can choose to identify patterns of partisan identification, partisan preference, the relationship between demographic growth and mobilization, and patterns in similarities and differences among Latino/a/x voters. Such deeper and more theoretically driven understanding is of course worthy of scholarship. However, an honest assessment of the impact such scholarship has had over the last thirty-plus years suggests that its impact in furthering the empowerment of Latino communities has been limited. No doubt we know more about the challenges of mobilization, turnout, and representational consequences related to Latino communities than we have ever known before, but that knowledge must be translated into viable and salient strategies that are aligned with the interests of powerful gatekeepers and stakeholders who currently dominate much American national politics.

Perhaps the rich and worthy scholarship contained in this volume will only begin to limit the detrimental consequences of the paradoxes of inclusion if scholars add this to the high intellectual expectations that they have of their work: that it also contribute directly to strengthening the fabric of our democracy by providing clearer outlines of how a focus on Latino communities can help more and more Americans see that the fate of Latino communities is intimately linked to the fate of the entire nation and especially the fate of future generations of all Americans. What I am suggesting is that those of us who benefit from the study of Latino communities accept the responsibilities of engaging with the normative challenges of making arguments about how greater Latino inclusion and related empowerment are likely to benefit broad cross sections of the American public that cut across the lines of race, ethnicity, class, and generational status that were used so effectively to marginalize Latinos in the 2016 election in a way that none of us predicted would occur, and that few of us predicted would be successful. We know what the consequences are of not engaging with the larger arguments of normative analysis with a purpose. We lived those consequences in the 2016 election, and many Latino communities must cope, and many suffer, with the consequences of the policies that have been enacted under the current administration. We who are scholars of Latino voting and elections are significantly protected from the limits of our scholarship. I suggest that our Latino communities generally are not in the privileged positions in which we scholars find ourselves. This reality, perhaps, is a final paradox of inclusion.

References

Fraga, Bernard L. 2015. "The Voting Rights Act Turns 50 Today. Here Are Three Trends in Minority Voting You Should Know About." *Monkey Cage* (blog), *Washington Post,* August 6.

Fraga, Luis Ricardo, and David L. Leal. 2004. "Playing the 'Latino Card': Race, Ethnicity and National Party Politics." *Du Bois Review: Social Science Research on Race* 1 (2): 297–317.

Frymer, Paul. 1999. *Uneasy Alliances: Race and Party Competition in America.* Princeton, NJ: Princeton University Press.

Discussion of the Latino Decisions Coverage of the 2016 Election

Joaquin Alfredo Angel Rubalcaba and Edward D. Vargas

THE AUTHORS CONTRIBUTING TO THIS VOLUME RELY HEAVILY ON POLLING data collected by Latino Decisions, bringing together several years of election data focused on the Latino community. This chapter focuses on the general methodology Latino Decisions employs in its polls, with a specific discussion of the data sets used by authors in the volume. Since its inception, Latino Decisions has leveraged cutting-edge methodological techniques to provide critical insights into the Latino community, while maintaining a strong commitment to high-quality and objective social science research and cultural competence in the Hispanic community. Latino Decisions, as the vanguard in Latino political polling, is comprised exclusively of credentialed researchers with established publication records at the forefront of their respective professions.

Latino Decisions has provided a wide range of services designed to inform and improve data-driven decisions for a diverse client base of leading companies, research institutions, policymakers, and advocacy organizations and political campaigns. Most frequently, Latino Decisions is engaged in polling the voting behaviors of the increasingly influential

Latino community. Accordingly, these surveys adhere to rigorous social science standards and rely on precise information about Latino demographics
to make sure respondents reflect the Latino electorate. In this chapter, we
highlight the most important aspects of the Latino Decisions' methodological approach in constructing several political polls between 2012 and 2016.

The data used throughout this volume are primarily comprised of the
Latino Decisions' Election Eve Polls for the 2012 and 2016 elections. Other
data sets used in this volume come from the Latino Decisions' state-specific
and national battleground surveys collected over the course of the full 2016
election season. The samples for each of these surveys are drawn randomly
from the most recent publicly available list of registered voters in the given
state or nationwide, and are based on Hispanic households, which are then
merged with third-party data to secure telephone numbers—both landline
and cell phone numbers. The inclusion of cell phone numbers is critical
due to the increasing number of households that have abandoned landline
phones across the nation.

Latino Decisions samples rely on a variety of methodological approaches specifically designed to obtain the most accurate and representative sample of Latinos. These samples have sometimes been simplistically
identified as "surname" samples, but in fact, the samples purchased from
a third party contain an appropriate percentage of respondents with non-
Spanish surnames, since we also use commercially available markers of
Hispanicity. To be clear, the sampling approach employed by Latino Decisions is not a surname-only sampling design. Typically, the number of
Hispanics with non-Spanish surnames hovers around 10% nationally, but
in some states, such as New Mexico, it can be as high as 20%, and Latino
Decisions respondent data match those proportions. Hispanic households
are typically identified first through a combination of Spanish-surname
lists, identified by the U.S. Census, as well as first and middle name lists,
as well as additional identifiers of Hispanic households. Census block data
on Latino population density are also used, along with additional market-
based, geographic, and consumer data collected and merged into voter files
to identify potential Hispanic households. Thus, Hispanic households are
identified by a wide range of techniques, of which the name list is merely a

starting point. Finally, all respondents are asked to self-report their race and ethnicity upon contact at the start of the interview. Only respondents who self-identify as Latino or Hispanic continue and complete the interview. Thus, the sample frame is targeted, but broad to cast a wide net so as not to miss any potential Latino respondents.

At the start of every interview, voter registration status, age, state of residence, and Hispanic identification are verified upon contact with respondents. For this type of research, we believe that using a registered voter list is far superior to a simple random digit dialing (RDD) of potential Hispanic households, given that a large percentage of Latinos are not registered to vote, and previous research has documented social desirability in overreporting registration among Latinos. Latino Decisions avoids respondent misreporting of voter registration by using the registered voter list as a starting point. This step was particularly vital, as the authors are utilizing the Latino Decisions data to make inferences about Latino voters.

One of the most important aspects of the Latino Decisions methodological approach is that surveying is conducted by fully bilingual interviewers. Whether it is in live-caller telephone survey format, or self-administered online format, all respondents are greeted in both English and Spanish, and surveys are conducted in either English or Spanish, at the discretion of the respondent. Up to five callbacks or recontacts are scheduled for each record to ensure that populations harder to reach are properly included. The sample frame, design, and survey instrument are created by Matt Barreto, Gary Segura, Gabriel Sanchez, and Sylvia Manzano, often in consultation with other Latino political scientists affiliated with Latino Decisions, and then translated into Spanish. Depending on the political status of the organization commissioning the survey, it may be deemed that it is a coordinated or an independent project, and a strict "firewall" is in place at Latino Decisions to prevent the collaboration or sharing of data or any project information during an election season. Once the election is over, data are integrated into a shared database for research purposes. The survey is administered under the direction of Pacific Marketing Research in Renton, Washington, and performed using a computer-assisted telephone interviewing (CATI) protocol, as well as the Internet companion computer-assisted self-interviewing

(CASI). All programming is performed by Pacific Market Research. The Latino Decisions' CATI and CASI software offers a superior ability to exercise tight control of the sample. Latino Decisions also monitors the history of every contact attempt to each record, ensuring that the times when respondents are contacted are varied to maximize response rates and to achieve a high degree of customization to fit individual project requirements.

Following the 2016 election a new debate emerged over how accurate exit polls and other polling data were with respect to Latinos. Indeed, projects that do not have the specific intent to focus on an accurate sample of Latinos typically do not have a representative sample (Barreto and Segura 2017; Barreto et. al. 2017). In contrast, the data provided by Latino Decisions, featured throughout this volume, represents the best available information to accurately illustrate the increasingly influential role of Latino voters in the United States.

The 2012 and 2016 Election Eve Polls

The Election Eve Polls have remained one of the Latino Decisions' trademark data sets, offering state-specific and nationally representative insights into the Latino electorate, and are consequently a focal point of the chapters in this volume. The information gathered in the Election Eve Poll series covers presidential, Senate, congressional, and in some cases local vote choices, as well as issues, priorities, and evaluations of both major political parties. The Election Eve Poll data series is used in each of the chapters throughout this volume. From year to year the Election Eve Poll changes slightly to match the election season and to meet the needs of each sponsor. Many authors reference the 2012 data to make inferences regarding changes over time in their respective states or topical areas; we therefore provide some discussion of both the 2012 and 2016 data sets.

Latino Decisions completed 5,600 interviews in each of the 2012 and 2016 Election Eve Polls. Those interviewed consisted of Latinos who had already voted or who were certain to vote in the coming November presidential election. Interviews were conducted via telephone with live callers, all of whom were bilingual, and interviews were completed in the language of preference of the respondent. In the 2012 Election Eve Poll respondents were reached at landline and cell phone-only households from November 1 through November 5 of 2012, and the interviews averaged twelve minutes in length. Approximately 25% of the 2016 Election Eve Poll respondents were reached via Web survey. The 2016 Election Eve Survey was conducted from November 2 through November 7, 2016, lasting an average of ten minutes.

Voters in the 2012 and 2016 Election Eve Poll were prescreened based on their vote history in previous presidential elections and date of registration to include a mix of new registrants and first-time voters. It is estimated that 20% of respondents in the 2016 Election Eve Poll were in fact first-time voters in a presidential race. Respondents were asked whether they had already voted early, and if not, whether they were 100% certain they would vote in the coming November election. Respondents who were not certain about voting in the upcoming November election were terminated. This same methodology has resulted in 90% of the respondents validated as voting in the election. Furthermore, the distributions on the variables of interests did not vary between the total and those validated.

Specific to the 2012 Election Eve Polls, eleven individual states were targeted with a minimum of 400 completed interviews to provide state-specific reliable estimates (this was the case for all of the states included in this volume). For the remaining thirty-nine states and the District of Columbia an additional national sample was completed and then combined with the eleven stand-alone state samples for an overall combined nationally proportionate sample. The national sample of 5,600 is directly proportionate to the Latino voter population nationwide, and it is weighted to reflect the known Census demographics for Latino voters.

For the 2012 Election Eve Polls, the national sample carries an overall margin of error of 1.8%. This is adjusted to account for the design effect resulting from twelve unique sample strata of varying size and the post-stratification weighting used to derive the national estimate. California and Florida each had 800 completed interviews, and each carries a margin of error of 3.5%. The remaining nine individual states sampled included Arizona, Colorado, Massachusetts, North Carolina, New Mexico, Nevada,

Ohio, Texas, and Virginia. These nine states had 400 completed interviews and carry a margin of error of 4.9%.

Specific to the 2016 Election Eve Polls, eleven individual state were targeted with a minimum of 400 completed interviews to provide state-specific reliable estimates. In Florida only, 800 interviews were completed. For the remaining thirty-eight states and the District of Columbia, an additional national sample of 300 respondents was collected and then combined with the twelve stand-alone state samples, weighted to proportional population percentages, to achieve an overall combined nationally proportionate sample. The national sample of 5,600 is directly proportional to the Latino voter population nationwide by geography, and is weighted to reflect the known Census demographics for Latino voters, most critically age, education, gender, and nativity.

For the 2016 Election Eve Polls, the national sample carries an overall margin of error of 1.8%. This margin-of-error is adjusted to account for the design effect resulting from twelve unique sample strata of varying size, mode differences, and poststratification weighting used to derive the national estimate. Florida has 800 completed interviews and carries a margin of error of 3.5%. The remaining individual states sampled include Arizona, California, Colorado, Illinois, New York, Nevada, North Carolina, Ohio, Texas, Wisconsin, and Virginia. These remaining states have 400 completed interviews and carry a margin of error of 4.9%.

A targeted application of the 2016 Election Eve Poll is demonstrated in Livaudais, Vargas, and Sanchez's chapter focused on Latino millennial voters ("Did Latino Millennial Voters Turn Out in 2016?"). They utilize the 2016 Election Eve Poll and one specific to Colorado to investigate the electoral power and mobilization of Latino millennial voters in response to racialized campaign rhetoric. The robustness of the 2016 Election Eve Poll series allowed the authors to focus the analysis on 1,172 millennial Latino voters, between the ages of eighteen and thirty-three years, who are difficult to reach and often overlooked in survey sample designs. This chapter also uses two Colorado-specific surveys that were utilized by organizations on the ground in Colorado to engage and mobilize Latino millennials specifically in that state. The power of this data set lies in its ability to look at internal variation within this subgroup, given the large sample size of a statewide poll and a sampling strategy specific to capturing likely millennial voters online in a millennial-focused poll. The millennial poll included live interviews of 400 registered Latino voters in Colorado between the ages of eighteen and thirty-three by telephone through both landlines and cell phones. The Colorado Statewide Issues poll included live interviews with 500 registered Latino voters in Colorado.

The Latino Decisions' webpage offers more about the Election Eve Polls (http://www.latinodecisions.com), including the toplines for the full national survey, with breakdowns for key demographic and political variables, as well as state-specific data points.

Polling the Battleground States

The Latino Decisions' 3-State Battleground Survey and National and Battleground State Poll are used in this volume to illustrate the opinions of Latino voters in emerging battleground states (Colorado, Florida, and Nevada) during the 2016 presidential campaign season. These pre-election surveys provide the ability to explore enthusiasm early in the campaign season, make inferences of important events during the election season, and track movement in important behavioral outcomes over the course of the election season.

In 2016 Latino Decisions interviewed a total of 3,729 Latino registered voters between August 19 and August 30 for the National and Battleground State Poll. Interviews were conducted in English or Spanish, according to the respondent's choice. Surveys were completed using a blended sample that included online surveys, and live telephone interviews on landlines and cell phones. For the seven individual states of Arizona, Colorado, Florida, Nevada, North Carolina, Ohio, and Virginia, Latino Decisions completed a minimum of 400 interviews for the National and Battleground State Poll to provide state-specific reliable estimates. The state-level results carry an overall margin of error of 4.9%. For thirty-seven remaining states and the District of Columbia an additional national sample was completed and then combined with the seven state samples and weighted for an overall combined nationally proportionate sample. The national sample carries a margin of error of ±1.6 percentage points.

Preuhs's chapter, "Colorado: Latinos and the 2016 Election," highlights the significance Latino voters played in the Colorado electorate during the 2016 general election and implications going forward. Damore's chapter, "Demography Realized? The 2016 Latino Vote in Nevada," describes how Nevada's political landscape was shaped by a growing number of engaged Latino voters in the Silver State. These chapters highlight the policy concerns of Latinos in key battleground states. The data used in these chapters also highlight the need to focus on down-ballot impacts and the need to better understand both the messages that resonate with Latino voters and the messengers (i.e., firefighters versus celebrities) whom Latinos trust.

Within the three battleground states of Colorado, Florida, and Nevada, at a minimum, 400 interviews were completed in 2016 between April 3 and April 13, to provide state-specific reliable estimates, and carry an overall margin of error of 4.9%. The 3-State Battleground Survey was designed by Latino Decisions and focused on Latino registered voters. Interviews were conducted in English or Spanish, according to the respondent's choice. Surveys were completed using a blended sample that included online surveys, and live telephone interviews on landlines and cell phones.

The Latino Victory Project/Fusion RNC Reaction Poll Series

The 2016 Latino Victory Project—Republican National Convention (RNC) Reaction Poll was designed by Latino Decisions to examine the response of Latino voters to the RNC and Donald Trump's campaign. Gomez-Aguinaga and Sanchez use this data series in their chapter "The Latino Rejection of the Trump Campaign: The Biggest Voter Gap on Record," to discuss how Latino voters responded to hostile campaign rhetoric directed at the Latino community. The Latino Victory Project—RNC Reaction Poll series was conducted in 2016, across four surveys, between July 18 and July 21. In each survey Latino Decisions interviewed 300 Latino registered voters, and all of the interviews were conducted online in English or Spanish according to the respondent's preference. The survey carries a margin of error of ±2.8 percentage points.

Conclusions and Future Research Plans From Latino Decisions

The research included in this volume made use of the most up-to-date and comprehensive data sets on the 2016 election. This resource has allowed for a rigorous analysis of Latinos and voting behavior across states. Given the changing demographics trends in both settling patterns of Latinos and the variation in age cohorts, the research in this volume testifies to the importance of collecting innovative data with an eye toward public policy preferences. This chapter provided an overview of the data utilized across this volume, as well as the methodological approach utilized during the data collection process. With detailed information about the various survey data available through Latino Decisions, readers can access these data for their own research.

The research team at Latino Decisions is constantly working on new ideas to bring the Latino politics research community the most innovative and accurate data on the Latino population possible. In addition to the data sets described here, some other data sets available on the Latino Decisions webpage. For example, in spring 2016, scholars were invited to collaborate on the 2016 Collaborative Multi-Racial Post-Election Survey (CMPS). The goal of the project was to create the first cooperative, 100% user-content-driven, multiracial, multiethnic, multilingual, postelection online survey on race, ethnicity, and politics (REP) in the United States. Eighty-six social scientists across fifty-five different universities collaborated. The survey's main focus is on attitudes about the 2016 election and candidates, debates over immigration, policing, and racial equality, and on experiences with racial discrimination across many facets of American life.

Contributors

Benjamin G. Bishin is a professor of political science at University of California, Riverside. His interests include questions of democracy, representation, identity and ethnicity, public opinion, legislative politics, Cuban Americans, and LGBT politics. He is the author of *Tyranny of the Minority: The Subconstituency Politics Theory of Representation* and recipient of the 2001 Jewell-Loewenberg Award for the best paper on legislative politics and, along with his coauthors, winner of the 2011 and 2014 Bailey Awards for the best paper on gay and lesbian politics, and the 2015 Award for the Best Conference Paper in the Law and Courts Section of the American Political Science Association (APSA). His work has appeared or is forthcoming in venues including *American Journal of Political Science, Comparative Politics, Comparative Political Studies, Journal of Politics, Legislative Studies Quarterly, Public Choice, Public Opinion Quarterly, Political Analysis,* and *Political Research Quarterly.*

Aileen Cardona-Arroyo is a senior analyst at Hart Research Associates in Washington, DC. Before joining Hart, she was an assistant professor of political science and the director of Latina/o studies at Pace University.

She received her PhD in government from Cornell University in 2017. Her research centers on the politics of Latinas/os and immigrants in the United States. Specifically, Cardona-Arroyo is interested in the dynamics of media coverage and public opinion on immigration, as well as the political participation of Latinas/os in the United States.

Ivy A. M. Cargile is an assistant professor in the Department of Political Science at California State University, Bakersfield. Her research focuses on Latinx elite and voter behavior. She is interested in how Latina political actors represent their constituents and influence policy outcomes. Her work has appeared in *Political Research Quarterly*, as well as in multiple books on the topics of immigration and Latinas as political actors.

Ivelisse Cuevas-Molina is assistant professor in the Department of Political Science at Fordham University. Her research focuses on self-reports of turnout in survey research and Latino political behavior, and she teaches in Fordham's Elections and Campaign Management program.

David F. Damore is a professor of political science at the University of Nevada, Las Vegas, a nonresident senior fellow at the Brookings Institution, and a senior analyst for Latino Decisions. Damore received his PhD in political science from the University of California, Davis. His research focuses on electoral politics and applied public policy. An expert on Nevada politics, Damore provides frequent commentary for local, national, and international media outlets, including the *New York Times*, the *Washington Post*, *The Economist*, and National Public Radio.

Luis Ricardo Fraga is the Rev. Donald P. McNeill, C.S.C., Professor of Transformative Latino Leadership, Joseph and Elizabeth Robbie Professor of Political Science, and director of the Institute for Latino Studies at the University of Notre Dame. His primary interests are Latino politics, politics of race and ethnicity, voting rights, education policy, and immigration policy. His most recent book is the coauthored *Latinos in the New Millennium: An Almanac of Opinion, Behavior, and Policy Preferences* (2012). He has published in the *American Political Science Review*, the *American Journal of Political Science*, and the *Journal of Politics*, among other venues. Among his most recent publications is "The Origins of the 1975 Expansion of the Voting Rights Act: Linking Language, Race, and Political Influence," in the inaugural issue of the *U.S. Latina and Latino Oral History Journal* (2017).

Barbara Gomez-Aguinaga is a doctoral candidate in political science at the University of New Mexico (UNM) and a health policy doctoral fellow at the Robert Wood Johnson Foundation Center for Health Policy at UNM, where she studies political and health disparities of minority groups in the United States. Gomez-Aguinaga served as a research and legal assistant for several years in different organizations such as the Migration Policy Institute, the Immigrant Legal Resource Center, and the New Mexico Immigrant Law Center. Her research interests lie in the effects of descriptive representation, elections and campaigns, and political communication.

Justin H. Gross is an associate professor in the Department of Political Science and the Computational Social Science Institute at the University of Massachusetts Amherst. His current research focus is on the role of ideological framing in the work of U.S. opinion elites. He also serves as senior consulting statistician for Latino Decisions, modeling voter turnout and choice.

Casey A. Klofstad is an associate professor of political science at the University of Miami, where he studies the influence of society and biology on political behavior. He is the author of *Civic Talk: Peers, Politics, and the Future of Democracy* (2011), editor of *New Advances in the Study of Civic Voluntarism* (2016), and author of numerous peer-reviewed articles in outlets such as the *American Journal of Political Science*, *Political Behavior*, *Political Psychology*, and *Public Opinion Quarterly*.

Jessica Lavariega Monforti is the Dean of the College of Arts & Sciences at California Lutheran University. She received her PhD from Ohio State University in 2001. Her research primarily focuses on the differential impact of public policy according to race, gender, and ethnicity. She is specifically interested in the political incorporation and representation of Latino/as, immigrants, and women. Her latest research examines how major forces such as technology, the military system, and immigration policy impact and are impacted by Latina/o youth. She has worked with organizations such as Texas Rio Grande Legal Aide, La Union del Pueblo Entero, and the South Texas Adult Resource and Training Center. Lavariega Monforti has co-authored two books and published more than fifty articles and chapters. She has contributed to several news articles and broadcasts, including in the *New York Times*, in *La Opinión*, and on NPR's *All Things Considered*.

Maria Livaudais is a PhD candidate at the University of New Mexico and a health policy fellow at the UNM Center for Health Policy. Her research interests include health policy and Latino politics. Her current work focuses on the impact of the Affordable Care Act on political engagement.

Xavier Medina Vidal is the Diane D. Blair Professor of Latino Studies and an assistant professor of political science at the University of Arkansas. Medina Vidal studied political science at the University of New Mexico and the University of California, Riverside. His research centers on contemporary issues in North American politics including U.S. Latino political thought, culture, and behavior, Mexican electoral politics, and migration. His work has been published in *Political Research Quarterly*, *Hispanic Journal of Behavioral Sciences*, and *Norteamérica*, among other academic journals.

Jason L. Morin is an associate professor in the Department of Political Science at California State University, Northridge. His research focuses on Latino politics, immigration, and representation. His work can be found various peer-reviewed journals, including *American Politics Research*, *Political Research Quarterly*, and *Social Science Quarterly*.

Stephen A. Nuño-Pérez is an associate professor in the Department of Politics and International Affairs at Northern Arizona University. He has a BA in political science from University of California, Los Angeles, and an

MA and PhD in political science from the University of California, Irvine. He is a research associate at the Leavey Center for the Study of Los Angeles at Loyola Marymount University and a regular contributor for NBC News-Latino, where he focuses on national stories that have an impact on the Latino community. He has written more than 200 pieces for NBCNews since 2012, and has written for Reuters, TPM, MSNBC, the *New York Times*, and The Monkey Cage Blog for the *Washington Post*. He does research in political behavior, race and ethnic politics, Latino politics, mobilization, and partisanship.

Adrian D. Pantoja is a professor in political studies and Chicano studies at Pitzer College. Pantoja's research focuses on the Latino electorate, U.S. immigration policy, and U.S. politics. His research has been published in nearly four dozen academic journals and edited volumes. He has written dozens of political blogs and policy reports. He has given over one hundred interviews for major domestic and international media. He is a senior analyst with Latino Decisions, a political polling firm surveying and analyzing the Latino electorate. As a political consultant, he has worked for the National Association of Latino Elected Officials, the Democratic Congressional Campaign Committee, the California League of Conservation Voters, the Natural Resources Defense Council, and other advocacy organizations working with the Latino population.

Francisco I. Pedraza (PhD University of Washington, 2010) is an assistant professor at University of California-Riverside with appointments in the School of Public Policy and the Department of Political Science. He is the coordinator of the Politics of Race, Immigration, and Ethnicity Consortium, www.priec.org. Pedraza's research centers on political attitude formation and political behavior, including Latino policy preferences and electoral candidate preferences, as well as the influence of immigration policy on health-related matters. He has contributed to the design and translation of dozens of nationally representative surveys over the last ten years, and was co-principal investigator on the 2015 Latino National Health and Immigration Survey.

Robert R. Preuhs is a professor in the Department of Political Science at Metropolitan State University of Denver. His research focuses on issues of racial/ethnic politics, state politics and policy, and representation. He is the coauthor of *Black-Latino Relations in U.S. National Politics: Beyond Conflict or Cooperation*, as well as author or coauthor of numerous peer-reviewed articles and book chapters in leading scholarly outlets.

Ricardo Ramírez is an associate professor of political science and a faculty fellow at the Institute for Latino Studies at the University of Notre Dame. His broad research interests include political behavior, state and local politics, and the politics of immigration, race, and ethnicity. His most recent book is *Mobilizing Opportunities: The Evolving Latino Electorate and the Future of American Politics* (2013). His research focuses on understanding the transformation of civic and political participation in American democracy by examining the effects of political context on participation, the political mobilization of and outreach to Latino immigrants and other minority groups, and the causes and consequences of increasing diversity among elected officials.

Zessna García Ríos is a graduate student in the Department of Political Science at the University of Arkansas. Her research interests include southern politics, voter education, and political communication and media usage.

Joaquin Alfredo Angel Rubalcaba is an assistant professor in the Department of Public Policy at the University of North Carolina at Chapel Hill. He earned his PhD in economics at the University of New Mexico, where he also maintained a fellowship in the Robert Wood Johnson Center for Health Policy. His research is centered at the intersection of health and labor economics in both applied and theoretical settings. Specifically, his research investigates health and labor market outcomes for some of the most vulnerable populations throughout the United States.

Gabriel R. Sanchez is a professor of political science and the executive director of the Center for Social Policy at the University of New Mexico. He is also a principal for Latino Decisions, the nation's leading research firm focused on the Latino community. Sanchez received his PhD in political science from the University of Arizona. His research explores the relationship between racial/ethnic identity and political engagement, Latino health policy, and minority legislative behavior. Sanchez is the editor of *Latinos and the 2012 Election: The New Face of the American Voter* (2015). A leading expert on Latino and New Mexico politics, he has provided political commentary to several state, national, and international media outlets, including *NBC Latino, New York Times, La Opinion, The Economist, Wall Street Journal, Los Angeles Times,* and National Public Radio, to name a few.

Lisa M. Sanchez is an assistant professor in the School of Government and Public Policy at the University of Arizona. She holds a master's degree in American politics and public policy and a doctorate in political science with distinction from the University of New Mexico. She is an alumnus of the APSA Minority Fellows program and the Robert Wood Johnson Center for Health Policy. Her current work focuses on the relationship between a rising U.S. Latino population and its electoral impacts within the U.S. Congress. She works on projects related to the intersection of legislative politics, race and ethnicity, and political behavior. Other research interests include legislative representation with particular regard to how minority influences affect policies such as health and immigration.

Juan Angel Valdez is a PhD candidate studying political science at the University of Notre Dame. His broad research interests include political incorporation, political participation, and the politics of immigration, race, and ethnicity. His research seeks to understand how local contexts, state laws, and the sociopolitical experiences of first-, second-, and third-generation immigrants influence the political incorporation of immigrant-based groups in the United States.

Edward D. Vargas is an assistant professor in the School of Transborder Studies at Arizona State University. He obtained his PhD in public affairs from the School of Public and Environmental Affairs at Indiana University.

His research interests include the effects of poverty and inequality on the quality of life, focusing specifically on how health, education, and social policy contribute to the well-being of vulnerable families.

Bryan Wilcox-Archuleta received his PhD from the University of California Los Angeles in 2019. He received undergraduate degrees from the University of New Mexico and a graduate degree from the University of Washington. His research explores connections between context and group-based identities among racial and ethnic minority groups in the United States. His work appears in *Political Research Quarterly, Journal of Race, Ethnicity, and Politics,* and *Research and Politics.*

Betina Cutaia Wilkinson is associate professor of politics and international affairs at Wake Forest University. She was born in Buenos Aires, Argentina, and immigrated to the United States at the age of six. Her research interests include racial and ethnic politics, Latino politics, public opinion, and political behavior. Her book *Partners or Rivals? Power and Latino, Black, and White Relations in the Twenty-First Century* won the 2015 American Political Science Association Race, Ethnicity and Politics Section's Best Book Award on Inter-Race Relations in the United States. She has served as an editorial board member of the journal *PS: Political Science and Politics* and as the president of the Midwest Political Science Association Latina/o Caucus. She is the recipient of the Wake Forest University McCulloch Family Fellowship and serves as an executive council member of the Midwest Political Science Association. Her research has been published in several political science and multidisciplinary journals including *Political Research Quarterly, Social Science Quarterly, American Politics Research, PS: Political Science and Politics,* and *Race and Social Problems.*